The Ludotronics Game Design Methodology

This book supports readers to transition to more advanced independent game projects by deepening their understanding of the concept development process. It covers how to make concepts sufficiently viable, ambitious, and innovative to warrant the creation of a polished prototype in preparation of a publisher pitch.

The book is divided into six sections. After a brief tutorial (Preliminary Phase), readers embark on a journey along the book's methodology. They travel through successive conceptual phases (Preparations, Procedures, Processes, and Propositions); advance through levels and action beats in each of these phases; master challenges (conceptual tasks) and overcome level bosses (design decisions) that become successively harder; collect items (fulfilled documentation tasks); and "win" the game by having progressed from a raw, initial idea to a full-fledged, polished game treatment.

This book is designed to support junior and senior year BA or MA students in game design programs, as well as novice indie developers and those in the early stages of their game design career.

J. Martin is Professor of Game Design at the Mediadesign University for Applied Sciences, Düsseldorf, Germany.

The Ludotronics Game Design Methodology

From First Ideas to Spectacular Pitches and Proposals

J. Martin

CRC Press
Taylor & Francis Group
Boca Raton London New York

CRC Press is an imprint of the
Taylor & Francis Group, an **informa** business

Designed cover image: Stefan Wetzel

First edition published 2024
by CRC Press
2385 Executive Center Drive, Suite 320, Boca Raton FL 33431

and by CRC Press
4 Park Square, Milton Park, Abingdon, Oxon, OX14 4RN

CRC Press is an imprint of Taylor & Francis Group, LLC

Library of Congress Cataloging-in-Publication Data

Names: Martin, J. (Professor of game design), author.
Title: The ludotronics game design methodology : from first ideas to
spectacular pitches and proposals / J. Martin.
Description: First edition. | Boca Raton, FL : CRC Press, 2024. | Includes
bibliographical references and index.
Identifiers: LCCN 2023007412 (print) | LCCN 2023007413 (ebook) | ISBN
9781032369624 (hardback) | ISBN 9781032368702 (paperback) | ISBN
9781003334682 (ebook)
Subjects: LCSH: Video games--Design.
Classification: LCC GV1469.3 .M3735 2024 (print) | LCC GV1469.3 (ebook) |
DDC 794.8/3--dc23/eng/20230322
LC record available at https://lccn.loc.gov/2023007412
LC ebook record available at https://lccn.loc.gov/2023007413

ISBN: 978-1-032-36962-4 (hbk)
ISBN: 978-1-032-36870-2 (pbk)
ISBN: 978-1-003-33468-2 (ebk)

DOI: 10.1201/9781003334682

Typeset in Times
by KnowledgeWorks Global Ltd.

Contents

Phase 03   Procedures

Phase 04   Processes

Phase 05   Propositions

Phase 06 Postmortems

Abbreviations & Acronyms

4X	explore, expand, exploit, exterminate
AAA	high-budget game
AI	artificial intelligence
AR	augmented reality
CRM	customer relationship management
CTF	Capture the Flag
DDA	dynamic difficulty adjustment
DLC	downloadable content
DM	Deathmatch
E3	Electronic Entertainment Expo
EVA	extravehicular activity
F2P	free-to-play
FPS	first-person shooter
GDC	Game Developers Conference
GDD	game design document
GUR	game user research
HUD	head-up display
IP	intellectual property
ISO	International Organization for Standardization
LGBTQ+	lesbian, gay, bi, trans, queer plus
MAYA	Most Advanced, Yet Acceptable
MMO	massively multiplayer online game
MMORPG	massively multiplayer online role-playing game
NDA	non-disclosure agreement
NPC	non-player character
P&P	pen & paper
PBL	points, badges, leaderboards
PSA	public service announcement
QA	quality assurance
QTE	quick time event
RPG	role-playing game
RPS	rock, paper, scissors
SAPS	status, access, power, stuff
SF	science fiction
TDM	Team Deathmatch
USP	unique selling proposition
VR	virtual reality
XP	experience point

Phase 01

Preliminaries

Introduction

Welcome to the Preliminary phase!

To start with a general orientation, each phase has a number of subchapters called "levels." In some phases, levels are linear; in others, levels are arranged in a non-linear fashion. Each level, in turn, is divided into "beats." This term denotes, to be discussed later in the book, the smallest unit of action within a dramatic structure.

This first phase, the Preliminary phase, has three linear levels that prepare you for your journey: *The Thing*, *The Map*, and *The Tools*. They will provide you with a sense of direction; a map of the territory and its cultural context; and the supplies and provisions you'll need to proceed and succeed on your path.

Finally, two disclaimers.

First, all the names of the works of art, companies, and brands mentioned under the Fair Use doctrine throughout this book—for purposes of analysis, criticism, and scholarly reference—are copyrighted or trademarked by their respective owners, even if they're not pepper-sprayed with superscript symbols. In the final Postmortem phase, every intellectual property is listed with full attribution.

Then, much has already been written, presented, and taught about game design—an immense corpus of theory, practice, and opinion that has shaped the way I think about games. Many sources from that corpus are referenced throughout this book. But there might be sources that express *specific* thoughts which I consider, in error, as my own. Wherever that should be the case, drop me a note and a reference, and the oversight will be corrected for. In later editions, potentially; but prominently on this book's companion website at *ludotronics.net*.

Enjoy your journey!

DOI: 10.1201/9781003334682-1

Level One

The Thing

Opening

Ludotronics is a paradigm and, building on that core, a design methodology for intermediate and advanced game designers, particularly late-term students and novice indie developers. It's built upon the notion—expressed three-quarters of a century ago by the industrial designer Raymond Loewy—that function alone won't necessarily generate beauty, but that there will be no beauty without order. *Ludotronics* will deepen your understanding of the concept development process; support your transition from term or pastime projects to more advanced independent game projects; and assist you in creating a game treatment that is sufficiently viable, ambitious, and innovative to warrant the creation of a polished prototype in preparation of a publisher pitch.

Certainly, *Ludotronics* offers benefits for beginners too, or for professionals. But industry professionals will have hammered out their own personal methodologies over time, and beginners might not want to commit to a methodology, any methodology, just yet. Also, beginners might occasionally be confused because the most basic nuts and bolts of the industry that usually go without saying will go without saying. Moreover, there's an abundance of terrific introductions to game design on the market, all aimed at beginners, and there's an equal abundance of explorations into specialized game design topics on the market, directed at professionals.

Now, what if you're a game designer to whom creativity and innovation come naturally, and your games are enthusiastically received? Do you need a paradigm or a methodology? Probably not. But you will still find a handful of tools here that you can pick up and put to use. Rare is the game that springs forth from the game designer's brain fully grown, armed, and armored like Athena from Zeus's skull.

If being creative *doesn't* come naturally to you, as it never came naturally to me, then you will already be appreciative of tools that support the creative process. Paradigms and methodologies exist to do just that. To riff on an old adage: you can't teach talent, but you can teach process!

Beat 1: The Concept

Ludotronics is not about game production or project management, code development or asset creation, game art, game writing, or marketing. It is about what's generally referred to as concept development: that path from coming up with a raw idea for a game to a fully developed game treatment. It is about a methodology that will help you whip ideas into shape until they are strong and sturdy enough to become the beating heart of your prototype, your killer proposal, and your game design document.

Beat 2: The Document

Talking of which. Hypothetically, you can use the *Ludotronics* paradigm to generate massive game design documents where everything's meticulously fleshed and figured out. But this might not be advisable; neither now on your journey nor later during development. Of course, the time-guzzling behemoths game design documents have become as a kind of industry standard do have their place if you know exactly where you're going, from franchise sequels and series installments to formulaic gameplay in well-known game types. (There's nothing wrong with any of these!) But as warehouses for fresh ideas and uncharted potentials, such documents have suffered severe criticism, on and off, through time. And for a reason. They're just not flexible enough for the rapid changes that are constantly called for when trying something new in highly collaborative environments, and it will vacuum precious time out of your project if your team tries to keep such a document's every nook and cranny current and consistent.

Instead, think of your design document as a "living" document, as it is often called. It should be solid, for sure, and convincing. Even elaborate. But thinking of it as a living document will prepare you for the onslaught of constant, sometimes radical change your concept is bound to undergo. Think *Thief: The Dark Project, Halo: Combat Evolved*, or *BioShock*—they all started out as entirely different beasts. What happens to your original idea during development will depend on your cocreative team of inspired professionals, led by the Great Coordinator & Midwife more formally known as producer. Who, together with department heads and maybe a line producer, or as a scrum master balancing the wants and needs of the team and the product owner, will help you lift the game out of your document and into the world. But what the world sees, most likely, will not be a faithful software version of what you once put down in writing—which was merely the foundation.

Beat 3: The Vision

Then there's the question of *vision*. As former German chancellor Helmut Schmidt once famously remarked, "people who have visions should go see a doctor." In the movie business, this sometimes manifests itself almost literally when a so-called script doctor is called in to provide emergency care for an overly ambitious screenplay that isn't holding up against actual filming. Overly ambitious game design concepts can be equally treacherous, tilting toward development hell when reality is introduced to great visions created by great egos.

Visions are internal representations. As such, they have a severe problem with resolution—way too high and way too low at the same time. Too high because our inner eye excels at sculpting vivid experiences sharply dissonant with what either technologies constrained by the laws of nature or reasonable budgets can realistically achieve. Too low because our inner eye merely perceives the predominant path of its own choosing, not that surprisingly elastic range of contingencies the game will have to accommodate when confronted with a diverse range of players.

What your game needs is not a grand, cosmic Vision with a capital V. What your game needs is a sound, reasonable, and practical vision that elegantly translates into your design goal as part of your treatment, your prototype, your proposal, and your GDD that will knock people's socks off through clarity, beauty, conceptual integrity, and the promise of joy.

Outlook

That's what *Ludotronics* will help you achieve. That's the thing.

Level Two

The Map

Opening

In this level, you will gain a rough understanding of what *Ludotronics* is about and how it works. Basically, it's your map and compass, with a basic overview of what to expect on your journey. It's all you need to get started.

Beat 1: The Paradigm

Perimeter, Dimensions, Territories

Ludotronics is a paradigm and a methodology, nothing more, nothing less. It's a structural and functional model that will lead you from your first idea to a game treatment that qualifies for a prototype and a killer proposal. It tells you *how* to make design decisions, not *which*. All design decisions, of any kind, will be *entirely* your own.

The perimeter will make you familiar with the nature of ideas, competitiveness, and conceptual integrity. The four dimensions will inform your game design from scientific, cultural, and technological perspectives. The four territories will set you up to make detailed design decisions.

Beat 2: The Center

Ludotronics

Right now, it bears the name of the paradigm and methodology. Eventually, *you* will be at the center of the map at the end of your journey.

Beat 3: The Perimeter

Thematic Unity and Market Research

These two elements are both simple and essential.

Market Research comes first. You should have rock-solid evidence that the game you have in mind is going to sell in a manner conducive to making everybody involved happy and not go broke. And in case you wondered: it's about market research, not marketing research. To design a game, you need to concern yourself with your prospective audience, not with marketing variables or distribution channels.

Thematic Unity comes second. For the vast number of design decisions a game requires, you need to develop a theme to which you and your team can anchor these decisions. A theme is your tool for making design decisions that are meaningful and coherent, not accidental and disparate. A theme, in that sense, has nothing to do with moral lessons or the message of a game.

DOI: 10.1201/9781003334682-3

FIGURE 1.1   The *Ludotronics* map.

Beat 4: The Four Dimensions

Game Mechanics, Ludology, Cinematology, Narratology

The four dimensions provide the structural organization for your prospective game. You can look at it this way: *Game Mechanics* provides the central nervous system, *Ludology* the musculoskeletal system, *Cinematology* the cardiovascular system, and *Narratology* the endocrine system.

While we should not overwork this metaphor, it gives you a fairly good idea how these four dimensions provide, and only provide, a game's generic system—it's you who will have to supply it with the spark of life through coordinating stimuli, robust bones and muscle tissue, fresh, oxygenated blood, and thrill-inducing hormones.

Now, why not leave it at that and work only with these dimensions? Or, the other way round, why not skip these dimensions and work only with the four territories introduced below, i.e., *Interactivity*, *Plurimediality*, *Narrativity*, and *Architectonics*, where you will make your actual design decisions?

This dimension/territory split has two reasons: conceptual completeness and the time-honored rivalry between ludology and narratology.

First, conceptual completeness. On a fundamental level, the *Ludotronics* paradigm pursues a holistic view of designing video games in terms of knowledge and expertise. What these four dimensions stand for, to that end, are the major fields of science.

> **Game mechanics**. This dimension represents all the principles and know-how that the natural and formal sciences contribute to game design.
>
> **Ludology**. This dimension represents the broad range of knowledge and tools from the social sciences to study how humans relate to games historically, psychologically, sociologically, and economically; to investigate how games are not only related to experiences and motivation and learning, but also to ideologies and violence and stereotyping; and to analyze an ever-widening list of aspects from the funeral games of antiquity to the virtual economies of MMOs.
>
> **Cinematology**. This dimension, in turn, represents the arts and art sciences. As a field of study, cinematology is not simply the study of film. It is the study of audiovisual techniques and experiences, artistically, historically, economically, and philosophically; the pursuit of the principles of art and design; and the research into empirical aesthetics and aesthetic perception and judgment. Not only does cinematology as a term capture the artistic aspects and aesthetic experiences of video games very well; it also includes kinesthetic conditions that can be carried

over from film camera, actor, and object movement to in-game camera, avatar, and in-game object movement. And, in case of VR or AR, player movement.

Narratology. This dimension, the field that studies the structure of stories and storytelling and its rules, stands for the humanities. Humans, as has often been pointed out, are storytelling animals. Humans tell themselves stories about themselves all the time, both in an endless internal monologue and through communicating with other humans. Language certainly doesn't constitute reality as it is "out there." But it constitutes the stories that we *tell ourselves* about this reality as soon as we leave the strings of symbols of formal languages behind that we employ to build ever more accurate *models* of reality. Thus, for the narrative aspects of designing and experiencing video games, the term narratology represents the humanities, including philosophy, history, literary theory, musicology, anthropology, or the study of religion—fields that, in turn, overlap substantially with methods and perspectives from the natural sciences, art, and social sciences.

Then, the time-honored rivalry between ludology and narratology. The two layer-construction of the *Ludotronics* paradigm curtails both narratology's traditional overlordship in matters of story and dramatic structure and ludology's traditional overlordship in matters of rules and mechanics. It does this by shifting actual design decisions away from these two fields into the territories, i.e., the respective intersections that *Ludology* and *Narratology* share with *Game Mechanics* and *Cinematology*. This ensures two things:

- *Ludology* still brings the study of player interaction and multimedia-based presentation to the table but is no longer the uncontested master of rules and game mechanics.
- *Narratology* still brings the study of dramatic structure and narrative presentation to the table but can no longer detach itself from rules and game mechanics.

As an aside, Jesse Schell's aesthetics–mechanics–story–technology tetrad from *The Art of Game Design* also defuses this rivalry, perhaps intentionally, by substituting technology for ludology and reassigning aspects of player–computer interaction to the former. This tetrad, by the way, is also an excellent model you can work with.

To wrap it up, the four dimensions inform the game's principal conceptual structure. Design decisions within that structure, in contrast, will be made in the four territories where these dimensions intersect.

All this, it should be added, will be a breeze in practice. By the time you reach the territories, you will have picked up everything you need to make interesting and informed design decisions.

Beat 5: The Four Territories

Interactivity, Plurimediality, Narrativity, Architectonics

The four territories are the intersections where the *Ludotronics* dimensions meet, and where most of your design decisions will happen. You can think of these territories as your prospective game's internal organs, pick any you like, it doesn't matter. What matters is that they provide the system's functional organization.

Importantly, these territories are more challenging than all the other parts on the *Ludotronics* map; they will confront you with distinctive design approaches and perspectives that are at times complex enough to leave the comfort zone. But don't worry! All four territories are "open-world" levels that you can travel through at your leisure, to pick what you need, and to return to when you feel ready and more secure.

Let's go through all four territories, briefly.

Interactivity. This territory inherits characteristics from both *Game Mechanics* and *Ludology*. As such, it covers interaction aspects from the perspective of the game, like rules and gameplay loops, and from the perspective of the player, like challenges and skills.

Plurimediality. This territory, the intersection of *Ludology* and *Cinematology*, governs design elements and design decisions from the two perspectives of functional aesthetics and holistic user experiences.

Narrativity. This territory, where *Narratology* and *Cinematology* meet, does not equal narrative, or story. Instead, narrativity is the quality or property that works of art often possess, in any medium, despite lacking identifiable plot or story elements. As a territory, *Narrativity* covers design elements that work toward conveying specific meaning for a memorable gameplay moment—visually, auditorily, kinesthetically, and mythologically.

Architectonics. This territory, the intersection of *Game Mechanics* and *Narratology*, is about the design and arrangement of the game's dramatic structure as a *holistic* structure that encompasses both the game's narrative elements and its mechanic elements like rules, difficulty progressions, and similar.

Along your journey, each territory will challenge you in different ways. Each comes not only with its own regional hazards and boss fights but also with its own splendid rewards.

Beat 6: The Methodology

Consistency, Adaptability, Efficiency, Effectiveness

Ludotronics has been specifically developed to support design decisions that are consistent throughout the game; to be highly adaptable without preference for certain game types; and to be efficient and effective in terms of getting started, replayability, and fun. But it's not the only conceptual framework in town! You can base your design decisions on different paradigms with different methodologies, which is perfectly fine and appreciated. There are many possible methodologies out there for different requirements and different temperaments.

Outlook

This should suffice for an introductory sketch of the *Ludotronics* paradigm. Everything else will follow smoothly and intuitively from these premises. Each term will be more fully explained in situ and, always with some necessary theory, turned into a tangible, practical tool.

Level Three

The Stage

Opening

If you want to create games that are not merely good but fresh and innovative, and perhaps directed at a more unusual and diverse range of players, here's some stuff and thoughts that might help you set the stage for that.

Beat 1: All You Can Use

At this book's companion website, *ludotronics.net*, you will find news, links, and updates, and an ever-expanding bibliography built upon the sources and resources referenced throughout the book. These are for you! The book can't follow every aspect down to its last detail and darkest corners. Natural sciences, social sciences, the humanities, and math—each of these fields will contribute aspects to design decisions, and all this book can do is scratch the surface and spark your interest. If you find rabbit holes that look inviting to you, don't hesitate to follow them down and discover the rich treasures they will lead you to.

But wait, there's more! The companion website will also provide you with supplementary material for download. To start with, there's a comprehensive collection of all key definitions, tables, and illustrations from the book in full color, to make your journey as comfortable and enjoyable as possible. Then, there's a set of templates and checklists for the tasks you have to accomplish during your journey, the challenges you have to master, and the documentation objectives you have to fulfill. All this material is free for you to use!

Beat 2: All You Can Ask

Alongside greater attention and an increasingly professionalized, maturing video game industry, markets and consumer identities have changed considerably. New audiences came to the table with immense combined buying power. These audiences not only want to play different and more diverse video games. They also want to see themselves *represented* in video games, for everything from being offered role models to becoming visible, understood, and accepted by society at large.

However, as in all tech industries, development floors and upper management tiers in the video game industry do not necessarily reflect this change. And while games increasingly feature women, people of color, LGBTQ+ folks, and other professionally and socially marginalized groups and subgroups, this does not always happen in satisfactory ways. Such game characters often lack agency, serve as motivational objects, are exoticized, or get things dead wrong.

Hence, whenever you want to create a game that touches upon groups and cultures you're not familiar with, you should take somebody on board from that group or culture. But that's just the first part of the challenge! In the humanities, particularly in postcolonial research, the concept of the "native informant" has been discussed extensively. Native informants are easily put under pressure—and are even prone to putting themselves under pressure—to conform to dominant narratives. Accordingly, inconvenient parts of their genuine narratives are always vulnerable to being discarded, or "foreclosed." Thus, as Gayatri

DOI: 10.1201/9781003334682-4

Chakravorty Spivak calls it, you have to start by "committing yourself to narrative and counternarrative." In other words, if you're on unfamiliar ground, you have to be attentive, receptive, and vigilant all the time.

Beat 3: All You Can Include

If you want to design and develop more innovative games in general, and more diverse and more inclusive game experiences in particular, make sure the words and images and actions in your game support your objective, and not undermine it with historical ballast and debts that might be invisible to you, but not invisible to others.

Especially the language we use plays an important, even formative role in that respect—how we see ourselves and others, and who even appears on our internal radars. That's why, as a critical example, "singular they" is used throughout this book. On the one hand, singular they has always been used by literary giants and regarded as perfectly grammatical and is even *explicitly recommended* by editorial style guides like the *Chicago Manual of Style* or Merriam-Webster's dictionaries and reference books. But beyond that, it lends support—surreptitiously or overtly, but always with the potential to effect visibility—to all those who don't fit into binary gender patterns.

In all likelihood, there will always be a substantial number of games where manly men can play a manly man and shoot at everything that moves. There's absolutely nothing wrong with that. Many players who are not manly men at all enjoy these games too! But the world has moved on. There can be, and will be, a growing number of different and innovative games for new and different audiences in equal abundance, and some of these could be designed by you.

Outlook

Now that you have completed the Preliminary phase and become familiar with the terrain, you can proceed to the Preparation phase—and jump right into the thick of the action!

Phase 02

Preparations

Introduction

Welcome to the Preparation phase!

As outlined in the Preliminary phase, each phase has a number of levels, sometimes in a linear, sometimes in a non-linear arrangement. The first level in this phase, *Level One: Spawning Ideas*, will engage you with the nature of ideas and how to produce ideas reliably in a disciplined fashion. For all practical purposes, this level constitutes your training level—not in the sense of a tutorial, but in the sense of a gym or dōjō that you want to visit again and again.

After that, you will proceed to *Level Two: Panning for the Core* to pan your freshly spawned idea and identify its core element, around which you will create a preliminary game concept later in the Procedure phase. This core element, in turn, will unlock three non-linear levels: *Level Three: Tough Investigations*, *Level Four: An Army of Avatars*, and *Level Five: Enter the Value Matrix*. You're free to tackle them in any order you like. But you must beat all three before you can proceed to this phase's boss encounter in *Level Six: Serve with Distinction*.

On the *Ludotronics* map, all the action in this phase takes place in the lower, or southern, part of the perimeter labeled *Market Research*. Which comprises "spawning ideas" as well because generating ideas that make sense has at least as much in common with research as with revelation.

This whole Preparation phase is iterative in principle. Like a gym or dōjō, as mentioned, you want to return to it again and again to get better at what you do and how you do it. Remember, gaining higher skill levels through persistent training can be intensely rewarding in and of itself!

DOI: 10.1201/9781003334682-5

Level One

Spawning Ideas

Opening

With ideas, it's not that difficult, it's not that simple. As Richard Feynman put it in his Caltech commencement address in 1974, the first principle is that you must not fool yourself—and you are the easiest person to fool. Basically, the whole process of developing your idea into a viable game concept consists of not fooling yourself, and you will be tempted to fool yourself every step of the way. However, tools that support the creative process are not only a great help if being creative doesn't come naturally to you, as mentioned in the Preliminary phase. They also help you to control your creative torrents when ideas *do* come naturally to you. Methodologies and paradigms exist both to support and to constrain.

Beat 1: Confusions

Fooling yourself begins with having ideas in abundance. Perhaps you can spawn dozens of ideas in one brainstorming session alone, and some of them look good on paper. The more experience you acquire, though, the harder it will become. That's because accumulated experience, training, and knowledge equip you with the mental apparatus to assess your ideas quickly and weed out those that lack originality, feasibility, playability, or market potential almost automatically. When that happens, ideas are no longer cheap. They're precious.

Another form of fooling yourself is pet ideas. Shaped by personal experience and cultivated for years, the perceived quality of a pet idea with its endless stream of exciting particulars is often an illusion, created by the combined psychological function of biographical significance and the sheer amount of time and thought it has consumed.

Neither clinging to a single idea nor producing great quantities of ideas haphazardly will get you very far. What you need is the practice and the experience that comes with discipline and challenge.

Artists sit down for a sketch or a drawing as soon as they can spare a minute. Writers write a number of words or pages per day or per week. Musicians practice their voice or their instrument every day for hours on end. What are you, the game designer, doing on a daily basis to hone your craft and develop your creative expertise?

Playing games is a good place to start, and it's a vital part of being a game designer. But you won't learn to design great games from playing games alone, in the same way that you won't learn to write best-selling novels just from reading best-selling novels or paint pictures to be acquired by Guggenheim just from visiting art galleries.

Thus, you also have to practice regularly. First, you create an idea. Then, you determine its characteristics and core aspects across the *Ludotronics* map's four dimensions *Game Mechanics*, *Ludology*, *Cinematology*, and *Narratology*. Finally, you figure out whether your idea holds up to expectations.

Walk into the wild, along this level's upcoming beats. Develop one brand-new idea per week. Create, sketch, analyze, rinse, repeat.

DOI: 10.1201/9781003334682-6

Beat 2: Constituents

Books that tell you how to spark ideas and be creative have always been a thriving genre. It won't hurt to read some of them. Advice differs widely, but what a creative idea is can be boiled down to a version of the following formula: a creative idea is the product of persistence, constraints, and an unfamiliar combination of familiar ideas, and the result should be original, interesting, and relevant. That's it. It's brief enough so you can learn it by heart.

> A creative idea is the product of persistence, constraints, and an unfamiliar combination of familiar ideas, and the result should be original, interesting, and relevant.

Let's unpack this formula and have a closer look at its constituents.

Persistence means intent and determination: you're chasing an idea and you're not giving up on it. Yet persistence doesn't mean you have to brood over it through the night and through the day. Rather, it means you should persistently *return* to it and give it another try. Taking breaks from conscious problem-solving is actually fruitful, and it works best if you're occupying yourself with something else during such breaks. This can be sports, a different task or problem, or simply getting on with handling your life for a good while. (Merely relaxing and loafing about rarely helps.) Elements of surprise might also be involved—when finally and suddenly everything falls into place on the one hand, or your idea turns out to be really clever on the other. You're not getting anywhere near such experiences without being persistent.

Constraints are desirable. Constraints can be genres and platforms, available technologies, prevailing market conditions and audience expectations, or the limits of your skills, knowledge, and experience. Whatever your particular constraints are, they define the space in which you can excel, and that makes them desirable. In this space, importantly, the value or relevance of your work can be *measured against that of other works*. But here's the tricky part. Your budget must not be a constraint but something that is *determined* by your constraints. It would be highly detrimental to your game if it could become a better game with a higher budget! Thus, you need to develop a clear mental picture of the constraints you face and choose to face, and then embrace them.

The third constituent, *combining familiar ideas to create something unfamiliar*, can be practiced with random input methods. Such methods have been around for a long time under many names. Among the most well-known is Edward de Bono's random word method. By design, it's used to solve defined problems by introducing a random word to the problem, to force the brain to think "laterally" along different angles and directions. Certainly, trying to come up with a game idea is not a defined problem in that sense, so we have to tweak it a bit. Pick a few words from a random word generator on the web—three is a good number—and try to find interesting relations between them to generate new and unfamiliar ideas. What's more, this technique is not restricted to words. You can also use random images or sounds or even events. With respect to words, you can also differentiate between nouns, verbs, and adjectives; each category brings its own flavor to the table. But mind, the focus is on practice, on honing your skills! It's less about results than about regular exercise. However, randomization isn't strictly necessary at an advanced stage. As a great example of combining familiar elements to create something unfamiliar, watch Feng Zhu's GDC 2015 presentation "A Live Art Demonstration of Creating Worlds through Design Thinking," especially the "Ask 'What If?'" section.

Finally, we need to unpack the formula's tail. *Original* means it's not a copy or a rip-off product. *Interesting* means it has to be, well, interesting—you can create something that is highly original but profoundly boring. *Relevant* can mean a lot of different things in the context of games. A game can become relevant as an industry-defining artistic, conceptual, or technological breakthrough, descriptions of which will grace presentation slides at developer conferences. Primarily, though, it should be relevant with respect to the playing experience. This can stretch from the prosaic to the profound, from simply not having wasted the player's precious time to fond memories for a lifetime, from an exhilarating afternoon to a startling personal insight, from a surge of pride for solving the game to deep emotional footprints whose traces linger for years. It is here that you should try and nail relevance. From there, fame and fortune might follow!

In closing, a caveat. Don't become attached too fast to an idea you generated. Starting from scratch is hard, and your idea might look much more promising than it actually is simply because it already exists. Which is just another path toward fooling yourself. Only keep that rare idea that clearly sticks out as superior and promising. Dispose of the rest.

Beat 3: Compartments

Now that you gained an understanding of what a creative idea is, what then would *specifically* qualify as a creative idea in game design? A lot more than you might think.

It can be a rule or a game mechanic. It can be an interaction with the device or with other players. It can be a rich, atmospheric setting. It can be a complex emotion or experience. It can be a character or a momentous interaction between two or more characters, a dramatic scene, or even a complete story.

Whatever it is, it will fall into one of the four dimensions of the *Ludotronics* map. A rule or a game mechanic will fall into the *Game Mechanics* dimension; an interaction into the *Ludology* dimension; settings and artistic elements into the *Cinematology* dimension; and a character, a scene, or a story into the *Narratology* dimension. Naturally, most ideas will come as packages that already comprise elements from all four dimensions. While this might sound innocuous, it is in truth highly undesirable and a challenge you'll have to face soon in the upcoming level.

Then, there's a bonus exercise to structure your ideas in ways related to games. It's based on Tracy Fullerton's "Below the Surface" exercise in *Game Design Workshop*. Here's how it works.

Take any event or sequence of events you come across. This could be assembling a bicycle or new wall shelves, or cooking and arranging a dinner for a large party, or gardening. Or, with narrative elements, a book you read, a movie you've watched, political or economic news you've followed. It could also be a particularly interesting event or endeavor from your own life, perhaps even the progression of a complicated relationship. Take this event or sequence of events and break it down to its structural elements: goals and subgoals; characters; moods; sceneries; rules that define what can and cannot happen; interactions and their constraints, i.e., which moves are allowed and which are not allowed; resources and their constraints; turning points and points of escalation that require more resources; and so on up to and including climax and reward. (Don't worry: all of these elements will be discussed more in-depth during the Process phase.)

What this exercise will do for you, over time, is to instill a way of structural thinking that you can then apply, both consciously and automatically, to your game ideas.

Outlook

Make these exercises part of your weekly routine; and don't abandon them when you're actually developing a game. Like an artist or a coder or a musician, you should always hone your craft. Also, these exercises will almost always compel you to do at least a little bit of research—in game-related fields, of course, but also beyond. That way, these exercises have the collateral benefit of rapidly increasing your general and specialized knowledge, which will make your ideas in turn more interesting and compelling.

Remember, most of what comes out of these exercises can be discarded as a rule. Not every sketch an artist makes becomes a painting. Only if your idea looks and feels like a killer idea, then you should put it in your *Ludotronics* inventory as a rough sketch and proceed with it to *Level Two: Panning for the Core*.

Level Two

Panning for the Core

Opening

To proceed, take the game idea that you created in the first level. To assess its strength, it needs some panning—think gold panning—to separate its core element—think gold nugget—from surrounding sediment. That's because ideas tend to come in packages, together with all kinds of fillers and decorations that attach themselves to your idea without the necessary baggage checks of critical design thinking. Getting rid of them and replacing them with more valuable elements is what this level is about.

Beat 1: Priming

Even if your idea is original, interesting, and relevant, or precisely because of it, it operates like an industrial-strength magnet for boilerplate material. That's your brain, primed for padding and scaffolding nascent ideas with presentable features, trying to help! There is no reason to assume that these features are the most worthy ones for your idea. More likely, they're standard formulas, tropes, and even straight-up clichés, and you're probably not aware of it as you're focused on what's fresh and new about your idea. If you let that happen, your *good* idea will become a poor game, your *great* idea a mediocre one, and your *killer* idea a good game that will be favorably received. That is not what you want.

Panning means extracting the core, the element or elements that truly define your idea. It's like extracting gold nuggets from a placer deposit. Whatever your idea's core is, it will fall into one of the four dimensions on the *Ludotronics* map:

- A *game-mechanical element* like an innovative rule, a set of rules, a mechanic for actions or decisions, or the gameplay loop itself.
- A *ludological element* like an innovative player/game or player/player interaction.
- A *cinematological element* like an innovative auditory, visual, or kinesthetic experience or combination of such experiences.
- A *narratological element* like an innovative story idea, plot point, journey stage, setting, or character.

All the elements just listed, from gameplay loops to interactions to plot points and beyond, will be examined in detail in the Process phase. At this point, a rough sense of direction and what to look for will suffice for productive panning sessions.

Beat 2: Panning

Let's look at four examples, one for each dimension.

First, let's assume your idea is a mobile puzzle game. The player assembles a functional space station from orbital junk, whereby each piece of junk has base values for momentum, speed, and rotation that change when moved and manipulated by the player, and only pieces with identical values can be joined

DOI: 10.1201/9781003334682-7

when they meet. These values in turn add up to the space station's total value at completion, which—together with playing time—is the final score. Sounds great! Then you start panning. Basically, it's an elimination game with a clever rule set at its core that clearly belongs in the game-mechanical dimension. Now define and describe that rule set in natural or symbolic language without referring to orbital junk or space stations in any way. That's your nugget!

Your next step would be to take that nugget and parse its space of possibilities. Let's do this right away. Is assembling a space station from pieces of junk the best possible use for this idea, and a mobile puzzle game the best game type fit? Could it be a multiplayer strategy game instead, perhaps an arithmetical brawler, if there is such a thing? (If not, can you invent it?) Could the game consist of levels, matches, stages, or missions? Could the game space be a map, a playing field, an arena, or something else altogether? What about the pieces of junk—could they be purry cats or giant mechs instead? What about game elements with special mathematical properties that are waiting for their turn in a dugout, cryo chamber, or special operations base?

Basically, to tease out your game idea's full potential, you have to parse as many options around its core as possible and see what fits best. This "pan and parse" strategy isn't exclusive to game design. To see a truly terrific example of it in action, check out Bob Shaw's *How to Write Science Fiction* and learn how his classic short story "Light of Other Days" evolved from a fairly interesting murder mystery sketch, *through this technique*, into one of the most anthologized sf stories of all time.

Next, let's assume you have an idea for a party game where the players' picnic basket was stolen by a group of mischievous, lively rodents, and players must catch all of them, one by one, by replicating their jumps and jolts and swings and switches. As the game proceeds, the remaining rodents become more clever, and the game harder and ever more entertaining. This time, the idea's core element is a player/game interaction that falls squarely into the ludological dimension. For the panning, you strip away the picnic basket and the rodents and describe the player/game interactions in abstract terms, how players must retrieve some in-game item by imitating adversary elements as fast and accurately as possible, and so on. After that, you again proceed with parsing. On the input side, elimination through imitation can mean a lot of things, constrained primarily by controller types. The adversary elements could be lively creatures of any kind or ballet dancers or circus artists or something else altogether. And what exactly players have to imitate and how, there will be no shortage of entertaining options. But maybe, and that's always a possibility, your first idea with the rodents turns out to be the most enjoyable! But you would never know that if you hadn't tried to come up with alternatives.

Then, let's pretend your game idea is about a neon-rainbow-colored bouncing ball that races through grim worlds with peculiar color palettes like shades of gray or primary colors only, populated by adversary elements that drain the ball's colors in specific ways until it's fully assimilated into the dominant color palette and the game is over. Certainly, there are rules and interactions involved, but the outstanding element is an aesthetic one that belongs to the cinematological dimension. Again, you would pan it down to an abstract aesthetic description, with the player trying to maintain their avatar's uniqueness against various types of uniformity. Again, other options will come to mind. The player's in-game representation, or avatar, could be a molecule, a stranded astronaut, a hapless eudaimon who fell among cacodemons. What you should focus on, in this case, are options for preserving uniqueness that promise to deliver spectacular aesthetic experiences.

Finally, let's imagine your game idea revolves around a player character who agrees to take money from a crime syndicate in exchange for certain information but has second thoughts. The character then tries to find or fabricate evidence to play the syndicate members off against each other in classic *Mission: Impossible* fashion (the television series, not the movies), so that they terminate each other without ever suspecting—and subsequently terminating—the player character. Now, this could also be a game-mechanical core with a clever rule set, but a narratological core seems to have more potential. And, perhaps, a gripping story is what you want! Thus, you strip away the money and the mob and pan your idea down to an abstract narrative core. Which, as it becomes clear now, is a variation on the classic "pact with the devil" tale! Which means that you have to parse even harder, to make that time-honored tale truly shine for a game. What if the player character were a sentient third-party code sequence in a military computer framework? What if the player character were a mighty mob boss in their own right in ancient Rome, and the syndicate were the Roman Senate? What if the loan were the ability to feel emotions, in exchange for the player character's experiences stored in their synthetic brain? Particularly when it comes to stories and characters, topics we'll look into in detail in the Process phase, you should do what Bob Shaw did with "Light of Other Days": aim at building the most emotionally interesting and rewarding narrative around your core that you can think of.

Beat 3: Parsing

As the preceding beats already illustrate the combined "panning and parsing" technique along four core examples, let's instead look at how you get the most mileage out of your parsing sessions in three easy steps.

First off, you should exercise panning and parsing regularly. Set aside 2 hours per week, for example, to generate an idea, pan it down, and parse as many elements for as many options as you can think of. With time, you will become so accustomed to this that you can leisurely create a staggering number of options in no time.

Then, specifically, parse different game types and platforms and controllers; different moods, settings, and literary genres; different rule sets, gameplay loops, and interactions; and so on—each individually and in combination.

Finally, when you have accumulated a decent collection of options, weed out everything that doesn't hold up to scrutiny until you have a new and improved game idea that fits your core element in the most interesting, most promising, and most exciting way.

Repeat these steps as often as necessary. If it yielded not one but several promising concepts, keep them. Chances are you will know which one to keep and which to discard along the upcoming levels of the Preparation phase, and certainly after beating its final level.

Outlook

You've beaten this level when you identified your original game idea's core element and its appropriate dimension; built one or more refined game ideas around your core that you're really excited about; and stored everything in your *Ludotronics* inventory!

With that, you'll have unlocked *Level Three: Tough Investigations*, *Level Four: An Army of Avatars*, and *Level Five: Enter the Value Matrix*. You can tackle them in any order you like. There, you will learn how to gather market intel, identify your potential players, and allocate value characteristics to your game idea that will set it apart from the competition.

Level Three

Tough Investigations

Opening

What you need to know when you set out to create a game, critically, is what games people buy, play, and enjoy. Which, against the background of the twenty-first century's information or knowledge economy, should be easy but isn't.

Beat 1: Searching

In contrast to traditional media such as newspapers or movies or television that rely heavily on advertising money, which is a forceful driver for performance transparency, you won't get any reliable sales and performance data for video game titles. Publishers have no reason to release verifiable sales and performance data above what's legally required.

Since that road is blocked, you have to take a few detours to find out how titles relevant to your game concept perform in the market. Alas, these detours are riddled with potholes.

"Best-selling games of the year," to start with, won't help you. They cover the usual suspects, that year's blockbusters, and only from retail sales. They don't reflect buyer behavior beyond best-selling games as a *category*. That's because retail sales dynamics are driven by the wedded pair of rapid inventory turnover and deep pockets for shelf space and promotion on the retailers' and the publishers' sides, respectively.

Then, "Top Sellers" or "Most Popular" sections on digital distribution platforms. These also do not tell you a lot. What data or formulas or dynamics drive these rankings is perfectly opaque from the outside, and a "most popular" game possibly just came out on top of the latest discount roulette.

Finally, there are digital distribution platforms that provide some statistics, and there are third-party developers who correlate and crunch publicly available data to make informed estimates about market performance and actual sales. All this worked reasonably well before the EU data protection laws kicked in. Since then, sales estimates from these sources have become a lot less reliable. Some studios and publishers even try to suppress such estimates, even though these services work with publicly available data.

To sum it up, the data horizon looks bleak. Particularly for indie developers, it has become progressively harder to calculate investments against returns. Nevertheless, you can and should collect all these kinds of data and put them into spreadsheets. They might be just ballpark estimates, but that's a lot better than nothing.

Beat 2: Studying

Besides collecting the data just mentioned, you should also keep track of what's going on all the time yourself.

You need to play games, talk to people who play games, roam game-specific community forums, and read different kinds of game reviews, not just those about polys and pixels. You can also check game ratings from aggregator sites, but these are viciously unreliable thanks to review bombing and other manipulations.

DOI: 10.1201/9781003334682-8

Keep monitoring which game types are thriving and which game types are struggling. Keep track of which titles become surprise flops or surprise hits and why. Keep an eye on crowdfunding platforms to see what types of games are funded and which are not. And always document what particular details players and critics are grumbling about with respect to games that otherwise perform really well. This data might turn out to be exceptionally useful for creating your game's value set.

All that should become part of your knowledge base. You have to have an idea about what's hot and what's not, and estimate how long it stays hot, if you want to develop games and make a living of it.

Beat 3: Scouting

Historically, researching mainstream media didn't make much sense for designing and selling video games. But times have changed. Customer demographics for video games went off the scales. People who aren't playing at least some video games have become increasingly rare, and they're not just playing casual–social–mobile games either. There's a good chance that the people you meet at the movie theater and the people who buy books at the book store and listen to music that's hot at the time are the very same people who might be willing to buy your game if it happens to meet their wants, needs, and expectations and the approval of their peers. If you look into it, you will even discover that very successful AAA games tend to pick up themes and motifs from best-selling books and award-winning movies released several years prior. *The Last of Us*, for example, as pointed out by Tim Rogers in his *Action Button* review, is clearly modeled after Cormac McCarthy's *The Road* and Alfonso Cuarón's *Children of Men*. This is no coincidence.

Should a story in the traditional sense be involved in your game concept, check what kinds of stories people are actually into at the moment. What are the movies and the movie genres that perform well? What kinds of books in which literary genres about what topics sell well? Figures are often available for the print market, but, again, rarely if at all for digital sales. To gain an even better, hands-on overview, visit a few book stores. Which authors from which genres are deemed worthy of precious shelf space? Which of these are even placed face out on the shelves instead of spine out? From those, read a few excerpts. For both movies and books, by what kinds of settings and characters are people attracted beyond genres and topics?

Then, aesthetics. What do people buy and listen to besides top hits? Are there identifiable music genres and moods that sell well across the demographics you have in mind for your game? Which artists and art styles in visual media are popular right now, with media coverage, exhibitions, and as a general trend? What are the prominent color palettes for everything from movies to advertising to websites?

To sum it up, your knowledge base isn't complete without data about what your prospective players buy and enjoy beyond video games. While your data sets from the previous beats primarily inform you about game-mechanical and ludological developments, mainstream media can tell you a lot about narratological and cinematological trends. All this will become valuable later to complement your narrative and aesthetic design decisions.

Which doesn't mean you have to conform to these trends! It's all about paving the ground for informed design decisions. You can build on trends if you want to; discard them if they don't match your vision; or extrapolate them to take them even further.

Outlook

If you have created a basic knowledge base that you can fill with data over time and put it in your *Ludotronics* inventory, you have cleared this level! To unlock the final level, though, you must also have cleared levels four and five.

Level Four

An Army of Avatars

Opening

In this level, you will develop a deep understanding of your potential audience. You will need this understanding later, together with your research data and your value set, to unlock the final level, transform your game idea into a game concept, and enter the next phase.

Beat 1: Audiences

To define your audience, you need to list the most prominent characteristics of your game idea. Will it have a strong story? Will it be multiplayer-focused? Will it be an old-school game or an oddball? Will it be easy for beginners or hard for everyone? How much of a time sink will it be? Will it be strong on customization or individualization? And so on, depending on game type and vision.

With that, you can build a model of your target audience and form a good mental picture of the type of players associated with these characteristics. Which, again, demands some research. Which platform or platforms would such players prefer? What can you find out about the frequency and duration of their playing activities? What is their physical gameplay context (while commuting, at home, etc.), their social context (alone, with friends or their families, with fellow clan members, etc.), or their psychological context (professional, competitive, ambitious, bored, pleasure-seeking, etc.)? There's a lot more to ask, so use your imagination.

For example, players interested in a game similar to *The Last of Us* would display very different characteristics than players interested in a game similar to *Threes*. (Duh!) The former would appeal to players who play regularly on their consoles or PCs at home, the latter to players who play regularly as well, but on their mobile devices and in much shorter sessions and probably rather en route. The former would appeal to players who like captivating settings and emotionally driven stories, the latter to players who love to find solutions for tricky problems. And so on. What other game types they like to play might factor in too.

You can work with terms like "core" and "mid-core" and "casual" when describing target audiences but *always* follow up with reasonable qualifications for these terms. People have different ideas about what they mean. As of now, video game design dictionaries are less reservoirs of systematic and scientific descriptions than haphazardly accumulated lists of industry lingo. What's more, not all term patterns or terms are productive. The pattern hard-core/core/mid-core/casual, for example, has one fuzzy "core" too many. Or take the term "softcore," which stayed mercifully buried for almost a decade until Bethesda pulled the stake out of its heart to revive it for the E3 in 2018.

What's more, "core" and "mid-core" and "casual" are often used as game attributes for convenience (a "mid-core game" or a "casual game"), but they're actually audience attributes that describe a range of behavioral characteristics. Here's a rough guide.

> **Core**. Players with core characteristics tend to be experienced players with serious skill levels and short fuses for tutorials, manuals, and slow beginnings; they tend to have clear expectations and preferences based on their media biographies and experiences with similar games; they're probably used to investing sizable amounts of disposable income and personal time

into games; and they tend to be focused on challenging playing experiences on the one hand, and quality in one or more of the four dimensions (mechanics, controls, graphics, narrative) on the other.

Emerging core. Players with emerging core characteristics tend to be experienced players with moderate to serious skill levels who might need some guidance for certain kinds of games but not for others; they tend to be open to new experiences because they haven't yet developed strong core preferences; they're probably already investing noticeable amounts of time and money into games but are both hesitant and unpredictable about when and where to do it; and they're looking for meaningful playing experiences.

Mid-core. Players with mid-core characteristics tend to be less experienced players with low-to-moderate skill levels who need some guidance and acclimatization; they tend to be open to new experiences because almost everything is a new experience; they're probably willing to invest moderate amounts of either time or money in games but not necessarily both or simultaneously; and they tend to be focused on having consistently challenging, but not necessarily meaningful, playing experiences. In a nutshell, games for mid-core players have to be as engaging as games for core players, but way more accessible in terms of purchase price, skill barrier, and time investment.

Emerging mid-core. Players with emerging mid-core characteristics might have some experience with certain games or kinds of games but will probably still need considerable guidance most of the time; they might be searching for new experiences because neither games directed at core players nor games directed at casual players fit their circumstances or interests; they're probably willing to invest discernible amounts of time in games but not necessarily matching amounts of money; and they tend to have no explicit focus beyond the desire to play games.

Casual. Players with casual characteristics are situational players who tend to need extreme accessibility to adopt a game but will later tackle high-frustration obstacles where even core gamers would falter; they usually stick to playing one game at a time, are not intrinsically inclined to seek new games with new experiences, and won't easily transition to a new game without heavy doses of marketing and peer pressure; they're prone to investing significant amounts of non-consecutive time as long as it fits into their professional and private schedules, but only a small percentage will actually invest noticeable amounts of money; and they tend to be focused on—or even addicted to—behavioral reward mechanisms.

By design, a few things are missing from this map. Devices play no part in any of these definitions because that field is shifting very fast—not too long ago, for example, the term "casual" was derogatorily thrown at console players and the games they played in general. What's also missing are player characteristics like "competitive," "social," or "community-oriented" because they're not exclusive to any one category. Certainly, players of party games are usually tagged as "casual," players of MMO strategy games like *Clash of Clans* as "mid-core," and MMO/MMORPG players as "core," for example. While there's some truth to it, there's too much overlap, and we shouldn't pile a set of sketchy correlations on top of another set of sketchy correlations. Instead, you should list "competitive," "social," or "community-oriented" as independent player characteristics for your potential audience.

All this is just a map, and a rough one at that. Like any map, it shouldn't be confused with the actual territory it represents, and there will be numerous individual exceptions. You can use these labels, but you should always back them up with precise explanations and specific player characteristics.

The next step, then, would be to translate your player characteristics into a catchy motivation statement. Here's how these could turn out for the examples mentioned above, a game similar to *The Last of Us* and a game similar to *Threes*:

- Experienced players who like survival- and exploration-driven action-adventure games with a strong human-interest angle.

- Recreational players who are drawn toward short, engaging problem-solving challenges that they can play while commuting or during breaks at work.

A motivation statement doesn't need not be true for every player. The point is that you are able to align your game concept's characteristics with *motivational models* that are well defined, well understood, and indicative of a numerically substantial audience against which you can calculate investments.

Store everything in your *Ludotronics* inventory: your game concept's most prominent characteristics, the corresponding characteristics of your potential players, and your player motivation statement. Much later, in the Proposition phase, a refined version of the player motivation statement will become part of your game pitch, and the player characteristics will become part of your proposal document to back it up.

Beat 2: Analytics

Next, generate demographic customer profiles from your primary target audience that you defined in the preceding beat. How old are they? Where do they live? What do they do for a living? How much do they earn? What other demographic aspects do you need to consider, perhaps ethnicity, education, political views, and so forth? Try to find out as much as you can about the aspects that make sense. And don't iron anything out—even if your potential players are fairly homogeneous with respect to playing characteristics, their demographic characteristics won't. Indeed, different and sometimes strongly contrasting characteristics within the same category should be the norm. But each characteristic should show some prevalence.

Then, there might be a secondary target audience that isn't defined demographically but is interest-driven with respect to specific aspects of your game. For games like *The Last of Us*, for example, there is probably a secondary target audience with a general interest in dystopian fiction. For games from *Wordfeud* to *Clash of Clans* to *World of Warcraft*, there are probably secondary target audiences with a general interest in competing or collaborating with real people. As a special case, there are secondary target audiences whom you need to convince in order to sell your game to your primary target audience. This is true, for example, for educational games where your primary target audience is a demographically defined group of kids, and your secondary target audience their parents or teachers.

Beat 3: Appearances

Finally, create a set of player personas. In the marketing disciplines, these are either called customer avatars or client personas; another term is player composites, as Morgan McGuire and Odest Chadwicke Jenkins call them in *Creating Games*. Your set will consist of a number of individual player profiles from your primary target audience, based on the characteristics that you compiled and defined in the previous beats. (As secondary target audiences are not defined demographically, you can't create meaningful player personas for them.)

Creating player personas involves creating characters complete with personal attributes and visual sketches, just as you would do for characters in role-playing games. So you'll have to answer a few more questions about them, based as much on research as on your personal experience. How do these players look? What do they wear? How do they behave in user forums and social networks? What else do they like besides playing games? Also, you should give them names and occupations, write up brief résumés, and provide them with motivations and even some quirks.

But that's all just preparation and documentation! For the actual personas, don't think of character sheets. Rather, think of trading cards. Keep it snappy and relatable! On the front, you can put a name, a micro-description ("Ambitious puzzle solver"), a crisp illustration that hits the right note between individuality and universality as elucidated by Scott McCloud in *Understanding Comics*. On the back side, you can put three crisp paragraphs that describe what they want (goals, aspirations); what delights them (key purchasing considerations); and what frustrates them (key pain points).

In brief, create people, not encyclopedias!

These player personas will do a lot for you. Later in your written proposal document, they will show that you did your homework. During concept development, they will disrupt unconscious tendencies to confuse your own wants and needs and preferences with those of your target audience. During development, they will make it much easier for you to think in terms of benefits (how would this knock these players' socks off?) instead of features (how would this make the game look even cooler?).

Throughout this process of defining and researching your target audience and creating player personas, keep in mind what has been touched upon in the Preliminary phase with regard to visibility, representation, counternarratives, and native informants. Especially when your developer team turns out to be very homogeneous, you can easily overlook, or even unintentionally exploit, demographics beyond your own. If you make such demographics visible through player personas that represent them with their actual experiences, preferably with some help and advice from people who are part of these demographics, chances are that your game too will include and represent them in meaningful ways.

Outlook

What you have created in this level are dossiers: your player personas with résumés, visuals, playing habits, and personal and demographic characteristics. All you have to do now to complete this level is to store these dossiers in your *Ludotronics* inventory! To unlock the final level, though, you must also have cleared levels three and five.

Level Five

Enter the Value Matrix

Opening

To win the boss fight in the upcoming final level of this phase, you need to create your value set, your key values, and your unique selling proposition, or USP. All three are about differentiation. Your value set differentiates your game from competing games through its blend of strengths and weaknesses and the richness and quality of its features overall. Your key values differentiate your game in one tangible way in each of the four dimensions. Your USP, finally, is about that one thing that makes your game not just different, but unique. For all three, you first need to construct a value matrix, as a benchmark against which you can make informed decisions.

Beat 1: Value Characteristics

Every game type has a number of elements and properties, which we call value characteristics, that are perceived as valuable by its respective target audience—each value characteristic on its own individual merit, and all together as their sum total. The specific value characteristics of the games you will compete against, together with their strengths and weaknesses, constitute your value matrix.

If your game concept offers a value set that is identical or very similar to games that are already on the market, people will wonder why they should buy and play your game. And if you pitch to a publisher, they will wonder too and ask why they should invest in your game, except as a knock-off product that will run on a high marketing and low development budget—and they wouldn't even need you and your team for that! Thus, differentiation. Differentiation means that your game delivers a combination of values and key values that no other game delivers for your target audience.

Beat 2: Value Sets

Your value matrix should be restricted to the specific game type or game types that most closely match your game idea. Still, the number of possible value characteristics is probably very high, which can become confusing. For that reason, you should create your value matrix not haphazardly but systematically, and you can use the *Ludotronics* framework for that. Your matrix will contain the *Ludotronics* map's four dimensions and two extra categories, "Customer Relationship Management (CRM)" and "Proposal." Here's a rough description of the possible values you can distribute across these six categories.

Game Mechanics. The *Game Mechanics* category can contain value characteristics like unusual game mechanics; engine type; performance; bugginess; distinctive technologies from physics engines to VR/AR; AI quality; etc.

Ludology. The *Ludology* category can contain value characteristics like freedom of movement; unusual interface or input technologies and controls; difficulty options; challenge quality; game length; player modes (single, multi, coop, MMO); challenge modes (Capture the Flag, Bounty, Solo Showdown); etc.

DOI: 10.1201/9781003334682-10

Cinematology. The *Cinematology* category can contain value characteristics like graphics quality; style; atmosphere; environmental detail; audio quality; music and sound integration; dialogue quality; voice actors; etc.

Narratology. The *Narratology* category can contain value characteristics like story depth; story integration; player agency with regard to story; character customization or individualization; etc.

Customer Relationship Management. The *CRM* category can contain value characteristics like available platforms; extra content (Mission Packs, DLCs, map packs); community features; mod-/conversion-friendliness; unusual revenue models; etc.

Proposal. The *Proposal* category should contain value characteristics like literary (entertainment) genre; theme; and USP.

All these examples are more or less generic. You have to populate these categories with values that fit the game type or game types that most closely match your game idea. In the next step, you will evaluate how strong or weak these value characteristics are in the most important games your game will compete against, and then add your findings to the matrix.

Beat 3: Value Matrix

In this beat, you will do three things, successively:

- select and research a number of published games your game will compete against;
- create a table or spreadsheet with one column for each game and as many rows as you need for the value characteristics you collected in the preceding beat;
- rate each value characteristic for each competing game.

You can use any rating system you like. But for something simple and powerful, the combination of a five-point scale with Harvey Balls is strongly recommended.

It's a five-point scale that can cover everything from existent to non-existent, from poor to excellent, from casual to committed, from disposable to persistent. The visualization provided by Harvey Balls will make everything instantly intelligible through five conditions: empty, one-quarter full, half full, three-quarter full, and full.

You can easily find and download a free Harvey Balls font from the web, to enter the five conditions with your numerical keys on your keyboard. Or, you can use your spreadsheet's pie chart editor to create your own set of Harvey Balls and populate your matrix via copy and paste.

There are alternatives to Harvey Balls, of course. You can use a scale with less or more than five points, and you can also use a different visualization tool. Radar or spider charts, for example, even though they have perceptual drawbacks that make some value comparisons hard to judge. Or strategy canvasses, as devised by W. Chan Kim and Renée Mauborgne in *Blue Ocean Strategy* and adapted as value curves by Tynan Sylvester in *Designing Games*; but these become overwhelming quickly with a large set of parameters. Finally, not to forget, you can always create your own visualization tools!

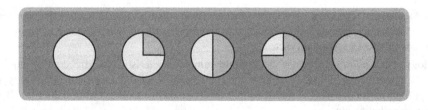

FIGURE 2.1   Harvey Balls.

FPS 1997–98	GoldenEye 007	Quake II	Unreal	Half-Life	Thief: TDP
GAME MECHANICS					
Own Engine	●	●	●	◑	●
AI Quality	◔	◑	●	◕	◕
Unusual Mechanics	◑	●	●	◑	●
LUDOLOGY					
Custom Difficulty	●	◑	◑	◑	◕
Multiplayer/Coop	●	●	●	●	○
Unusual Controls	●	●	◑	●	●
CINEMATOLOGY					
Atmosphere	●	◕	●	◑	◕
Environmental Details	●	◑	●	●	◕
Music & Sound Integration	◑	◑	◕	●	●
NARRATOLOGY					
Story Depth	◑	◕	◑	●	◑
Player Agency	◕	◕	◕	●	◑
Customizable Player Character	○	○	◑	○	○
CRM					
Multiple Platforms	●	●	◑	◑	○
Extra Content	○	◑	◕	●	○
Mod-Friendliness	●	●	●	●	○
PROPOSAL					
Entertainment Genre	Spy Fiction/ Thriller	Hard/Military Science Fiction	Science Fiction/ Science Fantasy	Near-Future Science Fiction	Dark Fantasy/ Steampunk
Most Likely Theme	Ghosts of the Past	[no identifiable theme]	Salvation	[find out for yourself!]	probably Balance
Most Likely USP	Movie Franchise	Pimped *Doom/ Quake* Clone	Atmosphere	Interactive Environment	Sound/Light Game Mechanics

FIGURE 2.2 Sample value matrix.

If you use the *Ludotronics* framework in conjunction with a five-point scale and Harvey Balls, your own value matrix might look similar to the sample matrix illustration, even if the value characteristics for your game will be different.

In this sample matrix, it's early 1999 and the refined game idea is a first-person shooter. Alternatively, the time is actually now and the game idea is a 1990s vintage first-person shooter! The column headers contain competing games; the row headers in each category contain value characteristics that fit these games; and the individual cells contain Harvey Ball ratings for each characteristic's existence or quality.

Now go and create your own value matrix!

Populate the column headers with the competing games you selected, and the row headers with the value characteristics from your research. Then, rate each value characteristic for each game. And don't forget to document your research and the reasons behind your ratings! Just as in the sample matrix above, not every rating will be self-explanatory or immediately plausible. Also, while this visualization technique puts everyone back on track in no time, even after a long hiatus, some crucial details might have been forgotten. Every visualization needs a documentation of its elements' origins and meanings.

Make sure everything's set and ready for the final level's boss fight. There, you will add empty columns on the right-hand side for different variations of your game idea, and perhaps add empty rows to various categories to try out value characteristics that are not usually part of your game type.

Outlook

As soon as you've stored your value matrix and your research and ratings documentation in your *Ludotronics* inventory, you beat this level! If you also cleared levels three and four, the final level has been unlocked and you are ready for the Preparation phase's boss fight.

But wait! There's one more thing. It's related to the topic of market data from level three. When you're doing your value characteristics research for the competing games you selected for your value matrix, also collect every piece of economic data for these games that's floating around, wherever it comes from. Budget figures, numbers of copies sold, retail price, download numbers, projected and actual development time, projected and actual budget, projected and actual profits, everything. Collect every postmortem you can find, every presentation, and any written material about the development process.

No matter how flimsy and unreliable that data is, you might still get lucky and catch some information against which you can compare your own estimates later in the Proposition phase.

Level Six

Serve with Distinction

Opening

Now that you did your research, defined your audience, and created your value matrix, the Preparation phase's moment of truth is here. To beat this level, you have to find the best possible value set for your game; its key values; and its unique selling proposition, or USP. After that, you'll have promoted your game idea to a game plan!

To start, add one or more columns on the right-hand side of your value matrix and create potential value sets for your game idea. Distribute your Harvey Balls and try out different combinations that look interesting and reasonable, and promise to deliver distinct and enjoyable playing experiences to your target audience.

Experiment, analyze, compare, improve! Can you get away with leaving some value characteristics out? Are there value characteristics you can't possibly compete against, because they are too strong or costly or both? Are there weaknesses you could improve on or new value characteristics you could introduce by adding another row at the bottom of a category? Would you rather go for a game that is well-balanced across all categories, or for a game that is insanely good in one category and bare-bones everywhere else?

This is only a small sample of all the questions you can ask. You have to find your own questions, based on your specific game idea, game type, and vision. In the following beats, you will learn more about this process and some of its invisible rules.

Beat 1: Pitfalls

The first rule is, you can't just copy a value combination that already exists, crank up its values, and call it a day. That's not how game design works. Or game development. Or the world, for that matter. Think combinatorial, not additive. Focus, don't spread. Compete on detail quality, not feature quantity. Create, don't clone, and specifically don't try and clone successful AAA games. When it comes to competing with genius ideas or monster budgets, your mantra should always be: *Not better is better, different is better.*

But still, maybe at some point you mutter to yourself, "now wait, this concept I have in mind is so awesomely awesome, why not just raise shed-loads of money, throw in and max out every possible feature, and make a game that can't possibly fail?" Well, first of all, it can and will implode from its own weight and fail spectacularly during development, owing to dynamics like ever diminishing returns for ever-increasing resources and other assorted obstacles. But even if that weren't the case, it will invariably fail in terms of quality. The more features you have, the harder it gets to turn them into benefits, and what you end up with is expensive clutter. The greatness of a game has nothing to do with the number of its features, regardless of their strengths. The greatness of a game has everything to do with a *particular choice* of value characteristics that will translate into a holistic, enjoyable playing experience.

Not better is better, different is better.

DOI: 10.1201/9781003334682-11

Design is about choices and trade-offs, and great design is about excellent choices and punishing trade-offs. It's not the player who should be burdened with choosing from an oversupply of features reminiscent of bloated word processors. That's not what "player agency" means at all. What's more, design choices are about *intent*—without which there can be no meaningful experience, no continuity, no flow.

In more practical terms, design choices interconnect with constraints all the time, from available technologies to desired age ratings. While the *Ludotronics* paradigm doesn't cover development, one of the most important constraints you want to familiarize yourself in this context is the "Pick Two!" principle of the famous Cost–Time–Quality/Scope production triangle.

All this you'll need to keep in mind when you choose your set of value characteristics.

Beat 2: Potentials

Among the immediately attractive options is to add a value characteristic that so far hasn't been served to your target audience by that particular game type. However, even if it's intimately connected with your game idea's core element, there are two caveats. First, there might be non-obvious reasons why this value characteristic is absent from this game type. Are you really the first game designer on Earth to have thought of adding it? You need to look into it very thoroughly, turn every stone. If there's a catch, you don't want to find it halfway into development. Then, for unique and original value propositions, no metrics exist to sketch out a profit–investment ratio and chances are that promoting the game will be much harder. You will have to explain a lot! Thus, publishers might be wary. Many are certainly prepared to take some risks with an innovative indie game. But it helps if you have some respectable research data and smart reasoning to back everything up. If that's the case, go with it! If it works out, you might become rich, famous, and overconfident.

Another attractive option is to look for a value characteristic that is served to your target audience but never seems to live up to expectations, either because it's crummy or so badly integrated as to be virtually useless. This is safer than the previous option, but don't let your guard down just yet. There might be a reason for this value's endemic feebleness that will become apparent during development with a vengeance. From the marketing perspective, though, it looks good. There are metrics to work with, and there's less risk involved overall. Then again, it's hard to explain credibly and succinctly why *your* game delivers this specific value for your target audience better than *all the other games* that already tried their hand at it. "We're not like the others, man, really!" can easily translate into promotional messages so full of braggadocio that they're liable to trigger a hypercritical response.

Finally, there's an excellent option with no strings attached. Instead of focusing on specific value characteristics to differentiate your game, you can create a value set that consists of a *new and exciting combination* of those value characteristics that your target audience reliably prefers and is familiar with. This can be a lot more innovative than it sounds, and it combines advantages from the other two approaches without their drawbacks.

Now, whatever option catches your interest, keep one thing in mind. Works of art can often be opaque and impenetrable or at least appear that way for a certain time and a certain audience. That's perfectly fine. But there is no hard rule that innovative games always have to be opaque and impenetrable. Innovative games are allowed to engage players and to spark joy! For these ends, you can follow principles like Raymond Loewy's MAYA principle for successful product design, "Most Advanced Yet Acceptable," or Jean Piaget's "Moderate Novelty" principle. (You can find a good introduction to the latter in Ginsburg and Opper's *Piaget's Theory of Intellectual Development*.) To follow these principles, your game should appear sufficiently familiar and sufficiently different at the same time. It shouldn't scare players away, but it should also promise new challenges and new experiences.

How do you do that? There's an old hat in every industry, not just the video game industry, that you should introduce one innovative element and leave everything else alone. That's not quite what Piaget or Loewy had in mind, but it can get you started, and you have the six categories of your value matrix to work with. Pick one of the four dimensions *Game Mechanics*, *Ludology*, *Cinematology*, or *Narratology*, or perhaps one of the other two categories, *CRM* or *Proposal*. Innovate the crap out of this one category with a new, exciting set of value characteristics. For the other five categories, create familiar value sets that your target audience will feel at home with right away. This allows you to find an ideal balance of novelty and typicality that's both innovative and true to tried and tested design and marketing principles. Later, you will be able to craft a golden ratio message that pitches familiarity and trust on the one hand, and a unique and innovative playing experience on the other.

Still, there's also a market for more radically innovative games, and there are also publishers who have an open ear for it as long as there's a reasonable investment-to-risk ratio. Another thing you can do is earn your money with games that are more commercially viable, and then follow your calling and invest some of your returns into games that really push the envelope.

Beat 3: Practice

Now that you know about the pitfalls and potentials from the preceding beats, you can rise to the challenge and beat this phase in three successive steps: create your value set, identify your key values, and define your USP.

Don't rush the first step. Create and iterate through as many value sets as you like until things begin to feel right and you have a winner.

From this set, then, you should be able to identify your key values, those values that are most important for your game's differentiation and your vision. Ideally, you have one key value for each category, and each key value is tangibly obvious and delightful for anyone who interacts with your game for the first time.

Yes, that sounds harsh. It hasn't always been that way—once upon a time, you could get away with a compelling value set and a sparkling USP. But in today's vibrant, crowded, and hyper-competitive indie games market, that's no longer the case. There are more indie publishers around than ever, and the number of indie games released each year keeps rising too. Indie game events, fairs, and festivals have become incredibly busy affairs. If your game fails to catch someone's interest within a minute, you won't get anywhere. That doesn't mean that your key values have to be innovative, or even new. It does mean that each dimension should have one key value that is instantly recognizable and delightful—a distinct aesthetic, a distinct mechanic, a distinct player interaction, and a distinct setting or, if your game is dramatically complete, crisp evidence of an engaging story.

What's more, having key values gives you an attractive advantage even beyond rising above the crowd. When you know your key values, you know what to hang on to with determination should worse come to worst during development and dwindling resources demand substantial cuts. To decide what to keep and what to cut, your key values and your creative vision together are a much better guide than your vision alone.

Finally, the USP. U stands for unique. It's one outstanding value characteristic of your game that conveys what's different and innovative about it. There are three basic options you can choose from, depending on your value set and key values. Your USP can be one of your key values; it can be an entire category that your game focuses on like none of your competing games does; or it can be, as mentioned, a surprising, well-balanced combination of value characteristics across all categories that immediately feels fresh and exciting.

Let's look at three examples, one for each strategy: two games from the previous beat's sample matrix and one indie game. In *Thief: The Dark Project*, there's one specific value characteristic that sets it apart from every other stealth or FPS game at the time. They took light and sound, which usually sit in the *Cinematology* category, and transformed them into game mechanics. That way, they created a brand-new entry in the *Game Mechanics* category for a playing experience that stealth games hadn't provided before. In the second example, *Unreal*, it wasn't an individual value characteristic but a whole category that made the game stand out. With their new engine, the Unreal Engine, they cranked up the entire *Cinematology* category to create environments with spectacular moods and atmospheres that hadn't been possible before. (Both *Unreal* and *Thief: The Dark Project*, it should be mentioned, also had substantial numbers of new value characteristics beyond that, well beyond the scope of even the most budget-intensive indie game.) In *Gone Home*, finally, it's neither one particular value characteristic nor a particular category that makes this game so outstanding. Instead, it's a distinct, well-balanced combination across all categories, from its quietly clever exploration mechanics to its evocative aesthetic elements and spatial design to its multi-layered narrative—all integrated through its well-designed world narrative, also called environmental storytelling, in such ways that everything in the game supports everything else for an instantly compelling and continuously rewarding playing experience.

While creating your value set, your key values, and your USP, you should regularly revisit levels three through five to ask yourself the following questions:

- Are there new or overlooked market conditions you should investigate?
- Will your value set, key values, and USP blow your player personas away?
- Are there new or overlooked competitors you should add to your value matrix?

Another question you should ask yourself at this point, based on all the information you gathered on your competitors, your game type, and the requirements for your value set, is the engine or engines you want to develop your proof-of-concept, your prototype, and later your game in. These are important decisions that will affect your concept development and eventually become part of your pitch proposal.

Outlook

If you have settled on your value set, your key values, and your USP, if you know your market conditions, target audience, and competitors inside out, and if you have a good idea about the engine or engines you want to use, then you've beaten the Preparation phase! Put everything into your *Ludotronics* inventory and don't forget to document all the background details and the reasons for your decisions.

And there's more! By beating all six levels of the Preparation phase, you have successfully promoted your game idea to a game plan. Congratulations!

The next part of your journey, the Procedure phase, will lead you across the northern perimeter of the *Ludotronics* map toward *Thematic Unity*. Along this phase, you will turn what is now your game plan into a game concept.

Phase 03

Procedures

Introduction

Welcome to the Procedure phase!

In *The Art of Computer Game Design*, Chris Crawford goes out of his way to stress the importance of both "topic" and "goal" to "establish the fantasies that the game will support and the types of emotions it will engender." This illustrates very succinctly the key aspects of what we will call the theme, the design-driven goal, and the desire-driven goal of a game in the upcoming levels.

This phase will take you to the upper, or northern, part of the *Ludotronics* map, for a journey through the essential aspects of thematic unity for game design. There are three levels you'll have to beat to upgrade your game plan to a game concept. The first level will introduce you to themes, motifs, and thematic unity as critical design tools. In the second level, you will develop the design-driven goal for your game, based on thematic unity, that you will polish down to a crisp, information-rich synopsis in the Proposition phase. In the third level, similarly, you will develop the desire-driven goal for your game, also based on thematic unity, that you will polish down to a powerful vision statement in the Proposition phase. Both the synopsis and the vision statement, that much should be obvious, are vital elements for a publisher pitch.

DOI: 10.1201/9781003334682-12

Level One

The Enchanted Theme

Opening

To make meaningful design decisions, you need a theme that keeps everything together. A theme prevents you, and later all hands during development, from making impromptu design decisions or design decisions based on personal preferences. It helps you to design games where every element is *valuable*, *relevant*, and *consistent*.

Beat 1: Experiences

What is a theme? Looking at lists of themes that are not downright hogwash, themes seem to be, or relate to, human experiences. Which can be experiences like ambition, fear, jealousy, identity, loyalty, forgiveness, or self-sacrifice, for example. But how these experiences relate to creative media like novels, movies, paintings, or games, which purportedly incorporate them, seems to be a rather complicated matter.

If you go and search for what defines the relationship between theme and creative media, it's like a game of musical chairs where a theme is what it is at the moment the music stops playing. It's the "broad idea" or "message" of a work, a "universal idea," an "outlook on life," the "central topic," what a work "is about," its "central idea" or "central point." This isn't helpful at all. Furthermore, what's supposedly not a theme—it's neither the "subject" of a work, nor a "motif," nor its "plot"—is far from enlightening either. Let alone applicable, even if you have a good understanding of what subjects, motifs, or plots actually are!

Trying to grasp the nature of theme through a dictionary approach will always lead you in a definitional circle right back to where you started. Which suggests that there is something wrong about the way theme is generally understood, or applied. Two things, specifically, seem troublesome.

To begin with, trying to understand theme through traditional approaches from the humanities leads into the domain of artistic and literary criticism. Now, analyzing and interpreting what a work's theme is and how it does what it does in, say, a novel, a movie, a painting, or indeed a game is exciting, and it can be exquisitely rewarding and enhance the overall experience. But analyzing and interpreting a work of art is certainly not a necessary part of enjoying it.

Then, and this is an important point to stress, theme is not primarily a tool for storytelling. It can support storytelling, as you will see in the Process phase, but you can tell stories just fine without developing a theme. The world is full of well-told stories from great storytellers who did not wrap their stories around specific themes. It could well be that one of the things that makes great stories great as an enjoyable, unified experience is that themes emerge from well-told stories. But that would once again point in the direction that storytelling *precedes* theme, and not the other way round.

Therefore, we will take a different approach and define theme as a *tool for design decisions*. Not just any old tool, but one of the most powerful tools in the game designer's toolbox. It will inform design decisions of any kind for the entire game, and that's why establishing a theme for a game falls firmly into the responsibility of a game *designer*, not a game *writer*.

Here's how it works. First, you create a theme, to be discussed in this level. Then, based on that theme, you create motifs based on that theme for all four dimensions of the *Ludotronics* map, also discussed in this level, and demonstrated. Finally, later in the Process phase, both theme and motifs will drive your

DOI: 10.1201/9781003334682-13

design decisions across all four territories of the *Ludotronics* map, informing choices for every conceivable game element.

We will define the theme for our purposes as follows: theme is a tool for design decisions that represents a human experience at the highest, but still useful, level of abstraction.

> Theme is a tool for design decisions that represents a human experience at the highest, but still useful, level of abstraction.

Let's cycle through a handful of examples to show why we need the limitation "but still useful" in our definition, beginning with "life." Life is an experience, obviously, and you won't get more conceptually abstract than that. But is it useful for making design decisions? No. Come to think of it, life isn't a theme but the *backdrop* for every possible theme.

Then, what about "death" or "love?" They seem better suited to serve as themes than life, but they're still too broad to provide top-notch guidance for design decisions. They qualify, but barely.

Finally, "danger." It's as abstract as it can get. But again, it isn't useful at all, only for different reasons this time. The range of possible motifs that danger could generate is immense, but these motifs would have very little in common, except for being, well, dangerous somehow. Thus, they wouldn't contribute to a unified whole or add up to a better understanding of danger. Compare that to "fear." Fear is equally abstract, but the motifs it could generate would indeed be able to add up to a better understanding of fear. Danger, looking closely, is rather a situation than a human experience. But "situation" isn't a reliable differentiator when it comes to deciding what qualifies as a theme and what doesn't. *Usefulness* is, together with abstraction.

You will find that there are many potential themes out there that are abstract enough and bring more substance to the table to aid design decisions than death or love. Some have been mentioned above, like ambition, fear, jealousy, or identity. Other great options are friendship, justice, power, or vanity. And so on. But go check and look for yourself! You will come up with a kazillion more.

Could you start out with a theme instead and then look for the best possible game concept that fits your theme? Absolutely. But a game concept will constrain the range of possible themes much more effectively than a theme would constrain the range of possible game concepts. Thus, the latter might lead to an arbitrary decision, not a deliberate or even necessary one.

Beat 2: Effects

The theme, as a tool, helps you create a coherent world where everything is connected by and through the theme. The game relates to your theme the way a compendium or handbook relates to its topic. The game can present theme-related aspects, attitudes, and approaches; provide conflicting or complementary viewpoints and perspectives; and might even offer competing or interlocking micro-narratives related to the theme. Alternatively, the game could offer a meta-narrative (or "grand" or "master" narrative) as a definite position. But one essential characteristic of video games is the potential to empower players to create their own narratives during play and make meaningful decisions, so it would seem undesirable to present an all-encompassing authoritative interpretation related to its theme. Which doesn't mean you can't do it if you want to.

Yet, what we cannot do, narratively and aesthetically, is to let things "just happen," the way most things just happen in real life. Even in aleatoric "made by chance" writing or music, words and sentences or notes and chords do not just happen. The element of chance that is introduced into these works of art is planned and systematic. In other words, *designed*. There is a fundamental difference between that which occurs naturally and that which is designed, between what happens in real life and what happens in a story, a game, or a work of art in general. We will dive much deeper into this topic through related concepts like contingency and unpredictability in the Process phase. At this point, it suffices to realize that thematic unity will make your design decisions non-random and a matter of, indeed, design.

Imagine your player character has to meet a non-player character to acquire a piece of information. It's part of your story line, and the piece of information is a plot point. Where should your characters meet? As you can observe in video games and other media as well, high on the list are offices, restaurants, bars, street corners, parks, maybe phone calls, and none of these have any dramatic function whatsoever. They should! Basically, there are two approaches to designing meaningful locations. One is to make that location count and use it to advance story or character or the world narrative, which we will discuss in-depth in the Process phase. The other is to advance the theme and highlight one or more of its motifs, which is the approach that interests us here. (The nature of motifs will be discussed in the next beat.) For example, if *jealousy* is your theme, the characters could meet in a department store at or around the jewelry section, which covers not just one but two motifs related to your theme: jealousy aroused by expensive, beautiful things one craves to possess but cannot obtain; and jealousy related to romantic love.

While all this is rather uncontroversial with respect to games with a cinematological/aesthetic or narratological core, there might be some confusion with regard to theme when it comes to games with a game-mechanical or ludological core. The discussion, most of the time, revolves around well-supported historical examples where games have shed their theme and theme-related elements over time and were reduced to their game-mechanical or ludological core. This often happens when a game becomes "professionalized"—with an infrastructure of core devotees, competitive tournaments, and increasingly standardized rules, requirements, and conditions. Think chess, for starters, where elaborately furnished and sumptuously decorated chessboards and set pieces, to support the fiction of imperial or feudal warfare, still exist for collectors and connoisseurs but are almost never used in modern professional tournaments. Think *Tetris*, which was originally released in the United States and elsewhere with a Russian theme or style that defined its look-and-feel through sound, music, graphics, and background graphics—less and less of which are to be found in versions aimed at professionalized players, up to and including the Classic Tetris World Championship. Or, as a final example, think of first-person shooter tournaments where all the visual candy supporting the underlying fiction is toned down or switched off, and tournament players go on a rampage when the host demands that they keep their own guns visible to provide a better experience for spectators. (Which indeed happened, back in the early days of esports.) But here's the catch. You cannot market your game to professionalized players when such players do not yet exist for your game. And to target existing professionalized players isn't such a good idea either. Why on earth should professional players abandon their favorite games, into which they've invested huge amounts of time and energy, and their dedicated and often tight-knit communities, for *your* game? At release time, you need to market your game to a broader audience by way of a broader appeal, and that's why you need a theme and theme-related elements in all four dimensions. Would *Tetris* have become such a staggering success without its theme-related elements? Probably not. Its look-and-feel and especially the music were instrumental in enthralling and mesmerizing players across all kinds of demographics. This is what you should aim at. If the mechanics of your game are well-designed, it might create its very own professionalized player base and infrastructure over time—which is a substantially more reasonable endeavor than to go and pry long-established games from dedicated players' hands.

Beat 3: Exercises

Now, to work with a theme, you also need motifs related to your theme. Here are three powerful practical reasons why you should always work with a theme and theme-related motifs:

- Working with a theme and motifs is a great way to make every design decision count.
- You and your team can discuss every design decision in terms of how well it matches the theme or one of its motifs. This prevents discussions about personal taste or preferences. How well something fits a motif, that's a topic everybody can contribute to in meaningful ways, regardless of their specialization.
- Along with your vision and your set of key values including your USP, it's your third magic item to guide you through the development cycle later. If you have all three, then you know

even better what elements to hang on to when funds run out, and you know even better what to implement and what to reject when your team (or your publisher) enters into the scope creep or feature creep phase. The ubiquitous advice given to game designers in such situations is to "hold on to your vision." But visions, particularly those with a capital "V" as mentioned in the Preliminary phase, are often joyfully impervious to rational decision-making. By triangulating your vision with your key values including your USP and your theme and motifs, however, you will never lose your bearings on the seas of ideas. You will always know which courses to follow and which to avoid.

Here's how you create a theme and motifs that relate to it. First, make a list of human experiences that might be a match for your game, are sufficiently abstract but still useful, and not entirely outside your wheelhouse. (When it comes to human experiences, you can research a lot, but not everything.) Envisage the different impacts each of these experiences would have on your game experience. Pick one that both fits your vision and has the potential to aid design decisions from levels to characters to assets to rules. Voilà, that's your theme.

Next, you need to derive motifs from your theme. To define what a motif is, we simply take the definition of a theme and reduce its abstraction level to a theme-related experience, activity, structure, action, representation, process, state, dependency, or similar.

> A motif is a tool for design decisions that represents an element associated with a theme at a lower level of abstraction: a theme-related experience, activity, structure, action, representation, process, state, dependency, or similar.

Creating your theme is the first step, creating motifs based on your theme is the second step, and making design decisions based on your motifs is the third step. Your theme is attached to your game as a whole; your motifs are attached to the four dimensions; and your design decisions for every conceivable game element are attached to the four territories—*Interactivity, Plurimediality, Narrativity,* and *Architectonics*—that you will travel across in the Process phase.

All this is less intimidating than it sounds. Imagine your player character is lost in the woods. How should the trees look? You can base their design on the game's art style, literary genre, or game narrative. All these will narrow your focus already, which is good and important. But these parameters are still too vague on a granular level. They rarely suffice to lead you to design decisions that are such a good match as to feel almost inevitable. However, if you have a theme like fear or spirituality or childhood with its corresponding motifs, it can guide your design decisions as to how the trees should look in very focused and distinctive ways.

Again, as with theme, there might be some confusion whether you really need motifs across all four dimensions. The answer should be yes, even for games with only the most rudimentary cinematological and narratological dimensions. Let's have a look at *Pong*. It's a very simple game, and it has a very simple and specific theme, "tennis." In the game-mechanical dimension, you can already see a clever design decision at work that is based on a tennis-related motif: by making the ball accelerate the longer it remains in play, the game catches the mounting tension during a prolonged game of tennis very well. In the ludological dimension, you can find another tennis-related-motif: by way of a segmented paddle, the player can interact with the ball in different ways and change its angle of return. For the cinematological dimension, the audiovisual presence of tennis-related motifs is rather obvious. Originally, crowd sound effects were considered too, but technically impossible to implement at the time. Finally, the narratological dimension. *Pong* certainly doesn't have a story. But playing *Pong* generates, in real-time, player narratives of a contest with a narrow set of dramatic arcs like "glorious win/crushing defeat," "tough match between equals," "comeback story," and a few others. So that's another takeaway here. If you have a game concept that doesn't include a story, look at the range of player narratives your game generates, and then tweak your game along your theme and motifs to define this range more precisely and more imaginatively toward a rich playing experience.

Generating motifs for your theme is a matter of brainstorming and research. For the theme "identity," for example, you could pick identity formation, identity crisis, and impersonation for the narratological dimension; symmetry, uniformity, and corporate identity for the cinematological dimension; mirroring, duplication, and pattern matching for the ludological dimension; and substitution, assimilation, and non-individual objects for the game-mechanical dimension. Motifs that can aid design decisions in the game-mechanical dimension are usually the hardest to find; but they can always give you ideas for imaginative rules and rule sets.

Outlook

If you have explored your options, decided on a theme, generated a number of motifs from that theme across all four dimensions, and stored everything in your *Ludotronics* inventory, you beat this level! With that under your belt, you can now proceed to create the design-driven goal of your game.

Before you leave this level, however, one final word on the nature of theme. If you happen to come across lists with "common themes" in books or on the web, often adding up to highly suspicious sum totals like 7, 10, or 12, and incorporating items like "Man Struggles Against Nature," "Love Is Stronger Than Death," "Crime Does Not Pay," or "Sacrifices Bring Reward," don't be fooled. All these "common themes" are supremely abstract all right, but they are not themes at all but stories on their highest possible levels of abstraction. (We will discuss the nature of stories in the Process phase.) As such, besides not being themes, they are singularly useless for making design decisions. What's more, most of them are *authoritative interpretations* that constitute the meaning, purpose, or indeed moral of the story in question. Which runs counter to the unique strengths of video games as an interactive medium, offering meaningful player decisions and generating individual player narratives, experiences, and viewpoints.

Level Two

The Design-Driven Goal

Opening

When we think of the goal of a game, we usually think along the lines of in-game outcomes—winning a match, retrieving the prince, or saving the universe. This isn't wrong. But remember, we're traveling through the *Thematic Unity* part of the *Ludotronics* map! That should give you a hint that more is at stake.

Beat 1: Precepts

What's at stake is that the in-game outcome of your game should align with the kind of game you want to design and the player experience you want to create. If these three components—which we will call the *game-driven goal*, the *design-driven goal*, and the *desire-driven goal*—fit well together, that's the holistic goal of your game. Here's an overview of its three components.

> The **design-driven goal** is the goal of the design and development process. It specifies and illustrates *player payoff* as a brief summary of growth, insight, and experience. Reworked and polished, your design-driven goal will become the *synopsis* for your pitch proposal later in the Proposition phase.
>
> The **desire-driven goal** is a powerful motivational message that makes the player *want* to play the game and achieve its game-driven goal. It specifies and illustrates the *playing experience*. Reworked and polished, your desire-driven goal will become the *vision statement* for your pitch proposal later in the Proposition phase.
>
> The **game-driven goal** is the game's victory condition, loss condition, or self-set condition (i.e., conditions derived from goals players set themselves). It specifies and illustrates *game completion* as a worthwhile and achievable outcome.

Before we proceed, a piece of advice: always be careful what you communicate! Your desire-driven goal, which will become your vision statement and the motivational message to go and play the game, is something you can and probably want to communicate far and wide. Your design-driven goal, in contrast, which will become your synopsis, will contain massive bags of spoilers, so you should restrict it to internal use and your pitch proposal. Your game-driven goal falls somewhere in between; you might want to communicate some of it in general (win matches, retrieve the prince, save the universe) but keep some or all of the details under wraps.

In this level, you will find everything you need to create your design-driven goal for your synopsis; in the next, you will learn how to create your desire-driven goal for your vision statement. For the third and final part of your holistic goal, the game-driven goal, you'll have to wait until you've entered the territories on the *Ludotronics* map. That's because your game-driven goal requires not general and conceptual, but very specific and practical design decisions that belong into the Process phase.

DOI: 10.1201/9781003334682-14

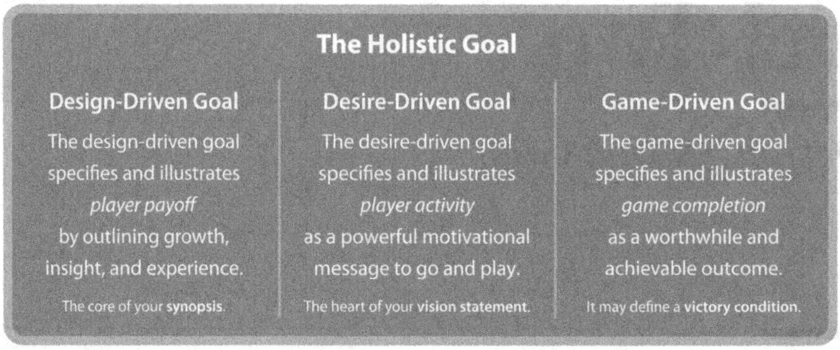

FIGURE 3.1   The holistic goal.

Beat 2: Payoffs

The first part of the holistic goal, the design-driven goal, is about planning the payoff for the player. Ideally, this payoff includes successful learning experiences; gaining insights into the game world and the game's theme; and experiencing settings and situations not normally available within the context of one's life.

Together with their respective frameworks, these elements look like this (the player, character, and story development arcs will be discussed in-depth in the Process phase):

- Growth (Player Development Arc)
- Insight (Character Development Arc)
- Experience (Story Development Arc)

This is also valid for games that are not dramatically complete. Even games with a pure ludological or game-mechanical core, from *Pong* to the game of Go, provide all three elements in one way or another. Let's go through these elements in some detail.

Growth. The growth component of the design-driven goal refers to the *skills* and the *knowledge* the player acquires and develops to reach the game-driven goal. Most of the time, it refers to advances in skill through predefined difficulty levels, open-ended high-scores, or matches against higher skilled opponents by competing for time, tokens (of every imaginable kind, from butchered enemies to stars or coins to cat snapshots), flawlessness of execution, number of victories (solved puzzles, correct decisions, defeated enemies, and such), or combinations thereof.

Insight. The insight component of the design-driven goal relates to a deeper *understanding* of the game world by encountering aspects associated with the game's theme, which in turn can and should support and encourage *attitude change* inside the game (but possibly also outside the game, including metagame aspects).

Experience. The experience component of the design-driven goal is provided by the *routes* and *resolutions* as part of the game's dramatic structure. In dramatically complete games, this refers to the story development arc along which the player has to uncover the conspiracy, save the universe, conquer the territory, escape the prison, or arbitrarily exterminate an important species. In games without stories, it refers to player-generated narratives as illustrated along *Pong* in the preceding level. In so-called goal-less games, it refers to arcs evolved from goals that players set themselves from the range of goals the game is designed to support.

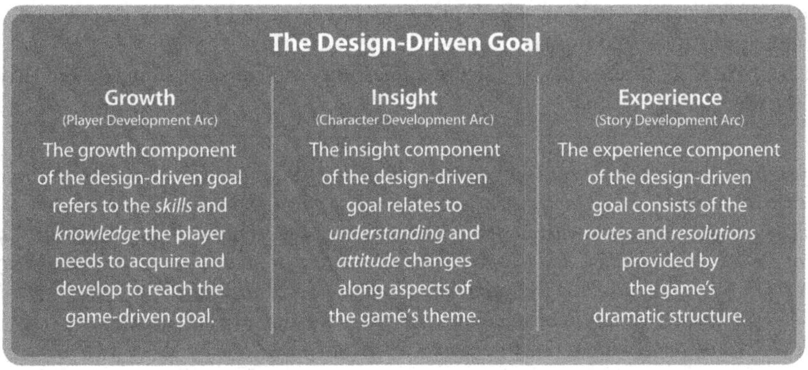

The Design-Driven Goal

Growth	Insight	Experience
(Player Development Arc)	(Character Development Arc)	(Story Development Arc)
The growth component of the design-driven goal refers to the *skills* and *knowledge* the player needs to acquire and develop to reach the game-driven goal.	The insight component of the design-driven goal relates to *understanding* and *attitude* changes along aspects of the game's theme.	The experience component of the design-driven goal consists of the *routes* and *resolutions* provided by the game's dramatic structure.

FIGURE 3.2 The design-driven goal.

Consulting your game concept and your player personas, you can now create your design-driven goal by answering these three questions about a typical player who played and finished your game:

- What did the player learn?
- What did the player understand?
- What did the player go through?

In the following beat, we will put this into practice with examples.

Beat 3: Patterns

This beat, mind, contains comprehensive spoilers for the single-player first-person shooter *Unreal*.

As mentioned above, a design-driven goal will become a synopsis and should be for internal use only. That's why you don't see them floating around on the web, except when they're of historical value or servers were hacked. Thus, while our examples will be actual games that exist, their synopses are reverse engineered for the occasion.

For our first example, we will imagine we're in the process of designing the 1998 single-player first-person shooter *Unreal*.

Our first question would be: what should our prospective players have learned by the end of the game? That's not too hard to answer in this case, as it's mainly about weapons and tactics. But many of these weapons are exotic and difficult to master, and there's a broad range of different enemies, each of them dangerous in their own strange ways.

Then, the second question: what should our prospective players have understood by the end of the game? That's intimately related to the game's theme, which we also have to reverse engineer. While we can't look into the heads of the developers or even know if they intentionally worked with a theme, there's strong evidence that "redemption" is the best fit. In brief, the player character is a nameless prisoner and shipwreck survivor on an uncharted planet, wounded and powerless, who becomes very powerful over time. The first insight to be gained here, which might sound familiar, is that with greater powers come greater responsibilities. Just by fighting the alien invaders on that planet, the player character becomes an ally of the native intelligent species, who might or might not come to regard the player character as a mythic savior figure during the course of the game. Attitude change is also involved, as an option: the more the player character cares for the suppressed natives, the more helpful they become by revealing secret passages and valuable equipment. (All these tropes around "natives," it should be mentioned, are fraught with historical ballast and narrative hazards.)

Finally, the third question: what does the player go through? From the prison ship to the numerous deadly locations on and around the planet and finally open space, the player goes through an endless string of successful escapes—each of which promises freedom, and possibly redemption. But there's always one more thing to escape from.

Now that we have a set of answers to our three questions, we can sketch our design-driven goal. It could read like this:

> *Escaped from a crash-landed prison ship on an uncharted planet, the nameless and initially powerless player/player character learns to control exotic weapons and acquire new tactics against ever more dangerous enemies on a journey toward redemption that touches upon questions of power, responsibility, and freedom. Uneasily drifting into and out of the role of a mythic savior figure who is supposed to free the planet from its host of alien invaders, the player/player character finally overcomes all obstacles and enemies and escapes into space in an emergency shuttle, but is left there with the only option to "drift and hope."*

Certainly, this is not a happy ending. Nor is everything lost. But, as a final insight, true freedom and redemption might have been gained by abandoning the logic of escape, by staying on the planet instead and deal with a whole pile of leftover problems from the invasion. (But as the logic of escape isn't abandoned after all, the game is able to keep scratching along, without fully embracing, the "white savior" trope that always looms perilously close.)

For our second example, let's have a shot at *Tetris*, a game without a story and with a game-mechanical core. Here, the answers to our three questions are a bit more condensed. The player must learn to manipulate the game pieces, tetrominoes, accurately and efficiently (growth). The player must understand how the different geometries of the tetrominoes behave, how they stack up, and what patterns they form (insight). The player goes from level to level with mounting time pressure, and with less and less room to maneuver, to prevent the playing field from filling up (experience).

Again, based on our set of answers, we can sketch our design-driven goal:

> *The player learns to move and rotate game pieces of different geometrical shapes that randomly appear and fall down a well with ever-increasing speed. To prevent these pieces from filling up the well, the player clears them from the playing field by arranging them into gapless, horizontal rows at the bottom of the well through foresight, pattern recognition, and careful maneuvering, with bonus points for completing and clearing two or more bottom rows at once.*

While growth and experience elements can easily be found for most games, insight is the element that often rests with your imagination. But rare is the game that doesn't offer any insights at all!

Consider, for example, a multiplayer arena shooter. Skill poses no problem. It will consist of advancing accuracy, speed, hand-eye coordination, combos, predictive aiming, and such on the one hand; and tactical and strategic knowledge to master challenges on the other, including map layout, weapon properties and contextual effectiveness, ammo cycles, power-up locations, and so on. For experience, this would naturally be a description of the events and sudden turns typical for a match in game modes like Deathmatch (DM) or Capture the Flag (CTF). But now, what insights should your player have acquired, and how would these relate to the game's theme?

While arena shooters, like any other game type, should *always* have a theme to guide design decisions, their themes are not renowned for facilitating profound insights into the cosmos. But we must consider what this game type is critically about. It could be insights about how one's own skills compare to others; how to keep one's cool and perform well under time or team pressure; or insights about, and advances toward, anger management as attitude change. In game modes where team performance is a factor, understanding and attitude change could be tied to qualities that make a good team player—which, in favorable circumstances, might translate into not being a self-centered jerk in real-life environments. Alternatively, it could be about learning to take the lead, deal with uncertainty, or mediate disputes, and whatnot. Whatever it is, *that's* what your design-driven goal should capture in this case.

Outlook

This should suffice to set you on track. After creating your design-driven goal, the next thing you have to make sure is that all three elements—growth, insight, experience—are fully compatible with the wants and needs of your player personas. Would those progressions in skill and knowledge, insight and understanding, and trials and tribulations toward game completion be a good fit? If not, you should either rethink your design-driven goal, rethink your player personas, or both, until they are a perfect match.

Your design-driven goal will accompany you throughout the Process phase to guide and focus your design decisions. After that, in the Proposition phase, you will rework and polish it down into a crisp synopsis, which is also often called log line just to confuse you.

Once more, be careful what you communicate. For the *Tetris* example, it wouldn't matter. But it should be plainly obvious from the *Unreal* example why your design-driven goal, and later your synopsis, should be for internal and pitch use only. Your prospective players would be rightfully angered if the game became comprehensively spoiled for them by way of a leaked synopsis.

Level Three

The Desire-Driven Goal

Opening

Reworked and polished, your desire-driven goal will become your vision statement later in the Proposition phase. But not only that! During and after development, it will become the key message around which you, and later your publisher's marketing team, will create the strategy and assets to promote and market your game.

Beat 1: Calls

Your desire-driven goal is, all things considered, the *call to action* to buy and play your game—a call to action that promises an exciting and rewarding playing experience. It links the game you want to create, your design-driven goal, with your game-driven goal as a worthwhile and achievable outcome for the player.

Like every call to action, your desire-driven goal must accomplish two very different objectives at the same time. It must command people's attention (the means), and it must deliver a powerful message (the ends). Each objective has its own specific set of strategies. The strategy set for commanding attention consists of being *simple*, *specific*, and *promising*. The strategy set for delivering a powerful message consists of the promise to *excite*, *achieve*, and *become*.

Let's unpack both sets, beginning with commanding attention:

- *Simple* indicates that your desire-driven goal must be easy to understand without any up-front knowledge about your game.
- *Specific* indicates that your desire-driven goal must offer concrete and identifiable details from your game.
- *Promising* indicates that your desire-driven goal must appear relevant to your target audience.

Next, the set for forging and delivering a powerful message:

- *Excite* captures the imagination by pitching the gameplay as an activity that is stimulating, delightful, and rewarding.
- *Achieve* promises challenge and, in extension, the right level of challenge so that mastering or beating the game is difficult to achieve, but can be achieved with the appropriate level of determination.
- *Become* communicates that mastering or beating the game brings about a meaningful and memorable transformation in terms of ability/expertise, attitude/perspective, or reputation/ status.

You will meet this set's three elements again in the Process phase as the three floors of the motivational building, to be populated with motivational elements that keep your players, once they were excited enough to start playing, spellbound and glued to your game.

DOI: 10.1201/9781003334682-15

FIGURE 3.3   The desire-driven goal.

Beat 2: Contrasts

To craft and calibrate your desire-driven goal, you need your game's key values, including your USP. Which should be obvious! If your desire-driven goal doesn't reflect them directly or indirectly, then something is clearly amiss.

Before we look at some fresh examples in the upcoming and final beat, let's return to *Unreal* to make the difference between the design-driven goal (synopsis) and the desire-driven goal (vision statement) more tangible.

To craft the desire-driven goal for *Unreal*, we need to check its value set in the context of its time. What are the game's outstanding value characteristics? What differentiates it from similar games from the same era? Luckily, we did all the necessary work in the Preparation phase!

In the *Game Mechanics* category, AI quality is a blast. In the *Ludology* category, there's a huge arsenal of unfamiliar weapons the player must learn to handle. As to coop mode, all competitors have it but one, so it's not a differentiating factor. In the *Narratology* category, it has a customizable player character, which is unique among its competitors, and it has an outstanding world narrative, also called environmental storytelling. But the game shines brightest in the *Cinematology* category, with its unmatched level of atmosphere and detail at the time. All this we have to convey with our desire-driven goal, but without giving away plot points or endings! So let's have a shot at it, and see how *Unreal*'s desire-driven goal might sound:

> *You are Prisoner 849, barely alive, and your prison just became much larger and more lethal. Escaped from the wreck of the crash-landed* Vortex Rikers, *you face a whole uncharted world waiting for you to make a mistake. Fight with strange and powerful weapons against hosts of enemies, each dangerous in their own terrifying way, from the claustrophobic confines of subterranean mines to breathtaking vistas of colossal canyons and floating villages under alien moons. Heroic defiance might not guarantee freedom, or make you the chosen one. But you can still hope that you're the lucky one.*

This encapsulates much of the experience that *Unreal* players tend to reminisce about, as Kaitlin Tremblay's and Alan Williamson's *Escape to Na Pali: A Journey to the Unreal* emphatically attests to.

As to our first strategy set, it's easy to understand (shipwreck, alien planet, escape), it's specific (*Vortex Rikers*, floating villages), and it's promising (intelligent enemies, exotic weapons, unique atmosphere).

As to our second strategy set, it should sound exciting enough for the primary target audience, and perhaps even for a secondary target audience with a general interest in science fiction. It promises a tough challenge, but a challenge a determined player can overcome. Its juxtaposed concepts (escape vs. freedom, being chosen vs. being lucky)—together with the game's atmosphere and mood and focus on exploration—promise experiences and insights with the potential to be meaningful and memorable. The customizable player character's been left out; while it would be desirable to convey it too, it can't be delivered "in character" and without breaking the message's mood and immediacy. It would make it less personal instead of more!

Comparing our sketches for *Unreal*'s design-driven goal and its desire-driven goal, the differences are numerous and vivid. The former is about facts and design, the latter about attractions and desires. The former is informational, the latter personal. The former crafts a summary, the latter promises an experience.

Don't let elements from one bleed over into the other. This will only dilute their respective powers.

Beat 3: Cases

Now that the differences are clear, let's look at a few more examples, so you can sketch desire-driven goals for different types of games with ease.

Let's turn from *Unreal* to its cousin, the famous stand-alone multiplayer arena game *Unreal Tournament*. Its sequel, *Unreal Tournament 2003/2004*, had a terrific vision statement; you can look it up on the web with the keywords "Reload. Rev up. Ride out." However, it had a new and rather curious game mode called Bombing Run that wasn't easy to portray, and its descriptions remained technical and the opposite of exciting. Let's try our hand at sketching a desire-driven goal for this game mode:

> *Be the one to grab the ball, execute a rushing play through enemy fire, and score a spectacular suicide goal—or pass the ball and protect your runner instead, by outmaneuvering, blocking, and mowing down hostile players with an incredible arsenal of futuristic weapons in an intense, coordinated team effort.*

It's simple (players get the idea even if they've never heard of Bombing Run before), it's specific (particularly the "suicide goal" option), and it's promising (as a distinctly new, yet sufficiently familiar challenge for the game's target audience).

It also covers all the bases from the second set: excite (gameplay), achieve (challenge), and become (transformation); the latter by evoking potential advancements in ability/expertise, reputation/status, and team-oriented attitude/perspective for this unusual and demanding tournament mode.

Next, let's do the same for an entirely fictitious third-person action-adventure game concept, set against the backdrop of the French Revolution. It might sound like this:

> *As a freed slave in the aftermath of the French Revolution, unravel labyrinthine plots and combat treacherous factions to save your friend and ally Thomas Paine from the guillotine—while searching for your ethnic identity, your own place in the world, and maybe your true self in the dawning age of nation states.*

It's simple (French Revolution, factions), it's specific (guillotine, Thomas Paine), and it's promising (engaging narrative, whodunit, action). There's excitement (revolution and conspiracies), achievement (cognitive and physical), and potential transformation (e.g., grasping the complicated dynamics between ethnic and national identity).

You can extend your desire-driven goal to explicitly include your USP. But if you do, it should not appear as a feature. It should appear as a benefit! Let's say our action-adventure game's USP was a highly sophisticated NPC system. What we shouldn't do, then, is to insert "with a highly sophisticated NPC system!" Instead, we should break up the first sentence after "factions" and proceed like this: *"Fight alongside and against persistent and believable friends and foes to save your companion and ally Thomas Paine from the guillotine."*

Our final example, the game of Go, is a tough nut to crack. Players stare at the board, sometimes forever, and take turns placing stones; the goal is to enclose board territory and capture opposing stones; and the higher point total from that plus first-move compensation wins the game. Translating that into a desire-driven goal wouldn't sound very enticing, so you have to think more holistically about what makes this game so attractive. With that in mind, the design-driven goal for the game of Go could sound like this:

> *Place your stones to surround more territory and capture more stones than your opponent in this most simple, yet most complex ancient strategy board game defined by intricate patterns,*

unfolding strategies, and dramatic reversals where victory is never certain. Become a member of a truly global community that will help and support you while you rise through the kyū ranks to earn your first dan.

Once again, it's simple (you place stones to surround territory and capture stones from your opponent), it's specific (reversals, community, ranks), and it's promising—for a particular target audience attracted by the promise of lifelong learning and being part of a global community.

And, once again, it covers the bases from the second set: excite (the gameplay), achieve (the challenge), and become (the transformation). Besides ability/expertise and reputation/status, the latter particularly touches upon attitude/perspective in terms of being competitive and supportive at the same time.

Optionally, as in the preceding example, we could incorporate the game's USP. For that, we first have to answer the question of what its USP is. Many of the characteristics the game of Go is praised for can be found in other games as well, among them having ancient origins, a global community, comparatively simple rules, a staggering number of possible combinations, and so on. A strong candidate, and probably our best bet, is its handicap system. Rare is the strategy game that enables players of all ranks and skill levels to compete with each other and enjoy the game without bending the rules to their breaking point. Turned into a benefit, it works best with the community part, where we can insert it like this: *Become a member of a truly global community to enjoy exciting matches with beginners and masters alike, who will help and support you while you rise through the kyū ranks to earn your first dan.*

That should suffice. Now you can sketch your own desire-driven goal!

Outlook

If you sketched your theme and motifs and your design- and desire-driven goals, and stored everything in your *Ludotronics* inventory, congratulations! Not only did you beat the Procedure phase, you also promoted your game plan to a game concept! Which will be your ticket to the Process phase.

Still, it won't hurt to double-check everything. Would your player personas still be excited about your game? Is everything in sync with your value set and your USP? Is the core of your game still what you thought it would be?

If in doubt, go back, dig deeper, change what needs to be changed. For term projects, a few initial flaws might not matter that much. But if you want to pursue a career as an indie developer and create games that captivate and delight your players, then your conceptual groundwork has to be a lot more robust right from the start.

Phase 04

Processes

Introduction

Welcome to the Process phase!

Before we plunge into the Process phase, let's pause for a moment. This is the longest and most challenging phase by far. However, only the two flanking levels, the integral perspectives, are meant to be worked through in the same methodical fashion as you worked your way through the *Preparation* and *Procedure* phases. The four levels in between will introduce you to a large array of challenging and often complex design approaches and perspectives that might or might not be relevant for your concept, applicable to your game type, or a match for the design approach you have in mind. Accordingly, all four are open-world levels! You can tackle them in any order you like, and you can pick and choose whatever you think is relevant. But don't skip anything merely on a whim! You might not know what's relevant for your game and what's not just yet.

Nevertheless, you'll have to face a wide range of design decisions in this phase. Always put everything down in your *Ludotronics* inventory, thoroughly documented, with all your research data and legends where needed. But there's more! If, at any point during your journey, you decide to make it a team effort, your inventory should be accessible for the entire team at all times. You can either use the tools you're already familiar with, perhaps from earlier efforts or term projects. Or you can go and pick a fresh set of platform-agnostic collaborative online tools—from wiki to brainstorming to project management solutions—that look promising and are inexpensive or free to use for small teams.

When you have beaten the head and tail levels on integral perspectives in this phase and roamed the open-world levels in between as far and wide as you like, you will have something that you didn't have before: a *game treatment*. Here's a principal, game-agnostic description of the progress you've made during your journey, and what you will have accomplished by the end of this phase:

> From an initial idea that you panned and refined on the first leg of your journey, you created a *game idea*. Later on, still in the Preparation phase, you added a *target audience*, *key values*, and a *USP*, and promoted your game idea to a *game plan*. Then, you sketched a *theme* and *motifs* and *design-* and *desire-driven goals* during the Procedure phase, which promoted your game plan to a *game concept*. Next, in the Process phase, you created a detailed description of its *rule system*, its *aesthetic elements*, its *dramatic structure*, and its *motivation* and *reward* systems, which promoted your game concept to a *game treatment*.

DOI: 10.1201/9781003334682-16

We will talk more about what it means to have a game treatment in the Proposition phase, but here's one thing about it that is very important. Your concept will become a game treatment only when everything is *typed out*, not just in your head or loosely sketched along keywords. Then, and only then, will it be a thing—tangible, copyrightable, at least in the United States, and yours.

Before you start, however, here's one more thing you should take care of, something that will make your life a lot easier down the road. For every game element you sketch during the Process phase—every mechanic, every rule, every value, every feature—sketch a complementary method for testing and balancing it! This will come in handy when you build your prototype in the Proposition phase. It might not sound like the most attractive and most desirable activity on your journey. But if you stick to it, you will be rewarded later by achieving a much better quality with less time, effort, and torment.

Level One

Integral Perspectives I

Opening

Now that you've worked hard to create and polish a viable game concept and trace out its principal premises as well as its marketability, you will proceed to sketch out everything that makes a game, from its motivators to its rewards, from its rules to its dramatic structure. It's here where you will transform your original idea of a game into your vision of an interactive playing experience.

Beat 1: Experience

But wait—what does interactive playing experience mean in the first place? According to books, papers, interviews, and the internet in general, interactive playing experience means just about everything and just about nothing. Descriptions and definitions seem to be ranging from the theoretical to the practical and from the sweeping to the particular.

To make this term more useful and pave the way for meaningful, deliberate design decisions, let's start with breaking down "experience" into the constituents that are applicable to our context. On one side, we have experience as *expertise*: developing skills, knowledge, understanding, and attitude toward mastery and competitive performance through motivational involvement. On the other, we have experience as *awareness*: perceiving ongoing events with and through emotional involvement.

As you can see, this presents a formidable obstacle to designing any kind of playing experience. We can't *design* motivational and emotional involvement toward expertise and awareness directly. And even if we could, players should or indeed *must* be allowed to create their own experiences in games, which are not necessarily the experience the game designers had in mind.

Thus, playing experiences can only be designed indirectly by designing game events that facilitate a certain range of possible experiences. From there, great design can make it happen that most playing experiences fall within the game's intended range.

At its core, therefore, the playing experience is about player motivation (toward expertise) and player emotion (toward awareness). In other words: playing experience follows player motivation and player emotion.

> Playing experience follows player motivation and player emotion.

Now we have to make this interactive, not to forget. Within the *Ludotronics* paradigm, player motivation and player emotion are methodologically tied to the four territories through the just-right amount of challenge (*Interactivity*), compelling aesthetics (*Plurimediality*), emotional appeal (*Narrativity*), and meaningful choices (*Architectonics*). Together, they comprise the interactive playing experience model of the *Ludotronics* paradigm.

Through each of these four territories, you will be able to roam freely later in this phase. But motivation and emotion are the two integral perspectives that you, as a game designer, need to know inside out. Both come with a few tough bites of theory. But chewing your way through them with determination will pay off in practice later.

DOI: 10.1201/9781003334682-17

FIGURE 4.1   Playing experience.

FIGURE 4.2   Interactive playing experience model.

Beat 2: Motivation

Previously, in the Procedure phase, we created two sets of motivational drivers for the desire-driven goal, with *simple*, *specific*, and *promising* in the first set, and *excite*, *achieve*, and *become* in the second. We can leave the first set behind now, as it is focused on attracting attention and marketing communication in general. It's the second set that is deeply involved in creating motivation. It will follow you throughout the Process phase and eventually link this first level to its final level in the context of goals and rewards.

   The three motivators from the second set constitute the three floors of what we will call the motivational building, with *excite* as its first floor, *achieve* as its second floor, and *become* as its top floor. *Excite* represents the first floor because it's hard to become motivated if you're not excited. It's where the interactive playing experience model from the preceding beat resides. *Achieve* represents the second floor. It's where the player action is, where the rubber hits the road. It can be populated in different ways, but we'll start with a balanced cocktail of activities, the player activity setup, to be introduced in a minute. *Become*, finally, represents the third floor, which tops off all the excitement and all the achievements with the promise of personal growth.

   Now, let's go in to check all three floors of our motivational building and say hello to the tenants.

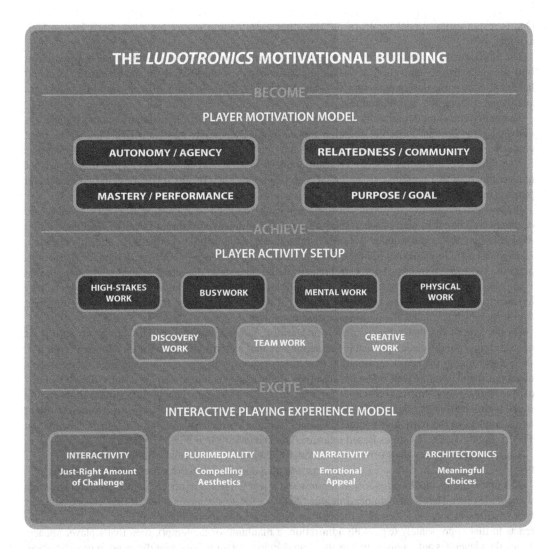

FIGURE 4.3 The motivational building.

On the first floor, as mentioned, reside the four elements of our interactive playing experience model: the just-right amount of challenge, compelling aesthetics, emotional appeal, and meaningful choices, each tied to one of the four territories.

The second floor of the motivational building can be populated with any motivational model or constituents that suit your game and your game type, including models you built yourself. We will revisit this floor in the context of goals and rewards in the final level and discuss different options. Right now, we populate it with an easily manageable set of activities that we will call the player activity setup. It's a cocktail of tasks that, if balanced in the right manner, makes these activities attractive, captivating, and worthwhile even though they are essentially work. The ingredients of this cocktail follow the seven types of work from Jane McGonigal's *Reality Is Broken*: high-stakes work, busywork, mental work, physical work, discovery work, teamwork, and creative work.

The tenants on the top floor need a more thorough introduction, and also a few remarks on research.

There exist all kinds of motivational theories, relating to needs, expectancy, arousal, and so forth, some of them stronger on the empirical side than others, some better at making testable claims or accurate predictions than others, on the whole they're too broad for our purposes. For game-based learning, two models are often used that are practical, applicable, and have a strong empirical heft.

One is a motivation model for learning, the other a motivation model for work. Let's have a look at both.

The motivational model for learning, called self-determination theory or SDT, grew out of research on intrinsic and extrinsic motivation. It was mainly developed by Richard M. Ryan and Edward L. Deci and later applied to game design by Scott Rigby and Richard M. Ryan. Its three primary building blocks are autonomy, competence, and relatedness.

The motivational model for work is also based on research on intrinsic and extrinsic motivation, put into shape and brought to public attention especially by Dan Ariely and Daniel H. Pink. In its most generalized form, it also boils down to three primary building blocks: autonomy, mastery, and purpose.

As you can see, autonomy is shared by both models. Mastery and competence, while related, are not quite compatible as a pair, and we will deal with that soon. Then there's relatedness in one model and purpose in the other.

Relatedness means exactly what you think it means: the need to connect with others, to take care of others, and be taken care of when things go wrong. Curiously, it's absent from the work motivation model. Which makes you wonder: not only is relatedness fundamental to cooperation and collaboration, which in turn are fundamental to mastering any substantial challenge in our time. Relatedness also supports the willingness to take risks, entrepreneurial and otherwise, not least because relatedness is also vital in case you fail. While we shouldn't put failure on too high a pedestal, it's certainly an opportunity to learn from mistakes, to see what works and what doesn't, and to push forward with better informed decisions, which is true for many things, including games!

On the side of the motivational model for learning, purpose is missing. This has to do with a set of underlying—and indeed reasonable—assumptions that subordinate purpose to autonomy. In a nutshell: according to the self-determination model, intrinsic aspirations and purposes are experienced as meaningful and promote well-being because they are products of autonomous decisions (driven by curiosity, creativity, enjoyment, the search for knowledge, and similar). Now, while this is theoretically sound within its framework, some evidence suggests that the three motivational factors from SDT might be incomplete in the particular context of games; see, for example, "Applying the Self Determination Theory of Motivation in Games Based Learning" by David Farrell and David Moffat.

Thus, the *Ludotronics* player motivation model will employ *four* primary building blocks instead of three, and each of them will come with two aspects that augment each other's essential characteristics.

The first building block consists of *autonomy* and *agency*. These are not the same—you can have one without the other. Here's an example. Imagine the player has to steal a diamond. If they can execute this task in different ways (e.g., sneaky, through an armed assault, or via blackmail), and the game world reacts to that appropriately (e.g., with admiration, a manhunt, or contempt), then that's player agency. When the player has autonomy, it means they can decide whether to steal that diamond in the first place.

The second building block consists of *mastery* and, in lieu of competence, *performance*. You can check out Carole Ames's "Classrooms: Goals, Structures, and Student Motivation" for a more in-depth introduction into this topic, but here's what it's essentially about. Mastery covers aspirations to become the best at a task, or at least to become as good as one possibly can. Performance covers aspirations to perform better than others—in other words, to win. The former roughly corresponds to intrinsic, the latter roughly to extrinsic motivation patterns. Yet, mastery-type players need performance goals too! Even with the best intentions to master something or other, it's often competition and extrinsic motivators that get mastery types off the couch.

The third building block consists of *relatedness* and *community*. Relatedness covers everything already mentioned: the need to connect with, and take care of, others; the willingness to take risks; and the opportunity to learn from mistakes. But relatedness does not necessarily include community. You can have great relationships with mutual support and everything without building or growing a community. Importantly, it's not relationships but communities that develop distinct cultures. Not always in good ways, mind—gaming communities in particular are often riddled with problems like exclusion, discrimination, and toxic behavioral norms. All this is part of the package, though, and that's what the term community brings to the table.

The fourth building block, finally, consists of *purpose* and *goal*. While more research needs to be done to test this hypothesis, observations indicate that the absence of purpose might be the factor that causes expectations to fail when SDT is applied to game-based learning or game design in general (research pending). In contrast to purpose, the complementary term goal refers to clear-cut goals that can be set, followed, and achieved. This comprises the game-driven goal, including all kinds of self-set goals that players might create along the way.

To sum it up, the four building blocks of our player motivation model are autonomy/agency, mastery/performance, relatedness/community, and purpose/goal. Now let's proceed to how this translates to learning!

Research into game-based learning explores how and what we can learn by playing games. Games are exceptionally good at teaching anything and everything. So good, actually, that we can say that *the motivation to play equals the motivation to learn*. To play a game well, we have to overcome challenges, and to overcome challenges, we have to learn. All the time. That's the nature of challenge. And what do you know—the widely familiar concept of *flow*, originally developed in the 1970s by the psychologist Csíkszentmihályi Mihály and subsequently expanded upon by himself and others, describes exactly that: *the state of flow is the completely focused motivation to learn and perform through constant challenge.*

The concept of flow, which we will examine more thoroughly in the second level in the context of *Interactivity*, is greatly preferable to the non-concept of "immersion," that favorite staple in game design lore, or its perfectly vacuous cousin "fun." If you detach immersion from the concept of flow, you'll be left with the conceptual equivalent of cotton candy—fluffy and tasty and sticky as a concept, but if you try to sink your teeth into it, there's essentially nothing there. You can be "immersed" in any media, from a blazingly high-tech virtual reality system at a cutting-edge research facility down to a cheap, worn-out paperback edition of a romance novel you read on your short bus ride to town. That's not very helpful. "Fun" is even worse. Attempts to catch the factors that make a media product "fun" without throwing entire experiences and emotions under the bus exist; but they only send you on a rollercoaster-like errand across human attributes and activities to a different flavor of vagueness. So let's stick with flow. When we examine its inner workings in greater detail in the upcoming level, as mentioned, we will also look at some of the criticism. But as a concept, it's much more sharply defined than immersion and powerful enough to hold our motivational building together.

Motivation to Play equals *Motivation to Learn.*

Beat 3: Emotion

Now that we have the keys to our motivational building, let's build a model for player emotion right in front of it that we will call the emotional landscape. For emotion, just as with motivation, there's a huge corpus of research. Some things are undisputed—that emotions influence behavior, for example, and have psychophysiological effects that include adaptation and appraisal, cognition, and motivation. Other aspects are debated, like categorization, functions, or relations to neighboring human experiences like mood and temperament. Depending on your type of game and your interests, you might want to dive into these and similar specialized topics; for an introduction and further sources, look out for Andrew S. Fox's *The Nature of Emotion* and Michael D. Robinson's *Handbook of Cognition and Emotion*. If you're working on a purposeful or serious game, you might also want to make yourself familiar with the difference between emotions and feelings, and how emotions and feelings in turn connect to memory formation. For both topics, "The Influences of Emotion on Learning and Memory" by Chai M. Tyng and others is a good start.

For our general model of the emotional landscape, however, we will pick the comparatively crude box cutter knife of dramatic theory, notably Aristotle's *Poetics*, to carve out a small number of equivalently crude categories. We will do that because it suffices for our purpose of gaining a basic understanding of emotions in the context of narrative structures, and game narratives in particular. Yet, we need to remind ourselves from time to time that dramatic theory is only a modest chamber within that vast edifice of scientific research into emotions and emotional experience.

In our first operation, we make just one deep cut. On one side of the cut, we have all the emotions that can be triggered in the player by visual, auditory, and kinesthetic means directly, i.e., through images, sounds, melodies, and movement. Without any claim to completeness, these comprise:

- Fear, joy, happiness, amusement, awe/wonder, sadness, sorrow, melancholy, nostalgia, loneliness, anxiety, terror, dread, disgust, nausea, revulsion, and similar.

On the other side of our cut, we have all the emotions that cannot be triggered in a player by visual, auditory, or kinesthetic means alone. These comprise, again without any claim to completeness:

- Pity, compassion, worry (for others), love, contempt, anger (not the kind directed at faulty controls), outrage, hate, admiration, envy, jealousy, resentment, grief, bitterness, and similar.

We can call the first group of emotions the "fear class" and the second group of emotions the "pity class." And, mirabile dictu!, it's these two classes that we find in the sixth chapter of Aristotle's *Poetics* and his definition of Greek Tragedy! There, Aristotle describes Greek Tragedy as composed of certain elements and characteristics like imitation of action and artistic adornment, and he closes with the statement that Greek Tragedy, roughly, "effects through pity and fear the catharsis of these emotions." Now, much has been written about the catharsis hypothesis, a concept that has so far resisted—or evaded— verification or falsification. But catharsis is not of immediate interest to us. Instead, we're interested in Aristotle's choice of pity and fear. Why these two? There's a well-established answer to that, deduced from Aristotle's definition of the tragic hero as a human being who must not be "superhuman," but have a character flaw that brings about the hero's downfall. Within this context, the audience pities the hero *and* fears that they could face a similar fate themselves someday. This defines the difference between our two classes. Emotions from the fear class are directly experienced through *identification with a situation we could see ourselves in*, while emotions from the pity class are indirectly experienced through *identification with the character or characters* by way of empathy mechanisms (possibly mirror neurons, but that's still a matter of debate).

This has repercussions for the way we design emotions in games. We can mess up spectacularly in two ways when we fail to recognize that *situation* and *character* are different loci of identification with different types of emotion and different types of experience—a direct experience by seeing ourselves in the game world on the one hand, and an indirect experience by empathizing with the game world's characters on the other.

It was dramatically and narratively highly developed interactive games, specifically, that messed this up and introduced a "locational" virus into these identification patterns that put everything in disarray. To isolate this virus, we need to undertake a detailed anamnesis. Based on the definitions above, what's been going on in non-interactive media for about 3000 years is this:

1. The dramatic situation the audience can see themselves in (fear class).
2. The characters the audience "identifies" with (pity class).

Now, in interactive games, our most popular strategy to create and convey emotions from the fear class consists of operating *directly on the player* with a sophisticated visual, auditory, and motion palette, and even kinesthetic effects like vibrations and pulsations in console games. All this is especially true for horror games. In games like *Silent Hill*, *The Suffering*, or *Dead Space*, players experience emotions from the fear class directly, not just indirectly by empathizing with game world characters.

So far, even this is not too different from Greek Tragedy; especially Aeschylus could frighten the audience out of their wits through well-placed effects. Now, if this fear class were all that's happening in interactive games, then there'd be no problem. But as soon as we create a dramatically complete game that also conveys emotions from the pity class, we have created a problem factory.

Our premise is that the player identifies with their player character. Therefore, in the tradition of Greek Tragedy and because it's just too obvious, we are tempted to convey the emotions from the pity class by letting things happen to the player character. But is our premise that the player identifies with the player character really true? And if it were true, would that help or be wise?

Probably not. To start with, the term player character itself already suggests a measure of identification that is misleading, because it obscures the fact that we merely deal with a player-*controlled* character. There's a difference between controlling a ball or being a ball, and that's also true for everything from cars to cybernetic super soldiers.

But there's more. What the player identifies with, first and foremost, is the player-avatar as a *representation of the player's actions*. This is not the same as identifying with a player-controlled character *as a character*. These are completely different mechanisms, which is and isn't obvious at the same time.

To boot, a major source of confusion is our indiscriminate use of the term "identify with." What we mean by that when talking about characters in non-interactive media, like novels or movies, is "empathize with," and that's what everybody understands, at least implicitly. But when it comes to player characters in interactive games, we tend to forget that. Here, we often use "identify with" as if it were indeed about identification, which is the opposite of helpful.

Thus, for a better understanding, we need to ditch the "identify/identification" terminology in favor of "empathy." (There are different flavors of empathy we'll get to in the *Interactivity* and *Architectonics* territories.)

Now that we got rid of the confusing term "identification," we can also see a lot more clearly that there are not two, but *three* loci of emotional involvement in interactive games:

1. The dramatic situation players can see themselves in (fear class).
2. The characters the players can empathize with (pity class).
3. The player avatar that represents the players' actions.

The third locus is exclusive to video games and comparable interactive media, and it triggers its own class of emotions. These comprise, again without any claim to completeness:

- Triumph, relief, jubilation, satisfaction, pride, gratitude, confidence, hope, guilt, remorse, shame, embarrassment, disgrace, regret, humility, disappointment, frustration, despair, and similar.

In non-interactive media, these emotions can only be experienced as part of the pity class through empathizing with the characters. In video games, however, where players have agency and can make decisions that have consequences, it is possible to trigger these emotions in ways that would be impossible to trigger with novels or movies: the player can experience guilt, remorse, shame, regret, pride, triumph, relief, etc. *directly* as a consequence of their own actions and decisions. To stress it again, this is unique to media that allow for agency, with video games as the most prominent example.

If Aristotle lived today and looked at video games as morosely as Classical Greeks looked at pretty much everything, he'd probably extend his original definition to *fear*, *pity*, and *guilt*. It's tempting to do just that. But to give this class of emotions a more positive spin, we will instead call it the fiero class:

1. The dramatic situation players can see themselves in (fear class).
2. The characters the players can empathize with (pity class).
3. The player avatar that represents the players' actions (fiero class).

Fiero is a concept that was introduced to the game design community by Nicole Lazzaro. It was quickly spread by others, deservedly, and became well-established as a term for the overwhelming feeling of accomplishment that includes triumph, pride, relief, and such, when players have overcome a major obstacle, triumphed in the face of adversity, won a huge victory, and so on. Most of these emotions are acknowledged and reflected within game worlds by design through rewards, acknowledgment by non-player characters (NPCs), and many other things. But not all of them, or always. For example, as David Perry and Rusel DeMaria observe in *David Perry on Game Design*, player emotions like pride often fail to be reflected within game worlds.

But this coin too has two sides. In the same way that our fear and pity classes also comprise positive emotions, the fiero class also comprises negative emotions. Among them are shame, guilt, regret, or disgrace that occur when a player fails to overcome an obstacle; suffers defeat; or makes life worse for their player character, their non-player companion characters, or other players' characters in coop or multiplayer games or MMOs.

Based on our understanding of these three loci of emotional engagement, we can now tackle the interference problems that occur when the pity class and the fiero class are confused with each other. Depending on mechanical aspects, some dramatically complete game types are traditionally more vulnerable to this confusion than others. Let's have a look at three major types.

Dramatically complete games with "detached" player characters, as we will call it, are usually unproblematic in this regard. Consider adventure games like *Syberia*, *Grim Fandango*, or *Tomb Raider*. While their protagonists represent the player's actions as player avatars, the player is not supposed to literally identify with Kate, Manny, or Lara Croft. Detached player characters have their own agendas, make their own decisions, and have their own lives. Kate or Manny or Lara represent the player's *actions* as player avatars; they don't represent the player as *player*. This leaves the emotional involvement structure largely intact. Players can see themselves in the dramatic situation (fear class), and they can empathize with the player character (pity class), who also happens to represent the players' actions (fiero class).

Then there's the type of dramatically complete games where the player is indeed supposed to be the player character in a way defined by John Romero. According to the latter's famous forum post, there was never a name for the *Doom* marine "because it's supposed to be YOU." Such games do offer stories, even if rudimentary. But they're not *completely* dramatically complete because they don't offer all three emotional classes: rarely is the player supposed to feel pity, hate, love, or grief. The pity class remains empty, or undefined, and that's why the structure of emotional involvement remains largely intact again. Players can see themselves in the dramatic situation (fear class), and the player character represents the players' actions (fiero class). That's it. This is similar to, but not identical with, games that are not dramatically complete, from *Pong* to *Forza Motorsport* to *Unreal Tournament*. Not only are the players' actions represented by the player avatar for the fiero class's range of emotions in these games. They also offer a residual situational in-place feeling at the point of one's paddle, wheel, or hand-and-gun that is able to evoke a rich subset from the fear class's range of emotions. But, like their not-quite dramatically complete *Doom*-type cousins, they do not offer emotions from the pity class.

It's the third major type of dramatically complete games that gives us trouble. These are games where the pity class is intact and the player character is supposed to represent the player, not just the player's actions. This is particularly true for role-playing games or games that employ role-playing mechanics in general—where players take on or project a virtual identity in order to make novel experiences in the game world, try out and practice different forms of self-expression, or both. With this combination, two incompatible identification routes collide: pity (identification via empathy) and agency (identification via representation).

Let's illustrate this dilemma with a stock example. In a historical game, the player character must choose between her fiancé, whom she loves, and her dream career. When this character chooses one of these options herself, the player can empathize and pity her for sacrificing either her love or her career. But that no longer works when it's the player who makes this decision. You can't possibly empathize with yourself, because that makes no sense whatsoever. And you can't feel pity for yourself, only self-pity, which is a completely different thing. In other words: with such a player character, you can't have empathy and agency at the same time!

Yet, many games want to have their cake and eat it too by endowing players with agency and with emotions from the pity class simultaneously. It's possible, to a certain degree; but only through an approach that contributes to video game narratives' bad rap. It's an approach that employs clichés as lowest common denominators, with easily recognizable emotions triggered by easily recognizable situations. These are so familiar to us that players can "feel" these emotions without really feeling them, without having to step in anyone's shoes, without having to empathize with anyone in any way. This is what makes dramatically complete games often so poor. It's not simply "poor writing," no. That could be remedied. It's a dilemma, and it is structurally related to the time-honored dilemma between dramatic structure and player agency, to be discussed in the level on *Architectonics* (which postulates that you can't have a dramatic roller coaster ride experience, similar to books or movies, and true player agency at the same time).

Does this mean that we cannot possibly accomplish a dramatically complete game that is emotionally meaningful and not poor? Fortunately, this isn't the case. Two converging approaches exist, at least. One is clever tinkering in the agency department, the other a well-established approach in the empathy department that focuses on the use of NPCs. To see what great design can accomplish by combining these two approaches, let's have a brief look at the games from the *Mass Effect* trilogy (minus the ending).

Clever tinkering in *Mass Effect* begins with almost unlimited player character customizability. On top of appearance and a wide range of character classes, abilities, and personal backgrounds to choose from, which all affect the game in one way or another, players can indeed build their player character's personality from the ground up. Then, the player can "own" the player character and, to a degree, project their own values, traits, and emotional make-up by choosing the player character's moral values through dialogue options and decisions. All this gives the player a substantial amount of agency. Different things happen in the wake of different decisions, which are frequently less about *what* to do, but *how* to do something. (The difference between *what* and *how* as a basic task design principle will occupy us in the *Architectonics* territory.)

Certainly, it's comparatively crude, and the choices are limited. But it's an ingenious way of providing players with the option to project at least part of their own personality and values onto the player character and have the game respond accordingly. It's still a simulation of agency, not true agency. But we don't yet have the technology to parse, interpret, and respond to the player's emotional and moral behavior consistently in real time.

But, as clever as this approach is, outside the agency department it has its limitations. In the empathy department, it still isn't enough to carry the player sufficiently deep into the rich palette of emotions that make up the pity class. That's where the second approach kicks in. There's an old quip where a seasoned, experienced character boasts they've "forgotten more things than you've ever learned," and this second approach fits that quip as it is one of the oldest tricks in the book. It's about letting dramatic turns or events with high emotional impact not happen to the player character, but to major NPCs—or Hero NPCs, as Chris L'Etoile calls it—to which the player character has become sufficiently attached. Originally, this served as a safety feature to protect players from emotional impacts that would take them too far out of their comfort zone. That's still important, but we can also use it to serve our purposes here. Remember, you can't empathize with yourself. You can only empathize with others, and that works better and more reliably when you empathize with someone who really means something to you. The games from the *Mass Effect* trilogy are chock-full of Hero NPCs one can care about deeply, providing the player with a rich subset of emotions from the pity class.

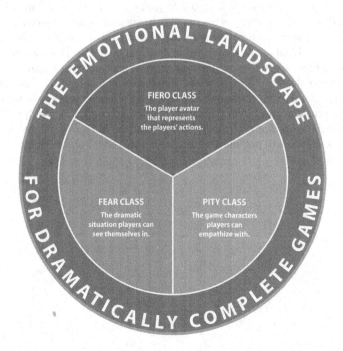

FIGURE 4.4 The emotional landscape.

Combining both approaches, the empathy/agency dilemma almost disappears. The player can enjoy both at the same time. They can enjoy the emotions from the pity class by empathizing with the fates of Hero NPCs, and they can enjoy player agency enriched by a limited amount of personalized emotions.

But let's not draw the wrong conclusions! Our *Mass Effect* example notwithstanding, it's not about complex technologies or staggering budgets. It's about designing and controlling all three loci of identification at all times throughout your game: the dramatic situation your players see themselves in; the characters your players can empathize with; and the player avatar that represents your players' actions. These three loci define the player's emotional landscape. If you want to design a dramatically complete game, controlling this landscape is as indispensable for your first indie title as it is for any AAA release.

There's one aspect we haven't touched upon yet but maybe should, particularly in the context of our *Mass Effect* example: romance options and love as an emotion from the pity class.

Do players really fall in love with Garrus, Samantha, Liara, Steve, or Tali, or characters from any other video game in general? Well, there are fringe cases like "Japanese man falls in love with/marries virtual idol/game character." But even in such fringe cases, these people do not fall in love with virtual characters, but with their *ideas* of these virtual characters. And whatever the future has in store for us in terms of pygmalionesque AI, at this point in time, the general answer to our question would be "no."

What players feel toward video game characters is not love, but strong emotional attachment. This isn't weird. Video game characters aren't special in that regard. Humans can, and do, develop deep emotional attachments to everything from dolls and teddy bears and plush bunnies to guns and hats and automobiles. In video games, it's this capacity that makes it possible to project the emotional potential of an in-game event, *including* romantic love between the player character and NPCs, into the mind of the player without having to make the player "truly" fall in love with an organized collection of pixels.

Outlook

Together, the motivational building and the emotional landscape define what your player will experience and how they will experience it. These models, or frameworks, enable you to make design decisions for numerous aspects across the upcoming levels. As a game designer, you really need to know a lot about motivation in general, and motivation with regard to your target audience in particular. If you want to design a dramatically complete game, you also need to know a lot about emotions in general, and emotions with regard to your target audience in particular. What motivates a player for a certain course of action and what doesn't? What elicits a specific emotion and no other? These are questions that you'll have to answer all the time, depending on your type of game and your specific target audience.

One last point. Design decisions for each class from the emotional landscape are loosely attached to design decisions in one of the four territories, marked by corresponding colors in the illustration's full-color version that you can download at *ludotronics.net*. Fiero interconnects strongly with the *Interactivity* territory, fear with the *Plurimediality* territory, and pity with the *Narrativity* territory. And in the fourth territory, *Architectonics*, you will pull the dramatic strings that hold everything together.

Level Two

Interactivity

Opening

Let's begin with a deeper look at the dynamics that tie this level's territory, *Interactivity*, to the just-right amount of challenge, its associated element from the interactive playing experience model that we developed in the first level.

It's the Goldilocks principle—a challenge that is neither too hard nor too easy, but just right. And we have a model for that, which we already mentioned: the concept of *flow*. If you've read more than zero books on game design, chances are that you have come across the basic flow model before. Thus, before we dive into it, two frequent misconceptions should be addressed. The first is the often foregrounded aspect of becoming oblivious to time; but that's a potential result and a benefit, not its mechanism. The second misconception is that this model hasn't evolved over time. Well, it did! A lot of research has been done since its inception.

In the following illustration, a lot of that research has been integrated, along with some necessary changes in terminology and visual presentation, for an integrated game flow model that you can use with *Ludotronics* or any other methodology. It processes and illustrates results from Csíkszentmihályi Mihály's original *Flow: The Psychology of Optimal Experience*; his consecutive research in *Finding Flow*; Massimini and Carli's "The Systematic Assessment of Flow in Daily Experience"; Falstein's "Understanding Fun"; Qin, Rau, and Salvendy's "Effects of Different Scenarios of Game Difficulty on Player Immersion"; and Lazzaro's "Understanding Emotions" and "Games and the Four Keys to Fun."

So let's unpack this. First off, for reasons that will become clear in a later beat, the term "skill" has been replaced with "proficiency," which covers not only skill, but knowledge, understanding, and attitude as well.

The letter "P" in the bottom left corner represents the player, who is learning to play a game, and the player wants to avoid both anxiety and boredom because neither are positive experiences. To avoid these negative experiences, the player's only available choice (barring the decision to quit playing altogether) is to return to the flow state. Thus, the player is highly motivated to do just that.

But that doesn't mean that P should never leave the flow channel, on the contrary! In both directions, states of mind exist that depend on different challenge–proficiency ratios. Some of these states of mind should be part of your design.

Above the flow channel, as an addition to the model's original challenge–proficiency ratios, resides "Fiero," the term introduced by Nicole Lazzaro as discussed in the previous level. The player's proficiency level is high, but the challenge is a bit higher than that, so that the player can experience fiero—triumph, pride, relief—when overcoming an obstacle that had been just out of reach before.

Below the flow channel resides "Control," which is also an important playing experience. The player's proficiency level is high, again, but the challenge is a bit lower than that, so that the player can experience control and enjoy everything they have learned so far.

Then, there are two states of mind for players with moderate proficiencies levels, "Arousal" above the flow channel and "Relaxation" below; these are also perfectly acceptable and enjoyable and should be part of your design. What's more, the integration of Fiero, Arousal, Control, and Relaxation as part of an enjoyable playing experience mandates that you shouldn't design the challenges for your game in a straightforward progression, but with crests and troughs in between.

DOI: 10.1201/9781003334682-18

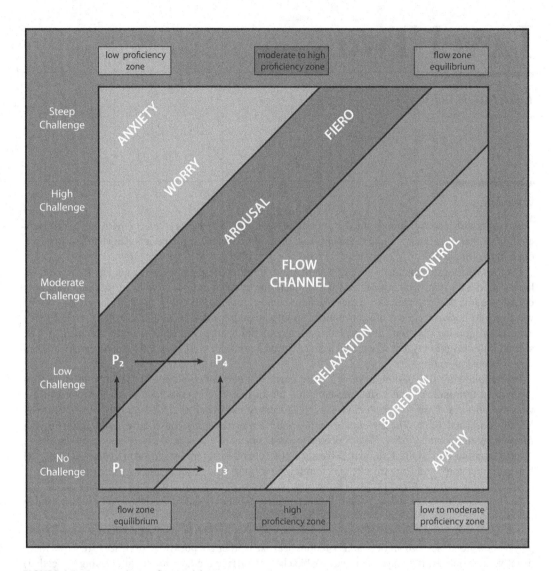

FIGURE 4.5   Integrated game flow model.

There are states of mind beyond these, however, that you should avoid. These are "Anxiety" and "Worry" (high and moderate challenge at low proficiencies, respectively) above the flow channel, and "Boredom" and "Apathy" (low challenge at moderate and low proficiencies, respectively) below the flow channel. These are not enjoyable states of mind.

In Massimini and Carli's original extension of the flow model, interestingly, the placement of "Relaxation" and "Boredom" below the flow channel was reversed. It was a hypothesis that made sense intuitively: without sufficient challenge, players at higher skill levels should be more easily bored than players at lower skill levels. Empirically, that didn't turn out to be the case at all. As various studies since then have shown, when players are not sufficiently challenged, boredom is more likely to occur at lower skill levels, while players with higher skill levels tend to fall back to a "relaxed" state when challenge decreases. Thus, if you give players the opportunity to leave the flow channel from time to time to experience Control or Relaxation, you make the playing experience actually more enjoyable.

Following this model, you won't have to (or shouldn't) design your game in such a way that it perpetually analyzes the player's performance and tries to wrap the optimal playing experience around them, so to speak. Instead, it allows you to follow three related design patterns:

- Provide *well-crafted* tiers of challenges. That way, the player can pick the difficulty level that is appropriate for them.
- Increase the challenges' difficulties in *up-and-down patterns* instead of increasing them continuously. That way, the player can both experience triumph, pride, and relief on the one hand, and enjoy hard-won increments in proficiency with control and relaxation on the other.
- Provide a well-crafted *range of solution options* for these challenges. That way, the player can pick different mechanics to mix and match their personal preferences and proficiency levels.

With these design patterns in place, the player will do the rest because they're highly motivated to stay within the flow channel, leave the flow channel for fiero and control (at high proficiency levels) and arousal and relaxation (at moderate proficiency levels), and return to the flow channel as a natural course of action.

All this, it should be mentioned, already addresses a lot of the criticism that's been leveled against flow as a productive model for game design purposes. The central argument is that the flow model not only suggests but even implies that design strategies like dynamic difficulty adjustment (DDA) should be used to keep players in the channel, and that, in extension, the flow channel can be easily abused to keep players glued to exploitative mechanics. As for the latter, retention and monetization mechanics are based not on flow, but on behavioral modeling conducive to hooking players to gambling mechanics. As for the former, it's certainly true that DDA, while sometimes helpful, contributes its own colorful problems to the design process and the playing experience. We will have a look at it later in this level. But for the flow model, DDA is neither implied nor important for several reasons.

To start with, the model's basic dynamics *inevitably* lead to growth and discovery because players must (a) constantly improve their proficiency levels and (b) constantly explore new opportunities for putting their improved proficiency levels to use. That's why, according to Csíkszentmihályi, the experience of flow is *always related to growth*, and not just any old growth, but *growth of the self*—a strong tie-in with our three components "growth," "insight," and "experience" from the design-driven goal that we created in the Procedure phase.

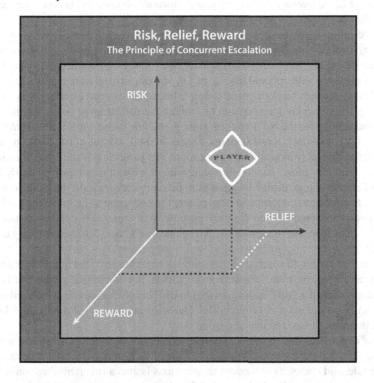

FIGURE 4.6 Risk–relief–reward pattern.

Then, as discussed, the flow channel is merely the safe ground to which the player always returns. To repeat, the player should be free, and even encouraged, to try out what's beyond its borders—to experience periods of fiero and arousal on the one hand, and periods of control and relaxation on the other.

Finally, there are design principles that accomplish this without any kind of DDA. The probably most successful of these is the concurrent escalation of *risk*, *relief*, and *reward*.

Greater *risks* that experienced players are willing to take are met by greater *relief*, i.e., more opportunities to restock staples like health, ammo, and so on, and greater *rewards* of any kind, from loot to experience points. Applying this principle means providing an interesting variety of interactive mechanics with different levels of execution difficulty, among which the player can choose in keeping with proficiency or preference.

You can see this design principle at work in many games, with numerous imaginative variations. It's what makes games from the *Mario* franchise enjoyable for players who widely differ in experience and expertise. For a detailed and comprehensive study of scalable difficulty in *Mario* games, Daniel Johnson's *Game Design Companion: A Critical Analysis of Wario Land 4* cannot be recommended highly enough. At every single moment, these games provide *choice*—about the preferred level of challenge and the preferred means to meet that challenge, which puts the player in control of their flow channel and offers great playing experiences with high replay values and opportunities for growth.

As a final remark, feedback isn't covered in this level, or in this territory. While it's an integral part of interactivity and vital for learning success of any kind, feedback in games is inextricably tied to visual, auditory, and kinesthetic elements that demand design decisions for the game as a whole along its various interfaces. Accordingly, feedback is discussed in the level on *Plurimediality* instead.

Beat 1: Rules

From Rules to Loops

Your first challenge in the *Interactivity* territory, and a formidable one, will be to create the best possible gameplay loop for your game.

First off, let's clear up a terminological confusion. A gameplay loop consists of a sequence of activities or sets of activities that the player engages in again and again during play. It defines the mechanical aspect of the playing experience. Your game can have one simple, well-defined gameplay loop. Or, it can have a core gameplay loop with optional side loops. Or, you can have an intricate structure of macro- and microloops. All that depends on your game concept, the scope of your game, and, not to forget, your budget. For *Pong*, the gameplay loop consists of moving the paddle up or down, hitting the ball at the desired angle, and waiting for the ball to return while predicting its velocity. That's what the player does again and again, faster and faster, until someone misses the ball and one of the counters goes up.

Don't confuse the gameplay loop with the game loop! The game loop is the piece of code that updates and renders the game from game state to game state with or without user input, all neatly clocked.

Eventually, of course, the gameplay loop needs to be represented within the game loop. To get from one to the other, from code to concept and from concept to code, and to facilitate the kind of communication that puts every team member on the same page, we will create a model that includes not only the code and the gameplay loop, but rules, rule sets, and game mechanics. That's the first leg of your journey in this territory!

For that, we have to start with something that sounds simple but isn't: the question of what constitutes a rule in games, and what constitutes a rule in video games. For non-digital games like board games or card games, the meaning of a "rule" seems obvious to us. This obviousness is reinforced by the fact that these games usually include a set of printed rules. But what are they, what do they do? Let's probe the game of chess, the game of Go, and the card game skat.

In the game of chess, the king's bishop's placement (f1, f8) in the initial game state is a rule. Its movement limitation (diagonal movement only) is a rule. One of its distance limitations (another game piece in its path) is a rule, and one of its movement terminations is also a rule (anywhere on its allowed path within its distance limitations). Beyond the rules that determine the King's Bishop's positional values, there are rules that determine the consequences of these positional values, like check or stalemate (or, for other game pieces, promotion, castling, or en passant).

Now, the bishop can also terminate its movement on a square occupied by a game piece of the opposite color and "take" that piece, and its movement is also limited by the edge of the board. These are rules too, but for reasons that will become clear later, let's put them aside for the time being.

In the game of Go, the free placement of a stone on any vacant intersection is a rule. The exceptions to that (self-capture, infinite repetition) are rules. The capture of a stone of the opposite color is a rule. Rules determine a stone's positional value in conjunction with other stones, and they determine territorial values scored by stones of the same color.

In the admirably complex game of skat, the procedure to determine the game value (also called hand value) is a rule. That a player has to follow suit, if possible, is a rule. That the set of trump cards constitutes a suit is a rule.

Along these examples, we can spot a pattern. Rules can define game states (e.g., the initial chess setup). Rules can define value states (e.g., positional values, territorial values, face values, trump values, or game values as in skat). Rules can define any action that leads to a different game state (moving the bishop in a game of chess, placing a stone in a game of Go, playing a card in a game of skat). Rules can define any change in values brought about by moving to a different game state (check positions; shifting territories in a game of Go; game value change through overbidding in a game of skat; game scores in general).

At this point, we need to go on a brief tangent about manuals to collect some insights that will then lead us back to our question. For the types of games we looked at so far, manuals exist that scrupulously list every single rule of their respective game. For pen-and-paper role-playing games (RPGs) or tabletop war games, it's similar, but also a bit different. *Their* rules and manuals are amended and superseded all the time; the tide of specialized rule books and expansions never ebbs; and the number of rules can grow so large with time that they overlap and contradict each other—necessitating even more rules. Nevertheless, in a perfect world, manuals for these game types would also list every single existing rule for each game, just like the manuals for chess, the game of Go, and skat.

Video games, in contrast, don't come with manuals that list all their rules, except for board or card game adaptations and similar. That's because a video game enforces its rules itself—in such a way that, for the player, *playing the game equals following the rules.* The player need not be told that they can't run faster or jump higher than the allowed values—they simply can't run faster or jump higher than that, and even exploits are less a matter of breaking the rules than breaking these rules' intentions. Manuals, if there are any, do explain some rules, but for different reasons. They do not explain rules in order to get players to follow them, but to help players to get started and better achieve their goals.

Now, beyond this substantial difference in rule enforcement, are board or card game rules and video game rules intrinsically different?

Judging by our examples with respect to functions and purpose, they aren't. Just as in board games or card games, rules in video games define the initial game state and the final game state. They define which interactions are allowed to move the game from one game state to another. They define value states, and how these value states change from game states to game state.

This doesn't mean that video game rules are always transparent or appear fair. What about headshots served by non-player characters from two miles away with a creaky 1888 commission rifle? Intermittent enemy invulnerability? Boss actions that feel as ad-lib as any rule of Calvinball? There's no rule book the player can consult, so whether these are rule violations or not is often the cause of dispute.

Regardless of how simple, complex, or exotic the rules of a game might be, this covers what rules do for all practical purposes. Importantly, game states, interactions, and value states can be left undefined. Or, they can be defined in more than one way to adopt zero as well as multiple states, options, or values. The rules can define two or more possible initial or final game states, for example, or define that there isn't an initial or a final game state at all. The rules can define *how* to interact with game elements but not *when* (at which point in time), or only *when* but not *how*. Time limits in chess games are "when" rules. A very simple arena shooter might have "how" rules but no "when" rules, so players are restricted in *what* they can do but allowed to use every rule at any given point in time between the game's initial and final game state. An arena shooter with spawn protection, in contrast, also has a "when" rule. Finally, a

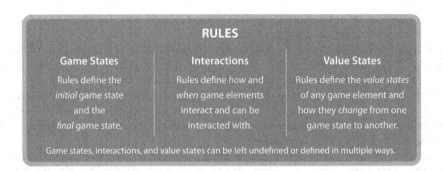

FIGURE 4.7   Rule characteristics.

game can leave game elements' value states undefined or define more than one value state for an element toward different conditions.

To wrap it up, a rule is a single, indivisible property of a game element, a class of game elements, or a game. But that doesn't make it the same thing as a piece of code! To become code, each rule has to be broken down into instructions and data. But within the confines and purposes of our model, it's as close to code as we can get.

From there, the next step on our journey from code to concept will take us to rule sets.

Whenever we have a large number of rules, the most sensible response is to collect closely related rules into *rule sets* that can be addressed through a table of content. A "king's bishop" rule set, for example, would contain its rules for initial game state, movement limitation, distance limitation, and movement termination. Then we have the two rules that we put on the back burner a while ago: that the king's bishop can occupy the square of a game piece of the opposite color and "take" this game piece, and that the king's bishop can't move beyond the boundaries of the chessboard. Neither rule is exclusive to the king's bishop, so it's more efficient to put them in different rule sets—one that deals with taking opponent's pieces and one that deals with universal properties.

For a video game, for example, we might collect the rules we need for walk, run, or jump to create "walk," "run," and "jump" rule sets, respectively. But this is flexible! If movement exists in your game but is only of minor importance, it might be more reasonable to bundle the rules for walk and run together into a single "horizontal movement" rule set or even create just one "movement" rule set that also contains basic jump rules. If you're designing a game that focuses on movement, in contrast, it might make more sense to create specialized, separate rule sets, i.e., rule sets for running jumps, double jumps, and so on.

Thus, we can define a rule set as a bundle of rules to establish a specific agent interaction. An agent, in that sense, can be everything from a simple process to a game AI to a player—everything that interacts with, and thereby changes, a given game state.

From here, our journey from code to concept, from individual rules to the gameplay loop, will take us to game mechanics. There are many different ideas out there of what a game mechanic exactly is, so let's put the definition for our model right up front this time: a game mechanic is a categorized collection of rule sets that define a specific player activity. Now let's unpack that!

First off, in contrast to rule sets, game mechanics are attached to the player, not to processes or game AI.

Then, also in contrast to rule sets, it's about activities, not interactions. In games, for example, where movement is needed but subordinated to more expansive activities like combat or exploration or puzzle solving, "jump" can be classified as an agent interaction, which makes it a rule set. Then we can take this rule set and organize it together with related rule sets—walk, run, dodge—into a collection that we call "movement." This, then, would be a player activity, which makes it a game mechanic.

As you can see, the difference between an interaction and an activity is not "out there." Instead, it's a matter of design and intent. Let's look at a few more examples. If you design a platformer that is all about movement, "jump" becomes much more significant, with particular modes of attack and perhaps combos. In this case, you can classify it as a player activity, which would make it a game mechanic in its own right. If you design a simple shooter, "pulling a trigger" would be an agent interaction in most

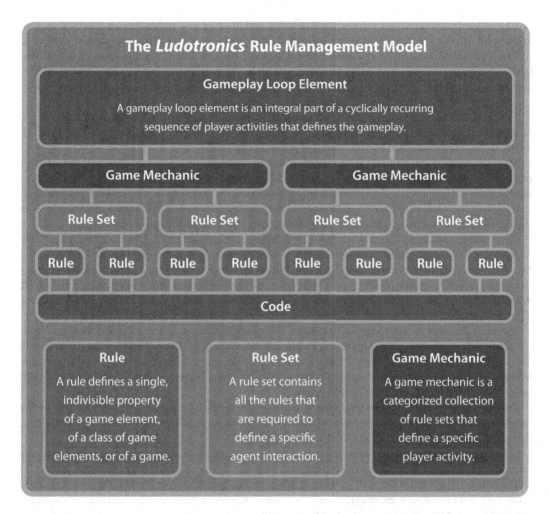

The *Ludotronics* Rule Management Model

Gameplay Loop Element
A gameplay loop element is an integral part of a cyclically recurring sequence of player activities that defines the gameplay.

Game Mechanic   **Game Mechanic**

Rule Set   **Rule Set**   **Rule Set**   **Rule Set**

Rule **Rule**   **Rule** **Rule**   **Rule** **Rule**   **Rule** **Rule**

Code

Rule
A rule defines a single, indivisible property of a game element, of a class of game elements, or of a game.

Rule Set
A rule set contains all the rules that are required to define a specific agent interaction.

Game Mechanic
A game mechanic is a categorized collection of rule sets that define a specific player activity.

FIGURE 4.8   Rule management model.

cases, with rules for pulling the trigger, waiting time between shots, and similar. "Shooting," in contrast, would qualify as a player activity, and therefore a game mechanic. Then again, for a more advanced shooter, that would be too coarse-grained! Here, you might split "shooting" up into individual game mechanics. The original "shooting" could become "projectile," with rule sets and rules for chamber status, recoil, muzzle climb, loss of aim, and so on, and then you would create separate game mechanics for, for example, "hitscan" or "indirect fire," each with their separate rule sets. Finally, consider "cover." Back when taking cover meant nothing more than moving behind an obstacle, it was part of the "movement" mechanic. Later, when taking cover expanded to "leaning out" or "peeking" around corners and obstacles, as in early *Metal Gear* or *Medal of Honor* or *Thief* games, it became part of a "shooting" and then of a "stealth" mechanic. Finally, when the concept of "cover" expanded even more, it became a game mechanic in its own right, introduced by games like *Kill.Switch* or *Gears of War.*

This is just one definition of game mechanics among many, and there are definitions that are more specific. But for our model, being less specific and more flexible is not a bug but a feature: it fully preserves game mechanics as a matter of design and intent. The concrete manifestation of rule sets and game mechanics in your game, aka game interactions and player activities, are not assumed, prescribed, or predefined by this model in any way. You, as a game designer, can make them all up, make them more granular, more sweeping, more numerous, or more uncommon, even screamingly unconventional. It will give you infinite options to try out something new and innovative, to remix old and worn-out rule sets into a new game mechanic that surprises and delights, and to adapt any game mechanic and fine-tune it to the spirit of your game. What if your player needs to reload a weapon? You could make it a rule set, like most games do. But maybe you want to introduce more realism, more suspense, or more opportunities for exasperation! Then you could promote "reloading" to a game mechanic, with different procedures and ammunition types for different weapons, the potential for misfeeds and jams, and procedures to clear these and other malfunctions under fire.

It's your design decisions that control what constitutes a rule set and what constitutes a game mechanic, based on factors like scale, common sense, game type, value set, theme, and target audience. In other words, it should be controlled by your intended playing experience.

Now we can loop back to our gameplay loop as the sequence of player activities that defines the mechanical aspect of the playing experience. As mentioned, you can model and visualize your gameplay loop in many different ways. And while we've built our rule management model bottom-up, from code to rules to rule sets to game mechanics to loop elements, there are indeed three good reasons why you should work top-down instead, starting off with sketching the gameplay loop for your game.

The first reason is about perspective. Think of game mechanics, rule sets, and rules as "features" and of gameplay loops as "benefits." The former is the design perspective, and the latter is the player perspective. From the design perspective, your game can objectively consist of great rules and rule sets and game mechanics which, from the perspective of the player, support a gameplay loop that subjectively sucks. Alternatively, you can design a gripping gameplay loop that is supported by well-known, even humdrum game mechanics.

The second reason is that gameplay loops and game mechanics operate in different domains. How rules, rule sets, and game mechanics interact with each other needs to be tuned and balanced in terms of *complexity*, whereas the gameplay loop, as it is executed by the player, needs to be tuned and balanced in terms of *playability*. And playability should always have the right of way. (Complexity will figure in the next beat, and balancing in the Proposition phase.)

The third reason, finally, is that game mechanics as such, with all their rule sets and rules and everything, do nothing. It's the gameplay loop where these rules are instantiated into interactions, activities, and a progression of *game states* that evolve over time.

Let's make up an example, a classic first-person shooter. We will call it *Shroom!* because we want it to be really colorful, and we want it to teach us a lot.

The four activities the player will go through again and again are explore (look for enemies, secrets, resources), fight (overcome enemies), solve (overcome obstacles, unlock secrets), and manage (pick up and manage resources like health, ammo, and power-ups).

At that stage, you can already check your setup against the player activity model from the motivational building. Does it have a well-balanced cocktail of activity ingredients? To recall, these ingredients are Jane McGonigal's seven types of work from *Reality Is Broken*: high-stakes work, busywork, mental work, physical work, discovery work, teamwork, and creative work. For *Shroom!*, we have high-stakes work (surviving in firefights), busywork (picking up ammo and health packs), mental work (cognitive challenges like obstacles and secrets), physical work (handling input devices for heavy loads of combat), and discovery work (exploration). That's quite a lot for such a simple loop, and maybe one of the reasons why this game type is so enduringly successful. And adding a multiplayer mode and a player community would even upgrade its cocktail to all seven ingredients through teamwork (CTF, Team DM, and other cooperative modes) and creative work (user-generated maps, mods, and conversions). But mind, the objective is not to cram all seven ingredients into your gameplay loop. It is to concoct a tasty, balanced cocktail with selected ingredients—ingredients, furthermore, that are at your disposal, and that you and your team can handle.

If you feel you're onto something with your loop elements, you can proceed to the next step and attach game mechanics to support them. Let's look at how this works for *Shroom!*

We can start with *Movement*, as the player should be able to move around! This game mechanic isn't dedicated to any particular loop element but will support every loop element that needs movement; in this case, all of them. For the loop element "explore," we need a *Navigation* mechanic to give the player a sense of location and direction; this could later become a map or a compass. For the loop element "solve," the player needs a *Use* mechanic to open doors or switch levers. And for the loop element "manage,"

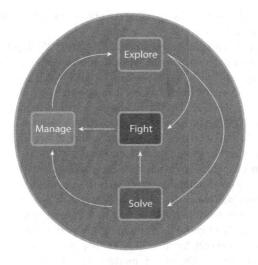

FIGURE 4.9 Gameplay loop.

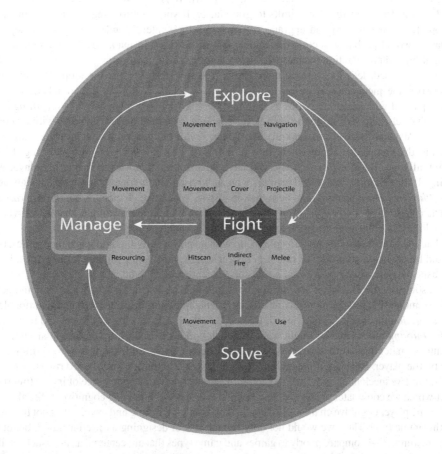

FIGURE 4.10 Gameplay loop with game mechanics.

some kind of *Resourcing* mechanic is needed, so that the player can monitor and manage their weapons, ammunition, power-ups, and so forth.

So far, every loop element has two game mechanics attached to it. We'll get back to them later for possible rule sets. That leaves the final loop element "fight." Theoretically, we could just slap on *Movement* and *Shooting* and call it a day! But "fight" is the most important loop element for this game type—it will affect and define the playing experience more strongly than any other loop element. And the central, defining loop element for any game, whatever it is, should be supported by more numerous, more interesting, and more differentiated mechanics, scaled to your particular game and game type. With respect to our example, *Shroom!* is combat-focused on the one hand, so we should support its "fight" loop element with a fairly substantial number of differentiated mechanics. On the other hand, it is a fairly simple shooter, and we wouldn't want its mechanics to approach titanic levels of granularity like *Phoenix Command* or *Operation Flashpoint*. Thus, a good solution would be to differentiate shooting into *Projectile*, *Hitscan*, and *Indirect Fire*, add a *Melee* mechanic to make it spicier, and a *Cover* mechanic to polish it off. That way, our loop element for combat would be supported by six game mechanics, which are neither too many (too complex) nor too few (not enough variation) for this particular type of game.

At this point, our gameplay loop sketch consists of four loop elements, three of them supported by two game mechanics and the fourth one—the most important one—by six game mechanics. For a simple, combat-focused game, this looks reasonably balanced. Other games will need more loop elements, a more complex loop structure, subloops, or a metaloop. Depending on the type of game, the gameplay loop and its attached game mechanics can become incredibly complex. In that case, you can always choose to work with other loop visualizations better suited to accommodate more granular information. You can use, for example, Emmanuel Guardiola's micro and macro loop system from "The Gameplay Loop: A Player Activity Model for Game Design and Analysis." Or you can devise your own means of visualization! However, there are limits to granularity. If you want to integrate, for example, all the microloops from your reward and upgrade systems with their interdependencies, your gameplay loop visualization would probably become indecipherable in no time. Instead, you should switch to other documentation and presentation formats like flow diagrams or spreadsheets.

Before we proceed, let's look at one more thing. You might notice that the loop element "explore" with its two game mechanics *Movement* and *Navigation* seems somewhat undercooked. The "fight" element is packed with player activities as it should be; the "manage" element has everything it needs; and the "solve" element will shine through clever challenges that the player can solve with a simple use key. But the "explore" element merely provides players with the general means to walk, run, or jump around, and the knowledge about where they're doing it! That doesn't seem very exciting. Is that an issue? Actually, no. Besides *Interactivity*, you have three more territories to make this player activity interesting. In this shooter, this would primarily be audiovisual and perhaps kinesthetic design elements from the *Plurimediality* territory, and perhaps some sparse narrative elements from the *Narrativity* territory. The important point here is, even though it's not an issue in our example, that a well-visualized gameplay loop can draw your attention to potential design challenges.

Now that you have sketched your gameplay loop with its player activities and game mechanics, the next step would be to sketch a number of rule sets for each game mechanic. To get your bearings, let's look at a few aspects with regard to *Shroom!*'s rule sets, except for the "fight" mechanics, which we covered already in some detail. The *Movement* mechanic would hold basic rule sets for walk, run, and jump but could also contain rule sets for more advanced movements like running jump, wall jump, or double jump. To the *Navigation* mechanic, as mentioned, we need to attach rule sets for waypoints and map-drawing. To the *Resourcing* mechanic, we might want to attach options to add, drop, or shuffle around items in the inventory, match ammo to weapon type, monitor health levels, and so on. Not everything needs to be done by the player. But even if you automate some of these activities, you'll need rule sets for them!

Finally, the *Use* mechanic for "solve." It's tempting to stock it with a wide range of interesting rule sets, on top of which we could later create ever tougher and ever more challenging cognitive tasks, aka puzzles. But giving the player cognitive challenges to crack, while both interesting and expected, is not the heart and soul of this game type. Thus, we would not only run the risk of designing a different game, but of implementing "features" that compare poorly to games and game types that are centered around such challenges. Always beware of those! And later, be careful about new features your team or your publisher would love to introduce during development. You don't always have to keep it simple, but you should always keep it focused. For our example, a "use key" with rule sets to press buttons, open doors, switch levers, etc., would suffice to give the player some tough nuts to crack but without turning *Shroom!* into a puzzle game.

Finally, you have to sketch your rules. Brace yourself—there will be a lot more rules to sketch than you can imagine! Later, you will need a good chunk of these rules for your proof-of-concept prototype, and all of these rules for a vertical slice prototype later.

For obvious reasons, we won't dive into the details, but here's a signpost to point you in the right direction. For a "jump" rule set, for example, you will need spatial values, time values, and control values from height and width to velocities to contexts and situations. If your game or game type is more movement-oriented, perhaps even a jump 'n' run, you will also need a whole lot of values and rules for how a jump "feels" to the player, which might include parameters like delay, friction, or ground composition. (For an introduction and further sources, check out Martin Pichlmair and Christoffer Holmgård's "You Say Jump, I Say How High? Operationalising the Game Feel of Jumping.") At this point in time, give all these rules and values your best shot, based on your experience and instinct. They will be far from perfect, or complete. You can and should add, scrap, revise, tweak, and polish your rules and values all the time, and when you start working on your proof-of-concept prototype, they will take shape and begin to shine.

When you have sketched and visualized your gameplay loop, attached game mechanics to the loop elements, and outlined your rule sets and rules, you can sit down and ask yourself all the important questions: is that exactly what you want your players to do again and again throughout the game? Would that gameplay loop appeal to your player personas? Will it support your theme? Will it support your key values, and would the mechanics provide a balanced mixture in the spirit of Piaget's Moderate Novelty and Loewy's MAYA principle? Does it vibe with your USP?

Should the answer be "no" to any of these questions, you might have a great loop on your hand, but it's a great loop for a different game, maybe one you want to design in the future. But it's not the right gameplay loop for *this* game.

Asking yourself these questions constantly will also prevent you from missing essential design factors in conjunction with your player personas. Consult them! One such factor, for example, might be "loop duration." If you're designing a casual game that people will play while commuting or during short breaks from work, you should design your loop accordingly. *Shroom!* most certainly doesn't fit that market. But if it did, you would want to design your two "explore–fight–manage" and "explore–solve–manage" routes in such a way that the player can decide which route to take, and that one of these routes can be completed in under 2 minutes. For an example, see Michail Katkoff's analysis of *Clash of Clans*.

Finally, let's return to the communication aspect of the rule management model. As mentioned, it is intended to support a rigorous and consistent design process throughout, be accessible and productive for everyone involved, and to facilitate communication.

> **The game developer** can take a game mechanic's rule sets, take these rule sets' individual rules, and break these individual rules down into codable components, all without losing the bigger picture.
> **The game designer** can design a game mechanic for one or more gameplay loop elements with the playing experience and the game's overall vision in mind, sketch its rule sets, and then sketch the rules for each rule set, all without losing their way among myriads of details.
> **The playtester** will naturally chunk related sets of interactions into player activities and experiences, which will reflect the design process based on this model in analyzable ways.

Conversations about game mechanics that are informed by this model are mutually intelligible for game developers, game designers, and playtesters alike. Design, development, and testing processes will benefit accordingly.

One last caveat: keep everything tidy! When you tweak even a single rule, check if you reused that rule for a different rule set, or that same rule set for a different game mechanic. If you did, rename the rule and the rule set or the game mechanic the tweaked rule belongs to—whatever is necessary. Keeping everything consistent at all times will endear you to your developers. Making a mess will not.

Beat 2: Reactions

From Interactions to Complexity

In this beat, as a warning, we will race through a dizzying array of abstract concepts that include determinism, randomness, unpredictability and uncertainty, contingency, and complexity. To be able to do that at all within the confines of this beat, we have to trim these concepts down, sometimes in Procrustean fashion, and jump into them as close to their contributions to our purpose as possible. That purpose, in the context of designing new and innovative games, is to offer you specific design perspectives on game outcomes and game interactions.

From every game state to the next, every output of every interaction between your game's agents—a simple process, a complex in-game AI, a player—is determined by the rules. But that doesn't mean that games are deterministic by nature. Applying the concept of determinism from math or physics, a game could be called deterministic when there is a causal chain from start to finish, and no randomness is involved in the development from its initial game state to its final game state at all. In other words, if the initial conditions are the same, the output will be the same. There seem to be games where that's not the case, as in match-based games, and games where that seems to be the case, like in point-and-click adventures, or adventure games in general. There, at least the initial state and the final state are perfectly defined, and you can only get from one to the other with the right input in the right sequence. But that doesn't make them deterministic. The question is, what are they then?

Here's the first important design perspective to answer that question, albeit indirectly: don't think in terms of endings! Final game states are much less interesting for the playing experience than they appear. What makes match-based games interesting is not that one player or team wins, but how that win comes about. What makes arcade-type games interesting is not that the player fails, but the measure of player success at the point of failure. What makes puzzle-type games interesting is not that the player succeeds in the end, but how, and maybe how fast, that success was achieved. One or the other also applies to game types like management, simulation, 4X, and so forth. In dramatically complete games that have a story, endings or multiple endings are certainly of interest, but only because of their plot structures and perhaps player decisions that precede them.

Thus, your design focus should shift to the *set of possible paths* that your player or players can follow from the initial game state to the final game state, no matter how determined or undetermined that final game state is. (On a deeper level, this perspective is equivalent to the narratological/game-mechanical perspective of "problem space," discussed in the *Architectonics* territory.)

Here's the second important design perspective to answer our question: don't think in terms of predetermined or undetermined, but in terms of predictability and, especially, uncertainty. "Predetermined," for starters, doesn't equal "predictable," just like in physics. Chaotic systems like weather patterns, for example, are deterministic, but predictions become less and less reliable, depending on how far you want to look into the future, until they become completely unpredictable. Schrödinger's equation for the evolution of the wave function in quantum mechanics is fully deterministic but not predictable outside of "determined probabilities." For game design, this means that even the most strongly predetermined games need not be predictable, let alone fully predictable. The same applies to solved games—a topic we will return to later—with solutions that are too complex to commit to memory. Players, to sum it up, enjoy even strongly predetermined games, as long as they offer an element of unpredictability, which is to say, uncertainty.

Now, with these two design perspectives under our belts, let's look at how they translate into design strategies.

There are at least four major strategies you can follow. One of them, creating unpredictability and uncertainty through plot structure, is discussed in the *Architectonics* territory. Here, we will discuss the other three, one by one: *controlled randomness*, *prepared contingency*, and *input complexity*.

First, *controlled randomness*. Why "controlled?" Can't a game have truly random elements? Leaving aside flavors of randomness that would engage us with various subfields of physics, the answer appears to be yes, it can. You can see it at work, for example, in the distribution of cards after a skat deck was properly shuffled, or every time you have to roll the dice. For video games, it's also possible but not desirable for at least four very different reasons! First, algorithms can't produce true randomness. You'd need cryptographic hardware, server-side or client-side, to create truly random values from statistically random physical input like thermal noise. Then, there's the rinse-and-repeat dynamic of video games. With truly randomized values, it's very hard to create the same input/output sequence twice, let alone limitlessly often, so it's almost impossible for the player to learn from past events. The popular learning-by-dying recipe would be severely curtailed. Also, truly random games are not enjoyable, except when the players don't know they're random. For the latter, Jesse Schell provides an astute example in *The Art of Game Design*. Children enjoy playing the truly random card game War only as long as they believe that they can affect the value of the next card through "magic" rituals. As soon as they're old enough to understand that the game is truly random and their rituals don't work, they lose interest. (As a related aspect, true randomness is also a factor in gambling addiction.) Finally, true randomness is truly random! For any observer, probabilities do not tend to behave in proper "probable" fashion; you will create all kinds of unintended playing experiences that are often baffling and rarely enjoyable.

Thus, if you decide you want to have randomness in your game, your design choice should always fall on *controlled* randomness. That could be deterministic and repeatable pseudorandom sequences, or it could be random calls from a set of precalculated values.

But mind, in contrast to true randomness, controlled randomness can become predictable too! In Pac-Man, for example, the ghosts' behavioral rules are fixed and can't surprise—except for the "frightened" mode in the earlier levels, where their movements indeed become random. However, as analyzed by Jamey Pittman in his seminal "The Pac-Man Dossier," the pseudorandom number generator for their random turns always starts with the same seed value. Thus, players are still able to optimize their game-play toward an optimal path and then stick to this path with great precision. (But Pittman also notes that relying on rote patterns might not be the optimal strategy for Pac-Man, as it leaves you stranded once you make a mistake.)

To wrap this up, let's look at two related design patterns that will help you decide how much controlled randomness you need or want to employ, both pointed out by Morgan McGuire and Odest Chadwicke Jenkins in *Creating Games*. First, even and especially in more complex games, a reasonable amount of randomness can *relieve* the player of the burden to plan ahead as far as possible and play as judiciously as possible. Then, if you design your game with less randomness, up to being a pure intellectual challenge on the order of chess or the game of Go, the more interesting and enjoyable it will become for ambitious and more professional players. If you design your game with more randomness, in contrast, it will increasingly appeal to players who'd rather relax and socialize. Rare is the drinking challenge that gets under way over a game of chess.

Let's turn to *prepared contingency* now, a very different design strategy to create unpredictability and uncertainty. First, we have to clear up the concept of contingency, which you will also meet in the *Architectonics* territory. Reality, as it appears to us, is contingent. Things that happen could have happened differently, but didn't. Certainly, nothing happens without a cause. But that doesn't lead to visible or experienced determinism because many if not most of these causes cannot be known with certainty, or known at all. One principal reason is that over time, ever smaller differences in initial conditions bring about ever greater differences in outcomes, just like in chaos theory. "True" first causes either fade into perfect obscurity, or they cannot be known at all, as they reside in a domain of physics that does not allow precise measurements under any circumstances. There are more aspects to it, but this should suffice.

If you want to use contingency for the purpose of game design, however, you need to employ what we will call "prepared" contingency, similar to why you need controlled randomness instead of just randomness.

The most noticeable examples for prepared contingency are memory games, Sudoku games, or crossword puzzles. Everything is set, deterministically, which is the "prepared" part. How the game or match evolves, though, is entirely contingent on the sequence of moves the player or players make. In *Uncertainty in Games*, Greg Costikyan explains this for crossword puzzles: all the letters are fixed in advance, but solutions are contingent on letters from crossing solutions that have already been found. Thus, for these and similar game types, everything is contingent on the player's first move. Which, more often than not, is even a random choice—players have to begin somewhere! And while such a first move, for example, the first memory tile a player turns over, is certainly "caused" by something along a chain of physiopsychological events, where a certain set of neurons and no other fired in the brain which caused the hand to pick up that tile and no other, these causes are not retrievable and cannot be known.

You can compare this design principle to the very first communication between strangers, an example loosely based on Niklas Luhmann's "double contingency." Anything you say to initiate a conversation with a stranger, let's say at a party hosted by Jack and Jill, is again "caused" by a chain of physiopsychological events. Yet, whatever you say—from "So, have you also been invited to this party?" to "Do you know Jack and Jill from work?" to "What's your opinion on Everett's many-worlds interpretation?"—*doesn't follow from anything,* and you could have said something else entirely. After that, however, all the communication with your new acquaintance will follow in some way from your initial utterance, subtly or overtly—just like your memory game will evolve from the first tile you turned over and your crossword puzzle from the first letters you dropped into the grid.

In contrast to life and what happens after that party, though, your final game state is entirely pre-prepared and fully determined. The number of potential paths in such games, though, can range from the tractable to the incomprehensibly huge—which will define part of the playing experience and should be a matter of intentional design. Prepared contingency is a form of unpredictability design that countless players enjoy immensely, certainly no less than any of the other forms of unpredictability design for games.

The third and final design choice, *input complexity,* will lead us into a vast, sprawling wilderness full of subsystems, self-organization, emergence, and self-improving agents. Again, as a refresher, it's about the number of possible paths between the initial and final game state and the measure of unpredictability and uncertainty the game provides.

Input complexity is very different from both controlled randomness and prepared contingency. This begins with initial moves: they are neither random nor contingent. In games with noticeable input complexity, the first move or moves are usually very calculated and optimized. So calculated and optimized, in fact, that they often become predictable and even standardized, like opening moves in chess. Over time, of course, such games deviate from any standard openings and become fresh and exciting. These later game states are certainly not independent of earlier game states, but they're not contingent upon them in the sense discussed above. Every input in these games, from the very first to the very last move, is deliberate and executed for a *reason.*

However, the level of input complexity in your game isn't an indicator of its quality. The indicator of quality for your game is how its level of input complexity fits the key values of your game and what your target audience enjoys. Thus, when you pick input complexity as your tool, you must develop a very good idea of how much of it you want to introduce. Most of the time, input complexity directly affects the number of possible paths between the initial and final game state—for match-based board games, for example, there's a huge difference both in possible paths and in input complexity between games similar to chess and games similar to Pachisi.

Again, there's a caveat, not unlike how controlled randomness can become predictable, as mentioned above. The number of possible paths in any game whose uncertainty relies on input complexity can shrink over time, even to the point that the game becomes "solved." That's because there's always a possibility that dominant strategies are discovered that make the game fully predictable, so that it can be won through "perfect play." Examples for solved games are the game of checkers or *Connect Four.* Are there games that are completely immune to becoming solved? Possibly, but it's hard to tell. So far, whenever computing capacities caught up with a game's level of complexity, it didn't take long until solutions were found—or at least proof that such solutions exist, as is the case with *Hex* (11×11 standard board). All bets are off.

Now it's time for a close look at the design challenges that high input complexity invariably entails; this will lead us deep into systems and subsystems and finally to modular design.

Input can come from many sources—from simple processes to complex AI to human players. In other words, from agent interactions and player activities, as you might remember from the preceding beat. On the system level of a game, all these count as subsystems that interact with each other directly or indirectly. The higher the input complexity of these subsystems, the more the complexity of the system as a whole will rise, and with it its unpredictability.

Here's something that is easily overlooked. The input complexity of a subsystem does not depend on the complexity of the subsystem! To unwrap that, we need to get a bit technical for a paragraph or two.

Players are the most complex subsystems your game will have. But for the game system, they're not necessarily more complex than any other agent in your game. That's because player input isn't arbitrarily complex. Instead, it's exactly as complex as your design allows it to be.

That's a crucial detail! For the system as a whole, the complexity of a subsystem equals the complexity of the input from that subsystem. The actual complexity of a subsystem behind its input is invisible and irrelevant to the system. But that's still not the whole story! For the system, the complexity of a subsystem's input is defined by the changes it causes within the system—in other words, how many other subsystems are affected by this input and how strongly. Even the most complex input doesn't count for anything when it doesn't impact other subsystems in ways that alter the state of the system as a whole. For rule sets and game mechanics, this impact will primarily appear as modified value states, but rules and rule sets can also be affected in many ways. The impact on the player subsystem primarily affects its input options that are provided by the system. Especially in complex games, however, not only the player's input itself but also its complexity can change through strategic adjustments, corresponding to changed assumptions and intentions. This, in turn, leads to another interesting aspect. In games that have more than one player subsystem, and the permitted input complexity is high enough, the input from these two player subsystems need not necessarily be of equal quality and equal impact to other subsystems because their *individual potential for game-related internal changes* can differ. Outside the system-level description, this will be experienced as the difference between weaker and stronger players. Who, as AlphaGo or AlphaStar first demonstrated, need not necessarily be human.

To wrap it up, the range and complexity of the permitted input—from processes, agents, players—as well as each input's permitted impact on the system as a whole—the game state—defines the possible number of individual playing experiences and shapes these experiences in profound ways.

Before we proceed to the challenges you have to face when designing systems of higher complexity, a few words on terminology. Throughout this beat, the term "complexity" is used in its general meaning as a system with many parts whose parts interact with each other in multiple ways. There are other, more specialized meanings, so don't mix them up. What hasn't been used, and actually been dropped after some deliberation, is the term "emergence"—a term otherwise liberally used in game design. There is no scientific consensus about the definition of emergence and its exact properties, requirements, and effects. But even if we pick more cautious definitions, these are not really compatible with what happens in games. One very useful description of emergence comes from Peter A. Corning. What differentiates emergent behavior from synergetic effects, according to Corning, is that the constituent parts of a system that display emergent properties are "modified, reshaped, or transformed by their participation in the whole." Another useful description by Mark Bedau and others, called "weak emergence," describes "new properties arising in systems as a result of the interactions at an elemental level." That's most probably not what we see in video games; what we see there, rather, are Corning's synergetic effects. This leaves "emergence" reasonably intact for expressions like "emergent gameplay"; but when discussing a game's system-level events, it would be misleading.

Now, the downsides. With higher input complexity, greater number of subsystems, and more and more significant interactions between these subsystems, there will be a higher number of possible paths for the player from the initial to the final game state. That's usually a good thing. But there will also be a higher number of possible game states that are undesirable—and the more complex your system is, the larger will be the number of undesirable game states that are also unpredictable, at least for practical purposes. When such an undesirable game state occurs, the game might behave erratically and crash or become unplayable or create impressive opportunities for hacks and exploits.

To illustrate this process, let's revisit our first-person shooter *Shroom!* and cook up a very trivial example that will get us into trouble. Items for our ammunition subsystem—clips with a certain number of bullets—are dropped by killed AI enemies. Items for our health subsystem—health packs—are distributed across the map. The player can pick up both ammo and health packs; the former replenishes their ammunition supply, and the latter replenishes their health for a health pack's standard replenishing value, but not beyond the player character's regular maximum health. All this should be familiar. But now you want these subsystems to interact with each other to keep the player in the flow channel. Your solution is to have a predetermined, fixed amount of health packs on any given map and a variable amount of ammunition, and the latter is determined by a ratio of remaining enemies to remaining health packs. When the level starts, with 100% enemies and 100% health packs, the ammunition dropped by killed enemies will be a default value of 100%, which stands for a predetermined number of bullets. When the percentage of remaining health packs becomes less than the percentage of remaining enemies, killed enemies will drop more ammunition, conforming to that predetermined ratio. And vice versa: if the percentage of remaining health packs is greater than the percentage of remaining enemies, killed enemies will drop less ammunition.

You can certainly see where this is going. To start with, when the player picks up the last remaining health pack on the map, your game will explode that instant over a division by zero under the hood. Moreover, experienced players are likely to catch on to this system and exploit it by systematically using up health packs for minimal damage in order to collect the maximum amount of ammo they can carry.

Of course, subsystem designers are rarely that naïve, and this mistake can be easily spotted and corrected for. However, the difficulty of catching interactions that cause undesirable game states rises *exponentially* with the number of interacting subsystems, the number of interactions between these subsystems, and the quality of these interactions—in other words, with higher complexity.

But, one might ask, why don't we just introduce a few more rules that solve the problem? One rule catches the divide-by-zero exception in our example, another rule checks how much health has actually been restored to the player character, and a third rule deals out some punishment when tracking data from the second rule suggests that the player is trying to exploit the original rule.

The answer is that this is a terrible idea for a whole raft of reasons. To start with, quick-fix rules in particular and special rules with a very narrow range of applications in general are "clutter rules" in *Ludotronics* parlance. They violate the principle of skill, style, and substance matter as discussed in the *Plurimediality* territory. They violate it because they're not professional; they don't contribute to original, recognizable patterns; and they don't work toward the rule system as an integrated whole. In other words, they're neither productive, nor interesting, nor in sync with anything else. In *The Art of Computer Game Design* and elsewhere, Chris Crawford refers to such rules as "dirt." This is a superb designation.

But that's not the end of it. Quick-fix rules introduce *additional* complexity into the system. As such, it's extremely likely that they will turn on you somewhere down the road in wildly unexpected ways. What's more, quick-fix rules sugarcoat the fact that the original rule or rule set that made them necessary wasn't such a stroke of genius in the first place and should be removed, or at least extensively reworked. Finally, a rule system should be carefully *pruned* at all times to remove unnecessary rules, much like a manuscript should be pruned to remove superfluous, unnecessary, and redundant words (you get the idea). Just like a writer searching for the mot juste, the just-right word, you should always strive for the rule that's exactly right.

Complexity has its price tag. You have to control for unwanted and potentially destructive effects, which becomes staggeringly difficult with greater numbers of subsystems and greater input complexity. But there are strategies you can use!

The first rule of complex system design is, never design a complex system from scratch. According to "Gall's Law," formulated by systems and child development theorist John Gall, complex systems that work have always evolved from simple systems that worked. (This doesn't mean that simple systems always work.) Complex systems designed from scratch, according to Gall, will never work and cannot be made to work by patching them up.

That's the first strategy. If you want to design a game with high levels of complexity, like a multiplayer strategy game or a game with in-game economics, for example, you should start with a simple system that has a manageable array of interacting subsystems. When this simple system works, extend and expand through variation and selection in a tightly controlled manner, step after step. With each successful step, your game will become a little more complex. When things fall apart, you can always backtrack to your last successful step. From there, you can either trace forward to find and eliminate the cause of the meltdown or try something different altogether.

The second strategy is modularity. As Tracy Fullerton points out in *Game Design Workshop*, you should keep your subsystems modular at all times. Because then, and only then, will you be able to make controlled changes in one subsystem and then observe and measure how these changes propagate throughout the system and affect other subsystems. This ties in with our rule management system that we developed in the preceding beat, which strongly encourages modular subsystem design in the form of rule sets and game mechanics. But what qualifies as a module, exactly? A module is a stand-alone component that you can build and test independently. That's important! For these ends, it needs to have its own well-defined interface with its own well-defined input and output protocols. In other words, each module needs to be a black box for every other module. It receives information, processes it, and returns its results, without any other module being privy to how it does all that. Finally, like a Matryoshka doll, many if not most of your modules will consist of modules. That's perfectly fine, provided you build your modules along these rules. It also makes life a lot easier—you can start off with conceptual black boxes and dummy modules that you can fill with life later, and you can easily fine-tune, repair, or replace a module that doesn't live up to expectations *without* having to fiddle with any other module. Because other modules aren't affected at all, and they don't care: every module is a black box for every other module. This is what modularity means. (It also means abstraction, but that would lead us too far astray.)

That's it! These are the design perspectives this beat introduces you to. In a nutshell: it's about possible paths between initial and final game states, not about endings; you can use either controlled randomness, prepared contingency, or input complexity to control the number of possible paths in your game and the just-right level of unpredictability and uncertainty; and you should build complex systems up from simple system and as modular as possible.

Beat 3: Revolutions

From Cycles to Circuits

In this beat, we will look at conflict design from two different perspectives: non-transitivity and feedback loops. What they have in common is that they feed back into themselves. Which, in different forms and ways, is vitally important for designing interesting and non-exhaustive playing experiences around *conflict*. This beat, again, offers you a particular design perspective. You can put it to use to create exciting conflict setups for your game.

Previously, when we examined rules and rule sets and game mechanics and how and why they interact with each other, we also looked at value states and how they can change from one game state to another. For non-transitivity, our first topic in this beat, we will focus on value sets that are associated with the rock–paper–scissors dynamic, or RPS.

We can look at RPS in two ways, as a game mechanic and as a rule set. The stand-alone game Rock Paper Scissors is clearly a player activity, which makes RPS a game mechanic. There, it defines the values of three elements, governs how they interact with each other, and has a rule set for when and how players can make their moves. In game design, however, we usually subordinate RPS to broader and more compelling player activities, which turns RPS into a rule set as part of a game mechanic. This game mechanic can then be attached to any element of the gameplay loop, particularly loop elements related to competition and combat.

For any game, RPS controls at least three game elements that compete with each other in non-transitive ways. Let's illustrate that with an example.

For a *transitive* relationship between three or more elements, imagine you're running a test to compare the long-range capabilities of a twentieth-century field gun, a field howitzer, and a mortar. In your first test, you find out that the field gun has a longer range than the howitzer. In your second test, you find out that the howitzer has a longer range than the mortar. Knowing that, you don't need a third test to compare the field gun and the mortar. There's no way that the mortar can have a longer range than the field gun when the mortar has a shorter range than the howitzer, which has a shorter range than the field gun!

That's what defines a transitive relationship. If A beats B and B beats C, then A will beat C. The same is true, by and large, for our artillery weapons' capacity to clear terrain elevations, only the other way around. When the mortar can clear higher close-by obstacles than the howitzer and the howitzer can clear higher close-by obstacles than the field gun, then we can be reasonably sure that the mortar will be able to clear higher close-by obstacles than the field gun.

That's not how RPS works. RPS elements have a non-transitive relationship. In the stand-alone game, paper beats rock and rock beats scissors, yet paper does not beat scissors! Here, if A beats B and B beats

C, then C beats A. In other words, a transitive relationship is a straight line with a beginning and an end, as in both artillery examples, and a non-transitive relationship is a cycle, as in the Rock Paper Scissors example.

Why would you want to create non-transitive relationships for game elements that stand in conflict with each other? The answer is fairly simple, but far-reaching. If your players must choose one element from a set of elements in your game, and one element is consistently more advantageous than all the other elements in that set, then most if not all players will choose that element most if not all of the time. That can be a weapon, a character, a military unit, a terrain, a branch from a technology tree, and a thousand other things, depending on your game type. Which element or elements the player selects is a *strategy*, and if there is a strategy that has consistently more advantages than any other possible strategy, that strategy is called a dominant strategy. You don't want to have dominant strategies in your game! Any dominant strategy will greatly reduce the number of possible paths and the range of possible playing experiences, as discussed in the preceding beat. Dominant strategies make your game less interesting, less enjoyable, less meaningful, and less rewarding.

To create interesting relationships for conflict, you can then increase the number of elements, the number of non-transitive relationships between these elements, or both. The best way to design your non-transitive relationships is, well, math! On the surface, you might have swords, spears, javelins, archers, and cavalry. Under the hood, you have numbers.

To give you an idea of how that works, and also to give you more ideas, let's take a look at a variant of James Grime's "Grime dice," as illustrated below; in case these are the print edition's gray scale

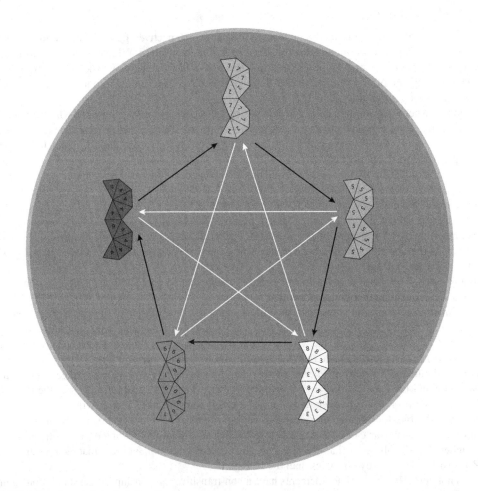

FIGURE 4.11 Corrected single Grime dice.

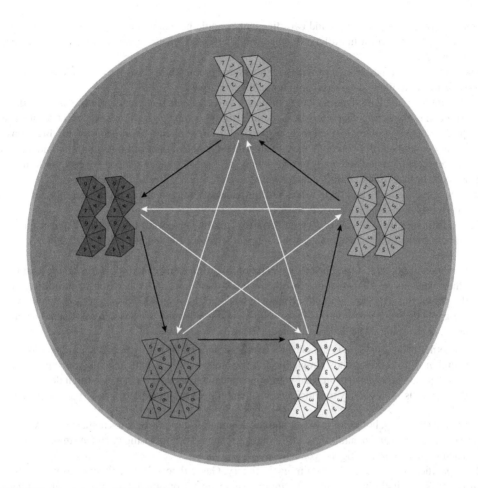

FIGURE 4.12 Corrected double Grime dice.

illustrations, you can download the full-color versions for better reference from the companion website at *ludotronics.net*. To implement Jon Chamber's correction for the green–red problem (two red dice performed better than two green dice on average in Grime's original setup, which they shouldn't), the setup has been converted from D6 to D10. The arrows between the dice indicate statistical advantages, for example, a red die would beat a blue die in the long run, or two blue dice would beat two red dice in the long run, and so on.

The beauty of this setup is that it forms not one but two non-transitive cycles, an external and an internal one. What's more, with two dice of the same color instead of one, the external cycle switches directions and the internal cycle stays the same! This, in turn, has an interesting side effect: you will always find a color that performs better on average against any two colors *at the same time* as long as you're allowed to determine the number of dice. Thus, no matter which colors your opponents might pick, their colors will either be next to each other on the external cycle or next to each other on the internal cycle. If the colors are next to each other on the external cycle, there will always be a color that has a better chance against both opponents on average in a two dice–game. If the colors are next to each other on the internal cycle, there will always be a color that will beat both opponents on average in a one die–game.

When it is possible to design such beautiful multiple and reversible non-transitive relationships within the constraints of physical dice, imagine what you can do under the hood without such constraints!

On the surface, then, you can map your values to anything. Combat moves for beat 'em ups, military units for strategy games, weapons for arena shooters, items for puzzle games, teams for sports games, amusement park rides for management games, technology trees for 4X games, you name it. The difference between one-die games and two-dice games could be mapped to different combat situations (offense or defense), terrain modifiers, damage modifiers, and whatever you can think of that makes sense in your game.

Importantly, these relationships provide no short-term predictability. All they provide are *statistical advantages* for more likely outcomes, not predictable outcomes.

If you want to create RPS dynamics in your game with elements that are clearly transitive in the real world, you can pull in more characteristics. In our artillery example above, we had two transitive relationships for range and obstacle-clearance, respectively. These already work in opposite directions, so they're easily combined. But you don't have to stop there! You can throw in field mobility and how long it takes to get them mounted and ready to fire. Additional factors you can include are cost, building time, ordnance cost, ordnance availability, damage value, and crew size. If well-balanced, the rules that govern these three game elements and their values will provide different advantages in different contexts as a non-transitive relationship on a broader level.

These advantages we will call *utilities*, a term that might ring a bell. Every time a player picks one game element over its alternatives in a given context, there are two mental processes at work:

- One mental process is the player's expectation that this element will perform better than the other elements in this situation. In other words, they have an expectation of its utility. For the player, this expectation might turn out to be right or wrong. However, your expectations as the game designer who controls these utilities mathematically are based on statistical advantages, in the same way that you calculate Grime dice outcomes.

- The other mental process is the player's anticipation of what their opponent would pick in this situation. While this sounds simple, it isn't. Because what you anticipate as your opponent's pick depends in large parts on what your opponent anticipates you will pick. And it doesn't stop there, because you will try to anticipate what your opponent anticipates you will do, and so on!

This sounds dizzying, both for the player and the designer. But in practice, it's manageable. As players, we have our heuristics and mental shortcuts to make decisions without losing ourselves in infinite-mirror rooms each time. And as a designer, you have math.

More specifically, it's the math used in game theory. Game theory is a mathematical model used in social sciences, particularly economics, to analyze the behavior of rational agents in conflict situations and their decisions regarding competition and cooperation. Thus, whenever you design non-transitive elements your players have to choose from that involve expectations and anticipation, you can use game theory as a tool. Even better, your elements are not restricted to items like swords, howitzers, technology trees, and so on. They can also be player decisions for plot points in conflict narratives.

To see how this works, let's look at the perhaps best-known example from game theory, the Prisoner's Dilemma. It's a standard situation, but with many variations, primarily in the form of different confinement values—some have 2, 10, and 8 years, others 1, 20, and 5 years, and so on. We'll stick with 1, 5, and 2 years, for simplicity's sake. In order to work, the original setup makes several restrictive assumptions, but we can eliminate the causes that necessitate these assumptions with a few narrative tweaks.

Imagine you're a burglar, and you've met another burglar, maybe while serving a short time in jail together or through a fence who buys and resells your loot, and you decide to pool resources and work together. Later, in the aftermath of an unsuccessful burglary attempt, you're both caught with your illegal burglary tools, but without loot or any other clear evidence that would link you to the crime in question. So much for the setup, now the game. You're alone in your cell, and a police officer visits you to tell you the following. If both you and your partner won't talk, both of you will be going to jail for one year for the possession of burglary tools. If you snitch on your partner regarding the burglary attempt, you're going scot-free, but your partner will be locked up for five years. If both of you snitch on each other, both of you can look forward to staying in the can for a period of two years. Then she tells you that she made your partner the exact same offer.

Your decision depends on what you think your partner will decide, which depends on what your partner thinks you will decide, which depends on what you think what your partner thinks what you will decide, and so on. In practice, each player's expected utilities for competing or cooperating depend on

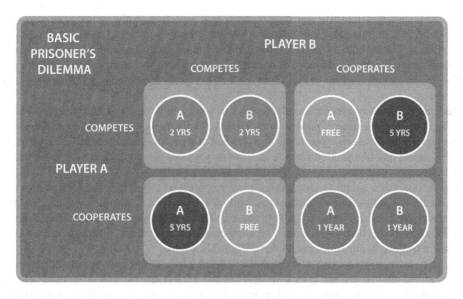

FIGURE 4.13 Basic prisoner's dilemma.

each player's anticipation of the other player's behavior, just like in an RPS match. And you can model these expected utilities and the best strategies to solve them with some manageable math. But there's more! In the case of the Prisoner's Dilemma, competing—which amounts to snitching—"dominates weakly." That's because, when both players snitch, both players can only do worse when they unilaterally change their decisions, i.e., from snitching to not snitching. The more general case of that, when neither player can unilaterally increase their expected utility by changing their strategy while the other player's strategy remains unchanged, is called a Nash equilibrium. Now, if that were all there is, and if all players always made rational decisions, then there would be no surprises and just one possible path. However, both the social side and the mathematical side bring more interesting things to the table.

On the social side, humans have a strong tendency to cooperate, which shouldn't come as a surprise. As a species of social animals, humans make cooperative decisions all the time, and these cooperative decisions aren't purely rational actions in the name of one's individual and immediate self-interest. Or, from another perspective, the social dimension is so strong that it becomes an important part of that very self-interest. Furthermore, players will remember their opponents' choices in match-based games and act accordingly in the following matches.

On the mathematical side, your conflict situation becomes more complex and more interesting when it doesn't provide a catch-all Nash equilibrium, so that the only purely rational way to resolve it is a so-called "mixed strategy." The trick is, each player can compute their optimal "decision mix" where it no longer matters what the other player decides! Mathematically, you take your opponent's utilities from the possible strategies and compute the value where these utilities are equal, which is usually a ratio. Here's an example that assumes two players and two possible strategies, to keep it simple. The first player computes 2/6; that's the ratio at which the second player's utilities become equal. The second player computes 5/9; that's the ratio at which the first player's utilities become equal. Then the optimal (mixed) strategy for the first player is to use the first strategy twice and the second strategy four times over six matches, randomly distributed. The optimal (mixed) strategy for the second player is to use the first strategy five times and the second strategy four times over nine games, also randomly distributed.

Do players actually compute optimal strategies? Yes, professional players do! Just look at poker players. But for your system design, it doesn't even matter whether they do or not, to enjoy the fruits of your mathematical toils. Whenever your players must choose between different weapons, items, units, map areas, technology trees, career paths, and so on, you can use your model to fine-tune your entire conflict setup very precisely, and you can also use it to fine-tune the decision abilities of your AI opponents for the just-right range of difficulty levels.

With these tools—non-transitive math, game-theoretical payoffs (roughly: utilities), mixed strategies, and infinity mirrors of mutual trust or distrust—you can create intricate and challenging relationships between items and agents both on and below the surface. You can control everything mathematically, test it relentlessly, and create the exact range of possible paths for your game that you want to create.

For the second part of this beat, we will turn our attention to feedback loops, which involve a similar design mindset.

As much as you want non-transitive relationships in your game instead of transitive ones, you want negative feedback loops instead of positive ones. To make the difference between these two immediately clear: the thermostat that keeps your home at a pleasant temperature runs on negative feedback, while the infernal squeal that fills your conference room when your mic gets too close to the speakers runs on positive feedback.

Positive feedback is a circuit or loop along which the output of a system is fed back to it as input. It usually articulates itself as a runaway effect that leads to extreme values of some kind. It's easy to build, both knowingly and unknowingly; it's pretty robust and hard to terminate; and it is often a side effect of agent interactions that haven't or couldn't be foreseen. Complex systems can create positive feedback loops without warning at any time, and with unpredictable results.

There are two major types of positive feedback loops in games. The first type is truly unpredictable and fed by all the math, rules, and cycles we've discussed so far. Once it kicks in, it creates effects that cannot be controlled or terminated through regular game interactions. It's a bug that needs to be fixed.

The second type primarily affects conflict-rich games with multiple agents or players. It manifests itself in a runaway effect popularly known as "the rich get richer, the poor get poorer." These are situations where being in the lead has intrinsic advantages that feed back *into itself* to widen the lead, often progressively. That's not just profoundly frustrating for those who try in vain to catch up. It's also profoundly uninteresting to play or to watch. To avoid positive feedback loops and keep everybody on the edge of their seats all the time, a game needs negative feedback loops that counter these effects in clever ways.

Here, good game design goes a long way. Not every solution that works is a good solution. The popular rubber band effect in racing games, where AI-driven vehicles never fall too far behind nor get too far ahead in thermostat-fashion, is a low-quality solution that is as transparent as it is annoying. While it is hard to come up with a better, different solution for more realistic racing games, it's certainly worth a try. (Rubber banding is usually categorized as DDA.)

For less realistic racing games, negative feedback solutions are easier to find because the game's rules are allowed and even expected to be more imaginative. The *Mario Kart* franchise is a renowned and remarkable example. Item boxes for leading players have a higher probability to contain less powerful and more defense-oriented power-ups. Power-ups for players that lag behind, in contrast, have a higher probability to be more powerful and attack-oriented. For a while, until this new setup was sufficiently tweaked, Nintendo went overboard with this solution in *Mario Kart 64* by introducing the truly nuclear "Spiny Shell," to be hurled toward the leading player as the most gratifying target.

This negative feedback strategy is extraordinarily successful, and not only because it counters the runaway effect. It also keeps games or matches with a mixed field of more experienced and less experienced players enjoyable and challenging for everybody.

Other game types need other solutions, for example, punishing encumbrance modifiers for more powerful weapons. Logistics become exponentially complicated the more troops or terrain a player amasses. More powerful spells inflict more powerful headaches and necessitate longer rest periods. A berserk mode kicks in after receiving substantial amounts of damage. And so on.

Another strategy is bottleneck design. It puts a crushing obstacle close to the end of the game that gives trailing players or the trailing team a chance to catch up. Famous examples are board games in the tradition of Pachisi, where only direct throws can bring pieces "home," or the "checking out" and "final double" rules in dart games.

There's a time-tested, game type-agnostic heuristic you can follow. If the player has to add assets in order to win (troops, territories, weapons, loot, friends, powers, favors, resources of any kind), make the game easier to play with fewer items of that kind. If the player has to get rid of items in order to win (cards, balls, debts, encumbrances of any kind, maybe clothing, depending on what you're into), make the game easier to play with more items of that kind. This principle can kick in right from the start or be delayed until a threshold value has been reached.

However, such matches shouldn't drag on for too long either. In certain cases, you might even want to drop your negative feedback loop for good on the final stretch to allow the leading player an "epic win." It all depends on your game type and your target audience.

To wrap it up for this beat, a few words on compensation. You can compensate for problems with fudging, which is a bad thing, and you can compensate for problems with tweaking, which is a good thing.

All your math under the hood should be rock-solid. If the math refuses to work out as intended, don't create special rules that will make it look like it's working out on the surface. Not only would such rules be clutter rules or dirt, as mentioned. Special rules to repair other rules will inevitably lead to weaknesses that will beg to be exploited. Chances are, some of these weaknesses will lead to dominant strategies, which will necessitate even more patches with even more clutter rules. And don't fall back on designing rules as arcane as telecommunication plans or health insurance options. You will never preempt possible exploits by obfuscation.

What you need to do, instead, is *tweaking*.

As a ground rule, symmetrical games need less tweaking over time than asymmetrical games. For a highly symmetrical game like soccer, rule changes are very rare. In the twentieth century, the entire set of soccer rules got along just fine for literally decades, until a general shift toward defensive playing styles triggered a round of rule changes to encourage more offensive strategies and tactics. Compare that to baseball! Baseball has major or minor rule changes almost every year.

The reason is this. In highly symmetrical games like soccer, the defending team and the attacking team do the same thing, basically, only in opposite geographical directions. So when a new technique comes along, it will benefit the attacking and the defending team equally and cancel out. That way, a new technique will make the game more interesting, not less. There are exceptions, of course, like the aforementioned rise of defensive soccer strategies. Baseball, in contrast, is so asymmetrical that a new technique or tactic or strategy or even slight advances in equipment will benefit either the attacking team or the defending team, but rarely both. That way, every half-inning will be dominated by the attacker or the defender, depending on who profits from that change. This diminishes the number of possible paths, which makes the game more predictable and less interesting. Thus, the rules are quickly amended to balance everything out and make every half-inning as interesting as it should be.

Now take a highly asymmetrical game like baseball, make it even more asymmetrical, add a third party, and you get *StarCraft*. The necessity to keep everything balanced, that each species will beat each other species on average 50% of the time over time with players of equal skill, while huge masses of players invent new techniques and tactics every minute, makes the *maintenance* of such a game as demanding as designing and creating it in the first place.

Asymmetrical games and non-transitive dynamics will always demand sustained tweaking after release, no matter how much prototyping, playtesting, balancing, and QA efforts were put into it before your gold master left the premises. That's a metaphor, of course. At less monumental scales, it will apply to your uploaded home-brew indie game as well.

Beat 4: Representations

From Rules to Realism

Now that we discussed what rules and game mechanics are, how interacting subsystems create individual and non-exhaustive playing experiences, and how compelling conflicts can be designed around mathematical models, let's look at the representational aspects of video games associated with the *Interactivity* territory, and how these representational aspects shape the *perceived realism* both in relation to game events and player input.

Let's start out with rules that represent or simulate aspects of bodily movements like running, jumping, shooting, or picking up items from the ground. For single actions, transitions from the realistic to the unrealistic are always vague and highly subjective. But there will be a point at which most players agree that, for example, a human avatar's allowed jump height or jump distance has stopped being realistic. That said, our assessment of what's realistic or not is often anything but realistic! A human avatar might be able to scale just a bit less than its own height in a standing vertical jump, which is pure fantasy, but the player might still "feel" that a trained person could accomplish this. Somewhere between that and twice the avatar's height, however, that feeling will certainly have evaporated.

Around such contexts, design decisions need to be made. Should the rules for a given game *be* realistic (capping vertical standing jumps at around 40 inches, or 100 centimeters), *feel* realistic (maybe allowing up to 60 inches, or 150 centimeters), or should realism be just thrown overboard (because scaling enormous obstacles with vertical standing jumps is a blast)? Obviously, your design decisions should depend on your type of game, its target audience, its key values, and its theme. Your decisions will be different if you're designing a training simulation, an arena shooter, or a beat 'em up. They will be different if you're designing a contemporary detective mystery, a high-adventure survival thriller, or a superhero brawler. But whatever you're working on, decisions need to be made. That is also true if your level of realism doesn't correspond to your game type or story type on purpose.

Then, you can and should extend this to any rule meant to represent or simulate activities and events in your game that exist in the physical world, which could include everything from lock-picking to persuasion. Here, the perceived realism depends on parameters like when, how, and how often such events occur, and how they play out in terms of success or failure. To illustrate how different mathematical models behind these activities and events create very different playing experiences, let's have a look at how probabilities shape the playing experience in pen-and-paper RPGs.

Probabilities in pen-and-paper RPGs with regard to skill use and difficulty levels depend on the type and number of dice. If your players resolve tasks by rolling a D100, a D20, a D10, or a D6, the probability distribution is uniform for every die roll. That's because every value has an equal chance of turning up. For a D100, each value has a 1% chance, for a D20, each value has a 5% chance, and so on.

If players roll any *combination* of dice, in contrast, the probability distribution isn't uniform anymore. Different values no longer have equal chances of turning up. You can see this at work if you compare a D20 system with a 3D6 system: the former shows an equal distribution and the latter a bell curve.

The important point is that differences in probability distribution will impact the playing experience in profound ways. To see how that works, let's drill down to the details. The principle behind such die rolls in general is that a player with an average skill level (in our example 10 in both systems, for simplicity's

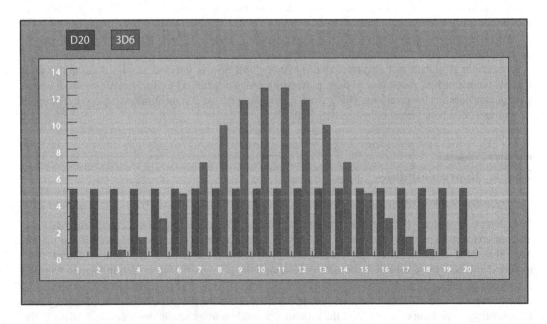

FIGURE 4.14 Probability distributions D20/3D6.

sake) has an average chance (50%) to succeed at a task with an average difficulty level (again roughly 10 in both systems). That might or might not correspond to how the world works, but it's a long-established convention where "average" difficulty is not equivalent to routine tasks.

In systems where players must stay below their target number, a character with average lock picking skills will successfully pick average locks about half of the time by rolling a 10 or less in both systems. But as soon as you leave that isolated sweet spot behind, things drift apart. In a D20 system, a one-point increase or decrease in skill level or difficulty level corresponds to a 5% increase or decrease of the chance to succeed, *proportionally* at every point. In a 3D6 system, in contrast, the chance to succeed is *disproportionately* affected by one-point increases or decreases in skill or difficulty.

Here's a simplified yet typical example where the range of possible skill levels maxes out in the neighborhood of 20. If your character has a better-than-average skill level of 12 in the D20 system, i.e., 10% better than average, their chances to succeed at an average task will also be 10% better than average, i.e., 60%. Now, if you raise a character's skill level in the 3D6 system by 10%, worth about 1.8 or 2 points, from 10 to 12, their chances to succeed at an average task are raised by a whopping 24%—that's a 74% chance to succeed! And vice versa. At lower skill levels or with higher difficulty levels, the player's chances to succeed at a task dwindle much more rapidly in the 3D6 system than in the D20 system. The same is true for modifiers; any bonus or malus affects chances proportionally in a D20 system and disproportionately in a 3D6 system.

This critically impacts the playing experience in many ways, not only for competition and combat, but for the entire dramatic structure. In the 3D6 system, even slight increases in skill grant disproportional advantages. But there's more! The probability values for the improbable and the probable are also different, and this impacts the dramatic structure in spectacular ways. The most improbable event in a D20 system, a good one or a bad one, occurs at a roll of 2 or 20, respectively, with a 5% chance for each—which is immense, if you think about it. In a 3D6 system, the most improbable event, again a good one or a bad one, occurs at a roll of 3 or 18, respectively. Here, each has a mere 0.46% chance to occur. Probable events, reasonably set between 7 and 13, will occur 67.58% of the time in a 3D6 system and 35% of the time in a D20 system, over time and all other things being equal. That's literally a dramatic difference—the D20 system will produce a lot more improbable results over time and yield a completely different dramatic structure that persistently veers toward the chaotic, the perilous, and the slapstick.

Over time, players will perceive a 3D6 system as being not only more realistic but also more predictable, and a D20 system as less realistic but maybe more exciting. Liberal use of steep modifiers can change these systems' basic characteristics in both directions, but your intended playing experience shouldn't depend on a Game of Modifiers.

Finally, if you've picked your general direction, you can fine-tune the playing experience further—neither systems with equal distribution nor with unequal distribution are all alike, respectively. Both a D100 and a D20 system have equal distribution, but the D20 system amplifies properties common to both. The chance to roll an extreme value, for example, grows from 1% in a D100 system to a whopping 5% in a D20 system. (In a 3D6 system, as you might recall, it's a mere 0.46%.) Likewise, unequal probability distributions also behave differently: if you compare a 3D6 system with a 2D10 system, the latter shows a flattened bell curve and more frequent outlier results at both ends.

With a 2D10 system, the extreme values 2 and 20 each have a probability of 1%, similar to a D100 system, and the chance to roll reasonably average results for average performances is around 58%. That is considerably closer to the 3D6 system's 67.58% than to the D20 system's 35% (or the D100 system's 37.5%). Thus, over time and all other things being equal, players will perceive a 2D10 system as more realistic than a D20 system, but it will give them perceptively more surprise results with interesting consequences than a 3D6 system.

To sum it up, how you design the mathematical underpinnings of your game in terms of representation and simulation has a distinct and powerful impact on the playing experience, which even extends to its dramatic structure. You can and should design these rules very precisely, with your target audience and your intended playing experience in mind.

Let's proceed to another important topic, the perceived realism of player input and the contentious issue of input realism. If you design your game's rules in ways that demand more or less realistic player input, what could be gained and what could be lost with respect to its playing experience?

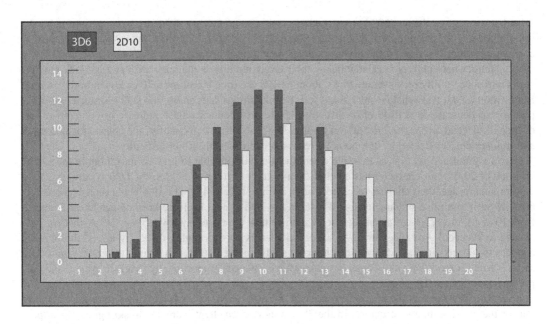

FIGURE 4.15 Probability distributions 3D6/2D10.

Usually, when you hear about a video game project X or Y or Z that built a prototype for a jet fighter game or a car racing game or a powerboat simulation game that was so realistic that only a fighter pilot or a Formula One driver or an offshore racing veteran was able to play it, you can be fairly sure it's a tall tale. Certainly, there might be exceptions, like the anecdote shared by pen-and-paper RPG legend Steve Jackson at the GDC in 1998, as related by Katie Salen and Eric Zimmerman in *Rules of Play*. According to Jackson, his team had built a driving simulation prototype that was so realistic that only a professional race car driver could handle it. While this indeed sounds like a tall tale, it might actually be true— Jackson was referring not to a "regular" racing video game but to his aborted *Car Wars* gaming center project, which was ambitious to the point of wrapping entire cars around players. But that's an outlier!

To gain a better understanding of player input–realism, let's stick to racing games for the time being. There are three major categories of car racing games on the market right now. With two of them, simulation and arcade, we're all familiar. The third category can be called grinders, with *The Crew* as a good example. *The Crew* isn't realistic, but it isn't arcade either. In both simulation- and arcade-flavored racing games, the point is to become a better player (but not a better driver in real life, we'll come to that). In *The Crew*, players do not primarily become better players through improving and mastering input controls and mechanics. What they're really getting better at is upgrading cars through a steady stream of grinding. And as soon as a player has a new car or needs a different upgrade kit for a different environment, the illusion of improvement and mastery up and dies. Granted, upgrading cars with fancy stuff is what people do in the real world too, that's realistic all right. But an experienced race car driver will nevertheless be able to hurl any off-the-shelf automobile down the track with miraculous precision. Vice versa, if you're an average driver, see how much your driving will improve if you find yourself behind the ultra-responsive steering wheel of a race-tuned high-performance engine. Good luck with that.

The basic design rule is obvious, not only for racing games but for any game type that can provide different experiences related to realism and input realism. If your primary target audience consists of simulation game aficionados, you'd better deliver on the realism part for an enjoyable experience. If your primary target audience is dedicated to arcade-style gaming, it makes perfect sense to support phantasmagoric maneuvers that would make Newton's head spin in his grave. If your primary target audience is more tuned toward role-playing experiences, then grinder-style games might be their thing. All, if done well, will deliver the intended experience to your audience, which doesn't mean that these categories are always clear-cut. Arcade-ish games can be simulation-flavored in some aspects, and so on. It all depends on your key values and the intended playing experience for your target audience.

But that's only half of the story. To get to the other half, we need to look at a contentious question attached to realism and input realism in games. Do players who get better at playing realistic car racing games become better drivers? What would it mean to design a car racing game that produces better drivers? There's a popular argument that goes like this. The more realistic the controls, physics, input details, and accompanying game graphics for a specific activity in a video game are, the more the player will learn about that activity and become better at it in real life. Following that logic, a player can not only become a better driver with the help of realistic driving simulators but also a better shooter with the help of realistic shooting games. That argument indeed exists: in interviews and articles, researcher and author Dave Grossman even refers to first-person shooters as "Murder Simulators."

Yet, think about it! Even with the most realistic shooter, what you're getting good at is handling a controller or a keyboard–mouse combination, not a knife, an M4 carbine, or a sniper rifle. Similarly, you will not become a better driver in real life and on the track by playing *Forza Motorsport, NR2003*, or even *Grand Prix Legends*. What if we threw in a full set of peripherals, from a racing seat with gear-shifter mount and foot pedals to a force feedback steering wheel, approaching Steve Jackson's *Car Wars* ambitions? Still, no. If you're a professional race car driver, you might be able to use outstandingly realistic racing simulators to get familiar with a track or practice a certain maneuver. But that's about as far as it gets. For shooters, likewise, even an M4 carbine gaming accessory will not make you a better shooter in real-life situations, let alone a better soldier or police officer (or mob enforcer, for that matter). You will get much better mileage out of visiting the shooting range a few times, or playing airsoft or MilSim. Military or law-enforcement professionals, just like race car drivers, can use simulation video games to prepare for certain situations, but that's again how far as it gets. (And even that has its limits; see Ed Smith's illuminating Vice article "In the Army Now: The Making of *Full Spectrum Warrior*.") Barring extraordinary contexts and circumstances, simulators can only complement, maintain, and support real-world proficiency levels, not create them.

What all this boils down to is a misconception. Car racing games and shooting games, even downright simulation-style, don't simulate driving or shooting. What these games simulate is a particular *experience* of driving or shooting, each game in its own distinct, uniquely crafted way.

That's what you, as a game designer, should aspire to. If you're designing a realistic game about the activity X, your question shouldn't be: *How can this game simulate X best?* Instead, your question should be: *How can your game simulate this particular experience of doing X best?* It's a completely different question that will lead you toward creating a highly distinctive game with its own personality that players can enjoy.

> A realistic game about the activity X should not try to simulate doing X, but a particular *experience* of doing X.

For this beat's final design parameter, let's look at the tension between in-game realism and input realism and the issue of quick time events (QTEs).

Let's start from scratch. Players often step in the shoes of professionals in games, like that ex-marine turned mercenary turned headhunter, a gladiator, a pilot, a sword fighter, a talented street kid, or the Batman. Rarely does that correspond to these players' personal real-life pursuits. Likewise, in most cases, these players control their in-game actions with a regular controller, mouse and keyboard, joystick, touchscreen, and similar, not with real guns, swords, combat aircraft, or roundhouse kicks. Now, how do you make these player actions look realistic and cool on the screen and not amateurish and silly?

The answer is that you do that by making player input more abstract, not more realistic. The higher your abstraction level is, the more accessible your game will become. In general, player input is translated into on-screen action through abstractions that map the latter to the former, and you should always consider very precisely the amount of input abstraction you want to offer.

You can create systems that are more enjoyable with less abstract and more realistic input, up to and including accessories like steering wheels or laser guns, with demanding combinations of keystrokes or button presses or gestures that the player has to learn, unlock, or both. This is great if your game addresses a target audience with "core" attributes who are not only used to but expect tough challenges and steep skill barriers, which we will discuss in the upcoming beat. But to make your game more enjoyable and accessible for less-skilled players or even players with "casual" attributes, you can create systems with less realistic and more abstract input—up to and including QTEs, which translate easy-to-learn player input into impressive on-screen action. An outstanding example of this is *Batman: Arkham Asylum*, demonstrated by Scott Rogers in *Level Up! The Guide to Great Video Game Design*. Here and elsewhere, QTEs map highly abstracted input to spectacular combat sequences and satisfying finishing moves that impart a sense, and the joy, of dazzling accomplishment for a broad range of players.

Granted, QTEs got a bad rap for "mash this unexpected button to pulp in a split-second or die," which even games like the *Tomb Raider* reboot sometimes fail to deem below their station. Another atrocious use of QTEs has been to give the player some flimsy semblance of control in cutscenes that stretch out forever, as in *Resident Evil 4*, which prevents players from skipping them. This is unfortunate! QTEs offer terrific abstraction techniques to provide enjoyable experiences in the *Interactivity* territory to non-core players. From the original *Shenmue* to games like *God of War* and *Heavy Rain* to mobile games like *Revolution 60*, QTEs have evolved well beyond "quick" and "time." You can even map them to moral decisions as, somewhat heavy-handedly, games from the *Mass Effect* trilogy do. QTEs can do all that without sacrificing perceived realism, without cutting the perceived cord of causality between player actions and on-screen events, without severing even once the player's continuous impression, however illusive, of agency, authorship, and control.

Beat 5: Readiness

From Skills to Challenges

To play a game well, the player needs to learn. What, how, and when the player has to learn something, i.e., the learning conditions of your game, should be well-designed and a good fit for your target audience. We can break these learning conditions down into three groups.

Proficiency spectrum. What are the proficiencies that your player must develop to beat your game or play it well?

Learning curves. How are the learning opportunities for proficiency progression distributed over the course of your game? This includes the questions of how much the player needs to learn before the game becomes enjoyable, and whether there's a point when getting better at playing that game becomes impossible or no longer makes a difference.

Playing preferences. Can the player tailor your game's difficulty settings and density conditions to their needs, and how?

For the first group, the proficiency spectrum, you have to deal with two different sets. The first set contains everything your player already needs to bring to the table. Most of that goes unnoticed, so go to infrared and look sharp! Among what goes unnoticed, for example, is being able to read, make deductions, recognize various patterns, use a mouse or a controller, differentiate colors, hear sounds, understand a language, and so on. For your game's accessibility features, this is where you have to look. Also, each game type has accumulated numerous conventions over time that, again, often go without saying—from the concept of power-ups in first-person shooters to the pretzel logic of adventure game puzzles. Find out what you're presupposing, and then look at your target audience. It may well be that the presuppositions your game makes need tweaking. This is especially important when you want to pull players into your game that are not used to this particular game type. But that comes with a catch; too much onboarding rarely fails to annoy experienced players.

The second set contains the proficiencies your player needs to develop over the course of the game to beat your game or play it well. Remember, your game *is* the learning experience your player needs in order to play your game! Not counting general physical or intellectual fitness training and a few esoteric exceptions, players don't train for a game *outside the game*, which can include practicing moves or

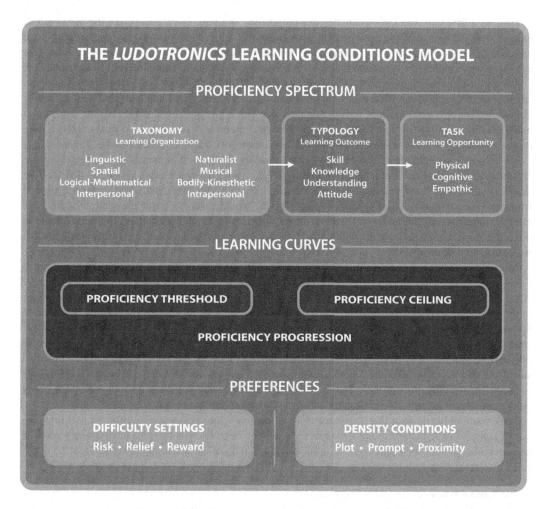

FIGURE 4.16 Learning conditions model.

combos or tactics against a game's AI. The game is the training! (This is one of several reasons behind humankind's preoccupation with games in the first place.)

All this should be meticulously planned. Your proficiency spectrum shouldn't come about haphazardly, as a mere afterthought to the challenges you throw into your player's path.

Planning your proficiency spectrum comprises three areas: your game's learning organization (taxonomy), its learning outcomes (typology), and its learning opportunities (tasks). Let's go through all three, bracketed by a practical example.

Let's say your game has a plot point where the player character is in the wilderness and must acquire an item, and you want to make it difficult for the player to acquire that item. After you thought about it for a minute, you put that item in a cave where it's hard to find; a ferocious mountain torrent between the player character and the cave; and an acutely ill-tempered bear into the back of the cave.

You could do it like this, and the sequence of beats might be enjoyable. But somewhere down the road, you have to make sure all this fits into the wider context of your game, which includes learning curves, variety, balance, and theme. Thus, there's a more organized way to go about it. It's a lot more demanding, however. Thus, we have to embark on an extended detour, at the end of which we will come back to this example and apply everything we have learned.

To begin with, you should not only have a plot point but also have an idea about the game's ending, or goal, and your theme and motifs from the Preparation phase.

Then, as a first step, you have to create your proficiency spectrum, with everything the player needs to learn over the course of the game to beat your game and achieve its goal. As a further step, you can organize this collection along a learning taxonomy of your choice. A learning taxonomy is a tool that can make your challenges' types and their distribution across your game more interesting and balanced.

Among the most easily applicable frameworks is Howard Gardner's "Frames of Mind." Here's a compilation of its more robust categories, or domains: linguistic, musical, logical-mathematical, spatial, bodily kinesthetic, interpersonal (social), intrapersonal (understanding of self), and naturalist (the capacity to make consequential distinctions). But you can also use frameworks richer in empirical evidence, like those compiled by Anderson, Bloom, Krathwohl, and others, often simply called "Bloom Taxonomy."

But let's stick with Gardner. You certainly don't need to use all eight domains and make your game "taxonomically complete." But it can inspire you to make your challenges more varied. To demonstrate that, let's pull up our third-person action–adventure game against the backdrop of the French Revolution from the Procedure phase. The challenges in this game would certainly cover the spatial, bodily kinesthetic, interpersonal, intrapersonal, and naturalist domains in some way or other. But what about the linguistic, musical, and mathematical domains? Could we make the game more interesting and enjoyable with associated proficiencies?

After some research, we realize that rhetoric and speeches are important characteristics of the French Revolution. What if the player character needs to become a better, more convincing speaker or writer? After all, Thomas Paine is their friend! What about the musical domain? Could we involve the player in the composition of the Marseillaise? Maybe the player character must learn the melody by ear from Rouget de Lisle, as contraband, when they share a prison cell together in 1793. Also, what if the player character at one time has to assist Lazare Carnot—who had studied with Benjamin Franklin and could plausibly be introduced by Paine—to solve applied math problems for the Ministers of War? It's not at all surprising that we rarely see these domains represented in games; neither input methods nor algorithms to handle them are readily available. But there's always a chance that you come up with something really simple and clever that enriches your game in ways you hadn't thought of before.

Next, you can break open that "proficiency" box and map your collection to different learning outcomes along so-called qualification typologies. As with taxonomies, you can pick any typology you like or even make up your own. But, as a recommendation, it pays off to differentiate between *skill*, *knowledge*, *understanding*, and *attitude*.

Skill as a repeatable, observable performance.

Knowledge as being able to recognize and recall facts and procedures.

Understanding as grasping complex processes and being able to apply knowledge in new and
   different contexts.

Attitude as changed or adapted behavior based on increased skill, knowledge, or understanding.

This set is loosely based on a variety of qualification typologies, including so-called "KSA" models (*knowledge*, *skill*, *attitudes*, or, more often, *abilities*), but reworked and broadened to dispel the rather limiting clouds of immediate workplace utility. All four elements are related, but not as closely as it sometimes appears. *Skill*, comprising proficiency, expertise, competence, and similar, is not the same as *knowledge*. You can have knowledge about something without being able to apply it, and you can be skilled at something without knowing how it works. Then, you can be skilled at something and know how it works, but you don't *understand* the underlying principles that would enable you to apply your skill and knowledge in different contexts and circumstances. Finally, you can be skilled at something and know a lot about it and understand the underlying principles, but you do not act on it or adapt to it by changing your *attitude*—your approach, your mindset, your strategy, and similar.

Here's an example. You're a good long-distance runner; that's skill. You learn how to train, do exercises and workouts, all in the right order, and prepare for races so you can run faster and farther; that's knowledge. You acquire insights into the mechanics of running and the complex physiological processes of your body so that you can avoid burnout and injuries, tackle shorter distances, or pick up other sports related to running; that's understanding. You enjoy all this so much that you resolve to keep up training hard and eating well every day; that's attitude.

For our action–adventure game against the backdrop of the French Revolution, a high-level typology sketch for its learning outcomes might look like this:

- Dexterity-based skills for action elements and cognition-based skills for puzzle elements.
- Knowledge about different forms of identity, and their respective historical contexts and developments in the eighteenth century.
- Understanding the nature of identity, the formation processes of identities, what identity means in different contexts at different times for different people, and its resilience or mutability.
- Attitude changes toward the player character's own identity and toward other forms of identity represented by non-player characters.

To repeat, not every skill needs knowledge, not every skill or knowledge needs understanding, not every attitude change has a skill attached to it, and so on. You can be great at repairing warp engines without changing your attitude, and you can resolve to eat well without understanding the intricacies of nutrition.

Before we proceed, though, we need to look at two possible sources of confusion that can mess up your challenge design.

The first, related to knowledge, is the difference between *recall* and *recognition*. If you can come up with a certain actor's name at a party or remember someone's street address, that's recall. If you can't remember that actor's name or your friend's street address, but you immediately know it's the correct one when you see it or hear it, that's recognition. In general, you can recognize far more things than you can recall. If your exam preparations are focused on recognition, and that's more often the case than you think it is, you will have a rude awakening during the test when you try to come up with answers that necessitate recall. Except when it's a multiple-choice test. Then, recognition will serve you well, provided it's sufficiently granular.

Thus, if you design cognitive challenges of any kind, popularly known as puzzles, mind the difference! Should the player be able to recall a vital piece of information, perhaps nudged by a subtle clue? Or does it suffice if they recognize a piece of information that is dangling before their nose? Both recognition and recall have their place. Always be aware of their difference.

The second possible source of confusion, related to both knowledge and understanding, is the difference between *procedures* and *processes*. Buckle up, it's going to be a rough ride.

In its most basic form, a procedure defines a sequence of steps, nothing more, nothing less. If you follow a cooking recipe, that's a procedure. Your knockdown furniture's assembly instruction sheet is a procedure. A military chain of command is a procedure. You don't let the chicken simmer for 2 hours *after* you removed its skin and bones, you don't tighten the screws *before* you insert the dowels, and you don't report the latrine malfunction to the Chairman of the Joint Chiefs of Staff *even* if you think it will prove decisive for the outcome of the war. (Unless perhaps you're at least a major general or rear admiral yourself.) Procedures can be mind-numbingly mundane or mind-bendingly intricate—neither difficulty nor complicatedness are defining attributes.

Processes are different, and their defining attribute is often some form of complexity. Unfortunately, in many fields like workplace organization, procedures are called processes all the time, which isn't helpful.

If you look for definitions of what a process is, most are variations on two themes. A process is either a set of interacting, interrelated activities to create a desired result or a process that uses, converts, or transforms inputs to create a desired output. Neither is particularly convincing, or helpful. To start with, procedures have outputs too, because outputs are the very idea of procedures. Then, by and large, processes outside standardized ISO definitions certainly have an output, but they don't have a "goal" or a "desired" output—think biological, chemical, social, psychological, mental, or evolutionary processes. Finally, the primary "output" of many processes *is the process itself*, while all other outputs, ranging from waste heat to self-aware human beings, appear as collateral benefits or collateral damage, depending on how you look at it. Legal processes, economic processes, or the scientific process have tangible outputs (court decisions, gross domestic products, knowledge), but in contrast to procedures (legal procedures, customs procedures, clinical trials), their primary concern is to *keep the process itself alive and running*: the legal system, the economy, the scientific endeavor.

From there, we can at least say this: complex systems like societies evolve with and through processes and cannot exist without them. These processes are continuous, in contrast to procedures, and thus more vulnerable to disruptions and interruptions. And while disruptions in a system can be easily observed, it's hard and often impossible to discern the reasons behind these disruptions, let alone find a remedy, without understanding the processes on which these systems are based.

A procedure-based challenge would be to create a puzzle where the player has to carry out certain actions in certain ways and in a certain sequence that is often time-sensitive or timing-sensitive. This is a very popular design that you can find in *Tomb Raider* and numerous other games. For process-based challenges, in contrast, think of the complex and often momentous decisions in games like the *Mass Effect* trilogy. If you create an alien society for your game, this society will have its *procedures* that the character can observe and add to their knowledge. The social dynamics behind these procedures, however, are based on *processes* that the player cannot observe directly, but needs to understand nevertheless to make better decisions. These, for example, can be processes that drive and define the alien civilization's cultural, legal, or military organization, which the player can then disrupt, maintain, or restore along their strengths, weaknesses, and sensitivities.

Before we leave the typology area, there's one more thing. Learning typologies often correspond to particular game types, which provides you with yet another opportunity for fine-tuning and balancing. *Skills* as repeatable, observable performances are often at the center of games with a ludological core, from arcade games to first-person shooters to simulations to party games; requiring dexterity, accuracy, quickness, speed, timing, stamina, and similar. *Knowledge*, the ability to recognize and recall facts and procedures, is especially relevant for games with a game-mechanical core, from chess to match 3 to strategy to 4X to management games and beyond. *Understanding* is often at the heart of games with a narratological or a cinematological core, where it is needed to follow plots, themes, or artistic patterns, from adventure games to RPGs to exploration games or visual novels. But understanding is also often important for games with a game-mechanical core that allow complex player input, like multiplayer strategy games or the game of Go. *Attitude*, finally, is applicable to all four dimensions. A game can demand attitude changes toward patience, self-discipline, team play, fairness, decisiveness, diplomacy, steadfastness, and so on, but also toward negatively connoted attitudes like ruthlessness and deceptiveness. But these are just trends, not rules! Don't let them keep you from doing things differently.

Now we can enter the skill proficiency's third and final area, where you turn everything into learning opportunities aka tasks. We will dig a lot deeper into the details of physical, cognitive, and empathic tasks in the upcoming final beat to wrap up this territory. But for our current purpose, they're sufficiently self-explanatory. Thus, we can finally conclude our detour and return to our torrents, our cave, and our bear, who've been patiently waiting for us while we were gone.

This time, instead of pulling the particular challenges that are attached to these obstacles out of thin air, we assume we have done our homework. We have our learning organization with the collection of proficiencies the player has to learn over the course of the game, and we have differentiated that collection into skill, knowledge, understanding, and attitude. We also have a theme, "negotiation," and we have our goal on which our proficiency spectrum is based.

For the goal, we'll imagine the following setup. The final boss is an earthquake. To survive that earthquake and beat the game, the player must negotiate treacherous, collapsing pathways across and between buildings, climb a steep precipice while dodging boulders and nasty showers of pebbles, and persuade an irascible harpy at the top of the cliff to pick them up and take them to safety. It's a cocktail of cognitive, physical, and empathic tasks that necessitate various types of skill, knowledge, understanding, and attitude. Now we can stack the obstacles in our example with tasks that make sense. For the torrents, the player must negotiate a collapsed bridge construction (cognitive and physical task), do the right thing and cool down the bear instead of attacking (empathic task), and climb to the top of the cave to retrieve the item from a barely accessible niche (physical task). Now, everything works toward what the player has to learn over the course of the game to achieve its goal and play it well.

If you follow these patterns, you can always make informed design decisions about what to put in the player's path and why. Most of the time, also, your challenges become more interesting because of it.

Let's turn our attention now from the proficiency spectrum to the second group of learning conditions, your game's learning curves and their associated design parameters, i.e., the proficiency threshold and the proficiency ceiling.

There's a mantra that threads all these conditions together. It's called "easy to learn, hard to master," known as Bushnell's Law or Bushnell's Theorem. In Dean Takahashi's *VentureBeat* interview, Blizzard's co-founder Mike Morhaime even refers to this mantra as belonging to Blizzard's core values. However, while this mantra is an excellent design philosophy, you should be aware that its original meaning was completely different from how it's understood today. In its entirety, Bushnell's quote—attributed to him around 1971, but without a verifiable source—has been handed down like this: "All the best games are easy to learn and difficult to master. They should reward the first quarter and the hundredth." Quarter? Yes, we're in arcade territory! A place and time when, from the design perspective, the goal of a game was to get the player to *insert another coin*, as Ian Bogost pointed out in "Persuasive Games: Familiarity, Habituation, and Catchiness."

While Arcade games are still around, their true heir are free-to-play games with in-game purchases. Thus, you can use this design philosophy in completely different, even mutually incompatible ways, depending on what kind of game you're designing.

If you decide to make your game free-to-play with in-game purchases, this mantra focuses your endeavor on its most important thing: retention. Retention once kept the stream of quarters running, retention today drives the F2P revenue engine by increasing the probability of in-game purchases over time. At the higher end of the F2P market, where incredibly high adoption rates are triggered by marketing budgets that go berserk at launch, even the slightest increase in retention positively affects the revenue stream, thanks to the power of statistical modeling. What's more, if you want your players to make in-game purchases as often as possible, forced failure must be part of your formula. Forced failure, in turn, necessitates reward structures designed along behavioral modeling—which, for example, keeps your player grinding on with well-placed soul-crushing obstacles, intermittent rewards, improbable numbers of near-misses, and other potent mechanisms that can push your game over the line and lead players from gaming as a sports or pastime activity into the realm of gambling and addiction. To create the math behind all this is challenging and beautiful, but its effects can become ethically dubious and corrosive. Certainly, that's not what you imagine your modest F2P indie game to become. The mechanisms that drive your revenue, alas, are basically the same.

But in case you're not designing an F2P game with in-game purchases, you can use this mantra in a completely different way, to make your game more interesting and enjoyable and rewarding right from the start. Here, "easy to learn, hard to master" means that the player can enjoy the game from the very first moment, but that there's also a reward for trying harder. In between, you can use the modified flow model to synchronize rising challenges with player proficiency.

That should suffice for the underpinnings; now let's look inside our learning curves box. The proficiency threshold (also called skill floor) determines how hard or how easy it is to start playing and enjoying your game. This means two things. The game can be accessible/inaccessible in terms of difficulty, and it can be accessible/inaccessible in terms of familiarity, in the sense discussed earlier in this beat.

In terms of familiarity, try to make a list of all the things that "go without saying" in the context of your game type, with all the conventions and player activities and interactions that evolved there over time, and check them against your intended target audience. If you miss something for a certain segment, your game won't be "easy to learn" for them. Correct for that with some imaginative onboarding that doesn't annoy the pros.

Then, difficulty. As "easy to learn" means "enjoyable from the start," you again need to reconcile the interests of more experienced players with those who just joined the party. Imagine your target audience consists of experienced players. Would it be okay then to design the game with a skill threshold that makes it barely accessible, perhaps inaccessible, for less experienced players? With the right target audience, such a strategy might not sound unreasonable at first. After all, you don't want your game's early levels to be boring!

There is a well-developed niche for games with merciless proficiency thresholds, like FromSoftware's *Dark Souls* or *Sekiro: Shadows Die Twice*. But outside that niche, it's almost always a mistake. First off, it won't win over players who are curious and might become part of your audience if your game gave them a chance. Then, the difficulty in most types of games cannot become arbitrarily high over the course of the game, so if you raise your game's threshold difficulty, you will have to flatten out your difficulty curves later. That way, besides losing less experienced players early, you will lose experienced players later, except by making your game shorter. In multiplayer games, moreover, where the difficulty can indeed become arbitrarily high, vast disparities in proficiency will develop even between experienced players, and the problem can't be solved by raising the threshold difficulty in any case.

At the end of the day, it's always better to make your game's initial difficulty more accessible for beginners.

In multiplayer games, you can go about it in several ways. One way is to design your game with a handicap system that allows players from every level of expertise to enjoy playing against each other. Another way is to equip less experienced players with the means to earn a few achievements early on. In arena shooters, for example, you can implement one or more "spammy" weapons that cannot but score from time to time. (There will always be a number of more experienced players who clamor to have them nerfed, but don't let that deter you.) Also, you can employ matchmaking, if that's within your means, even if the process of running matchmaking protocols and servers will give you serious headaches in return. What you can do, though, is fall back to the time when every player with a copy of the game and a broadband connection could host a game server over the web. That works just fine without matchmaking because players naturally flock to servers that suit them, and it's not hard to differentiate between offerings advertised as *n00bserv* or *{{{1337}}}_SniperCity*.

There are certainly a lot more options out there for all kinds of game types, and you can always use your imagination. But beyond that, you can defuse much of the threshold problem with just one rule: you should make your opening levels not difficult, but interesting. If you keep that rule in mind, together with the rules of familiarity discussed above, your game's skill threshold should do just fine, even if you find no catch-all solution to take care of everything.

Next, there's your game's proficiency ceiling (also called skill ceiling): whether or not, at some point in your game, getting better becomes impossible or no longer makes a difference.

Most multiplayer games, from the game of Go or chess to anything from shooters to strategy to simulation games, have no proficiency ceiling because the allowed input complexity from players is very high or even arbitrarily high, as discussed earlier in this territory. In old gunslinger fashion, sooner or later there will appear someone who's even better than you. This even applies to multiplayer games where player avatars' abilities are restricted by design, like *League of Legends*, *Defense of the Ancients*, or *Overwatch*. Players can always find new and surprising tactics and team tactics that push overall player proficiencies even higher.

Most single-player games, in contrast, do have a proficiency ceiling, be that shooters, strategy games, action-adventures, simulations, jump 'n' runs, and almost everything else. There will always be a point above which no additional success or reward can be gained. The player cannot beat such a game better than flawlessly—even if it takes 24 years to accomplish it, like Zero Master's *Doom II* reveal in 2018.

In most cases, you don't want your game to have a proficiency ceiling; not having one can give your game's replayability a considerable boost. But not all is lost if your game does have a proficiency ceiling! If your game is interesting, challenging, and enjoyable enough, players with come up with ideas all the time to make it harder and more challenging in unexpected ways—like self-imposed time limits or equipment restraints like no sword or knife only. The passion to break a game's proficiency ceiling in imaginative ways is strong in many players, which also gives you the design option to make your game mod-friendly and provide tools so others can make it more challenging for dedicated players.

Then, proficiency progression. If you think of the proficiency threshold as your opening and the proficiency ceiling as your endgame, the proficiency progression can be characterized as your long, long middle game. Its core question—how learning increases during play over time—is essentially a question of learning curves.

Your game *must* get its learning curves right in order to become a great game. For each learning outcome from your proficiency spectrum, you need to have a good idea about how long this will take players to learn on average, and in how many increments. Without that, you won't be able to coordinate and synchronize your game's learning experience with its playing experience, and you won't be able to establish flow.

Learning curves, as a term, has a scientific meaning and a popular interpretation. Scientifically, a steep curve means "rapid learning progress." In popular interpretation, a steep curve means "learning is hard and brutal." Depending on whom you talk to, you should be aware of both meanings.

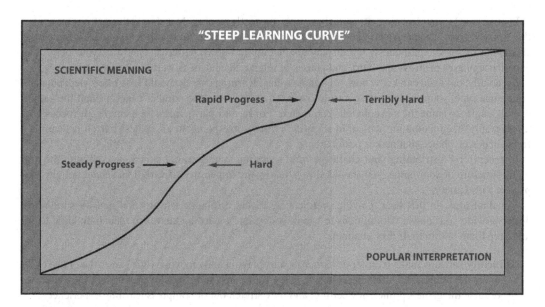

FIGURE 4.17 "Steep learning curve."

These are the questions you have to answer:

- For each learning outcome: into how many increments should you break it down?
- For each learning increment: how long will it take players to learn on average?
- For each learning experience: what kind of playing experience is the best fit for it?

At its most basic, an increment can be any of the following: mastering a new mechanic or a new combination of established mechanics; mastering a new puzzle type or a new combination of established puzzle types; gaining, recognizing, or recalling a piece of knowledge; understanding a plot point, a non-player character's motives, or the worldview of a group or society; adopt or abandon a strategy or an attitude; and so on.

You can sketch these increments by following your own experiences and making reasonable assumptions. Later during development, though, you should test these assumptions empirically and scientifically. For example, you can follow the approach of rational level design or rational game design, whose origins are somewhat hard to pin down, but a lot of work seems to have been done by developers at Ubisoft. Following this approach, you "atomize" each learning outcome into its smallest constituents and create learning curves based on empirical data and math. Your go-to sources should be Luke McMillan's *Game Developer* feature article "The Rational Design Handbook: An Intro to RLD" and Chris McEntee's "Rational Design: The Core of Rayman Origins," also on *Game Developer*. Plus, for good measure, Raph Koster's blog post on why "Tools Don't Stifle Art!"

But beware, not everything can be broken down into increments, and not every increment is easily digestible. (Rational level/game design accounts for that, so don't worry.) For a variety of skills from art to math to programming, there exist "Every x Tutorial Ever" cartoons where each step but the last looks ridiculously easy, but the last one displays, out of the blue, a preposterously perfect professional result. It's funny, it's hyperbole, but there's some truth to it. To reach professional levels, no matter for what, there will almost always appear obstacles out of the blue that can only be overcome by executing and mastering many different elements at once. Thus, not all increments should or can be alike. From time to time, there will be increments that pose formidable challenges to your players. These need more time to learn and provide a different playing experience. These should also, how could it be otherwise, correspond with your dramatic structure—discussed in-depth in the *Architectonics* territory—in ways that make sense! It doesn't always have to come down to boss fights, by any means. But boss fights are always a good default place because the player is expecting a formidable challenge and is prepared.

In other words, your learning curves will never be perfectly smooth. Nor should they! If you remember the "spikes" from the integrated game flow model discussed earlier in this level, your learning curves should not increase continuously but display distinct up-and-down patterns. That way, your player can experience phases of stress and fiero, and phases of relief and control as well.

Eventually, only you can know how your game's ideal learning curves should look like—dependent on your game type, your proficiency spectrum, your target audience, the number of levels, and the game's overall length, to name the most obvious parameters. For free-to-play games, for example, the occasional unbelievably steep mountain (which, in scientific terms, corresponds to an endless barren plateau) is a frequent design choice that makes perfect sense.

In general, by distributing your challenges and sculpting your learning curves in sync with the dramatic structure of your game, you should always follow the imperative of variatio delectat: delight your players with variety.

Our final topic in this beat, playing preferences, covers difficulty settings and density conditions. These provide your player with options to tweak your game's learning curves to their individual needs and keep them within their flow channel.

Difficulty settings make it easier or harder to start playing and enjoying your game; they raise or lower the proficiency levels necessary to enjoy your game and beat it or play it well; they lower or raise the game's proficiency ceiling; and they stretch out or compress learning experiences.

Density conditions control the frequency of challenges through shortening or lengthening the time between their occurrences; they control the number of challenges that occur simultaneously at any one time; and they stretch out or compress learning experiences.

Just like the playing experience, your game's learning experience needs to be flexible enough to accommodate a broad range of different players. Along the preceding topic, you have gained an understanding about how long it takes and how hard it is to learn anything in your game on average. But most of your players won't be average! Moreover, a player might love to put the pedal to the metal and encounter more and tougher enemies faster, but need to relax a bit between cognitive challenges, and need even more time between empathic challenges, for example, interactions with NPCs that require decisions. In other words, when you design your difficulty settings and density conditions, you should not look at it from the perspective of different player types, but different *playing styles*.

No two games are alike, so there are no master keys to design great difficulty settings or density conditions. However, there's no shame in simply letting the player choose from a well-designed set of difficulty settings, for starters! Even better, allow players to set the difficulty for different kinds of tasks, perhaps physical tasks or cognitive tasks, like *Shadow of the Tomb Raider* does. These difficulty settings, in turn, don't have to be completely static—some DDA within each difficulty setting could be involved, like in *Resident Evil 5*. But be careful with DDA. Players are a clever lot, DDA isn't too hard to spot, and they will game the system whenever they can. Also, make sure there's a mechanism in place that controls and recognizes DDA as a confounding variable. Only then can your game keep track of and communicate each player's true achievements and keep bragging rights intact.

Still, overall difficulty settings and even clever DDA are very crude tools, each in its own way, and you should always try to design more sophisticated options along which, knowingly or not, players can control their difficulty settings and density conditions themselves during play. While you have to find your own creative solutions, here's a handful of general principles you can work with.

For difficulty preferences, a general design principle that puts players in control—especially in control of their flow channels—is to design the game's challenge structure in such a way that it concurrently escalates *risk*, *relief*, and *reward*; this has already been introduced earlier in this level. Are you, the player, willing to jump down that suspiciously ladderless manhole for a rare power-up, and risk falling into toxic sludge instead of hitting that laughable excuse of a maintenance catwalk? Greater risks that experienced players are willing to take are met by greater relief, like health or ammo, and greater rewards of any kind.

Again, think *Mario*-type games that make use of this principle all the time. Or think of soft-gated open-world games, where certain areas are more dangerous than others, cleverly communicated so that

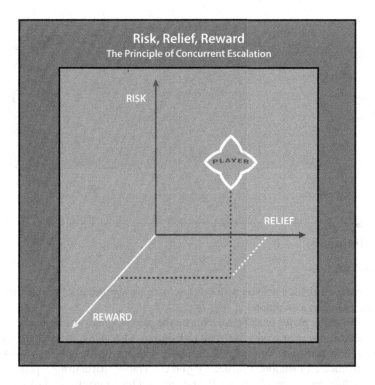

FIGURE 4.18 Risk–relief–reward pattern.

the player can make informed choices as to where to go, and when. Moreover, there could be secrets and secret areas that the player can only find and unlock above a certain proficiency level. And so on. Regardless of how you handle it, you should always aim at providing a joyful and satisfying playing experience not just to your average player, but to fast learners and slow learners and players with different levels of expertise alike.

Lastly, density. Before you can design your density conditions and give players a say in how often challenges occur and how many at once, you need to exorcise every incarnation of the abominable "x seconds" rule that has patrolled the marbled hallways of game design for far too long.

It's a rule that makes about as much sense as its dreaded cousin in the realm of dropped food. Players should at least be given the option to contemplate and explore, to savor sights and digest plot points, to process emotions and stress-test input controls.

Similar to difficulty settings, there is a design pattern that gives players some basic control over the game's density conditions: *plot*, *prompt*, and *proximity*.

Plot means that a challenge is triggered when the dramatic structure calls for it, which might or might not be caused by the player's actions. *Prompt* means that an impending challenge is signaled by hints or cues, and the player can respond when they're ready. *Proximity* means that a challenge is triggered when the player moves toward it.

The latter, famously employed in *Half-Life* and outlined in Ken Birdwell's *Game Developer* feature "The Cabal: Valve's Design Process for Creating *Half-Life*," lets players control density through self-confidence. If the player moves slowly and cautiously, challenges are triggered one at a time. If the player moves fast and aggressively, multiple events are triggered in rapid succession.

As always, you have to find your own creative solutions, but these patterns and principles will give you a head start.

If you have a lavishly designed proficiency spectrum with a great selection of learning outcomes, a proficiency threshold and a proficiency ceiling that make sense, great learning curves, and a number of options to give your player some basic control over how and when challenges occur, then you have all you need to make your game interesting and engaging from the first beat to the hundredth.

FIGURE 4.19   Density conditions.

Beat 6: Resolutions

From Types to Tasks

In the preceding beat, we already worked with tasks as learning opportunities through challenges. Let's drill into the nature of tasks a bit more.

Every task thrown at the player must be solvable by the player—that's the basic nature of gameplay. But solvability isn't the only requirement for good task design. Also, while every challenge is a task, not every task needs to be a challenge. You can task the player with non-challenging busywork, for example, as part of the work cocktail mentioned earlier. Or you can employ participatory play as taskless play, discussed in the *Architectonics* territory. Here, though, we will limit ourselves to tasks that involve challenges and compel the player to learn.

Not all tasks are created equal. Once more, for the purpose of designing games, we will simplify shamelessly and differentiate between three basic kinds of tasks: physical tasks, cognitive tasks, and empathic tasks. Before we look at them in more detail, let's map them to our learning typologies from the previous beat.

> **Physical tasks** are primarily connected to *skills* and *knowledge* and require control, coordination, and endurance. A physical task can be to defeat an enemy in combat; jump from one moving platform to another; or steer a vehicle through an obstacle course.
>
> **Cognitive tasks** are primarily connected to *knowledge* and *understanding* and require memory, analysis, and evaluation. A cognitive task can be to line up a row of symbols in the right way to open a crypt; or figure out how to move one's troops to outflank an opponent.
>
> **Empathic tasks** are primarily connected to *understanding* and *attitude* and require cognitive, emotional, and compassionate empathy. (Their respective differences in a nutshell: grasping someone's emotional state; feeling with that person; doing something about it.) An empathic task can be, over and above purely strategic reasoning, to grasp a character's motives or intentions or disposition in general and act accordingly; decide which party to join in a conflict; or weigh the ramifications of one course of action against its alternatives.

This model is not altogether different from the triad of physical, mental, and social tasks that the rational level/game design approach works with, as mentioned in the previous beat. But the methodology is different. While rational level/game design focuses on *skills*, the *Ludotronics* task model focuses on *tasks*. This focus, as discussed, allows us to break proficiencies down into the components skill, knowledge, understanding, and attitude. Then, while we can treat physical tasks and physical skills as identical for all practical purposes and cognitive tasks and mental skills as compatible, the ideas behind empathic tasks and social skills are quite different. (Beyond how we use them in this beat, moreover, the special nature of empathic tasks also informs an important design approach for dramatically complete games in the *Architectonics* territory.) Nevertheless, don't let that keep you! Rational level/game design

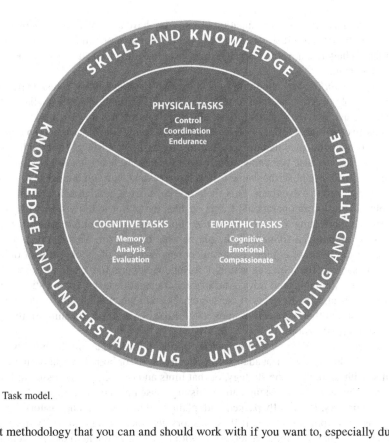

FIGURE 4.20 Task model.

is an excellent methodology that you can and should work with if you want to, especially during actual development.

This leads us back to the concept of flow and the general principle that the motivation to play equals the motivation to learn. The moment you take learning out of the equation, physical tasks become player interactions, cognitive tasks become puzzles, and empathic tasks become interactive storytelling. While these labels certainly have their place in general discourse, they don't provide you with meaningful paradigms to guide design decisions. "Player interaction" is too broad, "puzzle" too narrow, and "interactive storytelling" has serious drawbacks, also discussed in the *Architectonics* territory.

Regardless of type, well-designed tasks have three mandatory conditions and one optional condition.

Solvability. A task is solvable when its difficulty matches the player's present location on the associated learning curve.

Consistency. A task is consistent when it is constrained by its immediate context and the game's theme.

Recognizability. A task is recognizable when its nature is not itself a challenge.

Elasticity. A task is elastic if it can be solved at adaptable difficulty levels or in more ways than one.

Let's look at these conditions in more detail.

To ensure *solvability*, task design should always be guided by reasonable and justifiable expectations that the player has sufficiently progressed—in skill, knowledge, understanding, or attitude—to be able to solve that task's specific challenge. This applies to physical, cognitive, and empathic tasks equally. There's an additional aspect involved that is intimately connected to autonomy/agency from our player motivation model: *solving a task* should always be indistinguishable from *making a difference*. In other words, solving physical, cognitive, and empathic tasks should always have consequences that matter.

To ensure *consistency*, any task should naturally arise from its context and be related to the theme. You can't prevent tasks from being solved through sheer guesswork, but no task should only be solvable through guesswork. Physical tasks or empathic tasks rarely have a problem with following context and theme. Cognitive tasks, in contrast, often run rampant. A frequent challenge with clever puzzles, for example, is that it's hugely enjoyable to design them, whereas the prerogative should be that it's hugely enjoyable to solve them.

To ensure *recognizability*, you should always convey to the player what a task expects them to do. Players should be able to tell what kind of task they face. That shouldn't be a challenge by itself! Not knowing what the task exactly is leads to trial and error approaches and frustration. To prevent that, every task needs an operational frame. This frame allows the player to form a mental picture and identify the principal tools and strategies that are a match for this task. Never forget to establish such a frame! It's easy to forget, alas, because you know exactly what the task is about. Outside of video games, puzzle collections meticulously establish the frame for each puzzle and leave no doubts as to what set of tools and strategies are needed to solve them. This should be considered good practice for video game design as well. For physical tasks, an operational frame enables the player to tell whether it's about dexterity, accuracy, or timing, perfecting a certain interaction, combining different interactions, and similar. For cognitive tasks, an operational frame tells the player what to look for. This can be a missing piece of information, a certain piece of equipment, an unconventional use of a conventional object, the interpretation of a message, or the initiating action of a Rube Goldberg–like chain of events that solves the problem in deliberately complicated ways. And so on. For empathic tasks, an operational frame tells the player what exactly is at stake in terms of consequences and repercussions and scale, which often isn't altogether clear. Without that, it's nearly impossible for the player to run meaningful thought processes that lead to meaningful decisions.

Finally, you can add *elasticity*, which is entirely optional. Tasks that are designed with elasticity in mind are solvable in different ways, at adaptable difficulty levels, or both. It might mean that an opponent can be defeated with more than one strategy, or that hints and cues can be accessed to lower the task's difficulty. Here's a great example. Many natural history museums have a terrarium for insects that use camouflage and mimicry. It's usually packed with plants and brushwood, and visitors are challenged to spot as many insects as possible. Then, if these visitors get stuck or want to verify their discoveries or both, they can press a button to flood the terrarium with light of a wavelength that neither the visitors nor the insects can detect. However, every camouflaged insect is marked with a tiny spot that reflects some of that light in the visible spectrum. As you can guess, this is hugely entertaining for every age group. The beauty of this solution is that these markers are so tiny that the task *isn't automatically solved* by pressing the button. You still have to spot them, and you still have to identify which parts around these spots belong to an animal and which parts are brushwood! That way, the task's difficulty "degrades

FIGURE 4.21   Task properties.

gracefully" to manageable proportions for less experienced visitors. As a game designer, you can create similar or equivalent ways to make tasks elastic instead of frustrating by gracefully degrading their difficulty. All that without giving the solution away wholesale on the one hand, or encouraging players to fire up their second or third screen and check for solutions online on the other. But don't rush it! Give the player enough time or even a button before you flood them with hints through NPCs or otherwise, which is one of the more annoying aspects of the otherwise hugely enjoyable earlier *Uncharted* games and, more recently, *God of War Ragnarök*. Even better, you can give the player a choice, as *Shadow of the Tomb Raider* does, to activate or deactivate cues.

There's one more basic rule for task design that hasn't been mentioned yet. It's a negative rule, and it says that you shouldn't design tasks with "binary" solutions that solely depend on one specific piece of knowledge or one specific insight that the player either happens to have or not. Probably the most famous binary type are riddles, and many writers on game design mention them explicitly as that one puzzle type you should avoid, among them Bob Bates in *Game Design* or Zack Hiwiller in *Players Making Decisions*. But, as a thought experiment, could the riddle be salvaged if it naturally arose from its context and were related to the theme, for example, if the riddle of the Sphinx were given to the player at a multi-generational family dinner on Thanksgiving, and the game's theme had to do with aging? Yes and no. Under such circumstances, when the solution can be found through observation and circumstantial reasoning, it might be salvageable indeed—but only because it has ceased, under these circumstances, to be a riddle. In all other cases, use riddles only if you want to see most or all of your players strangled and devoured by the Sphinx.

Outlook

In the *Interactivity* territory, you learned what rules are and do, how they interact with each other and with the player, and how they can or should relate to reality and realism; about different ways in which values can relate to each other and to gameplay; about the demands of player proficiency and difficulty design; and about the range and nature of tasks and the challenges they represent. It's far from exhaustive, but it should give you enough perspectives and ideas to get started, and sketch this territory's game-mechanical and ludological elements for your game.

Do you have a good idea about your gameplay loop and its associated game mechanics? How the rules and values will work together in your game and process abstracted player input within the game world? How the game will progress based on that input? What your players have to learn, and how, and through what kinds of tasks? Do these tasks deliver to your player the just-right amount of challenge? Do they also support autonomy/agency and mastery/performance from the player motivation model?

If your answer to these questions is yes, congratulations! You just beat a very tough level.

Level Three

Plurimediality

Opening

The element from our interactive playing experience model that is associated with this territory is "compelling aesthetics." Aesthetics, in a game, comprises not only graphics, texture, sound, music, writing, voice acting, or look-and-feel in general, but also usability in its many forms, including player controls. That's because aesthetics and usability are two sides of the same coin, united by *function*. Every aesthetic element must serve a function, and every function must be an integral part of the game's aesthetic experience. That's what the *Plurimediality* territory, the intersection of *Ludology* and *Cinematology*, is about. It integrates design thinking from the perspective of functional aesthetics (the *Ludology* part) and the perspective of aesthetic experience (the *Cinematology* part). One can't be great without the other. Every element must connect with the theme in turn, and they all have to work together for a holistic playing experience that is consistent and compelling.

There exists some overlap between this territory and the *Narrativity* territory with respect to a number of aesthetic elements. Function and purpose, though, are very different.

> **Plurimediality is global.** Elements are designed and controlled from the viewpoint of *functional aesthetics* that work toward a game's thematic unity and consistent look-and-feel for a holistic playing experience.
>
> **Narrativity is local.** Elements are designed and controlled from the viewpoint of *narrative qualities or properties* that work toward conveying specific meaning in a specific dramatic unit for a memorable gameplay moment.

Like emotion or motivation, aesthetics is a multidimensional universe all by itself. It comprises thousands of years of varying perceptions of beauty (sociologically), the creation of beautiful objects (artistically), the commodification of these perceptions and objects (economically), numerous theories about beauty and what it consists of (philosophically), and the individual, subjective experience and appreciation of beauty (psychologically). While all this is useful and necessary for reviewing and analyzing video game aesthetics, for example, we need to extract a few simple aspects for our purposes that we can immediately apply to game design. Those simple, applicable aspects will be *skill*, *style*, and *subject matter*:

- *Skill* means that everything has to be, and look, professional.
- *Style* means that everything contributes to original, recognizable patterns.
- *Subject Matter* means that everything works together toward an integrated whole.

An amazing number of games display at least partial incompetence; leave a largely generic impression; or consist of elements that seem to have been assembled by throwing stones on the floor (an ancient divination technique). That's because skill, style, and subject matter have impressive enemies: *complacency*, *conformity*, and *clutter*. Complacency is when it's just good enough to be not offensively bad. Conformity is when it lacks differentiation. Clutter is when it lacks focus.

To forge compelling aesthetics, you have to overcome these enemies not once, but all the time. It doesn't mean, though, that everything has to be "perfect" in obsessive-compulsive fashion—perfectionism has

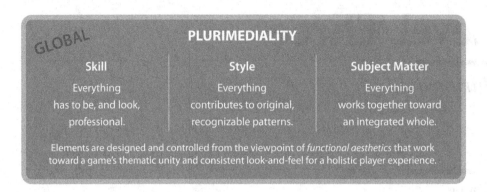

FIGURE 4.22 *Plurimediality.*

fractal properties and will never terminate. Instead, you should aim for "good," for "very good," and for "excellent" in justifiable proportions. Why not *only* "excellent"? Because not every nook and cranny in your game can be excellent; that's just another way of falling into the perfectionism trap. At some point, ever-increasing efforts will yield ever-decreasing returns, that's one thing. But it's also unsustainable and detrimental to a healthy work-life balance for you and your team during the development cycle.

Nevertheless, in order to create an outstanding game, everything has at least to be good. Moreover, substantial portions of that need to be very good, and some well-chosen areas must excel.

Regrettably, it's far too easy to drop the ball on skill, style, and subject matter. The primary reason for that is a psychological mechanism that is well-known but counterintuitive. To illustrate this mechanism, let's pretend you're applying for a job. Your three major skills are C++, linear algebra, and AI Programming. You also have a very limited command of French. While you wouldn't necessarily map your proficiencies to a scale, certifications and professional expertise make your three major skills correspond to 8, 8, and 7 on a scale from 1 to 10, which adds up to 23. Now you're tempted to add another 3 by including some basic knowledge of French, for a sum total of 26. In other words, you add everything up. After all, it can't hurt! More is more! And maybe, just maybe, something comes up, and your prospective employer sends you, and not someone else, to Paris or Montreal!

Alas, the people who will evaluate your skill set tend to build averages in their heads—i.e., the arithmetic mean. And suddenly, what would have been a perceived value of 7.6 without French becomes a 6.5 with French thrown in. You just lost more than 10 percent of your perceived skill value! (HR people know this, of course, but humans do not always act on their knowledge, even if they think they do.)

You've certainly recognized this mechanism already, and how it is rehearsed over and over during game development. The more half-baked design elements (or "features") are added by way of this reasoning, often aggravated by publisher pressure, the more your game's ratings will suffer—rated by critics who build averages in their heads. Indeed, a half-baked design element behaves precisely like the basic knowledge of French from our example: it's not professional enough (skill), it doesn't contribute anything really worthwhile (style), and it certainly doesn't integrate with anything else (subject matter). Money will be wasted. The game experience will suffer. Ratings will slide.

Without the consistent and recognizable presence of skill, style, and subject matter, there will be no beauty. Without beauty, motivation will drop. Humans are *strongly* motivated by beauty. Whether we see it in another human being or in a kitchen appliance, in a sports car or in a jail cell, in a work of art, in a virtual environment, or in a graceful diving catch. And whatever the prevailing concept of beauty happens to be, which can change dramatically over time and across cultures, or whatever lies in the eye of the beholder at a specific moment in time: skill, style, and subject matter are your best tools and your best bet to assemble something beautiful that will motivate and inspire.

Moreover, as a cultural force and a social experience that brings people together, beauty is also connected to the relatedness/community element from our player motivation model. Then, elements that function flawlessly and fit together support the mastery/performance element from our player motivation model as well. It makes it easier for the player to learn and become proficient. Clunky controls, convoluted menus, inscrutable or ambiguous objects, insufferable writing, or unintelligible voice acting are not the kind of playful, unnecessary obstacles that motivate players to overcome them through determination and effort.

Beat 1: Style

Squaring Efficacy with Enchantment

As established in the opening of this beat, *Plurimediality*, the intersection of *Ludology* and *Cinematology*, integrates design thinking from two perspectives: functional aesthetics and aesthetic experience. The former involves efficacy, the latter enchantment. The question is how to have both without sacrificing too much on either side.

Let's start with style. The question of style, from how to define it to how to find it, has a long and rich history. For our purposes, once again, we will rudely compactify this history into genre, period, and presentation styles, three practical categories that can be directly applied to game design.

> **Genre style**. Literary and cinematic genres as entertainment categories like fantasy, science fiction, science fantasy, western, mystery, horror, survival, romance, hard-boiled/noir, military, cyberpunk, and postapocalyptic.
>
> **Period style**. Art styles like Archaic, Classical, Byzantine, Tang, Muromachi, Kuba-Bushong, Realism, Expressionism, or Art Deco; architectural styles like Neolithic, Khmer, Romanesque, Aztec (Mēxihcah), Gothic, Victorian, or Bauhaus; and musical styles like Gregorian, Gagaku, Baroque, Romantic, Guoyue, or Postmodern. And don't forget typographic styles, for good measure, from cursive to movable type, from gothic to humanist, from Roman to Ming and beyond.
>
> **Presentation Style**. Artistic renderings, often simulating other media forms and media types (through advances in digitization and media convergence) that stretch from lifelike realism to comic/anime, from wood-block printing to papercutting to graffiti, from stop-motion to rotoscope, and many more.

The style elements that you pick from these categories constitute your basic *style set* that you can then tweak and refine. It will inform everything from game world to asset to character design. You can play it straight and combine mystery with "what you see right now outside your window" period style and lifelike realism. Or you can go and combine postapocalyptic with Western frontier towns and Gothic cathedrals in anime style, as in *Vampire Hunter D: Bloodlust*. Whatever you do, though, it should match your theme and set of motifs!

If you want to create an original, innovative style that the world hasn't seen yet, you *still* need to build upon styles that already exist—in the same way that new ideas are built upon what already exists, discussed in the Preparation phase. You can pick a style and modify it, or you can fuse two or more styles from the same category into something new. In the "Ask 'What If?'" section of Feng Zhu's GDC 2015 presentation "A Live Art Demonstration of Creating Worlds through Design Thinking," you can see these design principles in action.

There's one more ingredient that will be added into the mix: personal style. As soon as individual artists, possibly including yourself, set to work and create your game's artwork, personal style will naturally become part of your style set.

Now, putting your style set to use for architectural, level design, and character sketches, for example, that's challenging already. But where enchantment and efficacy really collide is your game's *interface*. Is it possible to make your interface match your game's style set in terms of genre, period, and presentation, and still comply with usability requirements?

What doesn't work is designing your interface following genre, period, or presentation styles as a fantasy, sf, western, horror, Gothic, or graffiti interface, or anything like that. Because that is a recipe for unreadability, incomprehension, and general disaster. You have to work with what people readily and

STYLE SET

Genre Style	Period Style	Presentation Style
Literary and cinematic genres as entertainment categories.	Period-specific art, music, architecture, typography, and similar.	Artistic renderings and simulations of other media forms and media types.

Original Styles can be created by modifying styles or fusing elements from two or more styles. **Personal Style** will be added by individual artists.

FIGURE 4.23   Style set.

intuitively understand, and that can neither be historical interfaces (just think how hard it is today to read original Wanted! bills in wood type letters) nor interfaces of the future (because we can't possibly foresee how these will look or work in their own usability contexts). Interfaces must be easily understood by people who live today, not in the past, not in the future, and not in a grim fantasy world with a lava-spewing volcano as their daily backdrop. So how can it be done?

The first step is to differentiate the interface into what we will call the *preference interface*, the *gameplay interface*, and the *inventory interface*. Together, they constitute your *interface set*. The preference interface is the place where the player determines how the game is played via option menus. The gameplay interface is the place through which the game is played along constant feedback data. The inventory interface is the place where the player manages and administrates gameplay-related data, covering everything from equipment to skill trees to log files to crafting. Obviously, different design parameters apply to each, and this differentiation alone goes a long way toward solving the problem of bridging usability and style, of joining efficacy with enchantment. Let's go through each interface's characteristics one by one.

The *preference interface*, without doubt, should be as user-friendly as possible. All the general rules for designing great user interfaces apply. There should be no pseudo runes, fake computer read-outs, garish backdrops, or blazing colors. Everything should be as easily locatable, recognizable, memorizable, and painstakingly obvious as possible.

The preference interface has only one job, and that job is to lead the player into the gameplay with the least amount of friction. Not before you get this right can you proceed and connect your preference interface with your style set. Still, less is more. Efficacy should always have the right of way, and that applies to unambiguous auditory feedback as well.

The *gameplay interface* is tasked with providing all the forms of feedback that your player needs in order to play the game, get better at it, and be at home in the game world. Thus, usability for the gameplay interface means different things for different games, different game types, and different types of players. You can't just apply a few hard and fast rules from usability design manuals. Instead, you have to approach your gameplay interface from the vantage point of specific functions, for which three basic classes are in use right now: the transparent, the overlay, and what has come to be called the diegetic interface.

- A **transparent** gameplay interface provides affective feedback data that is predominantly continuous.
- A traditional **overlay** gameplay interface provides superimposed feedback data that is predominantly discrete.
- A **diegetic** gameplay interface provides feedback data from objects that are part of the gameplay environment.

Clearly, every meaningful gameplay interface decision toward transparent, overlay, or diegetic design must be based on your style set and your theme. Let's walk through a few examples.

Transparent gameplay interface. If your player character is a Pleistocene hunter dealing with woolly mammoths and the occasional cave lion, a transparent gameplay interface that gives the player "affective" feedback data by indicating hunger, thirst, exhaustion, or injury through brief or persistent visual, auditory, or kinesthetic effects might be your best choice. Feedback on injury and shock, for example, could be indicated by a partial loss of vision through a stronger or weaker blur effect across the visual field. Such techniques can also be extended to reveal states of mind by showing how they affect the player character's perception, as in *Hellblade: Senua's Sacrifice*.

Overlay gameplay interface. If your player character is a Cold War operative in an espionage action-adventure, a traditional overlay gameplay interface might serve you best. It provides discrete, exact data, superimposed on the visual field, about everything from ammo counts to health and armor in percentage values; from available weapons or attacks to a line-of-sight indicator; and maybe some continuous data like a non-discrete stealth meter on the side.

Diegetic gameplay interface. If your player character is a space soldier who's always heading out for EVA or combat, you might want to employ a diegetic gameplay interface with an equipment-specific HUD and items like watches, pressure gauges, health monitors, motion trackers, and other objects that are functional parts of the character's environment. And for any kind of vehicle simulation, diegetic cockpit-type interfaces are certainly the best choice.

Mixed gameplay interface. If your player character manages a roller coaster park or a sports team in a construction or management simulation or commands the Procyon Uprising or the allied forces of World War II in a strategy game, a traditional overlay gameplay interface with a dash of diegetic office or command desk-type elements might be the best option.

You can mix and match, of course. But never forget that design is about decisions! Clutter is always ugly, and the less stuff you cram into your interface, the easier it will be to make these interfaces look fantastic. In an interview for Richard Rouse III's *Game Design: Theory & Practice*, Jordan Mechner—of *Prince of Persia* and *The Last Express* fame—relates that he always worked under the constraint that, at any time, the interface must be a pleasing experience for someone who happens to walk by and starts watching the screen. This is an excellent approach that will not only improve the playing experience but also generate buzz and get more people attracted to the game.

As a bonus suggestion, always keep an eye on creative and innovative continuous information design. There are a whole lot of human experiences that might be better and more cleverly represented that way than through discrete or numerical data.

The *inventory interface*, finally, will be the hardest part to sketch. It is both part of the gameplay and not part of the gameplay. It must be every bit as efficient as the preference interface and every bit as enchanting as the gameplay interface. It will consist, most likely, of many different parts with many different functions for many different purposes. Depending on your game type, players might need to switch between the gameplay interface and the inventory interface often, and then navigate a packed inventory interface.

For that, there's no one-size-fits-all recipe. But there's a principal approach that can help you get started. As it consists of two steps, we can call it the two-step approach:

- For the principal *categories*, you can use iconographic or diegetic design elements that the player has learned to recognize from the gameplay interface (enchantment).
- For *items* within these categories, you can use plain text and data design patterns the player has learned to recognize from the preference interface (efficacy).

Here's an example. Let's imagine a Mythos horror game where the player collects ancient tomes full of magic formulae; tracks and interviews people; receives testimonies, notes, and letters from contacts and institutions; travels to and investigates places; acquires and upgrades skills; collects herbs, plants, and whatnot to concoct potions for various purposes; obtains weapons and ammunition; keeps a diary with texts and sketches; and gathers assorted items for bargaining and puzzle solving. While all this is certainly not too fancy, the inventory interface will nevertheless be tightly packed!

The first step, now, is to design your iconography for the principal categories, using elements that the player can recognize from the gameplay interface. For our example categories, this could be a book with a pentagram on its cover for magic formulae; an address book for contacts; a file cabinet for evidence; a map with pins for travel; a stylized player character portrait for upgrades; a cauldron for potions; a knife or a bullet clip or both for weapons; a paper notebook for diary entries; and a pouch for assorted items. Alternatively, you can design diegetic elements around an office space—a book case that can be opened, an address book that can be flipped through, a searchable file cabinet, maps that can be drawn out from a drawer, a corner with training equipment, an apothecary cabinet, a duty belt, a paper notebook with flippable pages, and a deep pouch the player can rummage through. Either way, that's the enchantment part. And while it's organically connected to the gameplay interface, players can still find any principal category they're looking for at one glance.

The second step is to make the data behind your iconographic or diegetic design elements easy to read, easy to digest, and easy to manipulate. Your first choice should always be plain text—names and descriptions that make it a breeze for the player to find the right formula, the person, the place, weapon, or item; to skim evidence, notes, letters, and diary entries; to craft potions; and to upgrade skills, attributes, or sanity (if possible). That's the efficacy part. It makes it easy for the player to find what they're looking for, and it guides their decision-making processes.

With this basic two-step approach alone, your inventory interface will already satisfy all the conditions listed above for the preference interface—locatable, recognizable, memorizable, and as painstakingly obvious as possible—and remain organically connected to the gameplay interface as a critical part of the playing experience.

With the curious exceptions of "ranged combat" and "close combat," you can see this design approach at work in 2018 *God of War*'s excellent inventory interface. But you can also find the exact opposite approach, even in major action-adventure franchises like *Assassin's Creed*. There, plain text is used for principal categories and iconographic elements for items—which makes life harder for the player than it has to be. As you can't design immediately recognizable icons for hundreds of items, they are supported by fade-ins with scenic illustrations and descriptions. However, as there are no mnemonic links between the icons and their video illustrations, players *observably* trigger these video illustrations dozens and dozens of times to refresh their memory before making important decisions.

Now you can put this theoretical framework into practice. Choose your style set and sketch your ideas for your interface set. Everything should fit your theme, your target audience, your value set, and your USP. For your interfaces, you should collect everything that these will probably need to convey or could convey in principle. Put everything you come up with into one of three categories: the indispensable, the possible, and the unnecessary. (Don't skip the latter. If you don't document what you've already dismissed, it will pop up again and again.) Use the principle of constraints as your primary guide, and try to err on the side of less. Also, for every gameplay interface item that isn't on your indispensables list, try to think of a way to convey that information through *action*. This will push your game toward a tighter, more focused experience. Indeed, you should regard and assess gameplay interface elements as you would regard and assess cutscenes! What interface elements and cutscenes have in common is their seductive power to lure you into convenient cop-outs and dump information on the player that should really be converted into gameplay experiences and player action.

To document and communicate your ideas, finally, you should use *mood boards*, *sketches*, and *written briefs*. These three elements constitute your communication set.

Mood boards. For your mood boards, collect images that are similar to what you have in mind. To that effect, create a list of keywords based on your genre, period, and presentation styles, and start grinding through image search engines on the web, photo communities, stock photo sites, artists' and concept designers' portfolios, and similar. But don't stop there! Consult art books and classical paintings, graphic novels, cinematography examples, software and hardware interfaces for technical and military equipment, data visualization and infographics, dashboards of any kind, ideogram and pictogram sets, and display typography examples. And

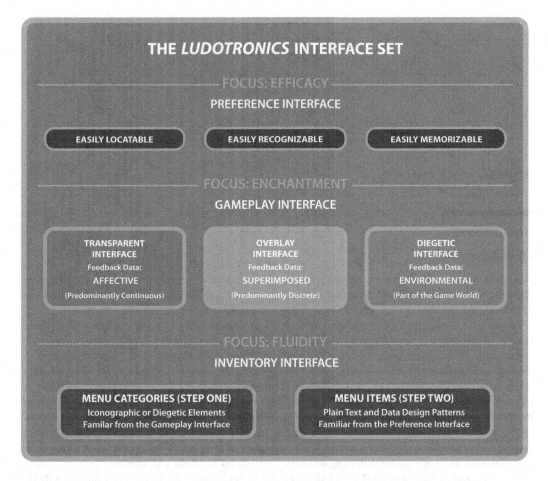

FIGURE 4.24 Interface set.

so on—depending on the styles you have in mind, you might come up with even more corners around which to peek.

Sketches. For your sketches, rough drafts that convey the principal forms and structures you have in mind for your style and interface sets should suffice. If you happen to be an artist, you can go beyond sketches and express your vision—there's no need to hold back.

Written briefs. Impressive mood boards and amazing sketches notwithstanding, written briefs are obligatory. Even if a picture happens to be worth more than a thousand words, these won't be the exact thousand words you have in mind. Your written briefs should reveal your reasoning behind your style set decisions, from genre to period to presentation style, and explain what your interfaces will require and why.

If you're an artist, you may want to follow the call of your profession and cast your envisioned style—genre, period, presentation—into concrete color and shape and proceed to palette and shading and to proportion and form. The same applies to your interfaces—if your professional focus happens to lie on communication and user interface design, draft away! If any of that is not your forte, rough sketches will do at this point. Later, though, you will need artists and designers whose forte it is, to create actual design work for your prototype and your pitch presentation. Then, your communication set will shine.

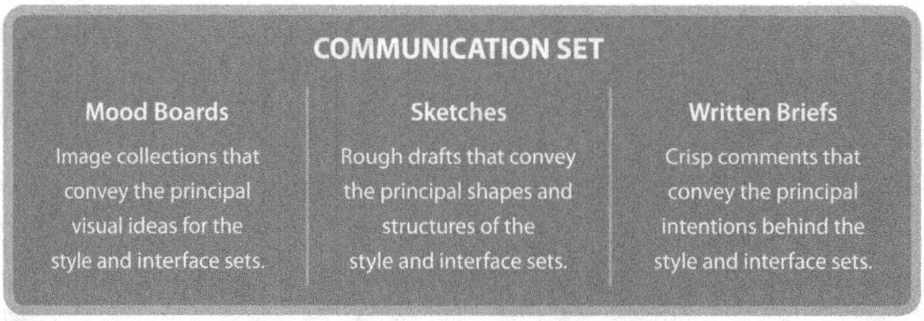

COMMUNICATION SET		
Mood Boards	**Sketches**	**Written Briefs**
Image collections that convey the principal visual ideas for the style and interface sets.	Rough drafts that convey the principal shapes and structures of the style and interface sets.	Crisp comments that convey the principal intentions behind the style and interface sets.

FIGURE 4.25   Communication set.

Beat 2: Space

Of POVs and Places

Any environment we bodily move through affects us both aesthetically and kinesthetically. Aesthetically through the sensory-emotional perception of the *environment* and kinesthetically through the sensory-emotional perception of our *movement* through that environment, including zero movement.

In movie cinematography, composition and camera movement seem to represent and convey these respective perception types well. In movie theory circles, however, many beg to differ. The understanding seems to be that in the realm of cinematography, vision (as aesthetic experience) always manages to reassert itself against movement (as kinesthetic experience). This supposedly holds true even with giant screens, preposterous resolutions, odd angles, and optical effects, calibrated to manipulate the sense of balance, including 3D cinematography. The reasoning behind it is: the more elaborate the on-screen movements are, and the more involving their choreography, the more forcefully will aesthetic experience reassert itself and push kinesthetic experience to the side. Sometimes, we might inadvertently react bodily to a movement on the screen, not unlike stomping on an imaginary brake pedal when riding shotgun. But once again, it's merely a fleeting and only temporary kinesthetic experience.

For video games, except those that include full-body player movement like rhythm games or VR/AR games, this might not be altogether different. But there's an additional factor to consider: the player actually *has* to move by using their controls. Thus, players manipulate with their own bodily movement the movement on the screen. Then again, these movements are highly abstracted; the player doesn't *really* perform a double-jump or dive under a table. So here, too, the aesthetic experience might reassert itself and override the kinesthetic experience. Nevertheless, the potential of providing kinesthetic experiences at least temporarily is there, and this is true for many different game types—from first-person action, where players physically lean to the side to "dodge" projectiles or look past their monitors in heated shoot-outs, to inadvertent movements in vehicle simulations or platform sequences.

What's more, many third-person perspective games, from *Tomb Raider* to *Uncharted* to *Zelda: Breath of the Wild*, have a distinctive characteristic that make their cinematography different from movie cinematography. These games have not one but two player-controllable reference points with the potential to provide kinesthetic experiences: camera movement and player avatar movement. (Technically, this also applies to first-person perspective games, where both reference points are merged into one.)

It should be added that neither of these two reference points is indispensable. Many games have no persistent or individual player avatar, like *Warcraft: Orcs & Humans* (which Ernest Adams calls the multi- or omnipresent interaction model in *Fundamentals of Game Design*); many games have no camera movement, like *Donkey Kong*; and many games have neither a persistent/individual player avatar nor camera movement, like *Tetris*. But if your game should indeed have reference points for movement, be it a player avatar that moves or a moving camera or both, you should put some serious thought into these movements, and how their kinesthetic experience can serve your game's theme.

As a reminder, *Plurimediality*—the current territory—is about global design decisions. This means that you have to decide on camera placement and camera movement on the one hand, and avatar placement and avatar movement on the other, in terms of game-wide consistency and a holistic user experience, not in terms of individual gameplay moments, which are part of the *Narrativity* territory.

For camera placement and movement, there's a whole catalog of questions you can ask yourself. Should your camera be fixed, tracking, or interactive? If fixed, where should it be placed? What are the benefits and drawbacks of third-person versus first-person cameras? Where should the player avatar be placed on the screen? How much zoomed in or zoomed out should the player avatar appear by default? And so on. Make yourself familiar with all the potential parameters that are a match for your game. Luckily, you will find information and advice for all this in almost every book on game design, and in numerous articles and presentations to boot. One inspirational place to start, even if you're working on a completely different game with a microscopic budget in comparison, is Remi Lacoste's GDC Europe 2013 presentation "Creating an Emotionally Engaging Camera for *Tomb Raider*." Always make your decisions fit your game type, your key values, your target audience, and your theme.

Before we proceed to address the intricacies of avatar movement, one final caveat with regard to camera movement. Its cinematographic potential is seductive. In-game camera movement has become so sophisticated that you can use it to tell or augment your story in spectacular and thrilling ways. But that thrill has to be paid for with player agency as blood money. The more you deploy your camera to let events in the game world narrate a story that your player cannot be allowed to miss, the more you have to curtail the player's freedom to control both their camera and their avatar. Effectively, you should resist the urge to constantly adopt what can be called embedded micro-cutscenes: taking control away from the player time and again, so they won't miss the spectacular effect X or the heroic attempt Y. There are cases where you can put embedded micro-cutscenes to good use, and we will come back to that in the context of rewards in the final level.

Now, avatar movement. Avatar movement is an essential game characteristic. Locally, it can express and amplify states of mind and emotions in specific situations. Globally, it defines a significant part of the playing experience. Certainly, the latter is particularly true for games where avatar movement is based on elaborate movement patterns, from vehicle simulations to parkour-inspired shooters like *Titanfall* or *Dying Light* and platformers like *Mirror's Edge*. But you can change the character of any game quite spectacularly by changing the way the player avatar moves.

Various types of movement, which is most often the case with first-person shooters, can also cause the player to experience dizziness, motion sickness, or headaches. But that doesn't necessarily subtract from the quality of the game—both *GoldenEye 007* and the original *Unreal Tournament* are great games that were both notorious for being able to induce terrible motion sickness or splitting headaches in a considerable number of players. VR games are also renowned for inducing nausea; but besides player movement, there's a whole range of factors involved, like latency, motion parallax, and refresh rate.

Avatar movement can also manifest itself in kinesthetic feedback. Usually, when we think of kinesthetic feedback, we think of controllers, joysticks, and other input devices with built-in haptic or vibro-tactile responses like vibrations or recoil. But kinesthetic feedback also works with less sophisticated control schemes, including the old-fashioned keyboard and mouse combination. You can design purely virtual kinetic interferences that act against the player avatar's movement and momentum, like surface conditions, headwinds, or centrifugal forces. The player avatar, for example, can react sluggishly under certain circumstances or can't easily be slowed down on an icy surface. Use your imagination! Kinesthetic feedback doesn't have to be real in the sense of bodily sensations, and it is not the exclusive domain of crafty controller schemes. It can also happen in the player's mind.

Let's turn our attention to the game space where all these movements take place. Game space can have two different meanings: one practical and one philosophical. The practical meaning applies to the space created by conceptual and technical level design. The philosophical meaning applies to what is often called the "magic circle" after Johan Huizinga, who coined the term in his influential *Homo Ludens*.

Like *Homo Ludens* itself, Huizinga's analogy of the "play-ground" as a magic circle or temple, i.e., a formally distinguished space with different rules that have to be acknowledged as such by the players, remains ludologically relevant. It has to be said, however, that we have become more critical over time of Huizinga's notion that the "laws and customs of ordinary life" no longer count within that space—no matter how special its rules are, they will in some form or other reflect prevailing power structures, and these power structures will always try to restrict access to it and define who counts as a welcomed member. Still, Huizinga convincingly demonstrates that there are *boundaries* between regular space and game space that one must cross in order to play.

When players cross these boundaries, they enter a space where some rules of the real world prevail, some do not, and others are substituted or supplemented by completely foreign, even bizarre rules that the player cannot yet know. Plus, the player cannot even know if any such unknown rules exist! Therefore, you should create transitional elements that lead the player from the outside, the space they occupy outside your game, to the inside, the space of your game world as a very special, very peculiar place. In other words, your transitional elements should create a *passage*.

Myth in general and medieval quests in particular excel at creating such transitional passages. For a mythical Hero's Journey, discussed in the *Architectonics* territory, this passage is often located around the player character's "Crossing of the First Threshold." For the player, it's the threshold that leads them into your game world.

To see how this works, let's look at *Pwyll, Prince of Dyfed* from the *Mabinogion* compilation of Welsh medieval tales. Pwyll (roughly: pu-ich) decides to leave his palace and go hunting. Together with his hunting party, he travels to the edge of the kingdom and sets up camp for the night. At dawn, he proceeds to his intended hunting ground, where he and his hounds get separated from his companions. He comes across a strange pack of hounds with shining white hair and glistening red ears. These hounds bring down a stag that they've hunted, but Pwyll shoos them away and sets his own hounds upon it. Whereof the other pack's owner by the name of Arawn appears, who identifies himself as "a King of Annwvyn," which is the Otherworld of Welsh mythology, and communicates his profound displeasure with Pwyll's unsportsmanlike behavior. The latter wants to make up for it, and Arawn gives him a set of tasks with very precise rules on how to complete them, all of which require switching appearances first and ruling each other's kingdoms for a year. Incidentally, this identifies Arawn as a Sídh (yes, you read that right, though it's pronounced with an initial "sh," and Arawn's also basically the good guy here), Welsh mythology's fairy folks who can change forms, among other things. And here, at this point, Pwyll's heroic adventure proper begins.

This tale contains all the structural principles of passage design, to lead your player from their own world into your game space. First, you lead the player to the threshold where ordinary space ends and game space begins. Second, you lead the player across the threshold. Third, you confront the player with the most important rules that apply to your game space, and in a dramatically complete game, these will also comprise moral rules.

Don't go about designing such passages, and this can't be stressed enough, in terms of storytelling or as expository dumps for your convenience. The focus is neither on challenges (*Interactivity*), nor on memorable gameplay moments (*Narrativity*), nor on storytelling and exposition (*Architectonics*). Elements from all three territories should and will be involved, naturally. But the focus is on drawing your player into your game space and confronting them with some of its basic rules, through spatial and audiovisual design.

You should always try to come up with creative solutions yourself, but you can work with two established elements, the loading screen and the introduction.

> **Loading screen**. The loading screen brings the player to the threshold that the player must cross to leave their own world and enter the game world. This crossing of the threshold happens every time the player starts playing.
>
> **Introduction**. The introduction sequence confronts the player with the basic rules of your game space that they need to know to meet its initial challenges. This introduction can also include moral rules and the game's mood.

The loading screen not only leads the player to the threshold; in later sessions, it also reminds the player of the entire initial passage—the crossing of the threshold into game space, and the basic rules of that game space. To accomplish this, the loading screen has to reproduce that passage in a nutshell: through a picture, an animated effect, a musical theme, a set of distinct sound effects, or similar.

Pulling this off is hard. You can start by analyzing how the initial loading screens of great games draw players into their respective game spaces, and how they remind them of the mood and the rules of these spaces every time.

Then, the introduction. Let's have a look at the introduction sequence from *Half-Life*, which, as Bob Bates puts it in *Game Design*, draws the player into its fictional world by placing them "authoritatively" into its "time and space." In Valve's legendary execution of this passage, the player has left their own world and their friends behind and has entered the game world. Along the tram ride, the player becomes familiar with the basic rules of this world, moral and otherwise: think of the Black Mesa Research Facility as Annwvyn, and its public address system as Arawn. The player is then pushed deeper into the game space, the Black Mesa laboratory. There, the player has to conform to some of its basic rules—settle into their job, suit up, and report for duty—before the adventure proper begins.

To design great passages, you can give your imagination and creativity a boost if you refrain from thinking about the world of the player and the world of your game along the lines of "real world" versus "virtual world." All experiences are constructs, without exception. They're never "out there" somewhere, they're always in our heads. Exactly where we have these experiences doesn't matter—in your local diner, in the land of Annwvyn, or in Black Mesa. Instead, as discussed, you should juxtapose the world of the player and your game world along the lines of rules and mood. Think of 1939's *Wizard of Oz*, for example. It pitches a sepia-toned rural Kansas against the Technicolor landscapes of Oz. The mood is different, the rules are different. But Kansas and Oz are both real in terms of experiences. (Plus, the land of Oz is indeed "real" in the novels—only the movie version makes Dorothy's experiences safe and non-threatening by turning them into a dream, a regrettable practice Disney later picked up on with their heavily laundered adaption of J. M. Barrie's *Peter and Wendy*.)

Another source of inspiration to try out new techniques for passage design is the concept of heterotopias, a term coined by Michel Foucault in "Of Other Spaces." The term heterotopia is a composite of "heterogeneous/non-uniform" and "topos/place." Literally, it denotes a place that consists of different places. It's a challenging concept in its original form, but, as always, we will extract only those elements that can facilitate interesting design decisions. The following three aspects of the concept of heterotopia seem to be the most productive in this regard.

The mirror characteristic. Heterotopias are outside of all places, but they are both real and virtual. With respect to the places they reflect and speak about, they can expose them as even more illusionary than themselves, or as being messy but altogether human through ill-conceived perfectionism. Think of Oscar Wilde's *The Picture of Dorian Gray* and Ira Levin's *The Stepford Wives*, respectively. Or, if you're familiar with neo-Freudian psychoanalysis, of Jacques Lacan's mirror stage.

The stage characteristic. Heterotopias are capable of juxtaposing several unrelated spaces in a single place, like the rectangle of a theater stage, a movie theater's silver screen, or the video monitor, each of which speak about a whole series of places that are foreign to one another.

The ship characteristic. Heterotopias are not public places. They are not freely accessible but always presuppose a system of opening and closing that isolates them and makes them penetrable. The inside, moreover, relates in peculiar ways not to one, but to many different places without being any of those places itself. Besides ships, think of airports, and also of rite-of-passage patterns.

That should suffice for inspiration. Whatever you do, always remember that *passage is structure, not story*. Arawn doesn't tell a story, and he doesn't dispense exposition. Neither does the Black Mesa public address system. Passages are not about challenges or plot points, they're about rules and mood.

Let's close this beat by returning to Huizinga's "magic circle" for one final aspect of game space, the fourth wall. Under certain circumstances, a game's magic circle can become porous, so that the game space seeps into the world of the player. While this is rare and always surprising, it's not unique to video games. "Breaking the fourth wall" is a very old technique from theater performances that was picked up by movies (e.g., Zucker–Abrahams–Zucker comedies) and television series (e.g., *House of Cards*, both the UK and U.S. versions). Traditionally, two major techniques have been employed: directly addressing the audience, as in *Annie Hall*, *Goodfellas*, or *Deadpool*, or addressing the play's or movie's own fictionality, as in *Moonlighting*, the Austrian TV show *Kottan ermittelt*, or, again, *Deadpool*.

The first technique is rarely found in games. Either the player avatar stands between this technique and the player as an obstacle, or the player is part of the fiction, particularly in games with first-person cameras, and addressed all the time accordingly. The second technique is still rare but makes more sense in games. Examples can be found in the *Metal Gear* series or in *Medal of Honor: Allied Assault*. It can be open and obvious, as in the former, or obscured, as in the latter. (The two soldiers in the "Lighting the Torch" level who can be overheard reflecting on life and the possibility that they're just disposable characters in a game speak in German.)

But there's a third option to break the fourth wall: referencing the hardware the medium is running on, or the audience's physical environment, or both. It's a technique that's much better suited for interactive media, mostly in the form of puzzles. It's very rare in non-interactive media, but it exists—just watch the *X-Files* episode "War of the Coprophages" and wait for the bug that crawls across your own TV screen. This option even has a name, paradiegesis. (According to E. W. Bullinger in *Figures of Speech*, the term originally denoted a rhetorical digression through the addition of "outside facts" that are "beside the case, yet help to establish it.")

The following paragraph contains spoilers for several games, so beware.

Famous (or infamous) examples are the mind-reading antagonist in *Metal Gear Solid: The Twin Snakes* (who literally reads the player's memory card and controller commands); the sea chart in *The Legend of Zelda: Phantom Hourglass* (which must be "stamped" by closing and reopening the dual-screened handheld console); *P. T.*, the playable teaser for Kojima Hideo and Guillermo del Toro's aborted shot at the *Silent Hill* franchise (puzzle pieces the player has to collect from the menu after pausing the game); and *Alien: Isolation* (where you'd better stop munching your tortilla chips while the mic's open). That's just the tip of the iceberg—just search for "fourth wall" on the internet for many more examples.

Crossing over from one space into another is never completely free of risk, physically as well as psychologically. Breaking the fourth wall can have unsettling side effects—even more so as games use it less for comedic effect but to amplify the uncanny. In other words, it intrudes, often violently, into spaces the player regards as their own, and as safe. Thus, as a game designer, whenever you let your game's magic circle become porous, whenever you let elements from your game world cross over into the world of the player, you should always be keenly aware of what you're doing.

Beat 3: Sound

From Score to Speech

This territory, as a reminder, is concerned with the game's overall characteristics in terms of usability and aesthetics. Therefore, sound will be discussed with regard to design decisions that apply to the game as a whole. The question of how sound elements can create and support emotions in individual gameplay moments is discussed in the *Narrativity* territory instead.

Game sound has so many aspects that we need to go about it even more systematically than usual. To start with, we'll break it down into the three major categories music, foley, and speech. The category "foley," without the customary capitalization, will serve as a shorthand for game sounds performed by Foley artists; field-recordings; digitally designed sounds; musical sound effects like fanfares, chords, arpeggiated chords, percussive effects, or short melodic phrases; and sound effects from sound libraries (which are in turn assembled from all the sources just mentioned).

Then, for each of the three categories, music, foley, and speech, we'll assign general functions, and later also specific functions, to define what they can or should do in a game, and look into their different types and modes. Here's the general roadmap to navigate this beat:

- **Category**: music, foley, and speech.
- **Function**: mood, feedback, and information.
- **Type**: type of music, type of foley, and type of speech.
- **Mode**: diegetic, meta-diegetic, and non-diegetic.

Your first design decision is about what sound categories you want to use in your game. Should there be music? Should there be foley? Should there be speech? It depends on what you want them to do in your game, what their functions will be. What makes some of these decisions tricky is that they often appear commonsensical and obvious, which they aren't.

Each category—music, foley, and speech—can serve all three basic functions listed above. They're all capable of setting the mood, giving feedback, and providing information. Let's take a closer look at these general functions for a better picture.

Mood affects or even controls player emotion. *Feedback* on player actions includes menu feedback and input feedback in all three interfaces, as discussed previously in this level. *Information* includes cues and explanations for understanding and interpreting any given element in the game world. Each function, moreover, can be met by temporary silence. The absence of music, foley, or speech can convey all kinds of mood, feedback, and information as impressively and efficiently as their respective presence. And between presence and absence, between full throttle and silence, there's the whole world of *intensity* to play with—from grandiose to minimalist to mesmerizing.

Accordingly, the questions you have to ask yourself are as follows:

- Will your game need music (score/soundtrack) for mood, feedback, or information?
- Will your game need foley (sound effect/ambient sound) for mood, feedback, or information?
- Will your game need speech (monologue/dialogue) for mood, feedback, or information?

Let's examine a few aspects of music, foley, and speech in more detail to demonstrate why you shouldn't take any answer to these questions for granted.

In *Aliens versus Predator* from 1999, you could play the game with the soundtrack CD mounted or without. The music is great. If it is on, you feel propelled forward with a sense of mounting suspense and epic adventure. Without the soundtrack, though, you are much more aware of your actual isolation and loneliness, and of the horror of being at the mercy of the environment. While both experiences are great, they're completely different. Hence, your decision to use music or not, and which music, is a decision that defines the playing experience in important ways. But there's more. In a dialogue between Ennio Morricone and Sergio Miceli in *Composing for the Cinema*, the metaphor of film music as a "guest" is introduced. Such a guest should not be invited just because they're always invited, i.e., just because most films—or games, in our case—happen to have music. That guest should be invited or not invited after careful considerations. As Morricone puts it, music should be present for poetic reasons. Otherwise, this guest would be useless and could even make a bad impression. Also, music shouldn't be a surprise guest. If it isn't carefully introduced and listeners are not prepared for it, it might not be able to fulfill its functions.

Regarding foley, in contrast, it's hard to come up with a game that can manage without it. Acoustic feedback is so vital, from menus to player actions to environmental cues, that a game without any foley is almost inconceivable. Even grunts, cries, and emotive sounds of any kind that are not speech are essentially foley. And even fairly recent games like *Zelda: Breath of the Wild* convey—except for cutscenes— what non-player characters have to say in written form while using foley to indicate speech.

Which brings us to speech. Especially in dramatically complete games, speech seems inevitable. It isn't. Speech can be conveyed through written text, or, as in *Zelda: Breath of the Wild* and many other games, a combination of written text and foley. Speech can be conveyed through symbols, think *The Sims*. Then, information can be conveyed by other means than speech, text, or symbols altogether. Naturally, that's much harder. Yet, speech is overrated precisely because it's so much easier to put something into words than it is to think about alternatives. What's more, speech can make things worse! Case in point, *Uncharted 4: A Thief's End* and *Uncharted: The Lost Legacy*. Like the entire series, these are hugely enjoyable games. But their disposable enemies have a rather limited set of dialogues in the manner of "Got anything?" "Nothing." "Check Over There. I'll go this way." "Sure thing, mate." And so on, over and over. Rarely are these dialogues warranted, if at all. The mercenaries should have followed their routes and procedures and used hand and arm signals to communicate observations and orders, if necessary, as professionals are wont to do. In addition, at no point are any of these dialogues needed to alert the player of enemy presence or reveal cues toward how to engage or evade them. And because putting something into words is so easy, it obscures the fact that *speech never comes cheap*. You need great dialogue writers, great voice talent, and the budget to pay them. In terms of quality, it is never cheaper to use speech instead of other means to convey mood, feedback, or information. Yet, to convey mood, feedback, and information, the use of speech is so natural as to be perceived as "free," so all this is easily forgotten.

Finally, silence. Sometimes, mood or information can be conveyed by the outright absence of sound, particularly music or speech. Most of the time, however, silence is more effective when it replaces music, foley, or speech temporarily. Thus, if you need silence, you also need music, foley, or speech in most cases.

When you know which sound categories you want to use, then you need to decide on which types you want to use and in what mode. Again, we will look at music first, then at foley, then at speech.

For music, type means the kind of music you want to employ—from a vast voice and orchestra apparatus that would put Gustav Mahler to shame to rock and rap music and synth landscapes to sparsely scattered notes from a lonely blues harp. The basic categories we will work with are *art music*, *popular music*, and *traditional music*. Certainly, these categories have fuzzy borders, especially when it comes to jazz, and each category contains a whole universe of styles in turn. Moreover, while the term art music is preferable to "classical" or "serious" music, it's not a perfect designation. However, in our context of designing games, these three categories are practical and manageable and serve our purposes.

Your type decisions should be based on the following criteria: your theme, your value set, and your target audience's preferences and expectations. The criteria should not be: personal taste, current hotness, easy availability. Furthermore, your budget shouldn't drive your principal decision but how you *apply* that principal decision. If art music is the best match for your theme, value set, and target audience, a full-scale orchestra isn't your only choice. What about a chamber orchestra? A woodwind ensemble? A string quartet? A solo artist of any kind, like voice, piano, violin, or concert flute? An a cappella chamber choir? There are plenty of options to choose from, and you will certainly find something that vibes with your criteria and your budget as well. Popular music also has a wide price range, most obviously in terms of whom you want to hire or what you want to commission or license, and how many songs or ambient compositions (not to be confused with ambient sound effects) you need for your game. The third principal type, traditional music, also opens up a wide range of possibilities, and we will get back to it when discussing its individual strengths and functions.

In all cases, keep the question of licensing in mind. For art music from composers that have been dead for a sufficient amount of time, you don't have to pay license fees for the music itself, but in almost all cases for recorded performances. Except, of course, you either perform it yourself or have it performed by musicians hired and paid by you. (And then, don't copy any published sheet music your musicians might need but buy copies from the publishers.) Yet, be careful—huge amounts of terrific art music exist that were written by composers who are alive, or by composers whose copyrights have yet to expire. For popular music, you almost always have to pay license fees, and if you pay a cover band to perform somebody else's music, that applies as well. And if you hire musicians who play their own music or indeed *write* music or songs for your game, yes, you will have to pay license fees! For traditional music, things are again a bit different. Traditional music is often license-free, but specific arrangements are usually not. So beware. Also, be both sensitive and sensible with respect to cultural appropriation. Borrowing expressions from a cultural group that is not yours without any involvement from members of that group is never a good idea. And be generous in giving back! Which could be granting your own arrangement back into the public domain instead of nailing it shut with a copyright claim.

The one thing you want to avoid at all costs are contracts where music licenses will expire after a number of years. You may think, well, in ten years, I won't care anymore. Don't. It's a pest for everyone involved. Maybe your game has become a classic by then. In that case, you will be forced to renegotiate license fees to keep selling your game, or let others sell your game, and you're not exactly in a position to bargain. Alternatively, if you go and take the music with expired licenses out of your game and replace it with something else, everybody will be rightfully salty and call you names. Don't attach yourself so much to a certain idea that others can take your game hostage. Instead, look around. There is so much talent out there, and independent talent at that, for art and popular and traditional music. For decent pay and with a decent contract, all this can be avoided and your game will be free to live and shine forever.

Next, let's drill down to music's specific function palette. These are functions that music can serve natively, beyond the three basic functions of mood, feedback, and information. You can think of it as a palette with the four primary colors evoke, illustrate, identify, and mesmerize that you can mix and match for all kinds of effects.

Evoke has everything to do with setting the mood and presenting and eliciting emotions.

Illustrate involves accompanying, intensifying, reacting to, and advancing dramatic developments.

Identify refers to presenting characters, cultures, locales, and motifs and make them recognizable.

Mesmerize contributes to keeping the player spellbound, engaged, and focused.

In the "evoke" section, you will need to develop a good understanding about mood and emotions as such, the specific mood and emotions you want to establish, and the musical techniques needed to evoke precisely the mood and the emotions you have in mind.

In the "illustrate" section, you must be able to carry out what is known as spotting sessions in the movie industry. In a spotting session, you figure out together with the composer and/or the musicians where the music should start in a level, where it should stop, what it should do in between and why, including doing nothing, and a host of dramatic details, all without wasting their time and/or embarrassing yourself. Moreover, in case your game isn't scripted to hell and back, you need the means to adapt your music in real time to what's actually going on during play. Long ago, there were engines and container formats like iMuse or MOD, now almost forgotten, that held a number of layers of the same track in different keys, tempi, types of instrumentation, and so on, plus a handful of transitional sections, that could adapt to actual player behavior. Fortunately, there's been a resurging interest in dynamic game audio, with new and improved dynamic music middleware you can choose from and use in the engine of your choice. But it's not an easy task—for an introduction, both Tim van Geelen's "Realizing Groundbreaking Adaptive Music" and Gina Zdanowicz and Spencer Bambrick's *The Game Audio Strategy Guide* are a good start.

In the "identify" section, think of musical motifs as RFIDs that you can attach to everything that the player has to identify in a "near field" or "contactless" manner, if you will. (Something very similar can be done with foley, but for different ends, to be discussed later.) The most well-known technique is the so-called "leitmotif" technique, of which the best-known examples in turn are Richard Wagner's operas and Ennio Morricone's movie scores. Leitmotif means that every character has their own musical motif, and when it is played, you know that the character has appeared, has been there, or will appear shortly; has been talked about or thought about by other characters; or this character's personal interests are affected in some way. There's more, but it should suffice to show how versatile leitmotifs can be. And character leitmotifs aren't the only game in town! You can attach leitmotifs to different cultures and different species. You can attach leitmotifs to locations, even to ideas aka motifs! And if you have a talented composer, which you should, they can weave such leitmotifs together into a soundtrack that not only "evokes" and "illustrates" and "identifies" but tells a deep and rich story about how characters, cultures, locales, and motifs relate to each other. This works for drama as well as for comedy. Just check Wagner's *Meistersinger*, where a lot of wit and humor and innuendo and outright punchlines are delivered through interwoven leitmotifs.

What Morricone or Wagner can also teach you is that leitmotifs are not the exclusive domain of melody. For the composition of leitmotifs for characters, cultures, locales, and motifs, you can choose from five different domains: *melody, harmony, instrumentation, orchestration,* and *timing*. Most of the time, leitmotifs combine several of these domains, but there's usually one or two domains that stick out.

Here's the rough guide. Melody is a string of notes that form a recognizable tune. Harmony is what happens when you play different notes at the same time. Instrumentation is the kind of instrument (including human voice) that you choose for performing the notes you have in mind. Orchestration is how you combine different instruments for a particular chord or a particular passage. Timing, finally, is the way how tones and chords form patterns over time—tempo, repetition, periodicity, rest (intervals of silence); the length of those notes, chords, and rests; and, in short, everything that is associated with beat or rhythm.

For simplicity's sake, some prominent sound properties are associated with these domains instead of having their own domains. Included in *melody* are musical scales with their different melodic

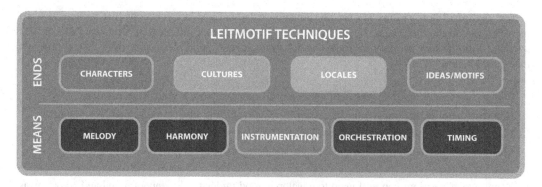

FIGURE 4.26   Leitmotif techniques.

characteristics, which is called "mode," and the frequency range that we experience as higher or lower, which is called "pitch." Included in *harmony* are the tonal or atonal relationships and hierarchies between different notes, which is called "tonality." Included in *instrumentation* is the tone color/sound quality that depends on the specific instrument or human voice as the source of that sound, which is called "timbre." So there's a veritable rabbit hole that you can follow down, a whole world of techniques and opportunities waiting for you to make your leitmotifs an unforgettable experience.

Then, there's the "mesmerize" section. Whenever the player has to focus on a repetitive task, that's where mesmerizing music should be considered. Being mesmerizing isn't equivalent to being repetitive, but there's a strong correlation. From all the spiritual endeavors in the history of humankind that require prolonged engagement and focus, it is hard to find one that doesn't involve some form of repetition by the individual or the group as an essential component. Dancing, singing, chanting, shuckling, you name it. For games, the most famous example that comes to mind is the A-type *Tetris* theme, the "Korobeyniki" folk song-arrangement by Tanaka Hirokazu. Traditional or folk music in general, all over the world, is strong in repetition—not only because repeating patterns are easily memorized, but because they are linked to repetitive actions in contexts of work or spiritual endeavors or, often enough, both. (And not always are these contexts joyful or pleasant.) Certainly, art music and popular music can be mesmerizing as well, from Johann Sebastian Bach's endlessly rising canon to Steve Reich's "Clapping Music" to Iron Butterfly's "In-A-Gadda-Da-Vida." But traditional music, that's the go-to.

To wrap up the music section, there's diegetic and non-diegetic music, which we call mode. These terms warrant an introduction.

On the surface, it's fairly simple. Diegetic music belongs to your game world in such a way that the characters in that world can hear it, or would in principle be able to hear it, while non-diegetic music can only be heard by someone who isn't part of that game world, usually the player. If you have a Washington DC level where your player character walks through a subway station, and there's a street musician performing Bach's chaconne for solo violin, so that your character and all the non-player characters in that metro station can hear it, that's diegetic. If your player character experiences rugged loneliness on a mountain top to that very same music, but there's neither a hidden violinist around nor a radio or other replay device, that's non-diegetic because only you, the player, can hear that music. Not even your player character can hear it! Especially games that work with period music, like *Mafia III* or *Fallout 4*, will have licensed music that plays as diegetic music through radio stations and car radios and such. Most of the time, though, such games will feature non-diegetic music as well, often in the form of ambient soundtracks that kick in when the player switches off the radio, leaves the car, and so on. You can also play with cross-diegetic effects, when originally non-diegetic music becomes diegetic, or vice versa. While it's frequently used for comedic effect, it doesn't have to. An unconventional example is Robert Altman's 1973 movie *The Long Goodbye*, where John Williams and Johnny Mercer's title song "The Long Goodbye" pops up again and again during the movie in different forms as blues song, supermarket muzak, hippy singalong, a Mexican brass band march, and whatnot, which is at the same time diegetic and non-diegetic, and eerily effective. (On a related note, the appearance of "The Long Goodbye" in *Star Wars: The Last Jedi* as casino muzak on Canto Bight is baffling.)

After music, our next stop for types and modes is the foley category. We can differentiate three general types.

Natural sounds. These are the sounds of nature and of living beings, humans included, that do not fall into the category of speech or emotive sounds (more on that below); sounds that are created by the movement of living beings and natural phenomena; and sounds that are created or modified by extraordinary spaces and environments. A common feature of natural sounds is that instances of the same sound are variable, fluctuating, and unpredictable as to their exact appearance.

Artifactual sounds. These are the sounds that emanate from artifacts or the use of artifacts, from tools and equipment and guns to machinery and technology in general. A common feature of artifactual sounds is that instances of the same sound remain constant under similar sonic circumstances, and their exact appearance is highly predictable.

Emotive sounds. These are the sounds from living beings that communicate internal states like emotions or wants and needs but are not speech.

That's very coarse-grained, and it has to be—categorizing all possible types of foley is a hopeless endeavor. And for our purposes, these three types suffice. The term "artifactual" roughly corresponds to how the term "artifact" is used by archaeologists for something made or modified and used by humans. (For us, though, it will also incorporate what counts as structures and features in archaeological parlance, i.e., artifacts that are not or not easily movable, and we're not restricted to humans as well.) The decisive point is that artifactual sounds are predictable, while natural and emotive sounds are not. If your tool or gun or generator or iron tower makes always the same sound or sounds in the same acoustic context, that's perfectly okay. If your wind or bird or human makes always the same sound or sounds in the same sonic context, that's weird. It will grate and attract attention. So if you deal with natural and emotive sounds, provide variation! Don't pepper your game with Wilhelm Screams unless all your enemies are perfect clones with the narrowest of emotive registers.

In contrast to music, and later also speech, foley does not have its own native function palette. That way, we can simply apply our three basic categories mood, feedback, and information: the sounds in a summer forest after a brief rain shower; the sound when you hit an enemy, pick up an object, or select a menu option; the sound a creature or enemy makes habitually before you can see it, or before it can see you. Let's have a look at these functions in more detail.

The mood function of foley. It certainly can create joy, sadness, and other emotions from the emotional landscape, but that's not what this function is about. Primarily, it's about establishing a sense of place, time, and context. You can use foley to evoke a certain historical epoch or a certain geographical region. You can use foley to convey a gigantic, commanding environment or a crushingly claustrophobic place, a mounting sense of urgency or feelings of peace and relaxation.

The feedback function of foley. It provides feedback on player action, either within or without the game world. Within the game world, for example, foley should indicate that the player has successfully dropped or picked up an item. Outside the game world, for example, foley should indicate that the player has added, removed, or rearranged an item in their inventory. As will be seen below, foley's feedback function is strongly connected to its mode.

The information function of foley. While it has many different duties, its most prominent function is to provide cues: distinctive and characteristic sound markers that are attached to anything that has the potential to be dangerous. Like the leitmotif technique discussed above, these markers work like RFID tags, and the player has a chance to recognize and distinguish enemies and dangerous situations instead of bumping into them unprepared. Moreover, these markers, or cues, should always be designed in such a way that they not only inform the player about the presence or approach of a certain creature or dangerous situation, but also about its type and its character.

In terms of mode, foley can also be diegetic and non-diegetic. On the whole, being diegetic or non-diegetic depends on the interface type that we discussed earlier in this level. Almost always, foley sounds from the preference interface, the inventory interface, and in some cases from a traditional overlay gameplay interface will be non-diegetic. In transparent or diegetic gameplay interfaces, foley sounds will almost always be diegetic. Yes, that's two different uses of the term diegetic here! But you can see how they relate to the exact same principle: things that are part of the game world, like an ammo counter on the side of your weapon and the cry of a bird, are diegetic; things that are not part of the game world, like your health meter and that pumping music whenever you join a fight, are non-diegetic.

In "A Conceptual Framework for the Analysis of First-Person Shooter Audio and its Potential Use for Game Engines," Mark Grimshaw and Gareth Scott differentiate diegetic sound events even further for multiplayer action along specified functions, for example, who triggers these sounds and who can hear them, adding the terms ideodiegetic, telediegetic, kinediegetic, and exodiegetic to the pool. If your game includes multiplayer action, you might want to check this out.

Finally, let's proceed to the types, special functions, and modes of our third and last category, speech. As certain schools of linguists put it, language is a tool to manipulate one's environment, with and through other humans. This "bio tool," together with opposable thumbs, has been essential for the enormous success humans have enjoyed as a species, by adapting to their environments and adapting environments to their needs. Indeed, to claim that language exists so that we can communicate with each other doesn't really mean anything—it's like saying that we are able to communicate in order to communicate. Moreover, animals can communicate just fine without being able to use language in the very specific and qualitatively different ways human animals can. Why is that important? Because if you think about language differently, it will open your mind to the versatility of speech and the numerous possibilities to utilize speech for different functions. Provided, of course, you decided to use speech in your game in the first place.

For our purposes, there are just two types of speech: monologue and dialogue. (Special cases are covered by mode, discussed below.) This sounds simple but isn't. Whatever you want to express through speech in your game, you should think about what you can accomplish with dialogue instead of monologue. Dialogue is much more natural and much more interesting, not least because dialogue is social. Monologues can also be interesting, but they should be used sparsely, and then to maximum effect.

Sadly, that's not what we see in games most of the time. If you think about it, most speech we find in games that we classify as dialogue is actually monologue. Why? A dialogue is a conversational exchange, a mutual exploration of observations, ideas, and intents, and it's about relationships. Speech that merely lectures or informs isn't dialogue, and even trading information doesn't constitute a dialogue, but a sequence of monologues for all practical purposes. Naturally, it's easier to write great dialogues if the characters, including the player character, have emotional bonds and shared interests or opposing interests that connect them in one way or another. And the reason is very simple—to write interesting dialogue, you need to have interesting characters and interesting relationships between these characters! So when your dialogues fall flat, it might not be the quality of your dialogues. It could be an indicator for a completely different problem, namely that your characters and the relationships between your characters need to be substantially rewritten.

Like music, speech has its own specialized palette of functions beyond mood, feedback, and information. Without wading too deep into linguistic waters, which is a polite way of saying that we will once more cut down and adapt a complex scientific domain with reckless abandon for our purpose of designing games, this palette has five sections that cover everything we need.

Inform. To describe external or internal states including intent; teach, educate, etc.

Inquire. To ask for information in order to learn something, be educated, develop, etc.

Influence. To request, persuade, order, command, convince, scare, inspire, etc.

Cultivate. To socialize, chat, assure, ascertain, introduce, etc.

Entertain. Aesthetic and poetic speech.

Let's turn once more to the abovementioned speech samples from the mercenaries in *Uncharted* and check them against this palette. Looking closely, you will notice something odd: they do not satisfy any of these five functions! They do not inform—nothing that is exchanged exceeds anyone's previous knowledge. They don't inquire—any fresh information in these situations would have been obvious and not in need of being communicated. It doesn't influence anyone—"this way" or "that way" is utterly random and devoid of directions. Neither do they cultivate relationships, nor entertain anyone. For the player, as has been said before, these dialogues serve no function either—they provide no cues for enemy presence or tactical options.

A great counterexample is *Oxenfree*. Not only is this game full of functional speech that informs, inquires, influences, cultivates, and entertains; techniques like dialogue time limits and interruptions (an ingeniously designed game mechanic, actually) make these dialogues appear exceptionally natural and meaningful.

But wait, there's more! If your piece of speech clearly serves one or more functions, then you have to ask yourself what function it serves with respect to the characters in your game world, and what function it serves with respect to your player. Answering both questions in a satisfactory manner is deeply important if you don't want to litter your game with dialogues that make players cringe in their seats. Here's why.

The player function of speech. If your dialogue serves one or several functions only for the player, and not also for the characters within the game, chances are these dialogues will sound like terrible movie exposition, the kind of screamingly unnatural informational exchange between non-player characters that would never happen that way in the real world—employed by the shovelful, for example, in games where the player character can approach guards in stealth mode, like in *Rise of the Tomb Raider*, regrettably.

The character function of speech. If your dialogue serves one or several functions only for the characters within the game, and not also for the player, these dialogues aren't doing what they're supposed to be doing. What they should do, as discussed in more detail in the *Architectonics* territory, is to advance the plot, portray a character, communicate an insight into the game world, highlight an aspect related to the theme or its motifs, elicit an emotion, advance player proficiency, or push the player toward the goal. All of that can be accomplished by one or more of the five functions inform, inquire, influence, cultivate, or entertain.

Thus, every dialogue should serve one or more functions, both for the characters in your game world and for the player. And these functions don't have to match! For example, characters within the game world can entertain other characters in the game world, which will provide the player with information about local lore. Guards that are bored out of their wits can socialize in a manner that may be highly entertaining for the player. And so on. Use your imagination!

On the player character's side, try to cut down on the inquire function, unless your game is a murder mystery or something along that line, and the player character is supposed to grill everyone on every occasion. Try to combine the inquire function with at least one other speech function. It will make it more palatable and realistic, and more probable in turn that a non-player character actually opens up. Combinations with the cultivate function or entertain function work great, but also as tit-for-tat with the inform function. And it works together with the influence function as well—to persuade, convince, or scare someone into delivering a piece of information is much more plausible, and much more interesting, than clicking through a sequence of questions on a dialogue wheel.

Finally, mode. Almost all speech that is used within the game world is diegetic—speech that the game world's characters are either able to hear or would be able to hear in principle. This covers regular monologue, dialogue, and every kind of recording, like voice diaries. It also covers every kind of remote voice commands delivered to the player character, from radio to telepathy, because all that is part of the world, and other radio operators or other telepaths would be able to listen in, at least in principle.

For speech, however, a third mode exists: meta-diegetic. Originally, this term was used for embedded stories and frame narratives. (Which were also called hypodiegetic or extradiegetic; it's amazing how many related terms live in this town.) Nowadays, the term almost always indicates some kind of reflective speech, the most prevalent being voice-over narration and soliloquy. Voice-over narration might be best known from film noir and soliloquies from *Hamlet*, but you can find both in other genres as well, including comedy. If you have a narrative designer on board, or you happen to be a narrative designer yourself, you can differentiate voice-over narration further: the narrator can be the protagonist, another character, or someone who is not part of the fiction. Following Gérard Genette's terminology in *Narrative Discourse*, these meta-diegetic events are called autodiegetic, homodiegetic, and heterodiegetic, respectively. Now you know!

Playing with meta-diegetic speech is versatile and effective as long as it isn't used to force-feed information to the player. If you use voice-over narration or soliloquies, it should serve dramatic purposes within your game that aren't just exposition and information. As a cautionary tale, this was precisely the case with the theatrical versions of *Blade Runner* and *Dark City*, where publishers forced voice-over narration upon the directors to deleterious effects. Plus, as meta-diegetic speech changes the character of a game in substantial ways, it should be intimately connected to your theme.

Finally, is there non-diegetic speech in games? Yes, but it's very rare. It might be a kind of "talking menu," either for serious games or as an accessibility feature, who informs the player about menu choices, moves, tasks, and so on. Some of these "talking menus" might even taunt the player on certain actions, for example, when the player wants to save or quit. But as soon as it connects to the narrative of the game, those voice-overs are better classified as meta-diegetic (heterodiegetic) narrators, like in *Bastion* or in *Edna & Harvey: Harvey's New Eyes*.

These examples are not exhaustive; it's a rewarding terrain for innovative and imaginative narrative design.

To conclude our speech section, some advice with regard to voice talent. If you want to make a professional game, you need professional voice talent. And if you want to make a professional pitch, and that pitch features a prototype that includes speech, you need professional voice talent too. This should be obvious. Yet, it often isn't. After all, can't we all speak, and haven't we even done it for years?

No. Like writing, drawing, dancing, running, throwing, cooking, and numerous other things we might do on a daily basis, there's a huge difference between an activity as such and that same activity as an artistic or athletic expression. And so it is with speaking. These are professionals who have trained and honed their craft for infinite hours year after year. That's what you pay them for. You're not paying them for reading lines from a screen.

When you choose and brief the voice talent that fits your game, be aware of the fact that games are a very intimate medium. Game designers have a habit of pushing their voice actors into overly dramatic poses to sculpt every line, remark, warning, or even throwaway gag into forceful theatrical expressions of utmost urgency. Which is completely at odds with how people act and speak even in critical situations. And never is more than one character allowed to speak at the same time! (Again, a great counterexample to all of this is *Oxenfree*.) Behind that lurks the idea that every single line throughout the whole game is immensely relevant and must be received and understood by the player at all costs. Which is often true for speech functions like inform and influence, but not for speech functions like cultivate or entertain. Bantering, for example, falls into the cultivate category, and bantering among combat troops in particular falls terribly flat in many games. Why? Because every line is conceived and performed like a rare gem worthy of the most prestigious comedy award. Also, it's not only perfectly natural that people don't understand every word, you can also use that for dramatic effect in combat situations, heated dialogues, and similar. What's more, you can use it to create specific emotions! A great example of the latter is the breakfast scene in *Alien*, after the ship's computer pulled the crew from cryosleep. The camera pans around the table, the crew members chatter away, but there's a palpable tension. And much of what they say isn't fully intelligible. As Ridley Scott later revealed in an audio commentary, that was on purpose. Being unable to fully understand a conversation makes people uneasy, anxious, and even fearful, which was exactly what Scott intended. And while games aren't movies, they're far closer to movies than to plays, where theatrical expressions and articulations are supposed to reach even the cheapest seats on the balcony with stupendous clarity.

Before we wrap up this beat and with it the entire level, there's one last thing: the soundscape.

The soundscape unites everything we discussed in this beat—music, foley, speech, and silence. It encompasses everything related to the game that the player can hear (with the possible exception of screaming cooling fans). Now, if you can weave all your sound events together into a distinct and recognizable soundscape, that will be a strong differentiator! It doesn't have to be pleasing to the ear,

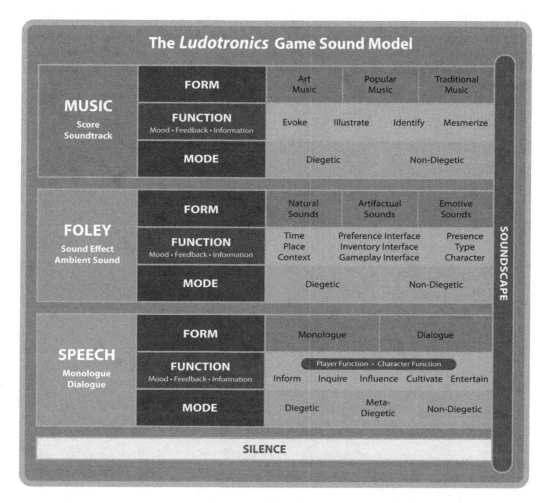

FIGURE 4.27 Game sound model.

necessarily, but it does have to be good. And memorable: when listened to, even much later, it should bring back emotions that the player felt while playing the game.

What's more, you can use the soundscape to fine-tune the playing experience, and even affect player actions by modulating it in ways that make it more pleasing or displeasing to the ear. You can subtly manipulate the player into staying at certain places longer than others, or leaving certain places earlier than others (real-life venues like stores or restaurants have done this for ages). You can influence the player's mood in ways that stimulate actions or decisions not only with music, foley, or speech, but also with your soundscape as a whole. If you want to develop a better sense of how soundscapes work and what they can and cannot do, try to listen to soundscapes in public spaces, like restaurants, stores, banks, and offices, and try to relate these to your affective attitudes toward these places. The soundscape is a powerful tool to work with that is often overlooked.

Outlook

Along style, space, and sound, we discussed a number of general design decisions on your journey through this territory toward functional aesthetics, thematic unity, and a holistic user experience. All of which you will later need for your pitch and your prototype, to be discussed in the Proposition phase.

Ask yourself: do you have a good idea, preferably a creative vision, about your game's functional aesthetics in terms of styles and interfaces, avatar and camera, spaces and passages, and a set of soundscape elements that rock? Is this vision compatible with your theme, your value set, and your target audience? Would you be able to sketch, present, and communicate this vision to designers and artists and writers in intelligible ways?

If your answer to all these questions is yes, congratulations! You made a big leap forward by beating this level.

Level Four

Narrativity

Opening

The motivational element from our interactive playing experience model associated with *Narrativity*, as discussed in the first level, is "emotional appeal." There is some overlap between this territory and the *Plurimediality* territory with regard to a number of elements, but not with regard to purpose. The difference is that *Plurimediality* is global and *Narrativity* is local. In the *Plurimediality* territory, elements are designed and controlled from the viewpoint of *functional aesthetics* that work toward a game's consistent look-and-feel for a holistic user experience. Here, in the *Narrativity* territory, elements are designed and controlled from the viewpoint of *narrative qualities or properties* that work toward conveying specific meaning in a specific dramatic unit for a memorable gameplay moment.

As mentioned in the Preliminary phase, the term *Narrativity* originates from film theory. It denotes narrative "qualities" or "properties" that lack identifiable plot or story elements. Thus, as *Narrativity* does not equal "narrative" or "story," it doesn't just apply to games that are dramatically complete. It's a vital part of any game, including purely "mechanical" games built around a set of game mechanics. Narrative qualities or properties can be attached to any *visual*, *auditory*, and *kinesthetic* matter, and also to a special class that we will call *mythological* matter, to be explained soon.

For each of these four domains of perception, you can differentiate two conceptual layers.

> Your specific choice and arrangement of visual, auditory, kinesthetic, and mythological **matter** for any given dramatic unit.

> Your specific choice of **narrative qualities or properties** that you attach to this matter, to fill it with life and connect it with your theme and motifs.

If this differentiation sounds somewhat artificial at first, it's because we don't usually reflect on these processes when we run them in our own minds. Imagine you want to create a painting. The first set of decisions would determine the medium (oil, acrylics, watercolors, pastels, ink, etc. on the one hand, canvas, paper, wood, glass, concrete, etc. on the other); *style* (realism, impressionism, surrealism, abstract, graffiti, etc.); tools (brushes, knives, sponges, spray cans, airbrushes, etc.); and subject (main idea, subject matter). The focus of the painting can be on the subject or main idea, which is what we usually assume, but it can also be on trying out a different medium, creating a new style, or working with novel or uncommon tools. Then you begin to paint. From that point on, the second set of decisions kicks in—artistic decisions around line, shape, form, color, value, space, texture. It's not exactly the same thing, but similar enough: it's your matter vs. the qualities and properties that you attach to shape that matter. Let's take a walk through all four perceptual domains, to establish their basic characteristics and peek into their respective toolboxes.

For *visual matter*, narrative qualities or properties can be established by the choice of color, color range, tint, shade, tone, surface texture, brightness, contrast, exposure, hue, saturation, luminance, temperature, fluorescence, sharpness, haze, blur, noise/grain, depth, resolution, size/dimensions, lighting, lenses, filters, camera angles, subjective/objective view, and many more. This should give you an idea of just how big this toolbox is. And you can invent or adapt your own tools!

Here's an example. Let's say there will be a level in your game—fantasy, contemporary, or science fiction, it doesn't matter at this point—where the player character must approach a mysterious stronghold

DOI: 10.1201/9781003334682-20

in the mountains. The stronghold and the mountains are your matter, and how they are arranged with respect to each other is your arrangement of that matter. That's the first layer. Then, with the help of your toolbox from the visual domain, you proceed to give that stronghold in the mountains the exact narrative qualities or properties that you have in mind, following both your imagination and your theme, or a certain motif. Are the mountains bleak and desolate, or are they smooth with sweet meadows and the occasional sheep? Does the stronghold look brooding and menacing, or rather like a robust place of refuge? Does the stronghold appear as an almost natural part of these mountains, or does it stick out as alien or even misplaced?

Your toolbox for *auditory matter*, to attach narrative qualities or properties to the three basic types of sound introduced in the *Plurimediality* territory—music, foley, and speech—is just as big. You can establish narrative qualities or properties through duration, loudness, timbre, pitch, intonation, modulation, inflection, rhythm, tempo, voice quality, modulation effects like distortion, reverb, or echo, and 3D audio effects, among many others, and don't forget silence and your soundscape in its entirety.

Let's say you want to apply music and foley while the player character approaches that stronghold from our example above. You have a harmony-based leitmotif for the stronghold and sounds that represent windswept cliffs, various player character footsteps for diverse and difficult terrain, and sporadic cries of a bird of prey circling over the region, but steering clear of the stronghold. Yes, all that belongs to the first layer! It is your matter and the arrangement of that matter. Now, to give this matter the exact narrative qualities or properties you have in mind, use your auditory toolbox. Is the bird of prey's cry more on the aggressive, predatory side, or does it evoke wide spaces and loneliness? Will the wind change in volume, or will it blow steadily at a certain force? And at which force? Will the sounds produced by the character player echo or reverberate? How will your stronghold leitmotif be arranged according to instruments, volume, tempo, and such, to make it appear outright threatening, uncanny, or subtly reminiscent of long-forgotten dreams?

For *kinesthetic matter*, we first have to examine kinesthetics in the context of video games before we look into its toolbox. The term kinesthetics itself is shorthand for two non-traditional senses: the vestibular sense for equilibrioception and the kinesthetic sense for proprioception. The first term refers to our senses of balance, acceleration (which includes both a sense of weight and of effort), and direction of movement. The second term refers to our sense of the relative positions and movements of body parts with respect to each other. The kind of kinesthetic matter a game can have depends on its control scheme and this scheme's level of abstraction. It can be delivered through combinations of player movement, avatar movement, and camera movement. We can differentiate between three basic types. The first type is defined by input on the highest abstraction level, as we find it in games that are controlled by keyboard and mouse, game pad, or touchscreen commands. The second type comprises games that are controlled by body movement, among them dance and rhythm games or certain kinds of sports and shooting games. These are either played without a controller, or with special controllers that mimic real-world tools, so that the input from physical movement in this type of games is on a much lower abstraction level than input in games of the first type. The third type consists of virtual reality games. Augmented reality doesn't constitute a type of its own, because AR games can belong to any type. All three types overlap a lot, but they do structure the field in ways that can aid design decisions.

It should be stressed that there is no difference in quality between these types, or in enjoyment potential. The first type is not "limited" in its input, and the third type is not "unconstrained." The true difference is that different levels of abstraction make different things possible and enjoyable. Would *Guitar Hero* be more enjoyable if players were holding real instruments in their hands within a VR environment? No, it wouldn't. It's the carefully crafted *abstraction* level that makes this game so enjoyable for so many people (including skilled musicians). Each type has its own potential richness of kinesthetic involvement.

Thus, not everything in your toolbox for the kinesthetic domain is applicable to every type. But there's more than enough to choose from: speed, acceleration, force, angle, momentum, torque, fluidity, sureness, smoothness, rhythm, balance, economy, consistency, variety, predictability, and more.

By now, the player character has moved into the mountain range toward the stronghold and needs to climb a steep hill in order to proceed. For the first type of games, you can simulate kinesthetic experiences like resistance, acceleration, momentum, and balance by manipulating the input/output patterns of mouse and keyboard, game pad, or touchscreen commands. That way, the player has to provide more sensitive input than usual at times, to avoid overshooting and uncontrolled sliding; or much more rapid and even frantic input instead, to scale heights, overcome resistance, and prevent the player character from sliding back. For the second type of games, these patterns could be mapped directly to a set of arm/hand gestures for a special controller, perhaps similar to the Wii Remote. For VR games, the third type, body movements could be added. For all three types, rhythm elements could be implemented to overcome obstacles, and fluidity and economy of movement could vary with terrain. Regardless of their respective abstraction levels, some physical movement is involved in all three types; each can provide a kinesthetic experience to some degree.

Mythological matter, the fourth and final perceptual domain, also needs a more thorough introduction. It is a special class with elements that resemble narrative or story elements. These elements are setting, location/environment, backstory, and lore, each with a dazzling array of tools. Among these tools are archetypes, memes (self-replicating cultural units), chunks (elements clustered into higher order units), associative relations, compression, simplification, exaggeration, metonymy/metaphor, and symbolism, to name a few.

But wait! Why do these belong into the *Narrativity* territory? Isn't it the case that setting, location/environment, backstory, and lore all "tell a story," and should belong into the *Architectonics* territory?

To answer this question, let's go back to our example, specify it as science fiction, and locate that stronghold in the mountains on a remote planet once settled for mining purposes. To all four compartments, we can attach narrative qualities or properties: the galaxy a few decades after an interstellar war (setting); a mining colony on a remote planet (location/environment); the history of that outpost before, during, and after the war and of the people who live there (backstory); the stories people from that outpost tell themselves (lore). What differentiates these elements from "regular" narratives is that they lack dramatic structure—no exposition, no inciting incident, no plot points, no rising and falling action, no climax, and no red herrings or Chekhov's Guns. All that is lost and can no longer be retrieved. It all happens before the game's story development arc begins! Also, there's no journey to be lived through for the character development arc, and no skills and abilities to be gained for the player development arc. (All three arcs are discussed in detail in the *Architectonics* territory.) What we're left with is a kind of abstract—which is what the artistic toolbox for the mythological domain, just as those for the other three domains, is literally about: *abstraction*.

What defines the mythological domain is that its elements are not altogether different from the abstractions of reality expressed through *myth*—traditional stories that explain the origins of a certain society or state of affairs, a certain practice, or a certain phenomenon. Such abstractions have a deep emotional appeal that can resonate over hundreds, even thousands of years. Of course, matter from our mythological domain will retain recognizable story elements, and these can become docking stations for actual story and plot elements. But here, in the *Narrativity* territory, these mythological abstractions operate in their own right on a psychological-emotional level, to be picked up by our "mythological sense," so to speak. Just like the other perceptual domains, the mythological domain provides you with specific artistic tools and expressions, which you can use to attach the exact narrative qualities and properties to your matter that you have in mind.

The player character, meanwhile, has reached the stronghold. The gate is closed. There is a side door nearby, and the player character tries to open it. It turns out to be locked as well, but then it's opened from the inside by a stranger. That stranger displays a haircut and adornments and clothes that remind the player of old records and stories about the very first settlers who had landed on this planet more than 300 years ago. Also, the stranger's legs seem to end in a pair of hooves.

For all four domains, an important question remains. How does narrativity work with respect to emotions? Let's look at music as a representative example. Music can't "have" or "express" emotions—it's not a human being, after all. So where do those emotions come from that we experience when listening to music? Following the musicologist and semiologist Eero Tarasti, loosely, we can argue that the sequence of emotions caused by a piece of music is what constitutes its narrativity. That would mean that music has no narrativity by and of itself, let alone any narrative, but certain qualities or properties that trigger sequences of emotions in the minds of the beholder *and* let the beholder interpret this experience in narrative terms. Similar dynamics have been observed from the psychological viewpoint, notably around the question of why people are drawn to sad music. As this question isn't altogether different from the

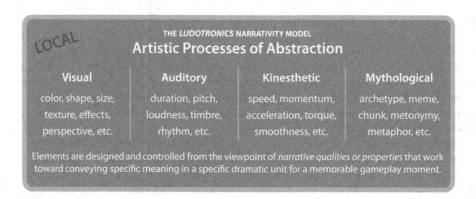

FIGURE 4.28   Artistic processes of abstraction.

question of why people go into theaters and watch tragedies, Aristotle's catharsis concept raises its hand; but again, its answers don't seem to have the explanatory power one might wish for. For the current state of research on sadness and music, Sandra Garrido's *Why Are We Attracted to Sad Music?* covers all the bases. But that's not the only unsolved question, or the first. When those qualities or properties can be "in" a piece of music, capable of triggering sequences of emotions that can be interpreted in narrative terms, how do they get there in the first place? Scientifically, i.e., psycho-physiologically, socially, anthropologically, and neurologically, we can't tell yet! The mechanism or mechanisms of how and why music can be "expressive" and trigger emotions still remain elusive. For the current state of research, the *Handbook of Music and Emotion: Theory, Research, Applications*, edited by Patrik N. Juslin and John A. Sloboda, will give you a comprehensive overview.

Thus, the only answer we can give at this point in time is a psycho-*philosophical* one, connected to art and myth, rather than a psycho-physiological one. Narrative qualities and properties are defined as that which is *retained* when it has passed through the *abstraction processes* that put them into art and myth. If you happen to be an artist, you will already be deeply familiar with these exact processes! Artists who work in or with media that cannot directly tell a story use these abstraction processes all the time. A symphony, a painting, a sculpture, or a modern performance dance: all these do not tell a story directly but trigger images and imaginations loaded with emotions, or sequences of emotions, in the beholders' minds, to be interpreted in narrative terms that may or may not refer back to those original stories. Often, they will refer back directly, when a work addresses well-known stories and experiences, like a sculpture playing on the Pygmalion myth, a painting depicting the Battle of Issus, an overture commemorating Napoleon's defeat, or a dance that reflects the ancient theory of the four temperaments. But the original stories do not have to be well known, or known at all. Or even exist! All this works just as well with stories that have sprung from the artist's imagination, experience, or, indeed, vision.

That's essentially what narrative qualities or properties are, and how they come about. It applies to art in the Louvre as well as to art in video games. But not in a direct and straightforward manner: artistic intentions cannot survive these abstraction processes fully intact, and they can't be fully retrieved by reverse engineering. Rather, through the narrative qualities or properties of works of art, the playing experience is artfully constrained by these artistic intentions. The playing experience is neither fully determined by them nor fully independent.

Don't worry—you don't have to be an artist or think like an artist to beat this level! What you have to do is to sketch two things. First, your matter and the arrangement of that matter (the first layer). Then, the visual, auditory, kinesthetic, and mythological elements your matter should convey (the second layer). You might even go so far and sketch a few abstraction techniques that you want to see employed. If done well, this will become the starting point for your creative team across all four perceptual domains— game artists of all kinds; sound and audio designers and composers; animation, motion, and camera designers; and game writers. As to the latter, there's the example of George R. R. Martin's contribution to *Elden Ring*; he exclusively created work for the mythological domain—setting, location/environment, backstory, lore—without being involved in the game's story and playable narratives at all.

As has been pointed out before, narrativity is a vital component in any game, including games with a purely mechanical core. It's *emotional appeal* that makes a game marketable to a broader audience, and from this broader audience might eventually leap the dedicated, maybe even professionalized player base you have in mind.

From the player motivation model, the relatedness/community element is strongly involved with the *Narrativity* territory—through the insights it provides into the game world, and into the characters who populate it.

Beat 1: Arrangement

Contrast and Congruence

From the four domains of perception just discussed, there will never be less than two domains involved in a game, with the possible exception of experimental or art games. Visual matter and auditory matter are always on board, and this is even true when they're temporarily absent—because in these cases, the absence of audiovisual matter *is* the matter (utter silence, e.g., or a black screen while the player character is in complete darkness or blindfolded).

As visual, auditory, kinesthetic, and mythological matter can all be employed for a single dramatic unit, you should know how these domains work together, relate to each other, reinforce each other, or interfere with each other.

Naturally, most people assume that visual matter has the right of way, but this is not what has been observed. There's been quite a lot of research into this, and for the mood and emotions that are experienced in a dramatic unit, sound almost always overrides even the strongest visual expression. The most exuberantly joyful amusement park ride will leave you in tears when set to Barber's *Adagio for Strings*, and the most innocuous family vacation slide show will deliver you a glimpse of the apocalypse when accompanied by Ligeti's *Requiem*. Or, for a more ignominious effect, watch the last minute of Maximilian Dood's YouTube review of the universally panned *Aliens: Colonial Marines*, which combines action footage from that game with the "Yakety Sax" theme from *The Benny Hill Show*.

Which, already, is an important design tool for specific gameplay moments. Creating incongruity by using sound that doesn't match the visual or narrative subject matter can achieve effects similar to the Kuleshov montage effect. When two different pictures are juxtaposed, Kuleshov showed, people interpret the meaning of the first in dramatically different ways dependent upon the nature of the second. That way, the second picture can "define" the first by providing cues for interpretation and solve ambiguities (or create them in the first place, as the case may be). Indeed, as a study by Baranowski and Hecht on "The Auditory Kuleshov Effect" indicates, juxtaposing visual matter with different auditory matter does the exact same thing. The Kuleshov effect works equally well when sound takes the role of the second picture.

Does that mean that visual matter is the runner-up in the domain hierarchy, right behind auditory matter? No, it isn't—narrativity related to mythological matter can, and does, strongly alter the way how visual matter is perceived.

To explain the reason for this and its practical use for game design, let's take a brief detour into media psychology and look at *agenda-setting* and *priming*. Both work in tandem and are related to memory and how we recall information. It's a three-step mechanism. First, certain aspects of a topic are highlighted over others. Then, these aspects are more easily recalled. Finally, with regard to this topic, decisions or certain forms of behavior in general are then *primarily* guided by our opinions about these *highlighted aspects*, and not about other possible aspects or the entirety of our knowledge about that topic. Priming effects, it needs to be remarked, have been milked for all its worth in scientific studies, and many headline-grabbing results can't be reproduced. But the foundation is solid—the first study on intentional priming by Iyengar, Peters, and Kinder in 1982, how media audiences evaluated the presidential performance of Jimmy Carter, has held up to scrutiny pretty well. Finally, perception itself is associated with memory. In the so-called sensory memory, a kind of ultra-short-term memory, the vast majority of sensory information is discarded within time spans ranging from 15 milliseconds to 2 seconds, or 3 seconds at most for auditory matter, according to current research. Processed further toward less volatile types of memory are only those pieces of information that we deem valuable, and we deem valuable what we either *are* focused on or *can* easily focus on. Which, unsurprisingly, will more likely be things attached to other things that we already know and can easily recall!

That's the abridged version, but it's all we need. Here's the point. You can use your mythological matter from setting, location/environment, backstory, and lore, or handpicked parts of it, to prime your player toward what they should *recall*, *expect*, and *focus on*. It won't override your auditory elements most of the time, but it *will* influence how the player perceives your visual matter, how they make decisions, and how they act on the basis of their perceptions.

In relative terms, we now have a hierarchy with the auditory domain on top, followed by the mythological domain, followed in turn by the visual domain. But where is kinesthetic matter located within that hierarchy? That, alas, isn't altogether clear. Partly because this specific question hasn't been studied a lot, partly because we have yet to unlock its true potential. Also, the power of the camera is somewhat diminished when compared with the power of cameras in movies. In movies, striking narrative qualities or properties can be established through special angles and special movement, including zero movement—think of Sergio Leone's extreme close-up Italian shot, Yasujiro Ozu's low-height Tatami shot, or Stanley Kubrick's interminable tracking shot. Outside of cutscenes, this seems very hard to accomplish in video games without cutting back on player agency. Thus, for all we know at this point, kinesthetics in games seems to have the weakest influence from our four domains of perception.

To wrap it up, the domain hierarchy with regard to player perception is, except in special cases, auditory, mythological, visual, and kinesthetic matter, from top to bottom.

You need to know this hierarchy if you want to work with elements that are in *dissonance* with each other within a dramatic unit: contrasting, conflicting, or even contradicting signals; incongruity, ambiguity, or uncertainty; and any other type of friction with the potential to create cognitive dissonance. Knowing this hierarchy, you can mix and match your domain elements with much better precision to produce your intended effect.

But you also need to know this hierarchy if you want to have your elements work in *consonance* with each other in a dramatic unit. Consonance doesn't sound as exciting as dissonance, but there are at least two important applications: intensification and clarification. Let's look into both, starting with intensification.

You might have heard about what has become known as the "misattribution of arousal" effect, an effect attested to by various studies. The most widely known of these studies is Dutton and Aron's "bridge" experiment. If you haven't heard about it already, its title will give you a hint: "Some Evidence for Heightened Sexual Attraction Under Conditions of High Anxiety." An attractive "interviewer" met unwitting test subjects on a suspension bridge with what the authors call "many arousal-inducing features"—think *Indiana Jones and the Temple of Doom*, with a 230-foot drop, wobbling, tilting, and so on. The equally unwitting test subjects from the control group met their "interviewer" on a much lower, solid wood bridge. As you can probably guess already, the test subjects from the suspension bridge were significantly more attracted to the interviewer than the control group, and this result was enforced by other, methodically more rigorous (but less spectacular) tests within the same study.

In general terms, strong emotions of one kind can intensify the attraction to something completely different. That's the "misattribution of arousal." This works not only with fear, as in the bridge example. Evidence from other studies suggests that misattribution of arousal also works with emotions like euphoria or anger, and even physical exertion. What's more, the misattribution effect supports not only positive attraction, but also its opposite—negative attraction.

As you can see, all this gives you a lot to work with. You can intensify any effect toward attraction or repulsion with clever layers of consonant narrative qualities or properties. For example, you can strengthen the bond between the player and a non-player character, a place, or an item. Or, you can make the player despise that character, place, or item much more strongly than without misattributed arousal!

For clarification, the second major application of consonance, we need to recall our psycho-philosophical model from this level's opening. Owing to the abstraction processes that went into it, the narrative qualities or properties of an artistic expression can never be unequivocal, never be straightforward, with respect to their meaning or interpretation. They're ambiguous, uncertain, even elusive, and

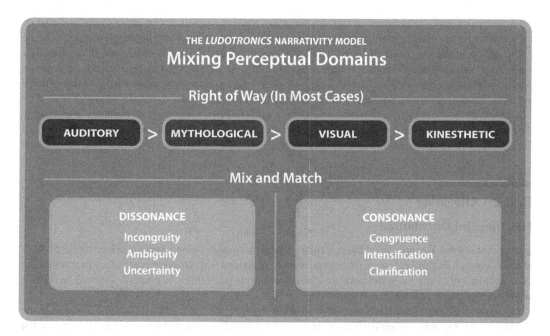

FIGURE 4.29 Mixing perceptual domains.

that's why people love to ask the artist to explain the "meaning" of their work. But for a work of art, any meaning and any interpretation can only be temporary and contextual. (That's one of the reasons why works of art can always surprise us with something new and completely unexpected, even after thousands of years.) But in your game, more often than not, you want your artwork to be understood! So you have to clarify, and you can use the narrative qualities or properties from one or more domains of perception to clear up ambiguities in another domain of perception. Again, the hierarchy is important. Especially music can "help" the player interpret certain characters or events correctly, clarify intentions, assess trustworthiness, rank importance, and more. Employing this tool, you can give the player a clearer picture without having to resort to explanations, particularly through speech.

Perhaps, during the course of this beat, some mischievous thoughts popped into your mind. With all these powerful tools at your disposal, from dissonance to consonance, from intensification and arousal to clarification and interpretation: is it okay to use narrative qualities or properties to mislead and deceive the player?

The answer depends on an unassuming detail: whether the misleading element is diegetic or not, a term discussed in detail in the *Plurimediality* territory. (In brief, if it's accessible to characters in the game world, it's diegetic. If it's only accessible to the player, it's non-diegetic.) Let's go through all four domains.

To fool or mislead, kinesthetic elements are not very useful, so we can leave them aside.

Mythological elements (setting, location/environment, backstory, lore) can be diegetic or non-diegetic. The player will have been confronted with some elements during gameplay (diegetic) and with some elements through marketing material, accompanying information, extended universes, and the like (non-diegetic). The former is allowed to mislead, the latter is never allowed to mislead. If there is a certain piece of lore that seems consistent and plausible but is in fact dead wrong, and the player has learned this piece of lore from a character within the game world, that's perfectly okay. If that piece of lore was printed on the box or came with the game description on digital platforms, that's not okay.

Elements from the visual domain that are diegetic may of course mislead. They do it all the time. But where would non-diegetic visual matter come from, if not from one of the interfaces? Being misled by one's interface will probably not endear you to your target audience. Breaking the fourth wall, as discussed in the *Plurimediality* territory, seems to be an exception. Whatever is referenced, however—the player, the menu, the hardware, the microphone—becomes part of the game world and should therefore count as diegetic.

Similar rules apply to auditory matter. Music, foley, speech, or silence that are diegetic and part of the game world are most certainly allowed to deceive the player. When some bouncy tavern tunes and a group of people singing cheerfully along lure the player into a den of vicious murderers, that's okay. If a smooth and relaxing non-diegetic track from the game's score provides the player with a false sense of peace and tranquility while some fantasy equivalent of *Tom and Jerry*'s Spike towers over them, that's not okay. Except, of course, you have a cartoon or comedy game in mind!

Think about it—if the player is misled or deceived with the help of non-diegetic elements, the player is directly misled or deceived by the designer. Except in experimental, art, or comedy games, it's very hard to come up with a hypothetical case where that would be conducive to improving the playing experience.

Beat 2: Allocation

Function and Distribution

Earlier in this level, we introduced the principle of narrative qualities or properties and the tools you have at your disposal. In this beat, we will discuss specific functions that narrative qualities or properties can and should serve in any given dramatic unit, and how narrative qualities or properties should be distributed over the course of the game as a whole.

Let's start with functions. Each beat—the smallest dramatic unit in a game, discussed in-depth in the *Architectonics* territory—should advance the plot, portray a character, communicate an insight into the game world, highlight an aspect related to the theme or its motifs, elicit an emotion, advance player proficiency, push the player toward the goal, or any combination thereof. The functions that narrative qualities or properties should add or support in a dramatic unit, how could it be otherwise, have the same line-up, but with one important exception: narrative qualities or properties cannot be used to advance the plot. Having no identifiable story elements is the very idea of narrativity, as mentioned before. What narrative qualities or properties can do instead is augment and enrich a story element or plot point with a specific emotional value. But that is a completely different function than advancing the plot.

All other functions are fine, and we will have a detailed look at four of them: portray a character, communicate an insight, elicit an emotion, and push the player toward the goal. As for the remaining two functions, highlighting aspects of the theme will be covered in-depth in the context of world narrative in the next and final beat; and we don't need to illustrate how player proficiency is advanced in terms of knowledge and understanding, as this is integral to how narrative properties or qualities work. For our demonstration, let's return to the stronghold in the mountains from the beginning of this level.

> **Portray a character**. A few paragraphs into Heinrich von Kleist's famous novella *Michael Kohlhaas*, a character is described thus: "The castellan, buttoning a waistcoat over his spacious stomach, came, and standing aslant against the rain, asked for his passport." If you visualize this castellan, you know everything you need to know about him, up to and including his poor moral character, which turns out to be as aslant, or »schief« in the original German, as his body posture and—eventually—the whole situation. Moreover, barring first-person perspective, you can use camera distance and camera angles to provide the player with even more psychological details about a character—here, you can learn a lot from classic "camera" angles in Marvel's or DC's superhero comics. Then, you can portray a character through sound, not only through leitmotifs or speech patterns but also foley: footsteps, the movement of their clothes, how they breathe or eat or sleep, and virtually any bodily function imaginable. Kinesthetically, the character can be portrayed through the way they move, not just the entire body, but eye and head movements, gestures, how they sit down and how they stand up, and so on. Mythologically, the character can display characteristics that relate to lore, location/environment, backstory, or setting. Among the things displayed by the stranger at the stronghold, remember, were a haircut, adornments, and clothes worn by the very first settlers more than 300 years ago.

> **Communicate an insight**. Let's say we want to give the player a new insight into this world, namely, that the people or their backstory or backstory-related lore might not be fully trustworthy.

According to what the player character's been told, the first group of settlers had built that stronghold and then vanished without a trace under entirely opaque, mysterious circumstances. Now you want to cast some doubt on that. The best way to go about is an accumulation of observations, not a single thing the player can either overlook because it's too subtle, or can't miss because it's straight-in-your-face. For the visual domain, the stronghold might just not look like something that had been built by settlers 300 years ago. It might appear too old for that. Or maybe too recent. Its design patterns could be outright puzzling for that period, or for any known period. Then, it could exhibit a particularly curious defense architecture that makes the player wonder about what kind of threat its builders had faced, and why nobody had deigned to mention it or any theory about it. And so on. In the auditory domain, narrative qualities or properties can underscore these doubts. The music, for example, can play with the stronghold's leitmotif in a conspicuous manner. Or, it could mix into it elements from a different leitmotif—one that is attached to an antagonistic force or place or event or non-player character, anything the player has learned to distrust. It's subtle, yes, but that's the nature of clues! The last two domains wouldn't yield much in this case. Communicating an insight through kinesthetic qualities or properties is certainly not impossible, but for our particular insight, it would be a stretch. And the mythological domain can't be used here because the insight is precisely about casting doubt on elements from the mythological domain, especially backstory and lore, so we would just be chasing our tail.

Elicit an emotion. At the beginning of this phase, we introduced the three classes of emotions that are relevant for designing games: fear, pity, and fiero. Emotions from two of these classes, fear and fiero, can be directly evoked through narrative qualities or properties—fear, joy, sadness, terror, as well as feelings of triumph and defeat. This applies to all four domains. Both the auditory domain and the visual domain are cut out for this job, and the mythological domain can "prime" the player toward any of these emotions, as discussed. In the kinesthetic domain, player movement (controller, body) and in-game movement (avatar, camera) can make the ascent to the stronghold terrifying or joyful (fear class) and elegant and triumphant or bumbling and disgraceful (fiero class). They can work together with the other perceptual domains to create an overall mood for the beat, like sadness or desolation, as well as sudden flare-ups of fear, joy, terror, regret, or resolve. For the third class of emotions, the pity class—pity itself, love, hate, jealousy, and so on—it's a bit different. Remember, emotions from this class can only be evoked empathically, through emotions displayed by non-player characters that the player can empathize with. Accordingly, these emotions cannot be directly evoked through narrative qualities or properties like the emotions from the other two classes. But they can intensify and sustain the emotions of non-player characters, so that the player character can emphasize with them more strongly and for a longer time.

Push the player toward the goal. Finally, all four domains again can be involved in pushing the player toward the goal. That could be visual cues of any kind that induce the player to hurry, dramatic music that communicates imminent danger, terrain that doesn't let the player rest for even a second, or having the player recognize a piece of lore that had seemed unrelated up to now, but suddenly looms large, and suggests—or demands—a particular course of action. Like, to apply our example, the peculiarly evocative anatomy of the stranger at the stronghold.

As you can see, you have many options to apply narrative qualities or properties. But beware! Don't try and cram everything into one beat. Just as with suspense and relief, or with action and relaxation, narrativity needs its own ebb and flow system over the course of the game.

Which, not incidentally, brings us to distribution, our second topic.

Every level in the Process phase demands sketching some conceptual map or other for the game as a whole, be that the distribution of emotions, challenges and learning curves, plot points, or subgoals and objectives. This level is no exception; its conceptual map is a sketch of the ebb and flow of *dramatic intensity*.

As with functions, intensity levels should vary. They can strongly affect the player's mood, and they should do so deliberately and purposefully. Moods relate to emotions, but they're not the same—moods need not be triggered by specific events; they last longer than emotions; and they influence the quality of emotions experienced in a certain mood. If you want to know more about it, "Distinctions Between Emotions and Mood" by Christopher J. Beedie and others is a good start. To sculpt your game's intensity levels, matter from all four domains, visual, auditory, kinesthetic, and mythological, need to be given their crescendi and decrescendi, their fortissimi and pianissimi, their fermatas and rests, across the whole map—as you would do for your plot, learning curves, or goal distributions.

The first impulse, which you should resist, is to force narrativity into lockstep with other distributions. Dramatic intensity can and should work together with plot points or challenges, no doubt. But if that's all what it's used for, in a one-to-one relationship with other territories, that would demote narrative qualities and properties to mere supporting roles. Instead, they should be designed, calculated, and outlined in their own right, not pressed into service to illustrate the plot or the action.

For the intensity distribution of narrative qualities or properties over the game as a whole, think less about dramatic structure and more about choreography. As an excellent starting point, check out Chanel Summers's rundown for the auditory domain in "Making the Most of Audio in Characterization, Narrative Structure, and Level Design." Its guidance and instructions for organizing "moods, intensity levels, pacing, dynamics, and transitions" can easily be adapted for the other three domains, and you can explore and expand from there.

As a collateral benefit, involving all four perceptual domains will meet different types of *learning styles*: visual, auditory, or kinesthetic. Indeed, these are three out of the four basic types of learning (the fourth being reading/writing). Is there a "mythological learning style?" Not in that exact definition. But when it comes to making sense of the world and of ourselves, the mythological domain just crushes it. Note, though, that this is about "learning styles," not "learners." Preferred learning styles are not an immutable characteristic; they can change with topic, age, and even the time of day.

With regard to distribution and dramatic intensity, there's one fundamental problem left to discuss: repetition. This problem pops up every time the player fails at a task and has to replay the same beat again and again.

For auditory matter, this problem is well-known and addressed in the literature quite a lot. Solutions, alas, are few and far between, and they usually apply only to specific types of games. In *Game Sound*, Karen Collins shows alongside her analysis of *Myst* how high dramatic intensity would be detrimental to puzzle-heavy games, where the player might be stuck for any amount of time. Thus, minimal, slow-paced, ambient audio seems to be the best choice for this type of game. But what about other types of games, particularly games built around high dramatic intensity? What about boss fights? Boss fights are designed to be difficult and frequently necessitate multiple replays by design! Then, different player types pose yet another problem, as pointed out by Richard Stevens and Dave Raybould in *The Game Audio Tutorial*: those who slowly sneak their way through a dramatic unit; those who blaze through it; and those who turn every pixel upside down before they leave (creepers, blazers, and completists, as they call them). Instead of solving our initial intensity problem, we now have two problems!

What is often recommended is adaptive sound, a topic briefly discussed in the *Plurimediality* territory. But adaptive sound alone doesn't fully solve the problem of forced repetition. And it certainly doesn't solve the problem for the other three perceptual domains. The epic vista that is revealed at the beginning of the boss fight, the spectacular monstrosity of the boss enemy itself, the sounds and taunts, the movements and combos, the arresting parade of mythical signifiers—all that, after the 10th or 20th rehearsal, will appear no less moth-eaten and irritating than the swelling strings with heavy brass stabs, or the emerging machine grooves over relentless techno beats.

Are there solutions that are more comprehensive? Possibly, but perhaps not for our cherished rinse-and-repeat mechanic. Player failure in games is almost always non-diegetic—when the player character dies and respawns, that death didn't happen in the game world. There are exceptions, certainly, like *Shadow of Mordor*'s undead ranger in combination with the Nemesis system. By making player failure diegetic, repeat encounters can take previous encounters into consideration and play out differently and with different intensities.

For non-diegetic repetitions and the rinse-and-repeat mechanic, you have to craft your own imaginative solutions.

Beat 3: Ambience

Memos and Memories

Although it falls squarely into the *Narrativity* territory, "environmental storytelling" hasn't been mentioned so far for two reasons. First, it's the level boss you have to face in this beat. Then, the term as such is somewhat misleading and not as productive as one might wish. Instead, we're going to use the term "world narrative," as introduced by Tynan Sylvester in *Designing Games*.

Here's why. The world narrative isn't about stories or storytelling at all. Instead, it's about information related to the game world that is embedded in the game world in narrative form. It delivers insights and meaning, not plot points and midpoints. What's more, the player can leave traces in the world to become part of the world narrative, which isn't something the term environmental storytelling suggests at all.

Moreover, the terms "narrative" and "narrativity" are more intimately connected to each other than either term is to "story" or "storytelling." You will find a more in-depth discussion of the difference between narrative and story in the *Architectonics* territory, but here's the rundown.

Story is about *what* is told, the content; it has an *ending*, or at least some perceptible kind of resolution or closure that may or may not encourage a sequel; any element that's not part of the story belongs to a *different* story; and it is *impervious to participation* (cue: interactivity).

Narrative is about *how* something is told, the structure; it is *open-ended* as new elements can join at any time; it can *include* not just one, but many stories; and it *invites participation* (think: social narratives, "grand" historical narratives, and so on).

Following these premises, the world narrative has two key functions.

The world narrative should **make the game world accessible to the player** (so that the player gains an understanding of the game world and can engage with it in meaningful ways).

The world narrative should **make player actions accessible to the game world** (so that the game world gains an understanding of the player and reacts to their presence in meaningful ways).

Let's start with the first. Making your game world accessible to the player is related to, but by no means identical with, exposition. Exposition is part of your game's dramatic structure, discussed in detail in the *Architectonics* territory. Within plot structures, for example, exposition prepares the ground for the inciting incident. The world narrative, in contrast, is much broader than that, and parts of it can and should be communicated even before the game is actually released.

On how to establish the world narrative in the visual, auditory, and, to a degree, kinesthetic domains, there's a whole world of books and lectures and presentations out there, and you can adapt almost any domain-specific tool and technique for this purpose. Thus, let's focus on the mythological domain. It's exceptionally powerful in that regard, but it comes with a caveat—while setting, location/environment, backstory, and lore are all well-suited to communicate parts of the world narrative, not all of these elements are universally accepted for that task, for historical reasons.

Let's begin with setting. The importance of the setting is uncontroversial. Not only will your game's setting influence your target audience's buying decisions significantly, as discussed in the Preparation phase. It will also do much of the heavy lifting that's needed to pull your player into your game right away.

This holds true for more general settings like science fiction, fantasy, final frontier, or contemporary; for more specific settings like Victorian steampunk or World War II; and even for that brand-new, very peculiar setting that you just made up. It's about personal interests, one way or another. Even people with more eclectic leisure-time pursuits make buying decisions, and these buying decisions are based on their preferences. For potential buyers of action RPGs, for example, it's the setting that will tip their scales in favor of *Dragon Age* or in favor of *Mass Effect*.

To communicate your setting and establish important parts of your world narrative efficiently, elegantly, and as early as possible, you can use your vision statement, your cover art, your game trailer, and—just for the record—a well-known IP.

The first line of communication to get your setting across is your vision statement, based on your desire-driven goal from the Procedure phase. It can be as elaborate as some of the examples we sketched there. For the purpose of the world narrative, however, it can also reveal a lot less or even be minimalist, like this example from Ernest W. Adams's *Fundamentals of Game Design*: "The game at its grittiest. No pads, no helmets, no refs, no field. It's just you and the guys, a ball, and a lot of asphalt. Choose up sides and go for it, two on two." It compactifies a good number of setting elements into vivid mythical tropes that are easily understood.

Next, you can disclose setting elements through your digital cover art, which should also be part of your passage design, as discussed in the *Plurimediality* territory. A vivid presentation of your game's style, space, and gameplay interface goes a long way toward communicating its setting.

Then, a trailer. As trailers aren't interactive, you can use cinematic techniques to communicate elements of your setting. Indeed, and this will probably raise some eyebrows, cinematic game trailers should focus on the setting through style, space, and atmosphere, to stimulate familiarity with and curiosity about the game world. A cinematic trailer is not a game; it's a completely different medium. To communicate actual gameplay, that's what a dedicated in-game trailer or demo should be for. Talking of which, there was a time when you could download a demo level or two from almost any game before and during release. You can still do that and provide your polished prototype as a demo, if you have one. But especially for shorter indie games, there's really no difference in terms of effort and time between downloading and installing a demo and downloading and installing the game. So even if you provide a demo, you should have communicated your setting sufficiently well by then.

Finally, the easiest and most convenient way to communicate your game's setting is when that setting is already well-known! As an indie developer, the only way to get there is to establish your own IP first, your intellectual property, to be discussed more in-depth in the Proposition phase. But if your studio is really large, perhaps, and you have a publisher who has a lot of confidence in you, you could try to obtain a license for a well-known intellectual property. Now, while the pros and cons of licensing IPs are outside the scope of this book, it's mostly about weighing up licensing fees against marketing costs; working on something cool and cherished; and struggling to carve out your creative space without upsetting the canon or the licensor. If your game is set a long time ago in a galaxy far, far away or in mines where dwarves dug too deep and disturbed a demon, or the player character has a double-0 in their name or fights vampires with a silver-plated titanium sword, players from your target audience have not only a solid buying incentive but can make meaningful decisions in your game world right away. As mentioned, however, this is only for the record. For an indie developer, it's an unlikely path.

Let's proceed from setting to location/environment. Its importance and usefulness to establish elements of the world narrative is even more uncontroversial than that of the setting. It has received a lot of attention, and world narratives communicated by great locations/environments keep receiving a lot of praise.

As mentioned, you can communicate elements of the world narrative in your locale or level with artistic abstraction techniques—archetypes, memes, chunks, associative relations, compression, simplification, exaggeration, metonymy/metaphor, symbolism, and so on. With these techniques, you can convey conditions like lawlessness, suburban affluence, repressed collective memories, economic upswing, simmering tension, grit and courage in difficult times, growing authoritarianism, rampant racism, and almost everything else you want that specific locale to convey.

What's more, these tools can also provide support for individual gameplay moments. For a specific beat, for example, your location/environment can convey a wrong turn, unnatural calm, spiritual potential, lingering malice, a decisive encounter, a momentous decision, impending loss, or comic relief. Not as plot points, mind—we're in the *Narrativity* territory, and these are elements of your world narrative. As such, they communicate aspects and perspectives of your game world by evoking specific emotions and conveying insights and meaning through narrative qualities or properties. They can augment and enrich a plot point, certainly. But the plot point must stand on its own. Plus, not to forget, these gameplay moments should always relate to your theme or an associated motif.

Let's demonstrate the difference between a plot point, an element of the world narrative that defines a level or locale, and an element of the world narrative that defines an individual gameplay moment with the help of an example. Let's imagine we're working on a first-person single-player game with a cinematological core and "identity" as its theme. The player character struggles to explore and preserve a precarious cultural identity that's been all but assimilated by an all-encompassing mainstream culture.

For our beat, the player character has been led to a hitherto unexplored urban district to find an artifact related to their culture. How would that scene play out if it were a plot point, a world narrative element that defines a level or a locale, or a world narrative element that supports an individual gameplay moment?

> *As a plot point.* Finding the artifact is an important plot point that presents new challenges and necessitates player decisions. The artifact reveals that the urban district where the player has tracked it down was the quarter where the very first immigrants from the player character's culture had lived and died, an important historic location that hitherto had been concealed or unknown.
>
> *As a world narrative element that defines a level or locale.* Finding the artifact reveals a new, recurring locale that the player can explore. Checking your theme, "identity," and your list of motifs, you decide on an urban district level that undergoes massive gentrification, to highlight the loss of locally defined identity when people are incrementally edged out of the neighborhood they had grown up, lived, and died in for generations.
>
> *As a world narrative element for an individual gameplay moment.* Finding the artifact should deliver a strong, emotional impact on the player. Checking your theme, "identity," and your list of motifs, you decide to design the living room and the personal belongings of the NPC who owns that artifact with all the telltale signs of personality changes brought about by neurodegenerative diseases like Alzheimer's, which is then reinforced by the NPCs behavior. This should also make the artifact more valuable for the player through the "misattribution of arousal" effect, as discussed previously.

Each of these three options, in turn, will affect subsequent design decisions. The plot point option will probably be well-suited to progress the main quest; the locale option to offer a collection of side quests; and the gameplay moment option might be part of a sequence of beats to let the player grow emotionally and change their attitude. The artifact can still be a plot point in the second and third option, even a momentous one, but it has to stand on its own feet. In both cases, though, your world narrative can make the plot point more interesting and emotionally more intense.

After setting and location/environment, the third element we want to look at is backstory. In contrast to the first two, backstory has been a bone of contention throughout the history of video games. One of the more radical views, expressed by Chris Crawford in *Chris Crawford on Game Design*, is that backstory is not part of the game and should therefore be dismissed altogether.

To some extent, this prejudice against backstory is a residuum from the early age of video games. With the technology available at the time, any backstory printed on the back of a cartridge box or inside a manual was way beyond what could be accomplished in code, and therefore not at all likely to correspond to actual gameplay in any recognizable way. The unlikeliness between a game's elaborate backstory and what actually happened in-game was every bit as astounding as the unlikeliness between box art and actual gameplay, as examples like *Space Invaders* or *Star Ship* for the Atari 2600 can attest to. As Chris Crawford put it in *On Interactive Storytelling*, you would "read grandiose tales in the manual and then confront orange and purple squares buzzing about on the screen."

Yet, backstories were not perfectly gratuitous even then. They served a marketing purpose, and that counts for something. Over time, though, all that has changed with advances in technology. Video games are now able to accommodate anything that cover art and backstory can throw at them. When backstory became translatable into code and thus into the game itself, it also became a full-grown world narrative tool. Today, its narrative qualities or properties can serve the entire set of dramatic functions that we discussed in the previous beat: portray a character, communicate an insight into the game world, highlight an aspect related to the theme or its motifs, elicit an emotional response, advance player proficiency, or push the player toward the goal.

One of the most widely used backstory tools to accomplish this are log files or diary entries to read or listen to that the player character comes across. In *Unreal*, as a venerable example, some of these little pieces of information portray the character who has left the note behind. Many communicate insights about the world, its inhabitants, how things used to be, and what has changed during the alien invaders' occupation. Many elicit an emotional response as miniature stories about hope, struggle, suffering, and defeat, and many push the player toward the goal, one way or another.

From the time on that diaries or log files were repurposed from modest puzzle elements to carriers of the world narrative, they've often been hailed as the knight in shining armor who had delivered games from the long-standing problem of communicating backstory through terrible exposition. Which it hadn't, of course. In-game, not all log files or diary entries are particularly plausible as to how, when, and why they were created and how they wound up in the player character's path. Also, many games took to clobbering the player with an endless assault of diaries, log files, voice recordings, and assorted news briefs. Which doesn't mean that this tool has become bad practice, far from it. It's a question of measure and restraint. There is a huge difference between a short, succinct log entry that delivers an emotionally charged glimpse into an unfamiliar world, as in our *Unreal* example, and an interminable holographic illumination reminiscent of a poorly delivered thesis defense. (Looking at you, *Horizon Zero Dawn,* an otherwise immensely enjoyable game.)

There's one crucial backstory issue, however, that can rarely be solved with diaries or log files: the backstory of the player character. *Unreal*, our core example, evades this issue entirely—the player will never know more about the player character than that she, or he, is Prisoner 849. Many other famous games also didn't bother with it in-game, like the marine from *Doom* or Gordon Freeman in the original *Half-Life*, relegating their backgrounds to guides or manuals. Diaries or log files might work with player character amnesia, another staple of game design. But beyond that, the background of the player character has to be communicated through exposition. Which, as part of a game's dramatic structure, is discussed in the *Architectonics* territory.

Diaries or log files and their many cousins—letters, tapes, voice recordings, or loquacious holograms—are all focused on individual and often private communication. They're not your only options! There's a huge box with tools out there to convey backstory through collective and often public communication, including signposts, blackboards, information terminals, banners, protest signs, graffiti, PSAs, news headlines, news articles, television or radio broadcasts, commercials, and many more. Then, it should at least be mentioned, there are peculiarities like codex entries and item descriptions that are neither private nor public communication. They're often attached to things the player can collect during gameplay; they're often so loosely integrated as to be almost non-diegetic; and they rarely reveal background information that truly matters. But they could.

There's one more tool, frequently used and misused, to deliver backstory we haven't mentioned yet: non-player characters talking to each other within the player character's earshot. This is a very dangerous tool. It tempts you to deliver dramatically relevant content, which is always a terrible practice. Instead, dialogues between non-player characters should communicate backstory through displays of emotion and attitude—for example, their conversation topic, language, body language, or word choice. So with that axe, be careful.

The fourth and final element to communicate world narrative in the mythical domain is lore. Earlier in this level, we used the remote mining colony to explore aspects from all four perceptual domains. In that context, lore was defined as "the stories people from that outpost tell themselves." That was meant literally. Lore is oral tradition, largely transmitted through non-recorded speech like tales, legends, proverbs, and jokes; through ballads, chants, and songs; and through rituals and ceremonies. Or, surprise, through no speech at all—for all the things that "go without saying" until the player character bumps into them, often unpleasantly. Any of these forms of transmission, in turn, might be reflected by cultural artifacts, some of which we will look at further below.

Here's an example. If your player character picks up information about that stronghold in the mountains from the colony's library, that's backstory. If a non-player character official mentions to you that some people who went there mysteriously vanished, that's still backstory. But when non-player characters are shocked that you want to go there to check it out, and try to dissuade you because "everybody knows" that the stronghold is cursed with bad luck and possibly infested with demons, that's lore. And that fanciful playground song you overheard, about the girl who went to the stronghold to learn what fear was? That's lore too.

Now, imagine you travel to a city that you never visited before. You visit the farmer's market and pester people with questions. What "secrets" should one know about this city? Have there been "strange rumors" lately? Are there things about which "y'all only dare to whisper?" Outside of games, this would not end well in any time period or setting. It's also tiresome for the player. Communicating lore by having the player milk a dialogue wheel to its last breath is not a recommended tool.

What you should do instead is give the player the opportunity to watch and observe, and then ask specific questions about what appears odd or inexplicable. For example, when non-player characters get uneasy over certain topics or have a habit of decorating their drapes with oodles of garlic, that's worth a question or two. Alternatively, you can let the player just go about their business until non-player characters are startled or begin to look at the player character askance. Then the player can try to find out where they inadvertently stepped on something sensitive that "goes without saying."

Here's how you can get started. Your tools, remember, are tools for artistic abstraction, to create pieces of art and elements of myth with well-defined narrative qualities or properties. Your player character can learn about local lore by listening to songs, chants, prayers, poetry, stories, tall tales, fairy tales, jokes and bantering, insults, proverbs and sayings, oaths, and all the "frozen metaphors" people use on a daily basis in their speech; by looking at paintings and photographs, sculpture, embroidery, quilts, rugs and tapestry, architecture and architectural peculiarities, and handicraft on the whole; by watching or attending festivities and festivals, rituals, ceremonies, celebrations, performances, children's games, and drinking customs; and by taking part in day-to-day activities in general. Many if not all of these manifestations of lore can tell a miniature story, but the story is not the point. The narrative qualities and properties attached to these manifestations are the point.

Now that we went through the elements of the mythical domain one by one, don't forget that these elements—setting, location/environment, backstory, and lore—and the elements from the other three perceptual domains—visual, auditory, and kinesthetic—should mutually reinforce each other. In some cases, if you do it right, the sum of your design decisions in all four perceptual domains can become so integral to your game and its gameplay that it elevates your world narrative to a character in its own right.

BioShock, as an outstanding example, integrates all four domains in such unique ways that its world narrative becomes a dynamic, living manifestation of its theme. Which, all things considered, seems to be "self-interest," from where it explores a range of related motifs from Objectivism's ethical egoism to naked greed along their impact on society and the individual. In their 2010 GDC presentation "What Happened Here: Environmental Storytelling," Matthias Worch and Harvey Smith pick one notable example from *BioShock* and demonstrate how the world narrative operates in this game. In that particular beat, the player character comes across a dead resident of Rapture, crushed to death by the vending machine he had attempted to loot. Not only does this scene represent, in classical nutshell technique, self-interest and its consequences, it also subtly entraps or seduces the player to adopt the very same behavior that this element of the world narrative exemplifies. Looting vending machines doesn't look like a particularly terrible act, but decisions of the same type will have to be made later, on a larger scale and with more substantial repercussions. Also, this element of the world narrative carries over into the game's *Architectonics* territory by fulfilling dramatic functions (it compresses the entire story into one single allegorical scene or beat, the "nutshell," as a type of foreshadowing), and into the *Interactivity* territory as well by teaching the player where to find resources (and adopt the questionable behavior all this is about). *BioShock*, after all, is a truly well-designed game, throughout all dimensions and territories.

To wrap it up, you should sketch everything you want your world narrative to convey, so that artists and writers, perhaps including you, can pick up the tools from all four perceptual domains and create a rich world narrative for your game.

Which is the first part of beating the level boss, and here's the other part. It's about the second, less voluminous key function of the world narrative: to make player actions accessible to the game world in ways that the game world gains an understanding of the player, so that the game world can react to the player's presence in meaningful ways. "Player," from here on, should always be read as a shorthand for "the actions and decisions made by the player and performed in the game world by their avatar, the player character," which is technically more correct, but unwieldy. The game world itself won't mind—as the player does not exist there, the game world cannot differentiate between player and player character in any case.

Now, how the game world reacts to player actions should always be determined by two parameters that go hand in hand: *what* the player accomplishes in the game world or not, and *how* the player accomplishes this or not.

Let's say the player decides to fight a formidable demon instead of bribing it or taking a different route altogether and manages to subdue it. That's the *what*. It's a brutal fight that lasts for hours until the exhausted demon gives up. That's the *how*. In what manner should the world react to it? People might hear about it through eyewitnesses or rumors, scribes might write about it in annals or chronicles, bards might sing about it, and demon lore pundits might analyze it on medieval talk radio. The important point is to scale the reaction correctly. The world should react to the event in principle (the *what*), and it should react to it in a manner appropriate to how the event played out (the *how*). How strong and how famous was the adversary? How difficult was it to overcome that adversary? How well did it go? Who has heard about it from whom, and how might the story have been embellished (or lampooned) along the way? Reactions don't always have to be appropriate, mind—information rarely travels unscathed. Non-player characters might recognize the player character and be awestruck because they've heard stories from a traveling bard about an epic fight, while all the player character did was win a fistfight against the bartender over an underfilled beer mug in Torgor's Inn.

Whether all this comes down to heroic recognition, comedic confusion, dramatic misunderstandings, or outright slapstick depends on the nature of your game and its theme. Moreover, all this doesn't have to be realistic, or even plausible. Frequently in medieval poems and tales, early Arthurian legends prominently among them, everybody in the story world knows, instantaneously and down to the minutest detail, what happens to important characters at any time, everywhere—when and how they succeed, when and how they screw up, even their intentions. Always create your own rules, deliberately, that fit your game world best.

Some games, like the *Red Dead* series or later installments of *Deus Ex*, track player actions through broadcasts or newspapers. *Hitman: Blood Money*'s "notoriety system," though, goes beyond that in interesting ways, as pointed out by Tynan Sylvester in *Designing Games*. Press clippings are generated after each mission that track Agent 47's actions not only in terms of "what," but also in terms of "how." Depending on how the mission played out, eyewitness accounts differ considerably, which also affects the quality of police sketch drawings. In that way, *Hitman: Blood Money* ingeniously establishes and intertwines both functions of the world narrative: players can engage with the game world in meaningful ways; and the game world reacts to these player actions in believable ways.

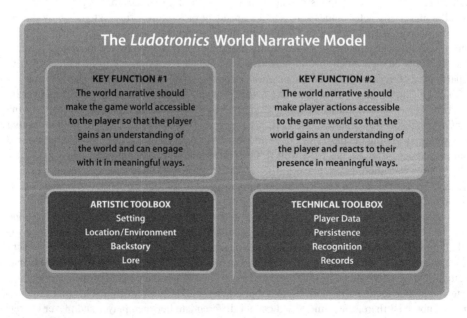

The *Ludotronics* World Narrative Model

KEY FUNCTION #1	KEY FUNCTION #2
The world narrative should make the game world accessible to the player so that the player gains an understanding of the world and can engage with it in meaningful ways.	The world narrative should make player actions accessible to the game world so that the world gains an understanding of the player and reacts to their presence in meaningful ways.
ARTISTIC TOOLBOX Setting Location/Environment Backstory Lore	**TECHNICAL TOOLBOX** Player Data Persistence Recognition Records

FIGURE 4.30 World narrative model.

This solution, moreover, enables the player to track and archive their own narrative path in a way that is deeply embedded into the game world. What players can record in other games, habitually in diaries or journals, is often not sufficient to keep track of all that has happened. Which is especially true for long and complex games like RPGs, as Allegra Frank rightfully laments in "RPGs Need In-Game Recaps to Help Us Out." Another option, popular with racing games, is a mechanic to record and replay player actions. A more recent and final example are photo collections—a technique that has evolved from fairly generic automatic screenshots to player characters making their own photos in-game with a smartphone, as in *Uncharted: The Lost Legacy*. There are certainly more options out there that you can find. But you can also try to come up with your own clever solutions.

All this should be part of your concept. Provide the means to make the world narrative accessible to the player, the means to make the player narrative accessible to the game world, and the means for the player to keep track of what has transpired. That way, player actions in the game world will not only have consequences. They will also have *meaning*.

Outlook

The processes of artistic abstraction, the tools and techniques to attach narrative qualities or properties to visual, auditory, kinesthetic, and mythological matter for meaningful gameplay moments and a memorable playing experience—all these will need top-notch professional input and execution from artists and writers. Among whom, of course, could be you. At this point in time, to beat this level, you don't have to create these elements. But you need to sketch out what your world narrative should convey. Which, importantly, also includes an intensity map for all four perceptual domains that corresponds to your level plan, your learning curves from the *Interactivity* territory, and your development arcs from the *Architectonics* territory.

Finally, as always, you have to ask yourself the familiar questions. Will these ideas and sketches vibe with your target audience? Are they compatible with your value set and your USP? Do they always draw from your theme and motifs? Do they support the player motivation model and connect the player to the game world in terms of relatedness/community, and infuse—through the power of emotional involvement—a sense of purpose and a worthwhile goal?

Should the answers to all these questions be yes, you have conquered this level!

Level Five

Architectonics

Opening

As defined back in the Preliminary phase, *Architectonics* denotes the design and arrangement of the game's dramatic structure as a *holistic* structure that encompasses both the game's narrative elements and its mechanic elements like rules, difficulty progression, and similar.

An advanced example that demonstrates this principle is Brenda Romero's *The Mechanics Is the Message* collection, especially *Train*, where the rules and the narrative are one and the same. A simpler and much more common example is the level boss. Here, ideally, all three dramatic development arcs—to be introduced soon—terminate in an event with player action at its center: a plot point from the story development arc; a journey stage from the character development arc; and a proficiency target from the player development arc.

In too many games, plot points and journey stages are not interlocked with player action but set up as cutscenes. Integrating all three development arcs into player action is at the very heart of the *Architectonics* territory. To get there, a lot of ground will have to be covered in the upcoming beats, from dramatic structure and empathic tasks to dramatic choice and player decisions to functional characters and the dramatic ensemble.

Not everything in this level will be applicable to games that are not dramatically complete. But dramatic structure neither equals story (we will come back to that in a minute), nor is it exclusive to dramatically complete games. Chess, the game of Go, *Tetris*, or *Unreal Tournament* are not dramatically complete games, but they are great games nevertheless, which they wouldn't be without a dramatic structure! Thus, we will also have a closer look at the dramatic structure of games that are *not* dramatically complete.

What this level will not do is go astray and venture into the vast, perilous, and beautiful realms of game writing. Game writing demands a book of its own. In a later beat, for example, we will discuss the various dramatic functions of non-player characters (NPCs) in scholarly detail, but we won't discuss how to write compelling characters that come alive in the game world.

Similarly, there's the difference between story (what happens) and plot (how it happens, i.e., the dramatic structure). There are useful definitions for both terms waiting to be picked from the shelf; but to sound out how they relate to games, we first need to take a detour.

One of the central topics discussed in the *Interactivity* territory is unpredictability in its different forms, particularly randomness, contingency, and complexity. For our purposes in this territory, we must draw another distinction: perfect information and imperfect knowledge.

Games whose unpredictability resides primarily in the *Interactivity* territory can be games with perfect information, like chess or Go or many video games with a game-mechanical core. Everything that can be objectively known and observed about a game state can be known by all players. (Subjective, unobservable information like intentions and assumptions, of course, remains objectively hidden.) Here in the *Architectonics* territory, in contrast, unpredictability is a function of subjective uncertainty, primarily produced by imperfect knowledge—information the player does not yet have and information the player does not yet know exists, all strategically positioned in ways we call *dramatic structure* and, more specifically, *plot*. That's where unpredictability resides in games that have stories—which, naturally, are strongly predetermined, no matter how many endings a game provides.

Importantly, stories are *designed*. As such, what happens in stories is neither random nor contingent (the concept of contingency is discussed in-depth in the *Interactivity* territory). What's more, everything that

DOI: 10.1201/9781003334682-21

happens in a story has to have discernible *causes*, or reasons. Otherwise, the story won't "work"—except with a theme relating to the idea that nothing we do makes much sense anyway because the quest for meaning is futile, like the Theater of the Absurd. Beyond causes and reasons, moreover, designed elements must have a discernible *purpose*. In a game story, in particular, the purpose of any event should be to advance the plot, portray a character, communicate an insight into the game world, highlight an aspect related to the theme or its motifs, elicit an emotion, or, and that's of paramount importance, stand in some relation to player proficiency and the game-driven goal. Reality can't possibly do that, thanks to contingency; reality can neither be coherent nor consistent in that sense. That's why reality is a poor writer of stories. What happens in real life is altogether too fantastic and confusing and too seemingly random on the surface to be enjoyable. Reality, after all, does not provide insights into itself. Science provides them, and so does art. Now, to be honest, purpose and insight as well as coherence and consistency are not the premier elements that come to mind when asked wherein video games traditionally excel. But games have evolved technologically, artistically, and professionally (in terms of craft and knowledge), and so have player expectations. Games are well on their way to become as sensitive and as vulnerable to being criticized for incoherence and inconsistencies as any novel, painting, movie, building, typeface, or television show.

Plot, now, is the story's dramatic structure. You might have heard of E. M. Forster's example where "The king died and then the queen died" is a story, whereas "The king died, and then the queen died of grief" is a plot. This covers causality, which is valuable, but there's a lot more that separates story from plot. A plot is a chain of causally related, significant events, organized and arranged into a specific sequence to create specific artistic and emotional effects, and to make everything that happens in the course of the story plausible and necessary. To "plot" a game or a movie or a novel is much more complicated and demanding than to create a "story." Consider how tightly any given story can be compressed into ever more abstract constituents. Even the most sprawling story can be zipped into an incredibly tiny package:

> *A smallish human inherits a piece of mind-enslaving jewelry, is advised to destroy it, and goes on a perilous quest to throw it into the fire of the active volcano it was originally forged in.*

You can't do that with plot. Plot can't be descriptively compressed. Moreover, plotting is an exceptionally demanding and merciless task that will occupy writers for extended periods of time especially when it's a *great* story.

> A plot is a chain of causally related, significant events, organized and arranged into a specific sequence to create specific artistic and emotional effects, and to make everything that happens in the course of the story plausible and necessary.

If your game happens to have a story, you will sketch it with a number of plot points for your story development arc in the upcoming beats, along journey stages for your character development arc and proficiency targets for your player development arc. For your prototype and your proposal, however, you will need someone with writing skills to develop the story and its dramatic structure to respectable levels. If you're a writer, of course, that could be you!

With regard to our motivational building, the *Architectonics* territory is strongly associated with "meaningful choices" from the interactive playing experience model, and through that with the autonomy/agency element from our player motivation model. However, as will be seen, it also connects to purpose/goal in important ways.

Beat 1: Partitioning

Quantifying and Qualifying

To establish a basic dramatic structure for video games, we need to differentiate between dramatic partitioning and dramatic development first: the playing experience is *quantified* by the former and *qualified* by the latter.

First, the dramatic partitioning.

Beat. A distinct event within a game level. It is roughly equivalent to the "beat" as the smallest unit of measurement in a screenplay, except it's not limited to story elements and doesn't have to be short. In games that are not dramatically complete, beats can correspond to a defined player action like traversing a series of platforms, arranging an item set to solve a puzzle, repel an attack, or reach a safe spot or save point.

Level. A unit that frames a specific goal (usually a level objective), place, time, motif, or player proficiency (if either change, it becomes a different level). It's roughly equivalent to the familiar dramatic unit of a "scene," but in terms of duration more similar to scenes in a stage play than to the considerably shorter scenes of a screenplay. The motif can either be a single motif associated with the game's overall theme, or a combination of closely related or interdependent motifs.

Sequence. A group of two or more game levels unified by common aspects of any kind, equivalent to how the term "sequence" is used in a screenplay.

Act. A major segment within a game serving a specific dramatic function, which can be everything from a single act to usually not more than five, equivalent to the familiar dramatic unit of an "act."

With the exception of levels, the partitioning scheme follows traditional play/screenplay patterns for both unit distribution and naming conventions. The level, moreover, echoes the original Aristotelian unity of action, place, and time, albeit with necessary adjustments—the addition of motif and player proficiency on the one hand, and the replacement of Aristotle's "original action" by the goal or level objective on the other.

However, while this is the most familiar pattern and a very effective one, it's not set in stone. It can be tinkered with, replaced by dramatic partitioning schemes of different cultural origins, or abandoned for something entirely new.

Then, the dramatic development.

Story development arc. This is an arc that evolves through effectively placed dramatic events, either by applying dramatic elements known from plays and screenplays (inciting incident, turning point, pinch, escalation, climax, and such), or by applying elements from different structures, both Western and non-Western, like kishōtenketsu, jo-ha-kyū, or repetition-break.

Character development arc. This is an arc that the player character goes through in the form of an inner journey, represented by structures based on Western and non-Western myths, prominently among them the hero's journey, but also Chinese box (nested narratives), nostos (the return home), or the medieval quest (very peculiar), often outwardly expressed through actual travels.

Player development arc. This is an arc that the player goes through by mastering challenges, among them well-placed and well-paced progressions of game mechanics and combinations of game mechanics, through actions and decisions.

Both the dramatic partitioning and the dramatic development structures are less like manuals and more like recipes. If you follow them, you'll probably create something delicious. But you're free to experiment with different setups and, possibly, create a whole new experience.

Nevertheless, the tripartite structure of the dramatic development is a core aspect of the *Ludotronics* methodology. Integrating the player development arc deeply and deliberately with the story development arc and the character development arc is the primary reason for the *Architectonics* territory's very existence.

Unfortunately, the latter two—the story and character development arcs—are often treated as if they were one and the same, which they are not. Apparently, just like Poe's purloined letter, the difference between the two is so obvious and in plain view that it eludes perception. To substantiate this difference,

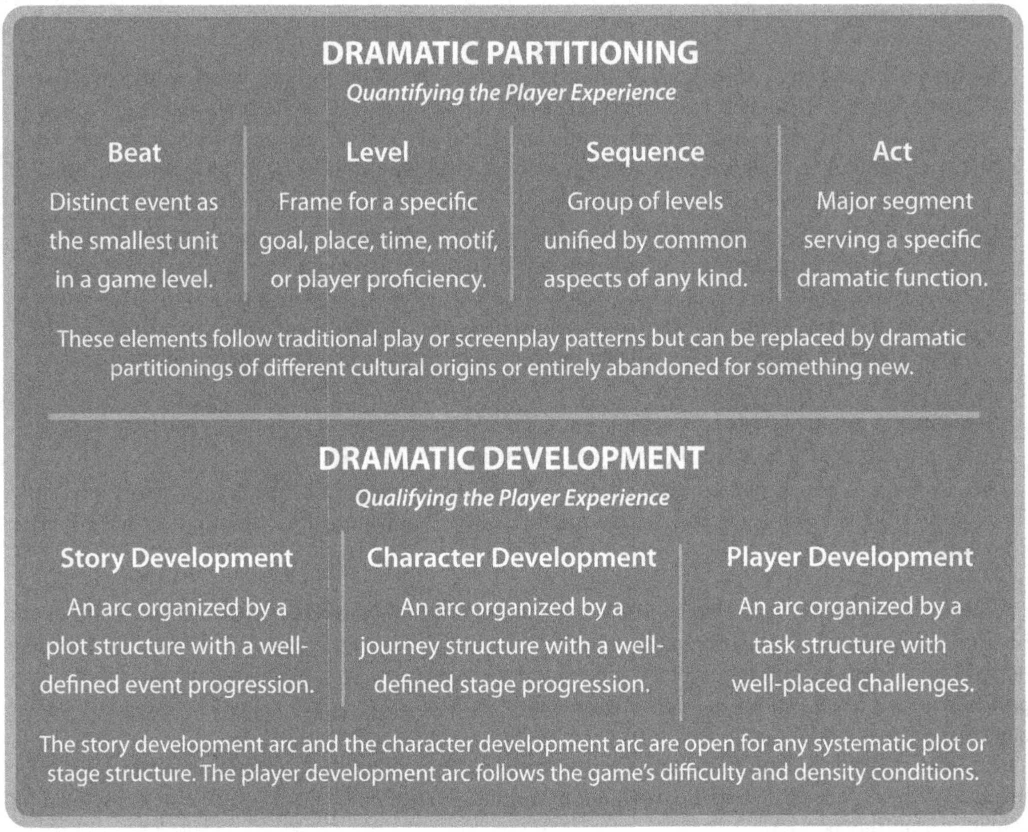

DRAMATIC PARTITIONING
Quantifying the Player Experience

Beat	Level	Sequence	Act
Distinct event as the smallest unit in a game level.	Frame for a specific goal, place, time, motif, or player proficiency.	Group of levels unified by common aspects of any kind.	Major segment serving a specific dramatic function.

These elements follow traditional play or screenplay patterns but can be replaced by dramatic partitionings of different cultural origins or entirely abandoned for something new.

DRAMATIC DEVELOPMENT
Qualifying the Player Experience

Story Development	Character Development	Player Development
An arc organized by a plot structure with a well-defined event progression.	An arc organized by a journey structure with a well-defined stage progression.	An arc organized by a task structure with well-placed challenges.

The story development arc and the character development arc are open for any systematic plot or stage structure. The player development arc follows the game's difficulty and density conditions.

FIGURE 4.31   Dramatic units.

let's look at two examples: the original *Star Wars* movie from 1977, deservedly famous for its adoption of the structure of the hero's journey, and James Cameron's *Titanic* from 1997.

For *Star Wars*, you might have come across those fringe discussions on the web on where the original *Star Wars* movie truly begins—when Leia's ship is pursued and entered by a boarding party, or when Luke receives Leia's message through R2-D2's holographic projection. That's a remarkably unproductive question from the category of not even wrong. First off, *Star Wars* begins when *Star Wars* begins, with the opening crawl. Next, the boarding of the diplomatic ship is the *inciting incident*, a dramatic element from plays or screenplays, and as such the beginning of the story development arc. Why is it the inciting incident? The screenplay—through several dialogues, first between Leia and Vader and then between Vader and Daine Jir—goes out of its way to emphasize that the violent takeover of a diplomatic ship is *not* business as usual. It's the first "imbalance" that the inciting incident is assigned to create, the first step toward upsetting the world's existing order. In this example, the imbalance will lead to the dissolution of the Imperial Senate and the Republic shortly thereafter. The world's balance is reinstated at the end through the destruction of the Death Star, courtesy of the stolen plans the inciting incident was about in the first place. Then, there's Leia's holographic recording that R2-D2 uses in its abbreviated form to lure Luke into removing that pesky restraining bolt. This is the kick-off for the character development arc, structured after the hero's journey, known as the Call to Adventure. It leads Luke in rapid succession to the journey's subsequent elements of the Refusal of the Call (Luke doesn't want to leave the farm), the Supernatural Aid (Obi Wan), and the Crossing of the First Threshold (leaving Tatooine and entering the Death Star).

Then, James Cameron's *Titanic*. Smack in the middle of the script, you'll find three consecutive scenes: Jack and Rose make love in a 1912 Renault Towncar in the cargo hold; Rose's fiancé discovers Jack's drawing of Rose and her telltale note; and the RMS *Titanic* hits an iceberg. These events, you probably guessed it, belong to different dramatic structures. On the one hand, there's Rose's "Apotheosis" or "Initiation," the "innermost cave" element from the hero's journey, as part of her character development arc. Making love in an automobile in the *Titanic*'s cargo hold is as innermost cave-ish as it gets. On the other hand, there's the fiancé realizing that Rose and Jack have an affair, and there's the *Titanic* hitting an iceberg. Together, they form the so-called Act II *midpoint* plot point from Syd Field's screenwriting paradigm, which spins the action into a different direction. (Why two events, the fiancé's realization *and* the collision? Well, it's a love story against the background of the sinking of the *Titanic*, not an action movie about the sinking of the *Titanic* with a love interest thrown in, that's one reason. Also, we know the collision will happen, so it can't spin everything into a different direction alone.) Thus, we have the midpoint's double-whammy from the story development arc and Rose's apotheosis from the character development arc neatly side by side in the middle of the script, exactly where they belong.

In both movies, *Star Wars* and *Titanic*, the story development arc and the character development arc operate on different levels but blend into each other so seamlessly and beautifully that their elements seem all of a piece.

The second thing we need to clear up, after differentiating between the story development arc and the character development arc, is how these arcs can possibly exist in games that are not dramatically complete, i.e., games with a game-mechanical or ludological core, or perhaps even a cinematological core, that have no story.

As you might remember from the Procedure phase, even a game like *Pong* runs the whole gamut of game-mechanical, ludological, cinematological, and narratological elements, however bare-bones. Still, it doesn't necessarily indicate that such games have a full set of dramatic arcs.

Let's have a look at *Tetris*. The player development arc offers four learning experiences: getting better at manipulating the tetrominoes; doing that faster; getting better at recognizing stacking patterns; and exploiting them more efficiently, up to and including bonus points. These are not easy learning curves, far from it, but they're not particularly expansive. For the story development arc, it's similar. There is no story, but there is dramatic development: the tetrominoes fall faster and appear more frequently. It's pretty basic, but it's a dramatic structure! Now, though, we run into a problem. *Tetris* has no character development arc. The reason is that *Tetris* belongs to a game type that lacks a continuous player avatar. There's no tiny construction worker on the screen who's spinning the tetrominoes and pushing them sideways.

However, when we consider game types that have visible avatars—paddles, rocket ships, plumbers, and so on—that are not only continuous but can undergo temporary or permanent change through power-ups or leveling-up, we do have a very rudimentary form of the character development arc. Such avatars, for example, can become faster or bigger or obtain new moves or accelerated fire rates. Or they can experience setbacks and become slower or smaller at times (like the paddle in the original *Breakout*). It's not a hero's journey all right, and it doesn't make such games dramatically complete. But it can be helpful, even necessary, to *think* along these lines during the design process and figure out how and when the player avatar can evolve in interesting ways. *Pong* does have a visible player avatar, but the paddle doesn't change over the course of the game to learn some backhand tricks, for example. However, if *Pong* had been invented a few years later, that might have been different.

Let's turn our attention back now to what every beat in this level is ultimately about: integrating the three development arcs into player action and harmonize them with theme, player motivation, and player emotion.

Integrating the three development arcs into player action is the most difficult step. When the *character and story development arcs* are at odds with each other, this often leads to the excessive use of cutscenes. When the *player and story development arcs* are at odds with each other, this can lead to ludonarrative dissonance, a term coined and introduced by Clint Hocking in "Ludonarrative Dissonance in Bioshock." In this specific case, it meant—along Hocking's line of reasoning—that the game offers a profound choice on the mechanical level whose equivalent on the narrative level it denies. But the term is also used now when the *player and character development arcs* are at odds with each other—when, for example, a game demands player action like killing and looting that is diametrically opposed to the player character's supposedly heroic and noble nature.

In the upcoming beats, a range of different techniques to integrate the three development arcs will be introduced, among them the concept of empathic tasks. Fortunately, harmonizing a game's development

FIGURE 4.32 The emotional landscape.

arcs with theme, player emotion, and player motivation is a lot easier. We will do that in three successive steps, starting with player emotions. For that, you need to refresh your memory of the emotional landscape model that we developed early on in this territory.

The three development arcs correspond to the three classes of the emotional landscape, fear, pity, and fiero, in the following ways.

The story development arc with its turning points and escalations is connected to the *fear class* as the dramatic situation players could, at least in principle, see themselves in.

The character development arc with its journey-like structure is connected to the *pity class* as a progression of dramatic hardships players can empathize with or relate to.

The player development arc with its player actions and decisions is connected to the *fiero class* through the dramatic representation of the players' actions.

The difference between "empathize" and "relate to" in the character development arc is the difference between emotions from NPCs (that the player can empathize with) and emotions from the player character (that the player can relate to as a series of basic human experiences around initiation and transformation).

To integrate these emotions in your dramatically complete game, you need to sketch events for all three development arcs across your dramatic partitions and assign to each event one or more emotions from the appropriate palette that you want your player to experience over the course of the game.

Now we can add *purpose*. Every single beat should either

- move the story's plot forward,
- move the character's development forward,
- move the player's proficiency forward,
- or move any combination thereof forward.

Every level, in turn, should have a group of beats that advance all three development arcs as distinct and meaningful bundles of plot, character, and player progress.

With the help of these purposes, eventually, we can harmonize our development arcs with theme, player emotion, and player motivation.

Moving the story's plot forward. The story development arc deepens understanding through exploring interesting aspects of the game's *theme*, questioning assumptions, and revealing new perspectives through the lenses of theme-related motifs.

Moving the player character's journey forward. The character development arc deepens *player emotion* by widening the player's understanding of the game world, deepening their relations with NPCs, and exploring their inner selves.

Moving the player's proficiency level forward. The player development arc deepens *player motivation* through pushing players toward the goal with physical, cognitive, and empathic challenges that continuously improve their skills, knowledge, understanding, or attitude.

That way, everything in your game will be integrated in meaningful and robust ways.

To the primary challenge, the integration of the three development arcs, we will return in this territory time and again, to approach it from different perspectives.

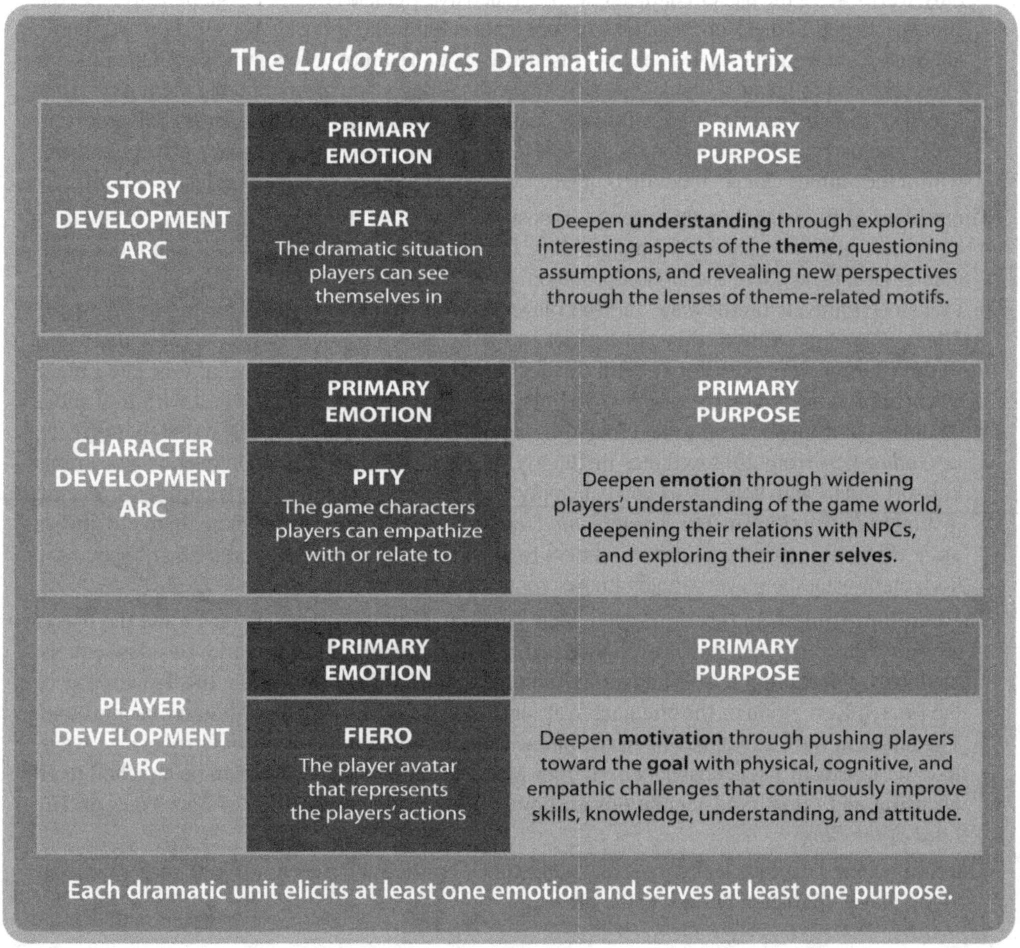

The *Ludotronics* Dramatic Unit Matrix

STORY DEVELOPMENT ARC	PRIMARY EMOTION	PRIMARY PURPOSE
	FEAR The dramatic situation players can see themselves in	Deepen **understanding** through exploring interesting aspects of the **theme**, questioning assumptions, and revealing new perspectives through the lenses of theme-related motifs.

CHARACTER DEVELOPMENT ARC	PRIMARY EMOTION	PRIMARY PURPOSE
	PITY The game characters players can empathize with or relate to	Deepen **emotion** through widening players' understanding of the game world, deepening their relations with NPCs, and exploring their **inner selves**.

PLAYER DEVELOPMENT ARC	PRIMARY EMOTION	PRIMARY PURPOSE
	FIERO The player avatar that represents the players' actions	Deepen **motivation** through pushing players toward the **goal** with physical, cognitive, and empathic challenges that continuously improve skills, knowledge, understanding, and attitude.

Each dramatic unit elicits at least one emotion and serves at least one purpose.

FIGURE 4.33 Dramatic unit matrix.

Beat 2: Prime Positions

Beginnings and Endings

Whatever structure you end up using, you'll always begin somewhere and end somewhere. In dramatic terms, you always need some kind of *exposition* and some kind of *closure*. Let's look at both in the order in which they usually occur.

In *Self-Editing for Fiction Writers*, Rennie Brown and Dave King hammer home one particular point they call R.U.E.: resist the urge to explain. R.U.E. highlights a problem that should be familiar to anyone who has ever played a dramatically complete video game. Namely, payloads of information packaged into awkward dialogues early in the game to explain what's going on. Which, as everybody agrees, is a terrible practice and should be avoided.

There are four basic situations that pose not only different challenges, but also different opportunities for your exposition: blank slate, widening horizon, familiar ground, and cold water.

The blank slate. In this first exposition situation, the player character is dropped into an unfamiliar environment, as in *Unreal*, and the player character has no more knowledge about the situation than the player. That way, you can take your time and weave the backstory into your gameplay, doling out bits and pieces in a suspenseful manner while the plot unfurls. Unfortunately, this only works when the player character is comprehensively clueless about the game world and the situation they find themselves in. One of the staple solutions to bring such a situation artificially about is character amnesia. It's been overused already and cannot be recommended. Other games have solutions to create a blank slate that are both complex and clever, among them *Assassin's Creed*'s "animus" setting. Which, initially, leaves the (nominally) primary player character from the frame narrative as conveniently clueless as the player, while the secondary player character within the animus can go about their business in a world in which they're perfectly at home.

The widening horizon. For this second exposition situation, the player character commences on a journey from a partially isolated place in the game world toward wider and more complex environments, like the Hobbit protagonists in Tolkien's novels. That way, more and more backstory unravels on the way, and the player can follow along without having to digest the *Silmarillion* first. (Often, this can be kicked off by clever passage design, a topic discussed in the *Plurimediality* territory.) With this technique, you can create a partially isolated place or corridor along which the player is led, step for step, into a widening world with ever more complex environments, up to and including an open-world where they can roam about freely, as *God of War* from 2018 executes brilliantly. The widening horizon, moreover, is a desirable kick-off situation in general, as you can apply what Jesse Schell calls J. R. R. Tolkien's "distant mountains" technique in *The Art of Game Design*. It creates a situation where there are always more things to explore and more wonders to see and more insights to gather *just* beyond the horizon of what the player already knows about the game world.

The familiar ground. In this third exposition situation, both the player character and the player are sufficiently and sometimes even thoroughly familiar with the game world. Besides sequels, obviously, this can be a well-known mythological or historical event, like the Trojan War or the French Revolution or the Vietnam War, or a well-known cinematic or literary background. The latter, in turn, can either be in the public domain, to be freely used in fairly elastic ways, like the worlds of Eschenbach's *Parzival* or Melville's *Moby Dick*. Or it can be attached to IP licensing and fairly rigid regulations and prescriptions, like the worlds of *Star Wars* or *The Lord of the Rings*.

The cold water. This fourth and most difficult exposition situation is a game world that is familiar to the player character, but not to the player.

For the fourth and last case, some workarounds exist, but not many. There's player character amnesia, as mentioned. Or a torrent of orders shouted at the player character by superiors. Or, it can be simply ignored, to the detriment of player motivation and emotion. Most of the time, alas, games fail to resist the urge to explain and serve an opulent dish of unwholesome dialogue.

Is there a recipe for the cold water situation that does not break the rule of R.U.E.? In a way, yes. It's hard to pull off, but you can try to create a temporary initial locale or situation that converts your cold water exposition to one of the other three categories, be that a clever blank slate, a widening horizon, or a locale so accessible that it counts as a familiar ground solution.

Should none of that work, there's a dirty workaround you can use that breaks the R.U.E. rule in a reasonably acceptable manner: the roll-up. Or, in more familiar terms, the opening crawl. Your exposition doesn't have to roll up or crawl, but it must throw the player within not more than three short paragraphs into the thick of the action. In the original *Star Wars* movie, everything flows from its opening crawl beautifully, and the two dialogues between Leia and Vader and Daine Jir and Vader reinforce and expand on the crawl's expositional message. Imagine the information from the opening crawl had been crammed into these dialogues! What's more, the audience wouldn't have had a clue as to what's going on for several scenes.

And it's not just *Star Wars*! There's a whole list of respectable movies that use this workaround, with *Unforgiven*'s two-paragraph roll-up as another famous example. Perhaps you have realized already that this workaround utilizes non-diegetic information, i.e., information that is only accessible to the player, not to characters within the game world. (Diegetic vs. non-diegetic information is discussed in-depth in the *Plurimediality* territory.) As such, it works even better with games than with movies. Unlike movies, games already provide a lot of non-diegetic information through its various interfaces throughout the game, so a roll-up stands out a lot less. Indeed, a succinct, powerful introduction that directly addresses the player can turn a cold water situation into a widening horizon situation. It can provide the player with enough exposition to create a familiar space in that world, and from that space you can lead the player into unfamiliar terrain at your leisure.

From there, let's move on to endings. First off, we will also look at games that are not dramatically complete, but not at games that have a match structure where the player either wins or loses against one or more opponents. Chess, skat, or the game of Go don't have "endings" in that sense. Nor, for that matter, have tournament shooters, match-based strategy games, brawlers, racing games, and so forth.

If your game isn't match-based, its ending will fall into one of four formal categories:

- Resolved endings.
- Unresolved endings.
- Mixed endings.
- Multiple endings.

Perhaps you expected something along the lines of happy or sad endings, but these and similar classifications are too dependent on personal, social, and cultural meaning and context to be a good foundation for design decisions. How happily, from today's perspective, does a pre-1960 movie end whose female lead character gives up her idée fixe (read: ambitions) and submits to becoming the male lead's loving housewife? Not very. From a formal perspective, though, this ending doubtlessly resolves the character development arc (and probably also the story development arc). Or, what if the character dies for a noble cause? Is that a happy ending? Not really. From a formal perspective, though, it resolves the story development arc! But then, it doesn't resolve the character development arc because characters—with rare exceptions—don't aspire to die for their cause.

Here are the rules. If every development arc is resolved or every development arc remains unresolved, the game's ending counts as resolved or unresolved, respectively. If at least one development arc is resolved and at least one development arc remains unresolved, the ending counts as mixed. If the game has more than one ending, depending on player performance or decisions (whereby each of these endings can appear resolved, unresolved, or mixed by itself), that counts as a multiple ending.

Let's go through all four endings one by one, so you can decide which option is the right option for your game. (Right now, don't worry about any of the upcoming parentheses with references to visible, internal, and proficiency goals; we will explore the nature of goals in detail in this territory's final level.)

The resolved ending. The world regains its balance, the player character's desires are met, and
    the player beats the game.

There's nothing wrong with resolved endings at all. In dramatically complete games, it means that the
world has been put back into balance or equilibrium (the visible goal from the story development arc); the
player character achieves what they aspire to (the internal goal from the character development arc); and
the player has beaten the game (the proficiency goal from the player development arc).

Importantly, the character's desire does not equal "inner peace" or some such, nor can it be superseded
by it. When a character sacrifices their personal desire or even themselves for a worthwhile cause (like
Rick in *Casablanca* or Jyn in *Rogue One*, respectively), the character development arc counts as unresolved (Rick still desires to be with Ilsa, and Jyn still desires to live).

In games that are not dramatically complete, a game counts as resolved if it has a conclusive ending
that is hard to achieve, and the game stops for good after that. Think *Desert Golfing* after the 2017 patch.
There are no more challenges left, and the player has achieved everything that can be achieved.

The unresolved ending. The world remains out of balance, the player character's desires aren't
    met, and the player fails.

In *Swords & Circuitry*, Neal and Jana Hallford argue that the player has put in too many hours into a
game and worked too hard to deserve to get "hit" with a bad ending. Let's think this through. To start
with, an unresolved ending should never "hit" anyone. Any dramatic arc's ending, resolved or unresolved, should make everything that has happened before worthwhile, relevant, and meaningful. For
what it's worth, this should allow both the story and character development arcs to remain unresolved
(the player character might even die, as in several hugely successful games). But what about the player
development arc and player achievement? Here, Neal and Jana Hallford have a point. If a dramatically
complete game is fully unresolved, i.e., the world's balance isn't restored, the player character's desires
thwarted, and the player has failed by design—well, that looks rather indefensible. Even the dismal world
of *I Have No Mouth, and I Must Scream* (which falls into the multiple endings category discussed below)
offers the player a slim chance for a half-decent ending. Thus, if you want to create a fully unresolved
ending, you need to provide a relevant, meaningful, and emotionally satisfying closure not despite but
because the player failed by design. Which, frankly, is pretty hard to pull off.

Games that are not dramatically complete, even those that become progressively harder until the
player fails, like arcade or management games, are almost never purely unresolved for one particular
reason: high-scores and tokens and badges and similar design elements that provide a measure of personal achievement. When the player fails but scores a personal record, that failure doesn't count as player
failure. It can even be a towering achievement, like reaching the kill screen in *Pac-Man* or keeping a
Dwarf Fortress alive for 200 years. Thus, as with dramatically complete games, endings for games that
are not dramatically complete are rarely if ever purely unresolved. But that's not to say it doesn't exist!
For a purely unresolved ending, as a cautionary tale, take *Desert Golfing* before the 2017 patch. The
game's algorithms sooner or later created an "impossible hole." That the event occurred was inevitable,
but when it occurred was unpredictable. That way, the game world didn't achieve equilibrium; the player
failed by design, not through any fault of their own; and any achieved score was rendered meaningless
since the impossible hole could hit the player at any state of achievement.

The mixed ending. The player beats the game, but either world balance or the player character's
    desires or both cannot be achieved.

In non-interactive media, there are only two options for mixed endings. For the first, the world is put
back into balance or equilibrium (story development arc), but the character fails to achieve their personal
goals (character development arc). As an example, in the miniseries *The Pacific*, the war is won, but the
central character is broken, in contrast to its twin miniseries *Band of Brothers*, where the war is won and
the central character's aspirations are met. For the second, the character achieves inner peace, but the
world remains in shambles. This is rare in movies, but frequent in television series. There, foregrounded

characters in individual episodes often resolve a local character development arc, but the story world's conflict remains unresolved (as it has to, in order to keep the series' story engine running).

In games, even if we exclude forced failure in the player development arc for the reasons discussed above, we have not two but three options. As long as the player development arc is resolved, the story development arc can remain unresolved; the character development arc can remain unresolved; or both story and character development arcs can remain unresolved.

For games that are not dramatically complete, mixed endings are not a good fit, as there is no character development arc that can succeed or fail. A game where the game world is restored despite player failure, or not restored despite player success, is probably not the experience target audiences would flock to, except for experimental or art games.

> **The multiple ending**. The ending turns out to be resolved or unresolved or mixed, depending on player actions and decisions.

A lot of ink has been spilled against multiple endings, and for good reasons. In *The Art of Game Design*, for example, Jesse Schell argues that not every ending of a story can be fully aligned, or unified, with the beginning of that story and its development over the course of the game. That is a good point. Then, others have argued that the player can never be sure to have gotten the best possible experience out of the game. That's another good point. Finally, story forks are rarely what they're cracked up to be, as they almost always have a lot of game content in common. Which is understandable from the development perspective, but disappointing to players who try out a different fork in a replay. Also, publishers are terminally ill-disposed toward bankrolling content that only a few players might actually see, which is also understandable.

All these are very sound arguments against multiple endings, no doubt. Does that mean you should stay away from multiple endings?

Well, no—except from classical "forking," which has largely been abandoned by game designers in any case. With forking, as a reminder, the player does A at some point in the game, which triggers event E, after which the game proceeds to ending 1. If the player does B instead of A, the event F is triggered, after which the game proceeds to ending 2. This strategy forces you to twist your design into all kinds of contortions just to keep it from forking exponentially.

What games do, and what you can and should do too, is focus less on "what" happens and more on "how" it happens, a topic we will return to in the upcoming beat. Roughly, if the player does A, event E happens, which leads to ending Z. If the player does B instead, event E' happens, which has slightly different qualities and consequences than E, and the game proceeds to ending Z', where things work out not as well as in Z courtesy of E'. It's still expensive and time-consuming, especially for an indie game. But it's a lot more feasible than forking, and even more so when A and B are tied to player performance.

Under these provisions, let's have a look at the two possible outcomes of a failed or less successful player development arc for a multiple ending that is neither fully resolved nor fully unresolved. When the player fails, this failure will more likely be bound, and quite naturally, to a failed story development arc, which is often tied to the game's victory condition. When the player development arc doesn't fail outright but is less successful, this will more likely be bound, again quite naturally, to a failed character development arc, as these two arcs are often closely related. For example, the player might have been just successful enough to meet the game's victory condition by resolving the story development arc, but the character development arc remains unresolved because the costs were too high (friends/team members died, etc.). Both cases, a failed story development arc and a failed character development arc, might equally incentivize the player to do a better job in a replay.

Here's an example. *Resident Evil* features multiple endings, each depending on player actions and player performance at certain key points over the course of the game. There's a perfect ending where the player character saves their partner (Rebecca for Chris's campaign or Barry for Jill's campaign) as well as a team member imprisoned in the lab (Jill for Chris's campaign and vice versa). Then, if only the respective partner survives, but the player fails to rescue the team member, the Tyrant is still defeated and the mansion destroyed, but a team member has been lost. Finally, if the player character fails to save both their partner and the team member, the mansion remains intact and the Tyrant remains loose

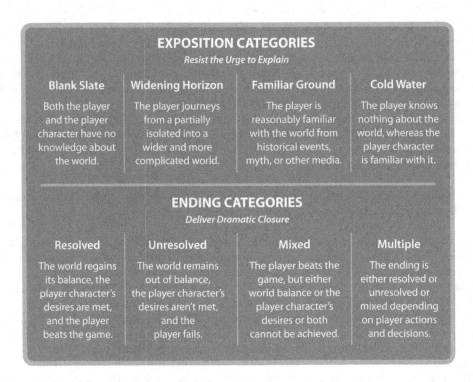

FIGURE 4.34 Exposition and ending categories.

in the forest. The *Mass Effect* trilogy, disregarding its atrocious final ending, operates similarly. There, many goals can be achieved with or without personal cost in terms of lost friends and team members, all depending on player actions and decisions.

Thus, if you think multiple endings will improve the playing experience of your game, and you have the necessary resources, go for it—but you should always focus on the "how," not on the "what."

In closing, whatever ending option you want to adopt for your game, resolved, unresolved, mixed, or multiple, it must always appear inevitable, in retrospect, with regard to everything that occurred before—events, actions, decisions. The ending can be a happy one, it can be a sad one, or everything in between. But it *must* make everything that has happened to the player over the course of the game worthwhile, relevant, and meaningful. What you want the player to experience at the end of your game is not an ending, after all, but *closure*.

Great beginnings and great endings are hard to pull off. Your exposition must lead the player into the game world without laborious explanations, which are detrimental to establishing emotions, and also without leaving them clueless, which is detrimental to establishing motivation. Your closure has to convey emotional truth and appear satisfying and inevitable with regard to everything that led up to it, especially player decisions. For both, you need an experienced writer, which could be you. But still— later during the development phase, which is outside the scope of this book, it might be a good idea to involve a writer with screenplay experience. Screenwriters in particular are well-trained in creating high-involvement expositions and satisfying closures.

Beat 3: Paradigms Lost

Mottos and Mantras

The differences between "story" and "narrative" have already been touched upon; in the *Narrativity* territory, for example, they motivate the adoption of the term "world narrative" over "environmental storytelling." Now it's time to carve out the practical differences between "interactive storytelling" and "interactive narrative," and how these differences apply to game design. To do that, we need to examine two design paradigms first: "show, don't tell" and "balancing story and gameplay."

Let's start with "show, don't tell." Stories cannot be separated from the medium through which they are told. For stories that are told through words, either orally or in written form, everything's in the *telling*. Dramatic dialogue and dramatic description, respectively, create emotions in the audience's minds. For stories that are told through a visual medium, the telling paradigm alone doesn't cut it. Here, the primary mode is visually compelling dramatic action that is *shown* to create emotions in the audience's minds. Thus, for this medium, the *show, don't tell* paradigm is a good fit. (You will often hear that the *show, don't tell* paradigm also applies to written media. In a way, that's not wrong—it's useful to keep your "urge to explain" in check. But beyond that, it's a dubious proposition because it entraps fiction writers in a cinematographic metaphor. You sing, not show, the anger of Achilles.) For a story that is told in an interactive medium, finally, *show, don't tell* needs to make room for a new paradigm, just as telling had to make room for *show, don't tell* for the visual medium. Neither dialogue delivered by NPCs (telling) nor full motion video cutscenes (showing) are adequate primary modes to advance the story, character, and player development arcs in an interactive medium like a video game.

Instead, everything should be designed to push the player through playable action toward plot resolution, character fulfillment, and the goal of the game. Therefore, our paradigm for games and similar interactive media will not be *show, don't tell*, but *push, don't show*.

Now, the argument can be made that the game shouldn't "push," but "pull" the player into the game like a reader is "pulled" into a story, an argument brought forward by Neal and Jana Hallford in *Swords & Circuitry*. Playable action and goals should be so enticing that the player cannot but be pulled toward it, without any need of being pushed. While this sounds sensible, games don't work like stories. A story pulls the reader along by keeping them curious about what's going to happen next, and this curiosity depends in no small part on the fact that the story can't possibly be influenced or changed by the reader in any way. Accordingly, being pulled into a story means, at bottom, that you can only *follow* the story and, under favorable circumstances, cannot *but* follow the story. This is very different from how interactive gameplay should work.

Consider this. What could it mean that a beat has to "push" the player toward an action, and finally toward the goal? A beat can, for example, provoke a reaction; trigger a movement; force a maneuver; demand a payment; present a puzzle; request an item; ask for a favor; call for help; give an order; require a decision; pose a problem; necessitate a response. This doesn't mean that there's no pulling! A beat can also, for example, provide information; make a suggestion; create tension; arouse curiosity; raise expectations; build anticipation; press to reconsider or rethink; present a surprise. Yet even there, the player isn't supposed to simply follow these pull elements, but to *act* on them. Hence, *push, don't show*, not *pull, don't show*.

> Push, don't show.

Is this paradigm valid for any game, always, and everywhere? Emphatically, no. *Tell* still plays an important role in visual media, and both *tell* and *show* fulfill important roles in interactive media. Also, there are decidedly less push-oriented games like kinetic visual novels, so-called walking simulators, and more introspective games in general, regardless of type. Or games like Kojima Hideo's *Metal Gear* series which combine show, tell, and pull elements in innovative and unexpected ways. But in many dramatically complete games, such *tell* and *show* elements—particularly non-interactive cinematics like cutscenes—are often mere vehicles to "solve" design issues around player agency and autonomy.

Then, there's the second paradigm, "balancing story and gameplay," which is inextricably linked to "interactive storytelling." This has been the dominant paradigm for a very long time, and there's a respectable corpus of research attached to it. But techniques have evolved that shifted away from "story" toward "narrative," for which the paradigm of "balancing story and gameplay" is not a good fit.

To make this more transparent and applicable, let's go for a walk. We'll visit the historic development of dramatic structure; its implications and challenges for interactive media; some of the classical techniques based on the "interactive storytelling" and "balancing story and gameplay" paradigm; and how the "interactive narrative" paradigm relates to more recent design techniques. To dispel potential illusions early, however: there is no magic bullet. All the techniques we will visit, the more traditional and the more recent ones, amount to clever tinkering. But different paradigms bring about different effects, and you might find some of them more useful and more desirable for your game than others.

In the beginning, dramatic structure equaled narrative structure. From Aristotle's *Poetics* to Gustav Freytag's Pyramid to Syd Field's Paradigm, philosophers and artists have tried to analyze, formulate, and refine the dramatic structure of non-interactive media to achieve the highest possible emotional impact on their audiences. From humble beginnings like exposition, climax, and dénouement with rising and falling action in between up to inciting incident, showdown, and resolution schemes peppered with intricate, precision-timed networks of plot points and pinches, dramatic structure has been used by artists to engage their audiences with relentlessly controlled experiences that enthrall and absorb. Dramatic structure became nothing short of a high-precision machine without tolerance for tolerances—in mechanical parlance, there's almost no room for "backlash" or "play." Now, adding player agency to that system is like throwing Charlie Chaplin's *Modern Times* character into the works. In games and comparable interactive media, the whole dramatic machinery rumbles and crumbles and breaks apart.

Which is another way of saying that for games and interactive media, *dramatic structure no longer equals narrative structure.*

In "Beyond Myth and Metaphor: The Case of Narrative in Digital Media," Marie-Laure Ryan discusses what is and isn't desirable for emotional "first-person" experiences in games. One of her examples, Tolstoy's *Anna Karenina*, reveals two momentous aspects for games. On the one hand, the dramatic structure can't throw all its plot points of pain and misery and suffering on the player without running into problems. On the other, plot points that are essential for the dramatic structure to work cannot easily be set up as player decisions.

With reference to Marie-Laure Ryan's essay, it has been quipped that not many players would be willing to kill themselves to make the game more interesting. But, on a side note, one shouldn't underestimate games—*NieR*'s third playthrough, for example, indeed presents the player with such a choice; and while it's "just" an alternative ending, it erases the player character's in-game existence along with the player's save files. Now, this is certainly an edge case. Ryan's observation remains true in less extreme circumstances. In the Process phase's first level on integral perspectives, you might remember, we went through the example of a historical game where the character has to choose between her love and her career. There, we focused on the problem of player emotion: as you cannot empathize with yourself, pity (identification via empathy) and agency (identification via representation) are mutually exclusive. In our current context, it makes Marie-Laure Ryan's argument immediately applicable for almost any kind of dramatic choice.

But it goes even further. For any given dramatic structure to work, the player can't even be granted unrestricted agency with respect to conflict in general! Some players will try to defuse conflicts. Others will try to over-escalate conflicts. Barring an unlikely army of Goldilocks players, the amount of possible player choices has to be curtailed considerably, just to keep things sufficiently interesting or from getting out of hand. The only way to guarantee that an indispensable dramatic event materializes is to take the associated dramatic decision away from the player and rob them of their agency—which, together with autonomy, as a reminder, is one of our critical motivational drivers from the player motivation model.

For all these reasons, it has more or less become accepted that dramatically complete games can't provide both—a screenplay-like roller coaster ride and substantive player agency. The traditional way to go about it, then, is to dig out a narrow channel between these two that can be navigated by "balancing story and gameplay." That's where this paradigm and its associated strategies originate.

The most popular strategy to navigate this channel, as mentioned, is to split the game into player action for the agency department on the one hand, and use cutscenes to convey plot points and dramatic decisions on the other. Another popular strategy is the illusion of decision-driven forking, with complex machineries of smoke and mirrors in the background to prevent the exponential growth of story lines that even a small number of successive player decisions beget.

More modern techniques, as mentioned, revolve less about "interactive story" and more about "interactive narrative." For a long time, the latter term was overshadowed by the former, but it's always been there and in use. You can find it in Mark Stephen Meadows's *Pause and Effect,* Marie-Laure Ryan's "Interactive Narrative, Plot Types, and Interpersonal Relations," Grant Tavinor's *The Art of Videogames,* or Tynan Sylvester's *Designing Games.* Now, it's more and more used by designers too—for an illuminating example, watch Miles Tost and Nikolas Kolm's presentation *"The Witcher 3*: Crafting a Compelling Narrative in a Believable Open World." The term was also used, and continues to be used, for AI approaches to algorithmic storytelling.

What's more, the terms "interactive story" and "interactive narrative" mirror many of the differences between "story" and "narrative," as discussed in the *Narrativity* territory. "Story" is primarily about *what* is told, the content; all that's not part of a story belongs to different stories; and stories are robustly impervious to participation. "Narrative" is primarily about *how* something is told, the structure; it is open-ended and can accommodate many stories and narratives; and it invites participation.

The openness to participation and the ability to accommodate many stories and narratives is particularly important in this context, as it allows "interactive narrative" to accommodate any number of *player-generated narratives.* Which leads us to our next waypoint.

Player-generated narratives are at the core of more recent design techniques that no longer navigate the narrow channel between story and gameplay, but try to integrate story, character, and player development arcs by giving the player a lot more leeway to play the game as they see fit. The perhaps most venerable technique here is soft-gating, which has been employed as early as *Gothic* and became more widespread later, with *Far Cry* or *S.T.A.L.K.E.R.: Shadow of Chernobyl* as memorable examples. Players can choose where to go and what to do, but—depending on overall progress and corresponding skill and equipment levels—not every choice is a healthy one. There will be some kind of stern warning, and if the player ignores it and then finds out that life is nasty, brutish, and short, they've no one to blame but themselves.

From there, along evolving technologies, it became possible to open up the game world even further, to give the player more and more to do and to decide—up to such decision-intensive games like the *Mass Effect* trilogy, *The Witcher 3: Wild Hunt,* or *Cyberpunk 2077.* However, games like that are handcrafted at an enormous price tag, with fact-tracking databases under the hood that compute player decisions and their consequences and determine less *what* happens, but *how* successive events will play out. (The difference between *how* and *what,* already mentioned, will occupy us in more detail in the upcoming beat.)

Breaking these and many related techniques down, the baseline is as follows. There's the story development arc where things happen along a predetermined plot with regard to the *what,* but that's not where the player necessarily spends most of their time. Next, there's the character development arc, where the player can more or less do what they want, possibly restricted by character traits. (There's a difference as to what you can do as Geralt in *The Witcher 3: Wild Hunt* or as Trevor in *GTA V.*) This arc can be filled with everything from exploring or going fishing to combat encounters and missions. But beware: these cannot and should not be fetch quests! Fetch quests might earn the player experience points, but they never build character. Then, in the player development arc, progress in skill, knowledge, understanding, and attitude is determined by events from both the story development and the character development arc. Finally, to close the circle, *how* things work out in the story development arc along its predetermined plot depends on what the player's been doing in the other two arcs: how far they've progressed in skill, knowledge, understanding, and attitude, and what kind of person they had decided to become in that world.

Thus, you're no longer "balancing story and gameplay." Instead, you're integrating the story, character, and player development arcs into a framework for different player experiences that largely correspond to your vision. That's an important paradigm shift. Consider this: balancing story and gameplay is a paradigm focused on trade-offs, on making concessions, on finding compromises. In other words, it's what the Harvard Program on Negotiation calls "positional bargaining" in a "fixed pie" situation. Both sides take their positions, argue for it, and make concessions to reach a compromise, i.e., give up something they want less in order to get something they want more. But for an integrated dramatic structure for games, you "broaden your options" instead, as the Harvard model calls it. If your design focuses on shared and compatible interests between the three arcs, you will find that the number of these shared and compatible interests is substantially larger than the number of opposed interests on which the paradigm of balancing story and gameplay is focused. The challenges, as enumerated above, are real, and they're not going away. What changes is your mindset, and how you try to solve these challenges.

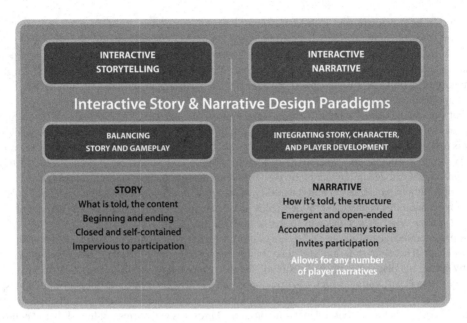

FIGURE 4.35 Story vs. narrative design paradigms.

Now, you might ask, how does that scale? At this point in time, you cannot automate any of this—as mentioned, the most well-known and successful games that use these and similar techniques have enormous amounts of handcrafted computations under the hood. There were and are attempts at automatization that should be mentioned, but they're not very helpful for various reasons. One attempt was to create stories algorithmically through abstraction: by wrapping procedurally generated story beats around the character development arc, particularly the hero's journey, like Chris Crawford's Erasmatron and Storytron or Ken Levine's "Narrative Legos." These attempts didn't exactly blossom. Other approaches that do produce playable and highly enjoyable games, up to and including *Crusader Kings III*, offer a cocktail of pre-established plot points or "beats," random table events, interaction rules, and probabilities tied to character traits to create individual player narratives that can be perceived as stories. However, they're first and foremost strategy games, and if you take the beats out of the equation, they're contingency simulators—in other words, they have more in common with life than with plot. Which doesn't make these games less enjoyable, far from it! But they're a different game type altogether. Then, there are language models based on deep learning that generate "story content" like *AI Dungeon* on the one hand, and there's the "AI Director" in *Left4Dead* on the other, who creates individual intensity curves by arranging encounters and events dynamically along player actions. These techniques have a lot of potential—great and rapid strides are made in AI technologies on a regular basis now, and you will be able to do more and more interesting things with them. But don't rely on them to tell a story that is well-structured, gripping, and not trivial just yet.

What it comes down to, therefore, is bricolage, or tinkering, and handcrafted design. That should sound familiar, as it's something indie games excel at. If you want to tell a story, but you also want your player to have agency, a great story development arc alone won't cut it. You also need great player and character development arcs—where players can make meaningful decisions and create their own player narratives, into which your story development arc will fit nicely. And don't think subplots! There's nothing "sub" about your character and player development arcs. Think narrative, not story. The plot of your story development arc is one element among equals.

As an example of how to bring everything together, let's pick up a fictitious game used for demonstration purposes in the *Narrativity* territory. It's a single-player game with a cinematological core and identity as its theme, where the player character struggles to explore and preserve a precarious cultural identity within an all-encompassing mainstream culture. One particular beat, where the player character finds an artifact belonging to that culture, is used there to carve out the differences between a plot point and an element of the world narrative—which, in turn, can either define a level or locale or an individual gameplay moment.

Finding the artifact is a plot point for the *story development arc* that reveals the urban district where the first immigrants from the player character's culture had lived and died. It's an important historic location that had hitherto been unknown, perhaps even deliberately concealed, which also increases the player's knowledge about the game world. At this new locale, the player character communicates and interacts with people who might or might not belong to that culture. They confront the player with ideas, biographies, and social narratives, prompting personal decisions and reflective choices that provide insights and promote understanding and attitude for the *character development arc*. Finally, exploring the urban district might bring the player character into dangerous situations and even conflicts and fights along physical and cognitive challenges, which boosts their skills. These, together with the player's progress in knowledge, understanding, and attitude, advance the *player development arc*. Every encounter and experience in one arc primes and prepares, complements, and consummates elements from the other two arcs.

That's how you integrate your story, character, and player development arcs. And you don't need a *Shenmue* budget for that! If it doesn't scale, cut down on the number of plot points first. That's where scaling problems hole up most of the time. And in an integrated interactive narrative, they're not as important as you think they are, neither for the story you want to tell, nor for the playing experience of your game as a whole.

Beat 4: Problem Space

Paths and Possibilities

Certain types of games, strategy games or tactical shooters prominently among them, are strongly defined by giving the player interesting choices all the time. However, these are choices and player decisions that arise primarily from the mechanics of a game, which belong in the *Interactivity* territory. Other types of games, action-adventure or exploration games prominently among them, give the player next to no interesting choices during play. These are also not very fruitful for the purposes of this beat. What interests us here are dramatically complete games that have a story *and* offer the player interesting choices.

To create a dramatically complete game that integrates the three development arcs by providing player agency and perhaps even a measure of autonomy, as discussed in the preceding beats, you have to design meaningful choices. But not every choice is alike. Lacking clear ideas about what constitutes a good choice in an interactive game and what doesn't, which also and especially includes empathic tasks, makes their design more difficult than it needs to be, and the results less compelling than they ought to be.

Thus, to design meaningful choices for the player, we need to go on another journey. It will lead us from *agency* and *autonomy* to *choices* and *decisions*, touch upon different aspects of *problem space*, and segue into two design parameters for *empathic tasks*—our very own "problem space" for designing interactive narratives, so to speak. Let's buckle up!

Agency is first and foremost about the question of whether player actions and decisions make a difference in the game world. Let's extend our example from the first level and imagine the player has to steal a diamond from a well-protected vault. If the player can execute this task in different ways (e.g., sneaky, through an armed assault, or via blackmail), and the game world reacts to these different actions in different ways (e.g., with admiration, a manhunt, or contempt), then that's player agency. If the player can make these different decisions but the game world always reacts in the same way, then that player agency is substantially diminished—no longer define these decisions who the player wants to be in the game world; they merely reflect personal preferences in playing style.

Then, *autonomy*. Having autonomy, the player can decide to a certain extent which goals they want to pursue. In our example, the player would have autonomy if they can decide whether or not to steal that diamond in the first place.

Thus, to establish agency or autonomy, the following things must happen: the player must be given a well-balanced set of choices; the player must be able to make a meaningful decision; and that decision must make a difference in the game world. So far, so good!

Yet game narratives, often enough, have a habit of offering choices with only one correct decision. This looks innocuous enough, but you might already see how that opens up a can of worms. If the player is given a choice that has just one correct decision, the player has neither a choice nor agency! Imagine you can choose between hot, medium, mild, or no salsa with your burrito, and you're abruptly shown the door if you don't choose "hot" as the one right decision. (Which it is, but still.) So in a vast number of cases, the player has to make decisions, but literally has no choice, and there's no agency involved whatsoever. All the player does is solve a puzzle disguised as a choice.

But offering two or more "correct" choices is only the beginning. According to Tracy Fullerton, who provides a great introduction to the nature of choices in *Game Design Workshop*, a choice is then and only then a true choice when the options on offer are neither obvious nor arbitrary from the perspective of the player, and when these options are *interesting*. And the way to make choices interesting is to design them as *dramatic* choices.

Now, what's a dramatic choice and how would you go about designing one? A dramatic choice offers the player decisions that have different consequences in terms of advantages and disadvantages. One decision could have short-term advantages, another long-term advantages. One could be of material value, one of spiritual value. One can be purely selfish, one unselfish. One can be based on fear, one on trust. And so on. (Game-theoretical conflict design, as discussed in the *Interactivity* territory, fits such patterns well.) But that's still not enough! To design a truly dramatic choice, you need to flavor its options with different *emotions*. And even *that's* not enough—to design a truly great dramatic choice, it must serve a function! Like any task, as discussed repeatedly, challenging the player to make a decision should advance the plot, develop the character, or teach the player something new—in other words, advance one or more of the three development arcs. And if you want to dazzle and delight, design your choices in such a way that their dramatic functions differ!

Here's an example. In *Hamlet*, Act III, Scene iii, the titular character is given the choice to kill or not to kill the King who murdered Hamlet's father and married his mother, as Hamlet now knows for certain. Here, the function is contingent upon the character's action. Had Hamlet killed the King at this moment, this would have advanced the plot, or story development arc, and the play would have proceeded and ended differently from the play we know. Hamlet's decision not to kill the King at this moment, in contrast, advances the character development arc. Hamlet's knowledge is deepened about the nature and requirements of revenge in this world, and the audience's understanding is deepened with regard to Hamlet's character and motivation.

On a meta-level in this dark, unfathomable play, Hamlet's fundamental choice throughout is to advance or not to advance the plot. Which, in turn, teaches us something else: that a choice can and should include the option of inaction as a decision that has consequences. According to Michael Bhatty in *Interaktives Story Telling*, the first game to offer the player choices that included a possible "inaction" decision was the interactive movie video game *Star Trek: Klingon* from 1996. Over time, this design element has become a lot more frequent. In the aforementioned presentation "*The Witcher 3*: Crafting a Compelling Narrative in a Believable Open World," for example, Miles Tost and Nikolas Kolm relate that inaction as an option was an important parameter for designing player choices in *The Witcher 3: Wild Hunt*.

We can even go so far as to say that without a function, there can be no dramatic choice. This raises an interesting question. Must these functions be known to the player to make decisions meaningful? As Sebastian Domsch remarks in *Storyplaying: Agency and Narrative in Video Games*, the player must have knowledge about the situation and the consequences of their decisions, otherwise these decision would be arbitrary and the choice not really a choice—but this knowledge doesn't have to be complete. It's perfectly okay if the player has to make decisions with incomplete information. Players, and humans in general, do it all the time!

Thus, functions as perceived by the player don't need to be fully transparent, and neither do they have to be true. We are free to attach hidden consequences to our set of choices that the player plausibly can't foresee and shouldn't know about just yet—particularly to prepare turning points, pinches, and similar in dramatically complete games.

As an example, let's look at Garrus' loyalty mission in *Mass Effect 2*. The choices on offer hook into the game's Paragon vs. Renegade mechanic, but what's going on here is more interesting than that. When Shepard and Garrus finally track down a guy by the name of Sidonis, who had betrayed Garrus and got the latter's squad killed, Shepard can let Garrus kill Sidonis or intervene to save his life. It's a situation full of tension and emotion. Does it feel right, for the player, to let Garrus kill Sidonis? Does Garrus' loyalty depend on this decision? (And, crucially, does the option to romance Garrus later in the game depend on this decision?) As it turns out, there are no negative consequences, Garrus being Garrus. Which comes as a great relief to players who just couldn't let Garrus kill Sidonis and made the decision to intervene, even if it meant failing their loyalty mission.

As long as the choice feels consequential and meaningful to the player, as this example shows, it is still a dramatic choice, even if its function isn't fully or correctly known to the player. Indeed, there was even a plan for a delayed plot twist attached to this mission, to be revealed in *Mass Effect 3*, which didn't make it into the final release. (That's from unverified sources, however, so take it with a grain of salt.) What this mission also does is develop the player's self-perception, and what they want Shepard to be in this game world, by forcing the player to make a *moral* decision.

Now, while every choice should be a dramatic choice, not every decision needs to be a moral decision. But it can be, and sometimes should be. Why are "moral" decisions important for our purposes? In the *Nicomachean Ethics*, Aristotle states that decisions are "most closely bound up with excellence" and "discriminate" character better than actions. To clarify, what Aristotle almost certainly seems to have in mind for the operative verb "discriminate" (κρίνειν) in this sentence is to indicate that a person's decisions let us "determine" the character or nature of that person. But, as a second layer of meaning, it might also convey the sense that a person's decisions "determine" that person's character or nature, which fits right in with Aristotle's model of virtue ethics.

Here's an excellent example, relayed by Anna Anthropy and Naomi Clark in *A Game Design Vocabulary,* how player decisions can "determine" character in that way. Early in the game *Affairs of the Court*, a choose-your-own adventure RPG, a symbol for good luck appears and the player character is asked by an NPC to make a wish. The context suggests, and the player accordingly expects, that this is a momentous decision that will greatly affect the course of the game somewhere down the road, not unlike what the player expects in our *Mass Effect* example.

Here too, no consequences follow, and the player has no way of knowing that. Which, counter-intuitively, greatly amplifies its effect! Anthropy and Clark call this unusual kind of choice "reflective choice," which indeed should become part of your game design vocabulary. Similar to making Shepard's decision, deciding on a wish in *Affairs of the Court* makes the player reflect on the wants and needs of their player character and what they want their player character to be. In other words, the player "determines" who they want to be in this world, in the Aristotelian sense, with a decision they expect to be a dramatic choice. From there, it affects the player's playing style and with it the player's actions and decisions. Reflective choices advance the player character arc, have tangible consequences for the gameplay, and are robustly immune to optimization strategies.

If you dig deep enough, you can find reflective choices, and different types of them, in a substantial number of games. In *Mafia III*, for example, the player can keep the player character's lieutenants happy or enlarge their own personal wealth (or, more pedestrian, they can roam around the city and ransack corner stores or refrain from it). Finally, there are games where the player is given the choice to refrain from killing. Traditionally, that's been a reflective choice, like in the original *Thief* games, where killing was neither rewarded nor punished. In later games, the game might reflect on it, as in the "Sorrow" sequence of *Metal Gear Solid 3: Snake Eater*. Then there are games like *Dishonored* and especially *Dishonored 2*, however, where killing or not killing adversaries can have consequences that affect the entire game world, up to and including multiple endings. It might still be a reflective choice, depending on the player. But tangible consequences make it very easy to turn moral decisions into optimization decisions, for example, to be rewarded with a desired ending.

Which brings us to our final topic in this beat, the problem space where all these choices and decisions "live." The term "problem space" is adopted from cognitive psychology. It's an internal representation in the player's mind, but it also exists in the game itself. The problem space comprises all the tasks that have to be solved, all the choices these tasks present, and all the player decisions these choices allow. When a

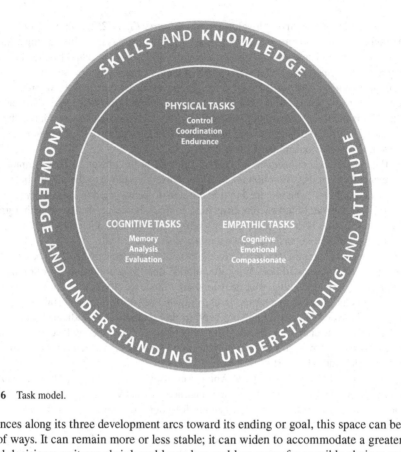

FIGURE 4.36 Task model.

game advances along its three development arcs toward its ending or goal, this space can be affected in a number of ways. It can remain more or less stable; it can widen to accommodate a greater number of choices and decisions; or it can shrink and leave less and less room for possible choices and decisions. (Deep down under the hood, this perspective is equivalent to the game-mechanical/ludological perspective of "possible paths," discussed in the *Interactivity* territory.)

Let's look at problem space from the perspective of our three task categories. Challenges, as discussed in the *Interactivity* territory, can be differentiated into physical, cognitive, and empathic tasks. These, roughly, correspond to the triad of physical, mental, and social tasks from the rational level/game design model on the one hand, and to action, puzzles, and player decisions in day-to-day parlance.

For physical tasks, which are designed around control, coordination, and endurance and primarily require skill and knowledge, the problem space tends to widen. More and harder tasks need to be solved with a wider variety of choices and ever more demanding decisions.

The same, by and large, seems to apply to cognitive tasks, which are designed around memory, analysis, and evaluation, and primarily require knowledge and understanding. But there are certain game types where the problem space not just widens but inflates rapidly over the course of the game. Life or management simulations, 4X games, and strategy games in general tend to evolve into ever more complex game states with escalating numbers of choices and decisions. This poses formidable design challenges, among them the question of presentation, to ensure that the player can keep track of all available choices and decisions without getting overwhelmed. But the key design challenge for controlling problem space in these games—as touched upon in Richard Rouse III's interview with Sid Meier in *Game Design: Theory & Practice*—is to ensure that the available decisions never become too obvious (not really a choice), never too arcane (impossible to decide), and never too time-consuming (neither too obvious nor too arcane, but bogging down the player with calculations).

Empathic tasks, finally, which are designed around cognitive, emotional, and compassionate empathy and primarily require understanding and attitude, have the opposite effect. For insight-driven or story-driven games, problem space decreases as the game progresses. In insight-focused game types, prominently among them educational games, it's the insight or learning experience the player is pushed toward that decreases the problem space over the course of the game. In story-driven games, it's a function of dramatic structure: the stronger and more tightly plotted the story is, the stronger the effect of diminishing problem space becomes. When the story progresses, more and more options fall to the wayside and fewer and fewer courses of action are available to the player, which equals fewer choices and less and less room for decisions.

Over and above, diminishing problem space in tightly plotted stories is also a function of suspense. If you have a story development arc, that story should be gripping. To make a story gripping and take the player on a wild emotional ride from start to finish in the Western dramatic tradition, particularly along Syd Field's paradigm, your story development arc needs to have a structure that includes an inciting incident, plot points, ups and downs, sudden reversals, and so on, and especially ever-rising stakes. It's this structure that leaves the player/player character fewer and fewer options until everything hangs on one final option that offers one particular choice with one particular decision for one particular heroic action whose success or failure will lead to triumph or tragedy.

This has been recognized by several writers, among them Brenda Laurel in her seminal *Computers as Theatre* and Richard J. Gerrig and Allan B. I. Bernardo in their *Poetics* article "Readers as Problem-Solvers in the Experience of Suspense." In Laurel's terminology, there is the "potential space," largely equivalent to our problem space. Initially, everything is possible in this space. When the story progresses (her primary example is *Hamlet*, befittingly), less and less is possible until only the probable is left. This, in turn, is diminished further and further until there's only one course of action left, the necessary. That's the climax of the story. The more possibilities and probabilities fall off, the greater becomes the suspense. And when the necessary finally kicks in, the audience must have the impression that it couldn't have happened otherwise. Gerrig and Bernardo, from a slightly different perspective, define suspense as the audience's belief that the quality or quantity of paths through the hero's problem space is diminished.

Classical and modern dramatic structures play with this diminishing problem space in wonderfully effective ways. One technique worth mentioning is the dramatic moment of delay (more intriguingly called *das retardierende Moment* in German). It's the promise of a different, non-tragic solution that, to employ Laurel's terminology, suddenly springs from the depleted repository of the probable as a glimmer of hope, only to give way to the necessary, the tragic solution, in short order. (The equivalent for comedies is the "everything is lost!" moment of delay shortly before the ending, which then gives way, conventionally, to a merry mass wedding.)

What about the other two arcs, the character development arc and the player development arc? Are they, too, sensitive to diminishing problem space and player agency? Luckily, no. The former doesn't have a problem space at all, and the latter is of a different nature. Let's have a look at both.

Whatever structure you prefer for your character development arc, the hero's journey or something else entirely, these journeys are already supremely abstract. And, while the player/player character can certainly make really bad calls, the journey itself is not about choices and dramatic decisions—it is about stages the character goes through for their internal development. In the hero's journey, some stages might look like decisions, like the Refusal of the Call or the Refusal to Return. But these aren't decisions because they aren't choices! Stage-based structures do not have a problem space where the possible or the probable can be depleted over time.

The player development arc, however, does have a problem space that can cause trouble. It is controlled by the game's *learning conditions*, particularly the proficiency spectrum and the learning curves, as discussed in the *Interactivity* territory. If the learning conditions are off, quite a number of things can happen to the player development arc's problem space, all of them detrimental to the playing experience. Among other things, the problem space can be depleted too early, or immoderately stuffed toward the end, or simply oscillate haphazardly between too much and too little like a drunken bandoneon.

Returning to the story development arc, where does all that leave us for story design in games and the story development arc's structure? For all that's been said, in this and the preceding beat, we need to square this diminishing problem space with player agency, and we have to do it by providing dramatic choices that allow the player to make meaningful decisions even late into the game.

Empathic tasks, evidently, are the crucible where solutions for this design challenge need to be forged. It's where we have to do things differently than other media. For the second part of this beat, therefore, we will look at two defining design parameters for empathic tasks: how to compose dramatic choices on the one hand, and how to handle the consequences of player decisions on the other.

For the composition of dramatic choices, we already know that we need to design more than one "correct" choice to establish player agency, otherwise it's just a puzzle in disguise. But there also exists a reverse misconception about empathic tasks: that *every* player decision needs to be accommodated by the game. Let's have a look at how player failure, by and large, is handled differently for physical, cognitive, and empathic tasks.

For physical tasks, imagine the player/player character tries to cross a superhighway on foot instead of walking up to the nearest footbridge because they're pressed for time. That doesn't work out because at this point, the player isn't fast enough to dodge the approaching cars, and the player character winds up under a car. Rare is the game that forks the story every time the player messes up like that, has the player character picked up by an ambulance, driven to the hospital, taken care of, and then arrested for public endangerment. Instead, you try again immediately in rinse and repeat fashion, or maybe your character leaves the hospital after a brief blackout, like in *GTA V*. In the same game, as a cognitive task, the player has to find a clever way to break into a closed supermarket without attracting attention. The player/player character kicks in the door, an alarm goes off, a dog begins to bark, and the siren of a nearby police cruiser approaches fast. Again, rare is the game that forks the story every time the player messes up like that, has the player character put into custody and scheduled for a court hearing. Then, in the same game, the player character is approached and questioned by the police, and how they react to that is set up as an empathic task. Here, suddenly, we have the misconception that we have to offer the player follow-up events for every choice in the set—instead of treating this task exactly the way we treat the physical and the cognitive task.

For every empathic task, there should be a small range of decisions that lead to success, at least two, and any number of decisions that lead to failure, and the player can succeed through understanding the situation or changing their attitude. Just as with physical and cognitive tasks, not every outcome of an empathic task needs to be accommodated. And just like physical and cognitive tasks, empathic tasks should become more challenging over time, across the whole range of cognitive empathy, emotional empathy, and compassionate empathy.

But mind the difference! As discussed, your empathic tasks need to accommodate at least two decisions that lead to success; otherwise it's not a choice. That's not strictly necessary for physical and cognitive tasks, even though many of these too offer more than one choice. For the physical task, the footbridge takes more time but is less dangerous. For the cognitive task, trying to enter the supermarket by cutting a hole through a roof window might be as feasible as pickpocketing the keys from the night watch who dozed off, but both courses of action need different skills and perhaps different attitudes. For the empathic task, when the character is questioned by the police, they can get along with the officers by acting polite or confused or self-confident, which makes for different experiences in the situation (and might even make life for the player easier or harder somewhere down the road). But there are options like acting blustering or aggressive or dumb or drunk which have the character promptly removed into the can, and that was it. Game over, rinse and repeat. All this leads us to our first rule of empathic tasks.

> **The first rule of empathic tasks**: there should be more than one choice that leads to success, and there should be more choices that lead to failure than choices that lead to success. And the game should provide exactly as many choices that lead to success as the game can handle without forking into a code version of Yggdrasil.

Our first rule of empathic tasks seems to leave us with one big, hairy problem, though. How do we get the player to make the effort to understand a situation or change their attitude if they can simply proceed by trial and error?

Physical tasks rarely have that problem. If the player isn't good enough to perform a task, they have to try again and again until they're good enough. Cognitive tasks are more susceptible to it. But it's quite conventional and even acceptable, except for educational games, to solve cognitive tasks through trial and error, even though we're supposed to use memory, analysis, and evaluation to find a solution. (Also, patience is in short supply, and second screen solutions are always seductively close-by.)

But it's actually less a problem than it appears. First off, there's the requirement to have more decisions that lead to failure than decisions that lead to success, and it isn't particularly enjoyable to play a beat over and over and grind through a number of wrong solutions just because you're too lazy to think.

More importantly, though, if each choice that leads to success has its own advantages and disadvantages, as dramatic choices should, chances are the player will not merely try to succeed, but try to succeed with the most advantages. This can only be accomplished by gaining an understanding of the situation. On top of that, solving an empathic task without trial and error becomes even *more* interesting and enjoyable if these advantages and disadvantages are player-specific in the context of their respective player narratives' wants and needs. That way, the player has a whole set of incentives to eschew trial and error. Certainly, there will always be players who try to optimize the outcome, but that shouldn't bother us—it doesn't bother us with physical or cognitive tasks; there are no indications that optimizers don't enjoy optimizing; and it might even boost the game's replay value.

In the example above, dealing successfully with the police officers by being polite and helpful can give the player character some advantage in dealing with the police later in the game. Dealing successfully with the police officers by being tough and self-confident, but with the just-right dose of respect, can give the player character some street cred instead. Or, staying firm and knowing their rights might also be successful, but actually not endear the player character to anyone. That brings us to our second rule of empathic tasks.

> **The second rule of empathic tasks**: the outcomes of successful decisions should be different enough to be perceived by players as being more or less advantageous, depending on each player's self-image and individual player narrative.

Now let's add emotions. Empathic tasks become even more interesting if they are attached to emotions from the fear class and the pity class, two of the three categories from our emotional landscape we developed in the first level. Emotions from the third class, fiero, will attach themselves to player success or player failure, perhaps in varying intensities depending on how well the player succeeded or how badly they messed up.

Hence, every choice of an empathic task that leads to success should have its own emotion or set of emotions attached to it. Let's start with the pity class, i.e., emotions from NPCs players can empathize with. A successful player decision in our example could make the officers happy, another could annoy them, and for a third they might feel contempt. Player decisions that lead to failure could make them angry or frustrated or resentful. (To develop an idea about these emotions, what might trigger them, and what the consequences would be, is indeed part of the empathic task the player has to solve.) Now the fear class, for the dramatic situation players can see themselves in. Again, different choices could trigger different emotions. The edgy solution would trigger fear or at least some anxiety; the polite solution possibly joy or delight to have gained new friends; the steadfast solution could simply come down to resolve and relief. (Not to forget, the emotional state of the player at the beginning of that situation should not be a matter of chance; design techniques like agenda-setting or priming that are cut out for this are discussed in the *Narrativity* territory.) Now we can define our third rule of empathic tasks.

> **The third rule of empathic tasks**: every choice on offer should have its own emotions from the pity class and the fear class attached to it, as well as follow-up emotions from the fiero class.

Finally, how do we deal with an empathic task that is set up as a plot point where something very specific has to happen?

If you think about it, the three rules of empathic tasks that we've defined so far are already quite sufficient to deal with it most of the time. Even the imperative that something has to happen rarely proscribes that it has to happen in exactly one manner, the second design paradigm that we will discuss in a minute. But okay, let's say you have a dramatic solution in mind that has to happen to a T, exactly as designed or written, to get the most dramatic and emotional mileage out of your plot point. Well, we have to amend the first rule then: in situations of paramount dramatic importance, only one choice is set up to be successful, and all others end in failure. But designing such tasks is hard and exacting—the

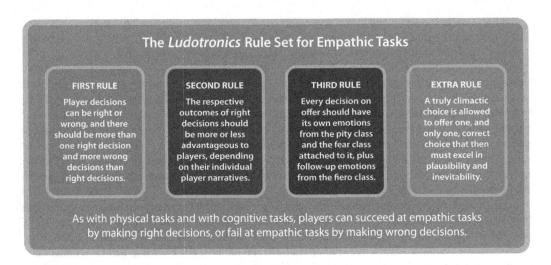

FIGURE 4.37   Rule set for empathic tasks.

successful choice must be even *more* convincing and even *better* prepared than any "regular" choice for an empathic task! Both the choice that leads to success and all the choices that lead to failure, in this case, must be impeccable in terms of plausibility and inevitability. To avoid clutter, we will formulate this amendment as an extra rule.

> **The extra rule of empathic tasks**: a truly climactic dramatic choice is allowed to offer the player one, and only one, correct choice, which must then excel in plausibility and inevitability.

To recap, player decisions can lead to success or failure; there should be more than one player decision that leads to success; there should be more player decisions that lead to failure than to success; successful decisions should offer different advantages and disadvantages; and successful decisions should deliver different emotions. Then there's the special rule that a truly climactic choice is allowed to have one, and only one, decision that leads to success, which then must excel in plausibility and inevitability.

What's already baked into these rules is the option to deal with diminishing problem space without removing player agency. When the story development arc advances over the course of the game, your sets of choices can provide fewer and fewer correct decisions—up to and including the climax that is allowed to provide only one specific choice that leads to success and to triumph, while all others lead to defeat.

When the problem space diminishes, and decisions that lead to success become more rare, these decisions must also become more plausible. Hence, decisions that lead to success have to be prepared more carefully, and the player has to be primed more thoroughly. To prime the player for correct decisions, you can employ, as mentioned, techniques like agenda-setting or priming that are discussed in the *Narrativity* territory. To prime the player against decisions that lead to failure, you can employ warning signs, even fairly prominent ones at that. Either they make the player wary, or they make the player realize in hindsight that they should have known better all along. When you have pestered your player/player character repeatedly with flocks of Crebain, for example, that's your warning sign. When they nevertheless decide to flag down a great eagle taxi to Mordor that can be easily spotted, they can then be discovered by such a flock and fried by the Evil Eye's minions without further ado, basking in the belated realization that this purportedly clever decision was ill-advised to begin with.

That's a good and feasible solution to preserve player agency along diminishing problem space, but there's another solution that is as good as this one, and perhaps even better. It's the second and final design parameter for empathic tasks, how to handle the consequences of the decisions that lead to success.

To design empathic tasks that fuel and deliver a tight dramatic structure along a diminishing problem space, but still integrate with player agency, you can design consequences that focus on "how" instead of "what." That way, you can give the player more choices that lead to success, and with that more agency, even during the climax. To illustrate this, let's assume there's a plot point late in your story development arc where the player has to make a specific decision, like trying to conquer an enemy base, escape from a prison, or kill the antagonist in a duel. All three decisions are very specific and leave little or no room for player agency.

Now, sit down and sketch the different levels of *abstraction* that your plot point permits. On the most abstract level, each decision is about the player/player character overcoming an obstacle to get what they want. That's as abstract as it gets! But it's not very helpful. What you have to do is to find the proper middle ground between your very specific choice and its abstract intent. In the first scenario, the enemy base has to be taken, all right, no way around that. But you could leave it to the player to decide how to achieve that—a full-scale assault, a commando operation, bribery, blackmail, perhaps negotiation, not all of which will be good decisions, or right decisions. In the second scenario, the more abstract version could be that the player character doesn't have to escape the prison but to regain their freedom, and escaping the prison is just one among several options to achieve that. (Use your imagination!) The more abstract version of the third scenario, finally, could be to remove the antagonist's power and influence from the game world. Again, this could be achieved in different ways, and some of these ways might be more interesting than killing the antagonist off.

Spoiler ahead for the ending of *The Witcher 2: Assassins of Kings*—but this is a fantastic example on many levels. After the problem space has been depleted, the game ends with a climactic duel. After the antagonist has been defeated, the player is given a choice: to kill the antagonist, or to let him fade into obscurity. Good reasons are attached to both options, and also different emotions. Here, you have it all. The possibilities and probabilities of the problem space are utterly depleted in favor of the necessary, but the player is still able to make a decision that counts, along their own reasoning and emotions and in line with their self-perception. The antagonist needs to be defeated (the "what"), but the player has agency and makes a meaningful decision (the "how").

In all these scenarios, it should be added, the game world should also react to it appropriately. It can become part of the world narrative, as discussed along *Hitman: Blood Money*'s notoriety system in the *Narrativity* territory. Or, as a simpler solution, NPCs can become more or less friendly or more or less helpful down the road. Or, even simpler, they can make an admiring or sarcastic or derogatory remark about it, and then just drop it. As an example, if you decide to collect the reward for Ciri in *Witcher 3: The Wild Hunt*, you're treated to 2 minutes of maximum cringe, followed by some furious dialogue lines, and then the whole affair is wrapped up for good by Ciri's remark that she'll "be over it" by the time they reach their next destination.

The important thing is, whatever solutions you come up with, whatever techniques you employ, it's much easier to make your game scale this way. In contrast to "what" consequences, "how" consequences do not automatically fork your story, and the choices on offer can be just as nail-biting, enjoyable, and satisfying.

But you have to work a lot harder on your conceptional design. As before, you need to develop your story line and translate everything into plot points. But you also have to create matching character and player development arcs, as discussed in the preceding beat; offer opportunities for the player to decide who they want to be in your game world; provide the player with choices at the just-right abstraction level; attach different emotions and advantages and disadvantages to these choices; and let the game world react to the player's decision—subtly or overtly, with a comedic flavor or a dramatic punch.

Beat 5: Participation

Pauses and Presence

Now that we have explored the nature of agency and autonomy, choices and decisions, and problem space and empathic tasks, let's turn our attention to participatory play.

By definition, participatory play is taskless play. No physical tasks, no cognitive tasks, no empathic tasks. It's just the player and their character, the level, and the excitement of being there.

This excitement can take different forms. Let's have a look at three of them that are probably the most relevant and most frequent: *suspense*, *spectacle*, and *communality*.

Suspense is the activity of waiting for something to happen, coupled with the pleasures and anxieties of anticipation. It's when you're standing on a hillside in a real-time strategy game, having arranged your troops into an effective battle formation, or so you hope, and watch the enemy's army approach. It's when you are playing a turn-based game or a multiplayer game and wait for another player to make their move. It's when you wait for your target to move into your crosshairs, hide in a basement, or cower under a tree in the forest at night in a horror or survival game. It's when you guard your team's flag and wait for the enemy's assault. It's when you ride an elevator to the topmost floor, or wait for the elevator to arrive. It's when you're at the plate and the pitcher takes their own sweet time. All these situations, and countless other situations like them, create participation through suspense. If done well, none of these are in any way less exciting for the player than answering a physical, cognitive, or empathic challenge.

Spectacle is the activity of marveling at the extraordinary. This can apply to elements from the *Plurimediality* territory, from the *Narrativity* territory, and from the *Architectonics* territory as well. It's not exploration, which is often a task, but it can be the result of exploration. When a dazzling landscape enraptures you. When you watch an epic conflict unfold. When you're listening to the sound of an approaching thunderstorm. When you appreciate a beautifully crafted item. Or, for *Architectonics*, when you contemplate a surprising turn of events. When you're enthralled by a sudden insight. When a mysterious character captivates you. When you're absorbed in an illuminating conversation. Every time the player is confronted with something extraordinary, there should be room to marvel, to appreciate, to digest.

Communality is the activity of partaking in something larger than oneself. Being a part of the Tenth mounted legion or the 1960s Packers or the march at Selma. A revolutionary movement, a sorority, a crime syndicate. A flash mob or a festival. In *Digital Storytelling*, Carolyn Handler Miller points out the similarities between highly participatory video games, especially MMOs, and highly participatory religious holidays, like Yom HaKippurim. The similarities are striking. Being part of something larger than oneself is established and expressed through customs, rituals, and ceremonies, the making of history, and the cyclical reenactment of that history. Myth, of course, is a powerful corollary. Certainly, communality is suffused with tasks of all kinds, physical, cognitive, and empathic. But it's not these tasks that create the rewarding emotional experience of participation for the player. It's the moment of commitment to such tasks by way of obligation, duty, or sacrifice.

There's another, different approach to taskless play, developed by Brian Upton in *Situational Game Design*. His three components of what he calls non-interactive play are *anticipation*, *interpretation*, and *introspection*. Anticipation certainly corresponds to suspense in our model, and elements of both interpretation and introspection are related to our model's spectacle. But there's a crucial difference between these two models. Upton's model focuses on outcome-oriented moves, developed within the player's mind during non-interactive play, to solve situations and resolve meaning. Our model focuses

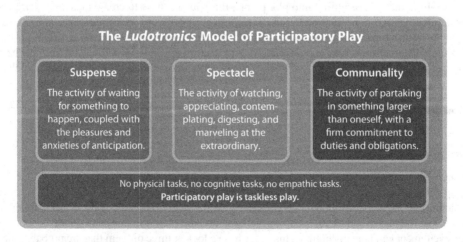

FIGURE 4.38 Participatory play model.

on taskless in-the-moment participation. Needless to say, both approaches can complement each other nicely. It's like two sets of tool boxes that you can mix and match, and each box is filled with endless possibilities.

Wrapping up this and the preceding beat, agency and participatory play are both essential design parameters. Their respective uses vary from game to game and from game type to game type. They always need to be handled with attention to detail. MMOs, for example, or horror games that are strong on terror and foreboding, are high on participatory play by design. Twitch or bullet hell games are low on participatory play by design. In between, there's a whole world of game types and games that handle participation differently, often in unique ways. They can inspire you to create and refine the playing experience for your game with the just-right combination of agency and participation.

Beat 6: Personnel

Personalities and Personifications

In this final beat in the *Architectonics* territory, we will take a look at characters against the background of *function*.

Counting among the first things you learn as a writer, usually, is that stories are about characters and not about things. *Star Wars* is not about the Death Star but about Luke, *The Lord of the Rings* is not about the One Ring but about Frodo, and *The Long Goodbye* is not about Madison's portrait but about Marlowe. That's true, but it's not the whole truth. What stories are about are these characters' wants and needs and the *emotions* attached to these wants and needs that drive Luke, Frodo, and Marlowe forward. But it's still not the whole truth! That Luke feels frustrated, Frodo desperate, and Marlowe disillusioned isn't meaningful in itself. What stories are about are the emotions of the *audience*, not the emotions of the characters. When, and only when, your audience reliably *feels* your characters' emotions by empathizing with them, then your story and your set of characters have justified their existence.

How your characters' emotions can be represented most effectively, in turn, depends on the medium. In a slightly different context a few beats ago, we differentiated between stories that are told through words, either orally or in written form; stories that are told through a visual medium; and stories that are told through an interactive medium like video games. For our current context, we also need to separate the spoken word from the written text.

In stage plays like tragedies or comedies, emotions are primarily represented through dramatic dialogue. In written media like short stories or novels, emotions are primarily represented through dramatic description. In movies, emotions are primarily represented through dramatic visualization. In each case, there's a secondary mode of representation: stage plays convey emotions also through visualization, and written texts and movies also through dialogue.

Interactive media like games have three modes of representation, each attached to one of the three development arcs and their corresponding emotional classes that we developed earlier in this phase. The player development arc, associated with the *fiero* class, is primarily represented through *player action*. The story development arc, associated with the *fear* class, is primarily represented through *dramatic visualization*. The character development arc, associated with the *pity* class, is primarily represented through *dramatic dialogue*. Each, in turn, can utilize the other modes of representation as secondary modes.

Mapping these aspects to game characters, we can now define their *principal* functions and how these functions are represented.

> **The function of the player character** is to want something the pursuit and accomplishment of which can be primarily represented through player action (with emotions from the *fiero* class) and secondarily through dramatic visualization (with emotions from the *fear* class).
>
> **The function of NPCs** is to help or hinder the player character and to elicit emotions in ways that can be primarily represented through dramatic dialogue (with emotions from the *pity* class) and secondarily through dramatic visualization (with emotions from the *fear* class).

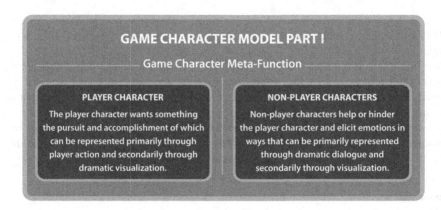

FIGURE 4.39   Game character model I: Meta-functions.

This does not always have to be true—the secondary representation might be missing, or even the primary one. Purely text-based games do not have dramatic visualization (but keyword input or text selection qualifies as player action), and kinetic visual novels have no player action (but dramatic visualization and dramatic dialogue). Nevertheless, this general differentiation applies to most cases.

Within this framework, we can proceed to explore the properties and qualities of functional characters in detail.

A good number of these properties and qualities will be informed by Melanie Anne Phillips and Chris Huntley's *Dramatica: A Theory of Story*. This theory has a reputation for pulling the uninitiated into byzantine mazes of narrative theory, a reputation that is mostly undeserved and brought about more by its technical vernacular than by its practical concepts. The aspects from this theory that have been incorporated in this beat's game character model are the composition of the *character set* with its role of the *contagonist*; the differentiation between *main character* and *protagonist*; and the notion of the *steadfast character*. These aspects enrich our palette of narrative techniques and are highly valuable for the purpose of designing dramatically complete games.

However, before we can start building our character set, two important concepts need to be introduced: the difference between functional characters and interesting characters on the one hand, and the history of archetypes on the other.

Functional characters, roughly, support the story's plot and the player character's journey, while interesting characters elicit emotions and deepen the player's involvement. In more theoretical terms, functional characters are attached to the *structural* mode of a narrative, similar to plot points and journey stages, while interesting characters are attached to the *rhetorical* mode of a narrative, similar to style or form or word choice. What exactly *is* structured by functional characters will engage us in a minute. While this difference between functional and interesting characters should always inform your design, it should be perfectly invisible to the player. The *functional* character who keeps spurring the player/player character on and into action by providing designated perspectives and arguments, and the *interesting* character who is an impressively sarcastic herald who enjoys fast horses, handsome knights, and the opportunities of diplomatic immunity, are one and the same! What connects the functional and the interesting aspects of a character is what motivates that character. Which, alas, is a game writing topic that belongs into a different book.

The second concept that needs to be understood—that is, beyond a passing familiarity—is the concept of *archetypes*. If you consult your books or your favorite search engine for story character archetypes, you will most likely be confronted with neat and tidy lists that contain a range of archetypal characters, along with their respective properties and explanations, "based on C. G. Jung." None of this is remotely true. Even if you manage to filter out lists of stock characters, which have nothing to do with archetypes in the first place, these lists neither reflect Jung's concept of archetypes, nor his archetypes! What happened here? It's not unlike a telephone game, only that the message, instead of degrading, was step by step transformed into ever more streamlined listicles. Considering the significance and prominence of the concept of archetypes for storytelling in general and our purposes in this beat in particular, let's saddle up for an excursion into its colorful history.

Everything begins with Jung's concept of a deeper layer of the unconscious, where images or motifs reside that are not personal memories. These images or motifs he calls "archetypes," a term adapted from philosophical traditions. One example of such an archetype is the *Shadow* as the unrecognized dark half of the personality, of which the "devil" is a variant. Another example is the *Magic Demon*, endowed with mysterious powers, as one of the most ancient conceptions of "god." This might sound familiar. But there are other archetypes, like the *Anima* as the all-merciful Great Mother and the *Animus* as the Father Figure, who together form the archetypal idea of the *Syzygy*. Then, there's the *Child* archetype, the *Maiden*, the *Dwarf*, the *Old Man* whose appearances include the king of the forest and animal manifestations, or the archetype of the *Spirit* whose workings for good or evil depend on conscious decisions. And so on. Jung's archetypes certainly don't compile into a list, and particularly in his essay "Archetypes of the Collective Unconscious," Jung explicitly *excludes* the possibility of a list of archetypes that one could then learn by heart. Also, in the same essay, he points out that the figures who appear in myths and fairy tales are not archetypes, but "stamped" and "handed down" forms that are *derived* from archetypes.

The second distinguished node in our telephone game is Joseph Campbell, who calls Jungian archetypes elementary ideas or "ground" ideas that manifest themselves not from Freud's personal, biographical unconscious, but from a "biological" unconscious. These ideas, in turn, appear in different historical environments and in different costumes as "bounded" forms, as Campbell calls it—as, for example, the archetypal "teacher of mankind," bringing great boons or fire, who has been "bound" into the *Trickster* or *Shadow* figure. This paints a subtly different picture. It's these "bounded" forms that Campbell attaches to the hero's journey, giving them names like the "supernatural helper," or the "herald" whose appearance triggers the crisis and the journey's Call to Adventure, or the "ogre" father who also appears as the Proteus figure of the *Shapeshifter*. All this is more familiar ground already, but not all of the items are familiar or bear their familiar names, and we're still far from having a coherent list.

Enter Christopher Vogler. In his seminal *The Writer's Journey*, he is the one who takes all these concepts and contexts and bakes them into the form most writers and storytellers are familiar with. He greatly simplifies, and simultaneously sharpens, the idea of archetypes toward practical usefulness. He does this by casting them as different aspects of the human mind, personified and endowed with human qualities, that "play out the drama of our lives." He further enhances their functionality for the purpose of storytelling by making them more flexible through abstraction and by curating their numbers, until we finally get our familiar list that contains only those archetypes Vogler deems most useful for writers— the shapeshifter, the threshold guardian, the trickster, the shadow, the herald, the ally, the mentor, and what Vogler calls the "higher self."

Yet, for the writer, this scheme poses a structural headache for broader casts of characters, when you don't have a small, ragtag group of adventurers who stick together throughout. Some characters might be integral to specific plot points but not to others, not least through their "interesting" characteristics, and become unavailable as functional characters when they're needed. Vogler defuses this by going a step further. He transforms these archetypal characters—who, as described, have already been substantially transformed from their Jungian beginnings—into *masks* that can be switched between characters. That way, different characters can play different archetypal roles at different times.

Which is a clever solution, but not a free lunch. While certainly streamlined, Vogler's archetypes— shapeshifter, guardian, trickster, shadow, herald, ally, mentor, higher self—are *still* very specific and not easily transplanted from one interesting character to another interesting character without friction. One potential casualty of which is the aforementioned character motivation: with this strategy, it becomes a lot harder to tie characters' functional and interesting characteristics coherently and conclusively together.

That's already a formidable headache, but something else adds into it. The hero's journey is certainly not the only possible journey along which character development arcs can be structured. Even for journey structures that are equally deeply rooted in Western culture, like the medieval quest or the return home, the usefulness of most of these archetypes decays rapidly, regardless whether they're personified characters or switchable masks.

Thus, we need to add one more node to our telephone game, and that is the functional character set as devised by Phillips and Huntley's Dramatica theory. It's a character set that is easy to learn, universally adaptable, and a breeze to apply. The Dramatica theory calls the characters in this set archetypal characters, carrying on that tradition. But we will stick to our own terminology of functional characters, to stress their structural aspects and dramatic functions.

Here's how it works. First, Dramatica switches from the terminology of *aspects*—aspects of the human mind or the unconscious—to the terminology of *arguments*. Next, it creates a collection of arguments that best represent the dynamics of wants and needs on the one hand, and help and hindrance on the other. Then, it *personifies* these arguments into a set of functional (archetypal) characters which, together, represent the problem-solving processes of the human mind. Not unlike Vogler, who defines his set of archetypes as a metaphor for the human situation, Dramatica defines its set of personified arguments as the "story mind." Finally, this story mind embodies the conflicting perspectives and proposals on how to overcome obstacles and satisfy wants and needs within the character's mind, including opposed wants and needs as antagonistic forces. (As an aside, this is not too far away from Gustav Freytag's view, which he expressed in 1863 in *Technik des Dramas*, that each dramatic character has a particular function with respect to the whole by representing a single common human trait.)

This might sound complicated at first, but it is really, really simple. It's a set with two groups. In the first group, there are four functional characters: the protagonist who personifies the pursuit of wants and needs; the antagonist who personifies the preventive forces of diametrically opposed wants and needs; a character who personifies help and conscience called the Guardian; and a character who personifies hindrance and temptation called the contagonist, to which we will return in a moment.

The second group also contains four functional characters: personified Reason, personified Emotion, a character who personifies trust called the Sidekick, and a character who personifies doubt called the Skeptic.

That's it—one set with two groups of four personified arguments, for a total of eight functional characters that you can learn by heart! As personified arguments, they're a lot more elastic than classical archetypes. In stories with larger casts, they can switch between characters easily, depending on the context, without becoming detached from these characters and their motivations. And they're also easily adaptable to alternative journey structures with very little friction.

Now, the contagonist. As indicated, the contagonist personifies hindrance and temptation. The concept has its predecessors—notably, it identifiably relates to the Shadow figure or the Trickster. But to consolidate these lineages into the functional character of the contagonist is perhaps Dramatica's most

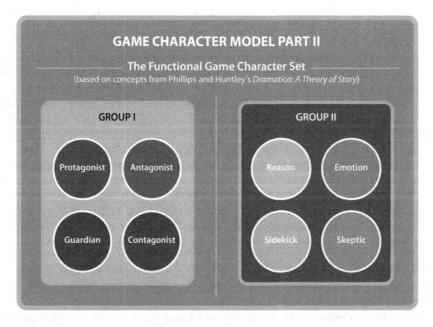

FIGURE 4.40 Game character model II: Functional character set.

remarkable contribution to the dimension and use of archetypes. The contagonist, as the "dark" counterpart of the Guardian, might or might not relate to the antagonist in ways that are similar to how the Guardian relates to the protagonist. Unlike the antagonist, the contagonist doesn't personify wants and needs directly opposed to those of the protagonist. Thus, the goals of the antagonist and the goals of the contagonist might or might not align, or might just loosely align, but they're rarely if ever identical. The argument the contagonist makes in the story, and that is its core function, is not brought forward by assault but by attractiveness, and its objective is not annihilation but seduction.

In the original *Star Wars* trilogy—of which particularly the first movie is used as a central example by Dramatica—the protagonist is Luke and the antagonist is the empire, later personified by the emperor. Each side wants to destroy the other. Vader, in contrast, is the contagonist: while his goals mostly align with the goals of the empire, he has his own agenda, and he doesn't want to destroy Luke but seduce him with the promise of unlimited power.

J. R. R. Tolkien's *The Lord of the Rings*, as another example, has many story subsets with their own local protagonists and antagonists and so on. But on the top level, where Frodo and Sauron serve as protagonist and antagonist, similar to Luke and the empire, the One Ring embodies the contagonist. Again, its goals are aligned with those of the antagonist, Sauron, but it wants to seduce, not destroy—and Gollum, as a classical mirror-character, is what Frodo will become if the One Ring succeeds.

As a third example, let's take a look at Ash in Ridley Scott's *Alien*. Ash doesn't "seduce" anyone, and he actively tries to kill Ripley when she finds out about Special Order 937 after gaining access to Mother, the ship's computer. But whether the crew lives or dies is none of his concern. All he does is subtly manipulate situations and influence decisions to protect the xenomorph, for later use by the corporation. With that, his goals align with those of the titular organism, but they're by no means identical.

As you can infer from these examples, neither the antagonist nor the contagonist have to be sentient beings. The antagonist can be a collective force like the empire or a force of nature like the Alien, and the contagonist can be a dangerous artifact like the One Ring or Ash, the synthetic person.

But we're not done. To repeat, the contagonist wants the same thing as the antagonist, roughly, and accomplishes that by seducing instead of annihilating the protagonist, or trying to. Thus, importantly, the contagonist is not defined by being good or bad. Neither is the Guardian! In Ryan Coogler's *Black Panther*, for example, the character who wants the exact same thing as the antagonist Erik "Killmonger" Stevens is none other than Nakia, T'Challa's former girlfriend. Through persuasion and implicit seduction, she tries to bring T'Challa to change his mind and reveal Wakanda to the world and use its powers to help the oppressed. That's exactly what Erik wants! (Albeit with some striking differences in method.) Then, there's T'Chaka as Guardian who, it turns out, brought about the world's imbalance and the ensuing conflict through his moral failure in the past. (That's a motif the later *Star Wars* movies also toy with, but neither as consistently nor as forcefully as *Black Panther*.)

With the concept of the contagonist safely under our belts, let's look at a few examples for the other functional characters in our set.

The first group is almost always fully loaded and carefully defined. In *Star Wars*, that's Luke as protagonist, the empire as antagonist, Vader as contagonist, and Obi-Wan as Guardian. In *The Lord of the Rings*, the first group from the top-level story line has Frodo as protagonist, Sauron as antagonist, the One Ring as contagonist, and Gandalf as Guardian. But there are many subplots and subordinated story lines in *The Lord of the Rings* that populate their first group differently; in one of these groups, for example, it's Saruman who embodies the role of the contagonist.

The second group from our functional character set, in contrast, rarely appears as fully defined and as clear-cut as in *Star Wars*. In *Star Wars*, it's Leia as Reason (making plans and all the rational decisions), Chewbacca as Emotion ("he likes to pull opponents' arms out when he loses"), Han as Skeptic ("that's suicide"), and R2-D2 and C-3PO as Luke's trusty Sidekick team who also provide comic relief. In more expansive works like *The Lord of the Rings*, these roles shift all the time between different characters—but, as context-dependent representations of arguments, they never come across as free-floating or arbitrarily assigned. The Sidekick role, for example, is sometimes embodied by Legolas and Gimli, sometimes by Pippin and Merry, depending on context and story line, with each team providing both trust and comic relief. And while Aragorn almost always embodies the role of Reason, the remaining two functions Emotion and Skeptic are forever on the move within and between different character constellations.

However, all this doesn't mean that you can only become creative with your functional character set's second group. *Alien*, for example, with its very intricate set for such a small cast, plays with the first group in clever and creative ways. Ripley is a covert protagonist for about 80 pages into the final script, and when she becomes the protagonist, interesting things happen. To see which, we need to wind back a bit. Earlier, when the movie starts, it looks as if Kane were the protagonist. After he dies, Dallas seems a good pick, and everything looks reasonably neat. There's Dallas as protagonist, the Alien as antagonist, the ship's computer, Mother, as Guardian, and there are enough clues to suspect Ash as contagonist early on. But there are also clues that something is seriously wrong with this constellation; one example is that the Guardian doesn't seem to do anything, least of all providing guidance to Dallas. When Dallas dies and Ripley is revealed as the protagonist, things fall into place. Ripley switches over into the first group. This gives her access to Mother, the Guardian, which she didn't have before, and in contrast to Dallas, she receives vital information (because she is the protagonist and Dallas wasn't). Later, Mother still continues to guide Ripley by continuously providing vital information about the ship's status. (Even later, the Guardian abandons her—but, as remarked, the Guardian isn't defined by being good or evil, and it's Ripley after all who messes up the self-destruct sequence.) There's a lot more going on, especially with respect to the second group. But it should suffice to give you ideas!

Just like reverse-engineering a theme, reverse-engineering a functional character set can be fun. But that's not what it's for. The functional character set is not a gotcha game, and there is no score. It's a structural design tool that helps you develop a full set of arguments for the "mind" of your story. Whether you want to use the whole set, use each functional character exactly once, or let one or more functional characters switch roles in different contexts, that's entirely up to you.

As our examples demonstrate, the functional character set scales from a tightly plotted blockbuster screenplay to a novel that spans six books in three volumes and took 12 years to write to a chamber play with a total of ten characters, three of which are a ship's computer, a xenomorph, and a cat. That's because the functional character set is a form, not a formula. Well, okay, it's also a formula. But it isn't formulaic! It's an incredibly flexible formula that you can bend any which way you want through the force of your own creative will, always providing you with a versatile and resilient structure that supports what you're doing and helps you keep track of all the roles or arguments in your game.

With this simple set of eight easily memorizable dramatic functions, you can go and sketch fresh, complex, dynamic functional characters that your game writer—which might be you—can flesh out and turn into interesting characters later on.

For our next topic, you might have noticed that the player character has never been called "protagonist" so far. The reason is that there's a functional difference between the protagonist of a story and the main character of a story. The player character can be both, or can be one or the other at different times, depending on your game's dramatic structure. Differentiating between the protagonist and the main character of a story is another contribution of the Dramatica theory, and it is again incredibly simple and immensely useful.

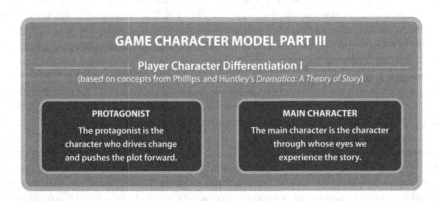

FIGURE 4.41   Game character model III: Player character differentiation I.

Here's what it is about. The protagonist is the character who drives change and pushes the plot forward. The main character is the character through whose eyes we experience the story. That's it! In any story, the protagonist and the main character can be one and the same, as Luke in *Star Wars* or Decimus Meridius Maximus in *Gladiator* or James Bond or Lara Croft or Nathan Drake. Indeed, this seems to be the default option. But then, there are Arthur Conan Doyle's Sherlock Holmes stories, Harper Lee's *To Kill a Mocking Bird*, or *Mad Max: Fury Road*. In each of these stories, we have a protagonist—Sherlock Holmes, Atticus Finch, Imperator Furiosa—who drives the story forward. And in each case, we don't experience the story through the eyes of these protagonists, but through the eyes of main characters—Dr. Watson, Scout, Max Rockatansky.

Differentiating between a protagonist and a main character can be particularly useful for game design, but not in the exact same way as in other media. If the player experienced the game through the eyes of the main character, while an NPC protagonist did all the heavy lifting, that wouldn't be very satisfying. The trick is to switch when needed.

Think of the great number of different levels and subplots and side quest, the three development arcs, and player agency and participative play. There's absolutely no reason to cast the player character as the protagonist everywhere all the time. To temporarily relieve the player from having to drive the story forward unlocks a huge range of design opportunities. For example, your game can start with the player character as a main character to defuse some of the classic problems attached to beginnings, as discussed earlier in this phase, after which the player character can grow into the role of the protagonist. You can design different story lines or subplots or side quests where the player character switches roles, depending on challenges and contexts. You can realize difficult plot points in more natural ways by casting the player character temporarily as main character and let a temporary protagonist make decisions critical for the plot, maybe with the help of soft cutscenes or even no cutscenes at all. Also, temporarily casting the player character as main character gives you more opportunities for the design of participatory play, as discussed in the preceding beat. It's a very versatile tool that you should keep handy.

Now, you might ask, whatever happened to the term "hero?" First off, the label "hero" can apply to the main character as well as the protagonist, so you'd never know whom you're actually talking about. Then, not all player characters are "heroic" in the sense of overcoming seemingly insurmountable obstacles, including themselves, and driving change. Finally, everybody is subjectively the hero of their own story, and involved in their own hero's journey or quest or return home in one way or another. All that makes the term "hero" fairly diffuse, which is the opposite of what a technical term should be. There are certain compound terms, though, like "hero's journey" or "hero NPC" (covered below), that have very specific meanings and are fit for use.

Let's proceed to Dramatica's third and final contribution to our game character model, the steadfast character. Since time immemorial, general wisdom has it that the central character of a story has to change, even "transform." This seems to go back to Egri Lajos' hugely influential publication of *Dramatic Writing: Its Basis in the Creative Interpretation of Human Motives* in 1946. Change is inevitable, certainly, because experience is inevitable—both in the sense of learning and in the sense of awareness, as discussed in this phase's first level. But that's not the kind of change Egri meant and everybody understood. Change, in this sense, means transformation, when characters transcend who they are and become better versions of themselves. If the character was greedy or racist, they become generous and accepting—a transformational change, often an internal shift in perspective, that paves the way to the story's climax and to mastering the final challenge. Moreover, Egri explicitly states that a fixed "nature" of a character constitutes bad writing. From there, the question of "has the central character sufficiently changed or not?" became everybody's favorite yardstick to separate "good" writing (highbrow) from "bad" writing (lowbrow).

This we should leave behind. There are terrific characters in great stories who "change" in the sense that they grow and do not cease to learn, but who do not transform their nature. Maximus in *Gladiator* is an excellent example, and so is Furiosa in *Mad Max: Fury Road*. (*Fury Road*'s main character Max Rockatansky, in contrast, does transform.) What Maximus and Furiosa are, in Dramatica parlance, are steadfast characters.

Like the protagonist vs. main character distinction, the transforming vs. steadfast distinction offers a greater range of design options for games that invite players to identify with the player character. If the

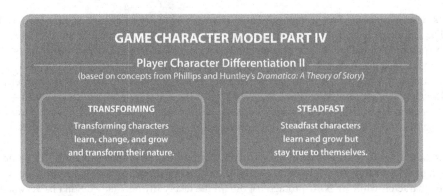

GAME CHARACTER MODEL PART IV

Player Character Differentiation II

(based on concepts from Phillips and Huntley's *Dramatica: A Theory of Story*)

TRANSFORMING

Transforming characters
learn, change, and grow
and transform their nature.

STEADFAST

Steadfast characters
learn and grow but
stay true to themselves.

FIGURE 4.42   Game character model IV: Transforming vs. steadfast.

player character is a detached character like Manny in *Grim Fandango* or Kate in *Syberia*, as discussed in the first level, then that character can transform as much as stories or journeys require without causing trouble. But in games like those from the *Mass Effect* trilogy, it can become very difficult to transform the player character against the will of the player without impacting player motivation and player emotion in undesirable ways.

Sometimes, it can be more opportune to design the player character as steadfast, as a character who overcomes obstacles and achieves their goals by staying true to themselves. But the most effective application is to give the player a choice—to transform or remain steadfast along a series of well-designed empathic tasks throughout the game. This hooks right into the "what" vs. "how" distinction from earlier beats. "What" the player has to achieve for the game's dramatic solution is fixed and doesn't fork, but "how" the player achieves it, through transforming or remaining steadfast, can modify the ending's circumstances, emotions, outlook, and so forth, preferably in ways that are compelling, plausible, and necessary.

There's one design aspect you should keep in mind that touches on both the transforming/steadfast differentiation and the previously discussed protagonist/main character split. When there's a split between protagonist and main character, the protagonist tends to be steadfast (Holmes, Finch, Furiosa) and the main character tends to be transforming (Scout, Max, even Watson at times). Now, while both transforming and steadfast protagonists can have fully developed character journeys, it usually makes more sense to attach the journey to the main character in such cases. Thus, if you indeed want to cast your game's player character as its main character, the character development arc with its character journey can safely remain attached to it.

To wrap up this beat on functional characters, we need to examine one more thing: major NPCs as "hero NPCs." A hero NPC is a special type of functional character related to Egri Lajos' concept of "pivotal" characters. However, before we can fill this concept with life, we need to get several things out of the way.

Against the backdrop of conflict, bad things happen to characters in games all the time. Often, these terrible things happen to the player character's friends and family, especially women, who must suffer to motivate the hero. This plot device, which has come to be called "Women in Refrigerators," has a bad rap for good reasons. But even if tragedies befall the player character directly, there's the *structural* problem we already discussed in a different context. As pointed out by Marie-Laure Ryan in "Beyond Myth and Metaphor," the dramatic structure of a game, in contrast to a novel, a play, or a movie, can't just throw all its plot points of pain and misery on the player, and impose unreasonable expectations or demands of actual emotional suffering.

Unreasonable expectations, on the one hand, because the player would need to *empathize* with their grieving player character—which, as discussed, necessitates a psychological distance to that character, as you can't empathize with yourself. Unreasonable demands, on the other hand, because if it does work, miraculously, it runs the risk of imposing an unacceptable amount of negative emotions on the player that might not meet the player's approval. There's no content descriptor for these kinds of negative emotions

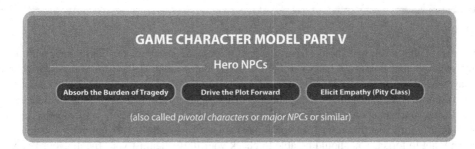

FIGURE 4.43 Game character model V: Hero-NPCs.

in PEGI, but it's recognized by ESRA, Iran's Entertainment Software Rating Association guidelines. While there's a lot to dislike about ESRA, to say the least, it has the content descriptor "Hopelessness," which specifies—among other noteworthy player emotions—the "deep feeling of sorrow due to the death of a lovable character."

Now, how and to whom *should* bad things happen in conflict situations so that they have an impact, but not drown the player in dreadful emotions?

Here, our "hero NPC" comes to the rescue, a term adopted from Chris L'Etoile's sidebar contribution to Lee Sheldon's *Character Development and Storytelling for Games*. Hero NPCs elicit empathy by "absorbing the burden of tragedy," a burden the designer can't and shouldn't impose on the player directly for all the reasons already enumerated. When a beloved character dies as a dramatic necessity, it shouldn't be a character beloved by the player character. It should be a character beloved by a hero NPC. That way, the player can empathize with the hero NPC's grief. They don't have to empathize with themselves, which is impossible, or weather the full impact of the loss, which is possible but ill-advised. Thus, hero NPCs absorb the burden of tragedy, elicit empathy, and advance the plot all at once, without imposing undue emotional demands upon the player.

To sum it up, if you want the player to experience a particular range and intensity of emotional suffering without harming the player or running afoul of self-empathy, you need to create distance. That distance already exists if your game features a detached player character, i.e., a character your player merely controls but not identifies with. (Functionally, detached player characters work like hero NPCs.)

Sometimes, though, if you can create the necessary distance, it might even work with a player character who isn't detached, as in the introduction sequence to *The Last of Us*. Not counting the game's ending, Joel is clearly a character that players can and want to identify with. But for the introductory sequence, if you look closely, you will find that Neil Druckmann—who wrote and co-directed *The Last of Us*—uses a number of *distancing techniques* to cast Joel temporarily as a hero NPC.

To start with, the introduction sequence is 20 years removed from the actual events in the game world and serves its expositional and motivational purposes before the bond between the player and the principal player character can be established. Then, while peppered with cutscenes and soft cutscenes, the introduction sequence's primary player character is Sarah. It's only during a brief part of the chase scene toward the end that the player controls Joel. Finally, there's a lot of *behavioral* distancing going on too, culminating in the beat where the player-controlled Sarah and her uncle Tommy are shocked and taken aback when Joel aggressively prevents them from picking up a desperate family at the roadside.

The whole introduction scene works as well as it does because these distancing techniques enable the player to *empathize* with Joel when Sarah dies. The player can feel Joel's pain and despair intensely on the one hand, but without being unduly burdened and overwhelmed by it on the other.

That should suffice. All this, from the functional character set down to hero NPCs, gives you an abundance of tools to sketch a cast of characters for your game that your writer, which might be you, can work with later—to provide them with motivations and make them credible, compelling, and unique.

Outlook

By the end of this level, you should have sketched a dramatic structure for your game, with a rough outline of levels and important beats on the one hand, and a rough outline for your story, character, and player development arcs on the other. If you're designing a game that is dramatically complete, you should also have some preliminary ideas about your game's exposition, ending, and functional characters, and what your game will offer the player in terms of agency, participation, and empathic tasks.

Rough drafts suffice at this point. But you'll need at least some details for your pitch and your prototype. And, not to forget, you should be able to check your drafts against your theme, your key values, and your USP, and against your target audience's player personas to see how they might react to them.

If everything looks good, congratulations! You have mastered this very tough level.

Secret Level: Story Specials

Opening

Exclusive to this fully revised new edition, please enjoy the continuation and extension of three topics around dramatically complete games that were merely touched upon before!

The following beats will sharpen concepts around character motivation and change, present alternative plot and journey structures, and widen your climactic palette with cinematic escalation and ending techniques that you might want to experiment with and convert into thrilling playing experiences.

Beat 1: Motivation

Of Traits and Change

For character design, as discussed in the level on *Architectonics*, you should differentiate between *functional* characters and *interesting* characters: the former support the story's plot and the player character's journey; the latter elicit emotions and deepen the player's involvement. These two sides, of course, must be made to fit together. When your game ships, every functional character must have become an interesting character. However, not every interesting character needs to be a functional character, and not all characters need to be interesting in the first place! Mostly, it's a matter of importance. But it should also be a matter of recurrence. Why, for example, should a merchant or blacksmith or bureaucrat the player has to call on regularly be bromidic, simply because they're not important? For characters that are not important but recurring, take a cue from 2018 *God of War*'s blacksmiths Sindri and Brok—*they* are certainly interesting, and they add a lot of local color to the world narrative.

As mentioned, it's *motivation* that connects the functional and interesting aspects of your characters. Providing motivation, mostly a combination of backstory and plot points, is the game writer's job, not the game designer's. But there's a sizeable gray area in between. Core personality traits—or attributes or alignments, whatever you want to call it—are an important part of a character's motivation and firmly connected to both its functional and its interesting aspects. Thus, there's no reason you can't or shouldn't sketch trait sets for your non-player characters, even your functional characters, as a game designer! Around which your game writer—maybe also you—can then create backstories and plot points that fuse these traits with motivations to make them interesting, plausible, and necessary.

Many techniques exist to sketch such trait sets. For starters, you can adopt the NPC motivation system from *Twilight: 2000*, to define traits for less important non-player characters quickly by drawing cards from a standard deck. The suits indicate four general traits of your choice that fit your setting (in *Twilight: 2000*, appropriately, these are violence, greed, sociability, and ambition for clubs, diamonds, hearts, and spades, respectively); the number values indicate trait strengths (2–4 "somewhat," 5–7 "moderately," and 8–10 "very" in *Twilight: 2000*); and aces and face cards define a suit's general trait in specific and prominent ways (the hearts suit's face cards in *Twilight: 2000*, for example, indicate wise, loving, honorable, and just for Jack, Queen, King, and Ace, respectively). At the other end of the spectrum, you can adopt any version of Timothy Leary's interpersonal circumplex and adapt it to your setting. As it is multidimensional and a lot more complex than *Twilight: 2000*'s NPC motivation system, it gives you a much wider palette of traits to play with for more important characters, perhaps even your functional characters. As the interpersonal circumplex has no in-built randomization, you have to create one yourself. A set of different sided physical or virtual dice, mapped to different areas of the circumplex, should do the trick in most cases.

DOI: 10.1201/9781003334682-22

Now, why is a sizeable dose of randomness so important? Humans, usually, have complex trait sets that they themselves deem perfectly reasonable and coherent. But, barring very experienced writers, it's very hard to *design* such realistic trait sets, especially when you try to create "reasonable" sets from scratch. That's because real-life sets have a whole lot of contingency baked right into them. Why were these genes expressed and not others? Why did these experiences shape our behavior and convictions more strongly than others? We're pretty good at rationalizing our own grab bags of biographical impacts and effects through the stories of our lives that we tell ourselves. (These, as a reminder, are not our lives, but our stories.) And yet, however improbable any given trait set might appear on the surface, there will be a specific perspective from which these traits line up and make sense. To create that perspective is the task of the game writer.

Besides traits, characters also have physical characteristics and emotional or mood states at various strengths. Many of these, and you should keep that in mind, will be various kinds of average! Applying a modified version of David Freeman's character diamond from *Creating Emotions in Games*, you can bestow a set of dimensions to each character: between one and three traits, depending on character importance; one physical characteristic; and one prominent or recurring emotional or mood state.

But wait! Before you start, there are four caveats you need to be aware of, the first two courtesy of David Freeman. First off, if you attach two or more traits to an important character, these should not fit together so well that your character becomes boring or a cliché. (Freeman's examples are "heroic, loyal, honest" and "swashbuckling, dry-witted, a bit arrogant.") Most of the time, luckily, your system's randomization element will take care of it. But you will almost certainly edit and rearrange some of your choices, and that's where you can easily fall into that trap. Then, don't think in terms of "balancing" or "trade-offs" either—that's also not how human trait sets work. (Freeman's bad choice example is balancing a "strong" trait like leadership with a "soft" trait like spirituality.) Your random element should take care of that too, but again, be aware of it when you edit and rearrange. Next, humans are capable of overriding character traits and emotional and mood states if the situation calls for it! (In pen-and-paper role-playing games, for example, the player would make a modified dice roll against their trait value in a dire situation.) Finally, traits or prominent emotional or mood states can change over time. Even your non-player characters should be allowed to grow emotionally and change over the course of your game!

To wrap up this beat, let's add a few words to character change. As discussed in the *Architectonics* level, there's the distinction between transforming and steadfast characters. Transforming characters, in that sense, often "transcend" and become better versions of themselves. If you're working with the Syd Field paradigm or a similar plot structure, this transformational change is the key event, after the midpoint, which paves the way to the story's final challenge and the character's mastery of that challenge. In this case, change is imperative to succeed. Similarly, if you have a steadfast character, it's this steadfastness that the character needs to cling to after the midpoint, hanging on to it by their fingernails, which then enables them to master the final challenge. When you design your dramatic structure, you should allow for one or the other or both. How it plays out, though, preferably involving factors like player performance and player decisions, that's a job for a game writer, and a very tough one at that.

Beat 2: Modification

Of Plots and Journeys

The level on *Architectonics* gives you a detailed look at plot structure and character journey, but limited to their most well-known paradigms: the Syd Field paradigm for plot structures and the hero's journey for character journeys. This beat will introduce you to alternatives to both.

Let's start with plot structures. As you might remember, the Syd Field paradigm—the predominant plot structure in the Western cultural sphere—is a three-act structure that encompasses the setup (inciting incident), the confrontation (midpoint), and the resolution (climax), with turning points and pinches in between. Let's look at three alternative plot structures: kishōtenketsu, johakyū, and repetition break.

Kishōtenketsu is a four-act structure that originated in China, moved to Korea, and eventually became a dominant paradigm in Japan. You can spot this plot structure not only in Japanese fiction but also in non-fiction and academic writing and in manga, where it is known as yonkoma, or four cell manga. Kishōtenketsu's four acts are constituted by the introduction (ki), the development (shō), the sudden turn (ten), and the conclusion (ketsu). As an example, here's the Japanese folktale "The Boy Who Drew Cats," as translated and retold by Lafcadio Hearn in 1898. A young acolyte, expelled from his home temple because he compulsively draws cats everywhere, arrives at a deserted temple. That's the ki, or introduction. After he has drawn cats on every screen in the temple room, he retires to a side chamber, because his former teacher once told him not to sleep in large open places. That's the shō, or development. In the middle of the night, he wakes up from horrible screaming and fighting; when it subsides, he falls back to sleep. That's the ten, or sudden event. Finally, in the morning, he finds the dead body of a huge rat-demon in the temple room, and the cats he had drawn on the screens have blood on their mouths and paws. That's the ketsu, or conclusion. Evidently, there's a lot of conflict in this story. But conflict in kishōtenketsu often plays out between notions, beliefs, and expectations instead of between characters, and the focus isn't necessarily on the fight or showdown. (Here, the fight is even entirely off-stage, not unlike furious battle scenes in Shakespearean plays.) It's a structure that's cut out to be used for smaller indie games, or for individual episodes within larger structures.

Johakyū, also from Japan, is the plot structure of traditional noh, kabuki, and bunraku plays, with slow beginnings and swift endings as outstanding characteristics. Its origins go back to Japanese court music from the Heian period, which in turn has its roots in Buddhist music imported from China during the Asuka period in the sixth and seventh century. Thus, if you want to try out this structure in creative ways, think less in "acts" than in "movements," with modulations in tone and an overall sense of acceleration. While its name suggests a three-act structure (johakyū means beginning/opening, development/break, rush/climax), it's actually a five-act structure. It begins very slowly with "love, peace, and happiness" in the first movement; builds up drama with "warriors and battles" (or events equivalent in intensity) in the second movement; and proceeds with "suffering and tragedy" to its dramatic climax in the third movement. After that, "journey and travel" with music and dance in the fourth movement ease out of the dramatic intensity, followed by a rapid conclusion in the final movement that ties up loose ends and returns to peace, love, and happiness. This structure certainly isn't small, and it gets a lot more complicated than this rough description suggests if you dive into the intricacies of noh plays in particular, with their elaborate variations and repeating microforms like clockworks within clockworks. If you want to read up on it, good places to start are Oba Junko "Jo-ha-kyū" and Hui Yu-Chun Lorena's *Japanese Noh Theatre: The Aesthetic Principle of Jo-Ha-Kyu in the Play* Matsukaze. But beware—the more complicated your structure becomes, the more it might confuse your target audience if you fail to prepare and market it correctly. Yet, it's a powerful plot structure that invites you to experiment with it and create memorable playing experiences.

Finally, repetition break. This doesn't need a lot of explaining: something happens again and again, with only minor variations, that establishes a pattern—until it happens differently in surprising ways that often involve a learning experience. You've probably encountered it many times, from fairy tales ("Three Little Pigs"), jokes (a priest, a pastor, and a rabbi …), or movies (*Groundhog Day*). This plot structure is highly memorable, highly persuasive, highly scalable, and can be embedded in other plot structures as well. Besides humor, it's also exceptionally effective for the uncanny, think *P.T.* or *Nightslink*—because humor and the uncanny are related in complex ways. Thus, if your game has elements of comedy or terror, this might be the plot structure you want to try out.

Let's move on to alternative character journeys. Here, the hero's journey has become the predominant framework in the Western cultural sphere. Journeys, as a reminder, are not about plot points but about stages connected to insights and personal growth, and they often involve outer and inner travels. Let's look at three alternative character journeys: nostos, the Chinese box, and—very briefly—the medieval quest.

Nostos is a character journey used in Ancient Greek literature. It translates to "return home," usually of an epic hero. Homer's *Odyssey* is an obvious example, but there are many other tales and tragedies that feature heroes who can't find their way back, need a lifetime for it, or are killed on arrival. There might be some historical background to that, related to a postwar power vacuum that led to the collapse of the Mycenaean palace culture and the beginning of the Greek Dark Ages. However, this character journey is not what you think it is, with neat successions of departures, wanderings, adventures, seductions, returns, and indoor massacres. Just look at the *Odyssey*! After the exposition, we meet Odysseus on an island, where he's been held captive for seven years by Calypso. From there, he travels to another island, where he tells his hosts a number of outrageous stories about his travels from Troy. (Mind that "wily Odysseus" is not the most reliable narrator.) His hosts, moved by his tales, help him to return to Ithaca, where he roams about quite thoroughly in disguise. Finally, he slays the suitors. If you dig into the nostos progression of this epic, you will find that it consists of stages that process and provide insights on hospitality (particularly eating), hubris, temptation, loyalty, and identity along Odysseus's outer and inner journeys. Like the hero's journey, nostos is a complex psychological construct, not an adventure flick with sea monsters. Adapting this journey framework for a game will certainly be taxing; but the resulting playing experience can be compelling and rewarding.

Next up, the Chinese box—also known as Matryoshka, nested, or frame narratives. In the Western cultural sphere, it was prominently employed in the Late Middle Ages (think Chaucer or Boccaccio), in nineteenth-century literature (think Mary Shelley or Joseph Conrad), and in postmodernist novels (think John Barth or Kathy Acker). However, it's most prominently and most famously used in the monumental Indo-Arabian folktales collection *The Book of the Thousand Nights and a Night*, where the nested narratives are at times six or seven layers deep (depending on how you count). Basically, it's a string of stories nested into each other, where the protagonist or main character on any given layer is told a story by another character, who then becomes the protagonist or main character in their own narrative layer. While these nested stories certainly have plot structures, they aren't plot points. Instead, they are "vertical stages" that teach protagonists or main characters on higher layers critical insights, which in turn enable them to grow and overcome challenges in their own narrative layer—or, in a comical manner, misinterpret what they've learned and make everything worse. In *The Book of the Thousand Nights and a Night*, not each and every nested story strictly follows this insight pattern, but it's pervasive and prominent up to and including the topmost layer of Shahryār and Scheherazade. Just like the nostos structure, the Chinese box is a very challenging framework for character journeys, particularly for smaller indie games. But imagine what you could do with it! Also, you can give each narrative layer its own distinctive plot structure, for example, kishōtenketsu or a compressed version of the Syd Field paradigm, and create a playing experience through multiple player characters like no other.

Finally, a few words on medieval quests. They're touched upon several times in this phase, up to and including the retelling of the introductory passage of *Pwyll, Prince of Dyfed* in the level on *Architectonics*. Authentic medieval quests are completely different from Hollywood sword-and-sandal epics or RPG quests. Nor can they, as it's often done, be pressed into the hero's journey paradigm, except violently in Procrustean fashion. They don't revolve around plot points but, again, around stages connected to insights and personal growth, almost always in the form of outer and inner travels. The thing is, you have to read them for yourself and savor their intriguing opaqueness and beautiful strangeness. In fact, the more you learn about medieval literature, the less obvious it becomes what these texts are about, which genre they represent, or what audiences they were directed at. Plus, take absolutely nothing for granted! Do we have sufficient knowledge, for example, to establish conclusively which concepts and practices courtly love, or "minne," represented in medieval times? No. At least, not if you ask a bona fide medievalist. What you should do is read—everything from the *Mabinogion* tales to the Pearl Poet's *Sir Gawain and the Green Knight* to Wolfram's monumental *Parzival*—and then adapt, create, and innovate!

Beat 3: Magnification

Of Escalations and Endings

In this beat, you will learn about a few more escalation and ending techniques. Most examples will come from movies. For convenience, certainly, but also to avoid spoiling dozens of games in a single beat. None of them will be easy to adapt for your game—as, more often than not, the clockwork-precision needed to produce their desired effects is limited by the demands of player agency. But that doesn't mean you shouldn't try!

Let's look at escalation techniques first. The final level of the Process phase on *Integral Perspectives II* introduces you to the goal escalation framework around importance, complexity, and urgency, which is focused on structure and challenge. Here, let's add to that seven escalation techniques that focus on emotional impact instead: proximity, magnitude, ticking clock, sudden time decrease, dilemma, becoming more personal, and severity of failure.

If you work with **proximity escalation**, whatever your player character fears most is coming physically or geographically closer. Think of Frodo approaching the land of Mordor and, particularly, its Evil Eye manifestation in Peter Jackson's movies.

Magnitude escalation is about a threat that is local at first but then grows larger and larger until it puts the entire game world into jeopardy. Think of *Invasion of the Body Snatchers*, where the replacement of humans through alien invaders escalates in magnitude from the neighbors to the entire town to the United States and finally the whole world. (As the studio insisted on changing the ending of the 1956 version by adding a frame story, the 1978 version catches this better.)

The **ticking clock escalation** is the time-focused equivalent to the proximity escalation. Here, whatever the player character fears most is coming closer and closer in time. Think *High Noon*.

In contrast to the ticking clock escalation, the **sudden time decrease escalation** pushes a dreaded event or the principal challenge unexpectedly up in time. Think *Aliens*—while the characters are still making plans for their survival, the discovery that the atmosphere processor's nuclear reactor is about to explode abruptly cuts down their time from 17 days to 4 hours!

Then, there's the **dilemma escalation**, when the player character is put in a situation that allows them to solve only one out of two or more challenges. Whom should the player character rescue on Virmire in *Mass Effect*? Whom should Batman rescue in *The Dark Knight*? You get the gist.

Often related to the dilemma escalation, and complementary to the magnitude escalation, is the **getting more personal escalation**. The threat the player character faces is at first more universal or professional, like a soldier who fights in the war, or an undercover agent infiltrating a cartel. But then they see this threat closing in on someone or something they hold dear, like their hometown or family. For an extreme example, think *Se7en*.

The seventh and final technique you can use is the **severity of failure escalation**, making the consequences for player failure in the game world more and more severe. Here, think *Alien³*, particularly the original screenplay and the 2003 Assembly Cut. Initially, failure to contain or kill the alien would lead to the death of the entire cast, which sounds severe enough. But after they managed to contain it, a corporate ship approaches, and failure to kill the alien in time would not merely lead to the cast being killed as unwelcome witnesses, but to bioweapons research with catastrophic results. Finally, when they realize that Ripley's pregnant with an alien queen, the failure to keep it out of the corporation's reach would endanger the entire human species.

Now, endings! In the level on *Architectonics*, you learn about the four ending categories resolved, unresolved, mixed, and multiple; like the goal escalation framework mentioned previously, these categories focus on structure and challenge. So let's again add seven techniques that focus on emotional impact instead: surprise, lost treasure, baddies win, not really the end, last scare, cliff-hanger/unfinished, and punch line. There are more, but these should suffice. Also, seven is an excellent number.

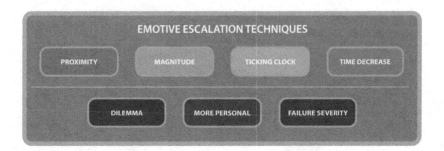

FIGURE 4.44 Emotive escalation techniques.

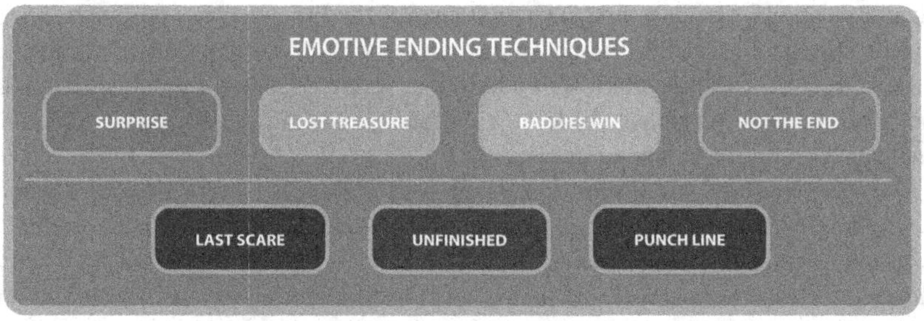

FIGURE 4.45   Emotive ending techniques.

While still a formidable challenge, most of these techniques are easier to pull off in a game than many of the escalation techniques introduced above. One big problem, however, is that these endings are not well suited for a multiple ending that depends on player performance and player decisions. Either way, you can experiment with them and perhaps find new and interesting ways to employ them.

The first is the **surprise ending** that makes you reconsider everything that has gone before, as in *The Sting*, *The Usual Suspects*, *The Sixth Sense*, or *The Game*. The second is the **lost-treasure ending**, as in *Raiders of the Lost Ark* or *Titanic*. Then, there's the **baddies win ending**, as in *Invasion of the Body Snatchers* (1978 version) or *Il Grande Silenzio*. Next, there's the **not really the end ending**, as in *Flash Gordon*, *Aliens* (watch the credits to the end and listen carefully), or the original *Doom* game (ditto). Also, there's the **last scare ending**, which you know from every horror movie since *Alien*. Furthermore, there's the **cliff-hanger/unfinished ending**, as in *Lock, Stock and Two Smoking Barrels* or *Thelma & Louise*. Finally, there's the **punch line ending**, as in *Some Like It Hot* or *Ferris Bueller's Day Off*.

Some people argue that if you know the ending of a novel or movie or game whose ending falls into any of these categories, then you have no incentive to read or watch or play it anymore. But if you look at the examples above, they've all become famous, and even iconic, because of their endings. Many people want to read, watch, or play them specifically for that reason! Also, many people who just read, watched, or played them want to do so a second time. As such endings often put everything that has gone before in a new light, this can make rereading, rewatching, or replaying it a compelling experience.

That'll do! These escalations and endings should give you a lot to dig in to, and a lot to play with.

Outlook

As you might have noticed throughout this secret chapter, the more you travel from structure and challenge to emotional impact and growth, the more you travel into game writing territory. But that shouldn't keep you from sketching ideas in these directions that your game writer—who might be you—can then take up and flesh out.

Level Six

Integral Perspectives II

Opening

Welcome back from your journey!

You can tackle this final level any time, no matter how many of the four open-world levels you traveled through or want to explore in the future.

Like the very first level in this phase, this one discusses matters independent of the type of game you envision. Back in the first level, we built models for motivation and emotion; now, it's time to build models for goals and rewards. Also, we will look at player failure and some interesting options to handle it.

Let's dive right in!

Beat 1: Goals

Among the seemingly indispensable elements that popular definitions of what a game "is" customarily contain is the so-called victory condition. This victory condition, in turn, is tied to a definable goal or, more restrictively, a "quantifiable outcome." From there, we can differentiate two schools of thought.

One school of thought excludes whole types of games that have no defined goal or quantifiable outcome from the category "game" altogether and throws them as "software toys" or with similarly endearing labels under the bus. For quantifiable outcome purists, RPGs from pen and paper to *World of Warcraft* don't qualify as games (quests are won, but narratives and characters keep evolving forever). Neither count *The Sims*, or *Dwarf Fortress*. Or, for some, story-focused games in general. What this embodies is an instance of game exceptionalism. For no other media format would anyone put forward such purely outcome-based definitions with a straight face. And while games from practically every game type can be lost—characters, Sims, and fortresses can perish, after all—quantifiable *loss conditions* are rarely considered game-defining by quantifiable outcome purists, which is peculiar.

The other school of thought tries to rescue these types of games for the category "game" by including goals that players set themselves. This isn't altogether wrong but leaves the door wide open for everyone and everything.

What you should do is follow the latter, by and large, but tie it to design decisions. We can reasonably demand that goals players can set themselves be compatible with the game's design-driven goal that you developed in the Procedure phase: growth (tied to skills and knowledge along the player development arc), insight (tied to understanding and attitude along the character development arc), and experience (tied to routes and resolutions along the story development arc). As a refresher, your game-driven goal is part of what we called the "holistic goal" of a game in the Procedure phase; the other two parts are your design-driven goal (the core of your synopsis) and your desire-driven goal (the heart of your vision statement).

Thus, for games without a quantifiable outcome, the design-driven goal's elements growth, insight, and experience should be tied to a range of possible goals players can set themselves that the game is *purposefully designed to support*. That way, we neither have to remove whole types of games from consideration, nor do we have to allow in everything that exists in the world and call it a game. All we have to demand is that the range of goals players can set themselves in so-called goal-less games must be anchored to purposeful design decisions toward player growth, insight, and experience.

DOI: 10.1201/9781003334682-23

FIGURE 4.46 The holistic goal.

Wrapping it up, we can now define the game-driven goal as such: it specifies *game completion* as a worthwhile and achievable outcome, which includes both the completion of partial and self-set goals, and may or may not define a victory condition.

Which doesn't necessarily exclude goals *beyond* your purposeful design. Never forget that players create goals of their own all the time, from legit to outrageous, even in games that have clearly defined victory conditions. Think speedrun, three hearts and no sword, or knife only. Think exploits, mods, and total conversions. In a way, think machinima and fan fiction! Additional goals like that aren't usually purposefully designed. But you can purposefully leave some room that allows players to create additional goals they enjoy and raises your game's replay value to boot.

Now let's move on to one of the most essential aspects of the game-driven goal: its affiliation with intrinsic motivation, as opposed to extrinsic motivation. This is a distinction from motivation theory that closely relates to self-determination theory and, again, the flow model, both discussed in earlier parts of this phase. Roughly, intrinsic motivation for an activity is driven by *personal interest* in that activity, and what can be gained from carrying out that activity in terms of personal growth, insight, and experience. Extrinsic motivation, in contrast, is driven by the *consequences* of carrying out an activity in a successful manner, consisting either of rewards or the avoidance of punishment. When you sit down and learn calculus because you find this part of math fascinating and want to know more about it, that's intrinsic motivation, and your goal to master calculus is an intrinsic goal. When you sit down and learn calculus to keep up with course requirements and get good grades, that's extrinsic motivation, and an extrinsic goal. When you sit down and learn calculus to get a better grade than all your classmates, that's also an extrinsic goal.

Now, you might have heard that extrinsic motivators don't work as well as intrinsic motivators, and that extrinsic rewards can even be detrimental to the development of intrinsic motivation. This seems indeed to be the case. It has been tested over and over with reliable and reproducible results. Learning French or calculus are not and should not be competitive tasks, and attaching such activities to rewards and punishments, like grades, makes it incredibly hard and often even impossible to enjoy these activities intrinsically. The world is filled with great literature, fantastic pieces of music, marvelous historic events, and fascinating scientific discoveries all of which people will never again in their life touch with a ten-foot pole after having been tested and graded on them in high school. (Nominally, grades have completely different functions than reward or punishment; but the way they're generally managed and the way they're generally perceived, it's reward and punishment all the way down.)

In this context, games do differ from other media. Having finished a novel isn't the goal of reading a novel, and having watched a movie isn't the goal of watching a movie. You read the novel or watch the movie because these are intrinsically enjoyable experiences. Only if you read the novel or watch the movie for course requirements or similar, then your goal is indeed to have read the novel or to have watched the movie. You get rewarded if you have and punished if you haven't. Again, while intrinsic goals are about experiences, extrinsic goals are about consequences. For games, the intrinsic side is manifestly the same—you play the game because it's an intrinsically enjoyable experience. But you also want to win the game, or beat it! Which is another way of saying that the goal is to have played it—successfully, that is.

In contrast to novels or movies, games have a *competitive* aspect that's baked right into their very nature. Thus, most of the time, games offer the joy of playing, which is attached to intrinsic goals, and also the joy of winning or beating the game, which is attached to rewards like hi-scores or badges or weapon upgrades or your status among other players and friends. Thus, rewards and punishments as extrinsic motivators are always already part of a game. Which, most of the time, is perfectly fine, except when it isn't—we will get back to extrinsic goals, their design challenges, and their range of rewards in this level's final beat.

Before we can put extrinsic goals on a hiatus, however, two more points. For the first, intrinsic motivation is related to so-called mastery goals, while extrinsic motivation is related to so-called performance goals. Or, more simply: "I want to be great at this" vs. "I want to win." Our player motivation model that we developed way back in this phase reflects this distinction by pairing mastery and performance into one motivational driver. It's the whole package that makes a game attractive and enjoyable to different kinds of players. And there's also a bridging effect between these two aspects. According to empirical evidence, and you can start with Kenneth E. Barron and Judith M. Marackiewicz's "Achievement Goals and Optimal Motivation," having lofty mastery goals doesn't necessarily translate into actual performance. In plain English, mastery goals alone rarely get anyone's behind off the couch. Performance goals do! Competition does! And once performance goals got mastery-type players going, mastery goals can kick in to provide long-term motivation.

As for the second point, many exceptions to all what's been said above exist. Especially games with a strong narrative core, like *Gone Home,* offer only intrinsic goals—here, rewards of any kind from the extrinsic range would be outright detrimental to the playing experience. And while games without victory conditions like *Dwarf Fortress* might offer some extrinsic goals, in this case bragging rights because your fortress lived longer than the fortresses of your friends, they don't contain explicit rewards from the extrinsic range either. Thus, they are probably more attractive to mastery-oriented players than to performance-oriented players.

From here on, let's focus on intrinsic goals and two sets of design principles attached to them. The first set of design principles is about *construction-specific* properties, the second about *completion-specific* properties. Let's start with the construction-specific properties of a well-designed goal:

- First, the goal must be *challenging*. Challenge means that obstacles must be overcome that arise from conflict, i.e., from competing goals that other game agents—be that tetrominoes, a great ape, the Persian army, or other players—pursue during the game.
- Then, the goal must be *structured*. Structure means that the obstacles that have to be overcome must be arranged in a meaningful order.
- Finally, the goal must be *representable*. Representability means that for each of the three development arcs, the goal must be representable in a specific dramatic mode.

Let's look at the first property. "Challenges" in games are generally understood as unnecessary obstacles by design. Following Bernard Suits in *The Grasshopper,* unnecessary obstacles are even a necessary condition for a game to be a game in the first place. There are two points here that need to be stressed. "Unnecessary" means that "necessary" obstacles cannot be part of a game. According to Huizinga's principle of the "magic circle," discussed in the *Plurimediality* territory, playing a game has to be *voluntary,* otherwise it's not a game. Then, "obstacles" should be defined very broadly, lest we fall back into the exceptionalism trap of quantifiable outcomes.

Another thing one can argue about is the term "conflict." Can there be games without conflict? Again, it probably comes down to how narrow or broad your definition of conflict is. There are non-Western storytelling traditions that are purportedly "conflict-less." However, at closer examination, such interpretations almost always turn out to be wishful thinking, with or without a dash of exoticism. Such traditions—like kishōtenketsu—are actually chock-full of conflict; it's how conflict is established, developed, presented, or solved that differs from Western narrative traditions. Thus, all things considered, you probably want to have challenges in your game that arise from some kind of conflict, so that the player can overcome or solve them to reach the goal, which can be a self-set goal.

The second property, that goals must be structured and that obstacles must be arranged in a meaningful order, effectively means that the obstacles that stand between the player and the goal of the game

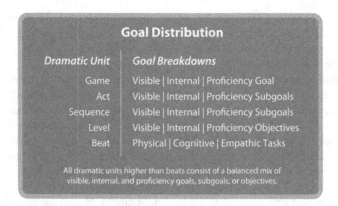

FIGURE 4.47   Goal distribution.

should become more difficult, more numerous, and more frequent over time, not the other way around, and in a controlled manner. For that, you need both a goal hierarchy and escalation techniques.

Your goal hierarchy is the breakdown of your game-driven goal into smaller constituents, to be attained individually by the player over the course of an act, a sequence, a level, or a single beat. With regard to these constituents, there's a whole bag full of terms that are in use, and any number of distinctions. What fits our challenge structure best, though, is a four-fold hierarchy along the terms *task* (beat), *objective* (level), *subgoal* (sequence or act), and *goal* (game), whereby levels, sequences, and acts can have as many objectives and subgoals as needed. As always, you can use a different structure or create one yourself! But this one has the just-right number of elements to allow interesting design decisions without being overwhelming, and the terms can be easily remembered.

You might notice that "task" isn't in the same semantic league as the terms objective, subgoal, and goal. That's intentional. Because within the span of a single beat, fulfilling a task should always equal the goal of that task. When the beat's goal is to take out a guard, the task is to take out that guard; if the beat's goal is to persuade a demon to let you through, the task is to persuade that demon to let you through; if the beat's goal is to find a stash of waybread hidden in a cellar, the task is to find that stash of waybread hidden in that cellar. You get the drift. Objectives, subgoals, and goals, in contrast, are not identical with any task, because the player has to perform a *series* of tasks to attain them—for example, break into a warehouse to find something valuable with which to bribe a demon to meet the level objective of gaining access to the dungeons. That way, by calling the goal of a single challenge a task, it is easier to remember that any goal at the bottom of the goal hierarchy needs to consist of one single challenge that cannot be broken down further. All this, obviously, has to be coordinated with your challenge structure and your learning curves, discussed in-depth in the *Interactivity* territory.

Next, your succession of tasks, objectives, and subgoals—your obstacles—must be in perfect sync with your game's plot points, journey stages, and proficiency targets in terms of *escalation*. As mentioned above, being arranged in a meaningful order means that your obstacles must become more difficult, more numerous, and more frequent over time, not the other way round. Plot points, journey stages, and proficiency targets, correspondingly, must become more important, more complex, and more urgent. Together, these elements constitute your goal escalation framework. Let's have a brief look at its three most fundamental elements and what they mean.

Escalation in importance. What the player/player character originally thought of as their all-important goal is again and again superseded by other goals, each considerably more urgent and important than its respective predecessor, up until the true goal of the game is revealed.

Escalation in complexity. The obstacles that have to be overcome to reach the goal become more complex than the player/player character originally thought, diversifying into more and more tasks that solidify into more and more objectives and subgoals.

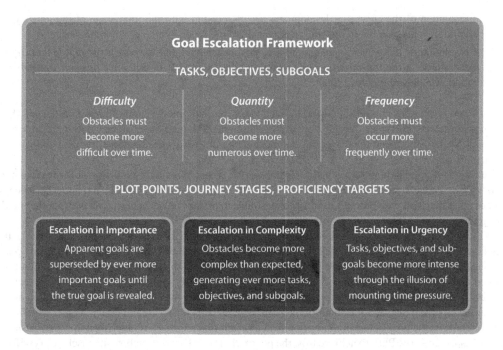

FIGURE 4.48　Goal escalation framework.

Escalation in urgency. The time to meet tasks, objectives, and subgoals becomes subjectively
shorter while the game progresses, not as timed tasks, but as a motivation- and emotion-driven
illusion of mounting time pressure.

Again, a basic example. The player character is an undercover agent whose goal is to infiltrate a gang
of small-time drug dealers, collect evidence, and bring its members to justice. Along the way, their plans
turn out to be a high-risk venture as the gang is trying to hoodwink a powerful drug cartel whose boss
has many friends in very high places and commands a large, ruthless, and well-trained militia. Then the
player character finds out that this militia is ready to strike at law enforcement key locations and even
government facilities to set an example and extend their sphere of influence. Finally, it is revealed that
these strikes are only a distraction, meant to absorb enough government forces to clear the way for an
impending foreign invasion. Here, you have a complete, if simple, goal escalation framework. Three
times, what looked like an important goal is superseded by a goal that is considerably more important.
Obstacles and difficulties mount, more and more tasks, objectives, and subgoals begin to emerge and
have to be dealt with in ever more rapid succession. Plus, there's a heightened sense of urgency, as the
invasion can only be prevented if enough of the cartel's preparatory operations can be foiled in time. All
the while, the player character must again and again rise to the occasion.

The third and last construction-specific property, that goals must be representable in specific dramatic
modes, is related to the dramatic structure of a game, as discussed in the *Architectonics* territory. To
summarize the main points and expand on them, this structure is defined by up to three different arcs:
the story development arc, the character development arc, and the player development arc. Games, as
a reminder, do not need all three arcs; they can do just fine without, or with only rudimentary, story
development and character development arcs. But for every arc your game contains, that arc requires its
share of the resolution in its primary mode of representation. For the story development arc, the character
development arc, and the player development arc, respectively, these representational modes are the *visible goal*, the *internal goal*, and the *proficiency goal*.

The resolution of the story development arc, associated with the resolution of the plot, should be
representable in this arc's primary dramatic mode, which is *dramatic visualization*.

The resolution of the character development arc, associated with the final stage of the journey, should be representable in this arc's primary dramatic mode, which is *dramatic dialogue*.

The resolution of the player development arc, the proficiency goal for which the player literally needs to be at the top of their game, should be representable in this arc's primary dramatic mode, which is *playable action*.

All three resolutions can be supported by secondary dramatic modes, and often are, to deepen their respective impacts: the story development arc by dramatic dialogue; the character development arc by dramatic visualization; and the player development arc by dramatic visualization, dramatic dialogue, or both.

But mind—experimental games and art games exist, where this might be different for reasons that make sense. Perhaps your game is one of these games! With respect to a holistic playing experience in games other than that, however, it's usually not desirable to replace any primary mode with another mode altogether.

What does all this mean in practice? Here's our trusty boss fight example again, only this time it's the final boss. It's the final *challenge* that will solve the conflict, and everything makes sense at this point because the player has been led here through obstacles that were distributed across the game in a controlled and *well-structured* manner. To succeed, the player has to apply every move and every combo and every trick in the book that they've learned over the course of the game. This is the resolution of the player development arc, and it's about *player action*. Also, this boss is the main antagonist who has to be overcome as the goal of the story development arc, and this must be accomplished in *visible fashion*, perhaps spectacularly. Plus, to achieve this, the player character has to rise above themselves to confront this antagonist as the goal of the character development arc, articulated and reflected upon by the player character's peers through *dramatic dialogue* in the form of words or cheers or huzzahs or letters of appreciation or admiration, and possibly love.

That should suffice for the construction-specific properties of a goal; let's turn to its completion-specific properties. Any goal, subgoal, objective, or task in your game should be *unambiguous*, *attainable*, and *valuable*.

The goal must be *unambiguous*, which is equivalent to being clearly communicated.

The goal must be *attainable*, which is equivalent to corresponding to the player's learning curves on the one hand, and it should remain attainable even when the player fails or makes a mistake on the other.

The goal must appear *valuable*, which means that its resolution should not only be desirable and rewarding, but credibly communicated as such.

As for the first property, we need to clear up immediately that no superordinate goal has to be unambiguously communicated from the start, nor should it. It always applies to the goal at hand, be it a task, objective, subgoal, or goal. What's more, what's communicated doesn't have to be true in the sense that it truthfully reflects what's going on in the game world. It just means that whenever a goal is communicated, there should be no doubt as to what that goal is, no matter if the assumptions behind it are genuine or in error or a decoy.

Now, for the subject matter of being unambiguous, this isn't trivial. In the *Interactivity* territory, four conditions of task design are discussed, one of which is *recognizability*. (The other three are *solvability*, *consistency*, and *elasticity*.) Being unambiguously communicated (from the designer's perspective) and being recognizable (from the player's perspective) are obviously equivalent, and they're practically identical for beats/tasks. For the player, understanding the nature of a task, objective, subgoal, or goal should never be a challenge in itself.

Another aspect is that communicating your goal unambiguously *once* may not suffice. While playing a game for weeks or even months, and playing several games at the same time, it's easy to forget what any specific goal was about—irrespective of how unambiguously it once was communicated! When you give the player some means to refresh their memory in some way, keep in mind that the gameplay context will differ. Even if your communication was perfectly unambiguous at the beginning of a task or objective, it might no longer be that unambiguous after the player proceeded halfway through it, paused playing for a week or two, came back, and now pulls the original missive from the menu. Never forget that communication and meaning are context-sensitive and context-dependent.

Now, the second property, being attainable. This is a lot less trivial than it sounds. For one thing, every task, objective, subgoal, or goal must correspond to the player's learning curves. Thus, your obstacles must not only be in perfect sync with your game's plot points and journey stages, but also its proficiency targets in terms of skill, knowledge, understanding, and attitude. All that comes with a huge load of parameters that you need to juggle successfully.

On top of that, each goal should still be attainable when the player fails or makes a mistake. Failure is usually the part that your design already covers—the player might have to respawn, reload, or similar, and can then try again. What's often not sufficiently covered is the second part, when the player makes a mistake—wandering off in the wrong direction, making an unexpected decision, killing a crucial informant, and so on. During development, many of such issues will be caught by quality assurance (QA) testers, provided it's part of your publisher agreement. But you won't have that for your prototype. Thus, you have to step into your players' shoes and find out what mistakes they can make. You need to ensure that a mistake doesn't leave the player stranded—wandering around aimlessly, reloading game saves at random, consulting the internet. Think, for example, of proximity triggers for scripted events that go awry, observable even in shipped AAA games with lots of QA testing. If the trigger range is too small, players might pass it by and never know why they got stuck. If the trigger range is too large,

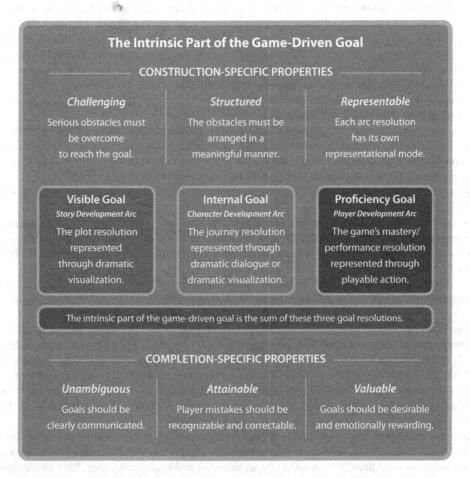

FIGURE 4.49 Intrinsic part game-driven goal.

exploration-focused players might trigger it from a distance, a location, or an angle you hadn't thought of, from where they can't properly react to that event or even don't notice it at all.

Finally, there's the third completion-specific property, that any goal must not only be valuable but also appear valuable. If you prepared a five-star dinner for your friends or family, you don't slap it on metal food trays with a crusty ladle. You arrange and serve it to your friends or family in ways that make it shine. On the side of the player, similarly, every goal should be perceived as desirable and rewarding, which you can only accomplish by presenting it in the right way.

That's what you should know about game-driven goals to get started. Only when the intrinsic goal of your game has all the properties it needs, three construction-specific and three completion-specific, will it be a great goal.

Being challenging, structured, and representable on the one hand, and being unambiguous, attainable, and valuable on the other, isn't tied to any game type. It's important for games as different as *Tetris*, *Mass Effect*, *Civilization*, or *Super Mario Odyssey*. It's also not tied to how ambitiously designed that goal is, from retrieving the prince at a construction site to saving the universe in six hyper-dimensions. Whatever your game-driven goal happens to be, it's the sum and the qualities of its basic properties that will make it a great goal.

Beat 2: Failure

While player failure raises a good deal of design questions, the fact that players expose themselves to the possibility of failure is not a mystery. For one thing, all three development arcs have in-built characteristics that make the possibility of failure outright necessary for an intense and fully enjoyable playing experience. The story development arc is driven by the game's visible goal, with the wants and needs of the antagonist standing in the way of the wants and needs of the player character. The higher the stakes, the more rewarding the playing experience. The character development arc is driven by the game's internal goal—the player character has to overcome their limitations to transform and transcend or remain steadfast and hold their ground. The more tempting the inner demons, the more enjoyable living up to one's true calling. The player development arc, finally, is driven by the game's proficiency goal—the player has to overcome physical, cognitive, and empathic challenges. The more formidable these challenges, the greater the triumph of winning or beating the game. Then, there's learning. When we decide to learn something, we do expect failure. Perhaps not sweeping failure, that it turns out to be impossible to acquire the skill, knowledge, understanding, or attitude we set out to acquire. But we certainly expect temporary failure. It would be hubris to assume invincibility or infallibility, and hubris is the straightest path to terminal failure.

To sum it up, everything we undertake that is linked to challenges or learning or both is fraught with risks, and humans wouldn't be where they are if they hadn't evolved to not just manage but indeed enjoy risks and the possibility of failure. A lot of social psychology is involved, certainly. But at the bottom, there's evolutionary pressure.

From there, let's examine some important design questions. Prominent aspects associated with player failure are player safety and punishment. You need to have a good idea about the implications of both.

Player safety is first and foremost a matter of preserving progress. The player should be safe in the knowledge that the time and effort they invested is not lost or wasted. The player should be safe in the knowledge that sudden interruptions from the outside world during gameplay won't lead to unresolvable conflicts. The player should be safe in the knowledge that they are allowed to try out and create their own playing experiences without being punished for it. All this shouldn't be controversial. But if, when, what, and how often a player should be able to save a game state during play has been a matter of dispute for decades.

Hardware restrictions that made saving a game complicated on earlier consoles should all but be a thing of the past. And while developers like to balk at the request to make increasingly complex game states savable on a medium, this shouldn't be an insurmountable obstacle either. Both challenges and solutions in development are getting more demanding and complex all the time.

Probably the most spurious argument against game saves is that the option to save, or even the knowledge that the game has been saved via autosave or checkpoints or task completion, would "break immersion." As discussed at length in this phase's introductory level, "immersion" is a non-concept anyhow, and nobody's "immersion" was ever "broken" by the option to put a bookmark between any two pages of a spy thriller or a period romance.

Then, punishment. We will define punishment as a rule set or a game mechanic that maps the occurrence of player failure *within* the game world in some way or other to consequences *outside* the game world, with non-diegetic costs for the player. In its most basic forms, the failure to keep the player avatar in the game, or keep it alive, necessitates inserting another coin or reloading an earlier game state. None of this is part of the game world.

Let's work our way through a set of game types and see which aspects need further analysis.

Retention-focused games. In retention-focused games like coin-operated arcade games or free-to-play games with in-game purchases, punishment abounds. After player failure, players either have to start from scratch or pay up in some way or other. If players don't pay up with money, they have to pay up with waiting times, protracted grinding periods, and other assorted cruelties informed by behavioral modeling. All of which certainly counts as punishment, but punishment is an integral part of these games. It cannot be abolished without substantially altering the game and the experience players have sought in these games, or been persuaded to seek.

Competitive games. In competitive games that pitch the player against other players, failure means losing the match. Losing a match alone hardly counts as punishment; possible consequences would. But the consequences of failure in competitive games hardly count as punishment either. Depending on game type, the player might lose a brief period of time until the next match begins. Or, as is often the case in arena shooters, the player loses little to no time but instead all their collected weapons and armor and power-ups. But losing time, equipment, power-ups, and so on as a consequence of failure is an integral part of the gameplay loop and the very playing experience this loop provides. Other possible costs of failure, like not being able to buy better weapons and other equipment for the next match, are not punishments but the absence of rewards. (Behaviorally, though, withheld rewards often do work and feel like punishments.) Most importantly, however, all these consequences are almost always consequences within the game world, justified by their respective narrative fictions.

Permadeath games. In permadeath games, a category that comprises everything from arcade-type games to *Tetris* to most roguelikes to *Dwarf Fortress*, the erasure of all progress after player failure is again an integral part of the design, and the very playing experience target audiences for these games are looking for. Add to that popular self-imposed permadeath challenges for any game, even open-world games like *The Legend of Zelda: Breath of the Wild*.

Single-player games. In single-player games of any type that are neither retention-driven nor permadeath games, going back to an earlier game state is the traditional way to handle player failure. That alone isn't punishment. But losing substantial chunks of progress, equipment, or resources of any kind as a consequence, or having to watch or skip through the same cutscene over and over, all that certainly counts as punishment for several reasons. To begin with, none of these punishments are true game world consequences: the "true" in-game consequence would be the death of the player character, not the loss of progress or resources. Then, lost progress, lost resources, or inexhaustible cutscene confrontations have to be measured in time, which means that player failure within the game world is paid for with the player's time outside the game world. Sending the player back to an earlier game state is, in most cases, a basic and necessary design choice. But none of these additional measures are necessary design choices by any means.

All in all, punishment for failure in retention-focused games and permadeath games is a necessary part of the design, and losing a competitive multiplayer match doesn't count as punishment in this sense. Historically, however, the latter wasn't always the case for competitive games—but we wouldn't want to reintroduce the original Olympic spirit of Ancient Greece where the winners were lavishly rewarded by their communities, but the losers shamed and humiliated, and runners-up not even remembered except in very unusual circumstances.

Disputed ground, first and foremost, are single-player games that are neither retention-type games nor permadeath games. Let's look at *Aliens versus Predator* from 1999 as a warm-up example; the differences between the original release and its Gold Edition update in 2000 reveal several details of interest.

Gameplay in *Aliens versus Predator* is demanding, most of the enemy placement is randomized, and some levels are very large and can stretch out forever, especially when players become progressively more cautious. In the original release, there was no game save option within levels, called episodes. The whole level or episode was lost when the player messed up, and particularly difficult levels could fill your day with an endless stream of rinse and repeats. Did these punishing requirements seem to be a good fit for the primary target audience? They probably did. Did these punishing requirements rhyme with the game's theme? Absolutely. Plus, while its USP was something different altogether, namely three playable species, the missing game save feature was almost certainly part of its value set. So, everything was groovy! Except that it wasn't. The game was painfully downgraded in game reviews because of it, and players were not amused.

There are two major problems involved with this missing game save option, one game-specific problem and one general problem. The game-specific problem is that the developer team wanted to force their exact intended playing experience on the player. It is a recurring flaw that is also reflected in the infuriating contrivance that the motion tracker stops working when the player character pulls down the helmet's infrared eyepiece. (A type of artifice spiritually resurrected with fanfare several years later by *Doom 3*'s "there is no duct tape on Mars.")

The more general problem with the missing game save feature is that the developers tried to translate the exposure and vulnerability of the player character into the exposure and vulnerability of the player. As has been discussed at the beginning of this phase, players experience emotions from the fear class by seeing themselves in the game's dramatic situation. They should not experience emotions from the fear class because the game threatens them with losing substantial amounts of time outside the game world. Of course should the player be terrified! But the player should be terrified along the lines of adrenaline-fueled brushes and battles (*Interactivity*), terror-inducing audiovisual and architectural design (*Plurimediality*), emotional tension in memorable gameplay moments (*Narrativity*), and a gripping dramatic structure (*Architectonics*). The player should not be terrified along the lines of possible interruptions and mistakes, shy away from trial and error, and become too afraid for in-game explorations as these would likely be too costly.

One year later in the Gold Edition, players were able to save the game at any time throughout a given level, but, depending on the selected difficulty (Training, Realistic, Director's Cut), only a limited number of times. Which turned out to be a fairly decent solution that didn't sacrifice the original idea in its entirety. And while it would still be preferable to let players decide how they want to play, it struck a good bargain between the designers' vision and the players' needs. The motion tracker/infrared contrivance, though, remained.

For console players, not to forget, the experience of not being able to save the game within individual levels was the traditional status quo, owing to technical constraints. (And non-console players could become quite furious when console ports wouldn't implement a game save feature for the personal computer, with *Halo: Combat Evolved* or *Alan Wake* as renowned examples.) Many of these constraints have been removed over time, and modern console games have both autosave and game save features. Many titles, however, like *Resident Evil 7: Biohazard*, still retain traditional "save point" mechanics where players can manage a number of game saves but can only save at certain locations within the game. Customarily, such locations were and are imaginatively designed—sleeping couches in *Ico*, typewriters in older *Resident Evil* titles, save crystals in early *Tomb Raider* and *Final Fantasy* games, or camp fires in *Dark Souls* or *Rise of the Tomb Raider*. (Whereby *Rise of the Tomb Raider* deserves special mention for its wildly misleading save slot system.) Why, then, without the technical constraints of the past, do many console games cling to such seemingly antiquated habits? Surprisingly, the answer has probably not to do with punishment, but with rewards, and we will save the answer to this question for the next beat.

On top of everything that's been discussed so far, there's another argument against punishing the player through loss of progress, loss of equipment and resources, cutscene repetition, and similar. As has been pointed out several times, all three development arcs are about challenges and learning: progressing in skill, knowledge, understanding, or attitude. Now, if the player fails to learn, games already react to that by withholding intrinsic rewards—important plot points, items, or regions cannot be unlocked; NPCs are no longer willing to help and assist or might even grow hostile; gameplay becomes repetitive as new mechanics or new combinations of mechanics fail to appear. Thus, for the best possible playing experience, in which flow plays a critical part, games must always *facilitate learning* by making it as exciting as possible. Each development arc provides the player with intrinsic motivators to learn as part of the playing experience. In contrast, any form of time loss outside the game world is not a withheld intrinsic reward, but an extrinsic motivator qua punishment. And what do we know about punishment? Is it a great motivator to facilitate learning and conducive to great learning experiences? Not at all. For all we have learned about learning, from behaviorism onward, punishment is the worst possible mechanic you can apply.

Actually, what these and other real-world punishments for in-game failure really provide is a meta-layer of competition *against the game itself.* That cannot be what you want as a game designer. Don't force your player into competition with your game! Don't forget that "play" also carries the meaning and the freedom to try things out without being punished or humiliated for it.

Let's move on to an argument from the opposite end of the spectrum, that there should be no game save mechanics at all because there should be no player failure that would make game saves necessary. This seems to have been forcefully argued by Chris Crawford in his 1995 essay "Barrels o' Fun," but the references to that effect and the generally abridged quotations are plainly misleading. Nowhere does Crawford's essay posit that there should be no player failure. Instead, its threefold argument reads as follows:

- Players should never have to start over after dying, being punished for it by losing all their progress.
- The game should spare the player the tedious task of saving, reloading, and file management; instead, it should take the player back automatically to the most recent convenient starting point, so they can try again.
- Game situations that can only be solved by repetitive trial and error with numerous save–die–reload cycles are not well-designed.

This, indeed, should be utterly uncontroversial in its entirety. And during the last 25 years, many games have adopted design patterns that do just that. Certainly, many players do want to handle and administer multiple game saves manually for various reasons—which has also been taken care of by many games that provide both an autosave feature and game save slots. And that's how it should be! For the best playing experience, your game should not only make it as easy as possible for the player to get back on the horse and try again, instantly, but also offer a mechanism for players who like to exercise some control over the process.

But the save–die–reload cycle, after all, even if imaginatively obscured by sleeping couches or typewriters or other solutions mentioned above, cannot be part of the game world proper. Naturally, there are game designers who aspire to do things differently, which brings us to this beat's final topic: the search for innovative failure mechanics. At their best, such attempts couple an innovative game mechanic with an imaginative narrative to keep the consequences of player failure largely, or even entirely, inside the game as part of the game world.

These attempts are dominated by two approaches. The player character is either already dead and therefore cannot die, or the player character doesn't die but is rescued and resuscitated. The latter has a variant, perhaps best known from *World of Warcraft*'s "ghost run," where the character's physical body dies, but their spirit remains alive with the option to resuscitate the body and reclaim their equipment. In most cases, these approaches come at the cost of time, equipment, and advantages, but these are in-game costs as they take place in the game world. In other words, they're diegetic costs, in contrast to all the forms of player punishment outlined before, which are non-diegetic costs.

An outstanding example of the "already dead" approach would be the undead ranger Talion from *Middle-Earth: Shadow of Mordor*, who gets even stronger through dying—a narrative device mechanically complemented and reinforced by the game's Nemesis system for persistent non-player characters. Other examples are *Planescape: Torment* and, in similarly intriguing ways, *Dark Souls*; the latter with an equipment retrieval system not unlike the one mentioned above.

An outstanding example for the second, the "rescued just in time" approach, is the "buddy system" in *Far Cry 2*. After the player chooses a character, all other playable characters become "buddies" who will rescue the player character after player failure. Which doesn't come without in-game costs; again, this narrative device is complemented by imaginative rule sets. Another example would be the *Gears of War 2* single-player campaign, where, at least on lower difficulty levels, the player character can be revived by non-player character teammates. Then there's the call to Valhalla in *Final Fantasy Legend II*, where Odin restores the player character *right back to the battle* on the promise to fight him at some point in the future. (But the player can decline the offer and return to a saved game state instead.) *BioShock*'s regenerative "Vita Chamber" devices also fall into this category, roughly. It's a solution that seems not altogether convincing at first but is vindicated later by being strongly embedded in the narrative.

There are other approaches than these, of course, but they're comparatively rare. One is the rewinding of time, as in *Prince of Persia: The Sands of Time* or in *Life Is Strange*. The former even has a meta-diegetic (autodiegetic) narrator as a backup solution who declares "that's not what happened" when the player character runs out of magic sand and dies. And then there are unique imaginative solutions for a game or series of games, like the famous "synchronization failure" in *Assassin's Creed*. On a side note, picking up on a plot device from Philip José Farmer's fabulous *Riverworld* novel, a game could design player character death as a travel system to known, unknown, or otherwise inaccessible locations.

Thus, there is no recipe. Each of the existing approaches is only applicable to a certain range of narratives. For your game, in general, you're on your own. The most promising places to find a solution that fits your game world are the *Interactivity* and *Architectonics* territories: it's almost always the combination of innovative game mechanics and imaginative storytelling that provides outstanding solutions for this challenge.

Beat 3: Rewards

In this level's first beat, we looked at intrinsic goals and how these relate to our motivational model developed at the beginning of this phase. Now we will look at extrinsic goals and rewards in more detail, after which we will weave intrinsic and extrinsic motivation, goals, and rewards together into a stratified reward system that you can use, adapt, or expand for your own game.

First, we need to pick up on our discussion of how intrinsic and extrinsic rewards either complement or interfere with each other.

On the one hand, there's a whole mountain of scientific evidence from studies and meta-analyses that extrinsic goals are detrimental not only to intrinsic motivation, but even to creativity. One basic test comprises two groups of people who are given the same task. One group is promised an extrinsic reward for that activity, like sweets or grades or money, depending on age and context, while the other group is not. Invariably, the group that wasn't promised an extrinsic reward enjoyed the activity more, repeated that activity more often without being explicitly tasked with it, and scored higher on a creativity index, if measured. What this means is that extrinsic rewards, except in very specific circumstances, reproducibly and reliably override whatever makes an activity or a task enjoyable in itself.

On the other hand, games have a "dual" nature, as discussed, courtesy of being competitive at heart, serving both mastery goals and performance goals. The player can enjoy the gameplay intrinsically as a rewarding activity and, at the same time, enjoy extrinsic rewards for getting better or beating or winning the game. So does it mean that there's no problem involved with mixing intrinsic and extrinsic rewards when it comes to games? Sadly, no.

In *Designing Games*, Tynan Sylvester is highly critical of extrinsic rewards for all the reasons enumerated, and rightly so. When an enemy drops loot after being killed by the player, his example goes, the player's intrinsic motivation to fight that enemy within the context of the game's setting is severely compromised. This is plausible and convincing. Many games ride piggyback on this dynamic, to turn the game into a slot machine where the next extrinsic reward is always right around the corner. So keep playing. And don't stop. Or contemplate. How, then, can we handle extrinsic rewards when they seem both supportive and detrimental to an enjoyable playing experience?

Here's a solution. It's not a magic bullet that works everywhere, but it works well enough most of the time. That solution is to align intrinsic and extrinsic goals and rewards with your development arcs in ways that make sense. Your story development arc and your character development arc should provide intrinsic goals and rewards toward the player's wants and needs; their appreciation and deeper understanding of the game world; who they want to be in that world; and emotions from the fear and pity classes. Your extrinsic goals and rewards, in contrast, should be provided by the player development arc toward player progress; proficiency goals; and emotions from the fiero class.

Mapping this to Sylvester's example of the loot-dropping enemy, the design rules could be like this. First, killed or captures enemies should only "drop" things that they would plausibly carry. (This should reduce the number of loot-kills.) Then, if an enemy carries anything of value, it should never be random but extra plausible in ways that could be expected, perhaps even actively sought out by the player. (This takes several addictive slot-machine mechanics out of the equation.) Valuable items, finally, should be specific items that help the player character in the context of a task, objective, or subgoal. (Reducing the amount of non-specific valuables like gold or coins or any other in-game currency reduces the number of meaningless killing sprees to upgrade equipment, buy better weapons, and similar.)

This will make your game world a lot more plausible as well. Soldiers, for example, would leave their valuables in the camp or with the baggage train, not schlep them around on duty or on the battlefield. But if an enemy is on their way to buy a new set of armor, they could be expected to carry either cash or items of exchange matching their intentions. And a specific enemy who might be in possession of a map or other tactical information could be pursued by the player for that very reason. Also, what about enemies who don't carry any valuable items, don't pose an immediate threat, and might, in certain situations, even be unarmed? Here, the player would have to make up their own mind what to do, instead of being perpetually pushed toward loot-kills for gold or experience points.

The latter, sadly, we see way too often. *Assassin's Creed: Origins* is a good example. It's an excellent game with a dazzling and beautiful game world, but in the reward department, it effectively assassinates intrinsic motivation. The never-ending cycle of looting and killing to upgrade equipment and, especially, gain experience points lures the player into meaningless extermination sprees against enemy soldiers and the local fauna alike. Also, as soon as the player character has acquired the hidden blade, the player must jump through hoops to regain the ability for non-lethal takedowns. But why would they—non-lethal takedowns bring no experience points; they're useless against higher level enemies; and the player can't even hide the body! To top it off, pocketing loot and experience points is accompanied by audio-visual cues straight from the *Bejeweled* department. Add to that a most uninspired tutorial level, where everything is about introducing basic combat and climbing and looting, and nothing about amazement and wonder and awe. Yes, it's still a terrific game—but it could have played in a whole different league.

By keeping extrinsic rewards out of the story and character development arcs, the decision to kill an enemy can become a matter of necessity, a matter of assessment, and a matter of character. All of which makes the gameplay vastly more interesting. But for the player development arc, it's different. The very fact that the player becomes better at something can both be an intrinsic reward in the context of mastery goals and an extrinsic reward in the context of performance goals. To extraordinary player achievements, you can attach everything from high scores or badges to player status or access to additional game content, and so on, as types of extrinsic rewards that we will examine in more detail below.

Reward alignment in this sense, it should be stressed, has nothing to do with the business practice of aligning rewards with desired employee behavior. Reward alignment in this sense is about aligning your intrinsic and extrinsic goals and rewards with their proper development arcs.

Doing that isn't trivial. That's why you need a reward system for your game with two registers. One register is for intrinsic goals and rewards. Even if your game is not dramatically complete and offers no genuine story or character development, there should be intrinsic goals and rewards attached to the game's general dramatic structure and to the player avatar. The other register is for extrinsic goals and rewards for player progress and player proficiency, attached to the player development arc. There are games, as discussed, where extrinsic rewards might be detrimental to the playing experience—where, for example, player progress is exclusively attached to understanding the game world and other characters, and perhaps to attitude. In such cases, you might decide to use only the intrinsic register for your reward system, which is perfectly fine.

Let's build a reward system that is both a model and an example, with a final illustration toward the end of this beat.

For our intrinsic register, we will apply everything we've discussed in this and the first level of this phase. For the extrinsic register, our reward system will utilize the toolbox of gamification. This might sound curious at first, because the term gamification refers to the use of game design processes and mechanism in non-game contexts. But what the gamification toolbox contains is a well-organized collection of extrinsic motivators adapted from game design, ready for use. Plus, importantly, the reward system of a game is not a game!

Let's start with the extrinsic register. Gamification has a mixed reputation, to put it mildly, and both its good reputation and its bad reputation are largely warranted. Gamification can be a force for good and enrich our experience, and it can be a force for evil that seduces us to waste our time and talents. On the evil side, gamification can mask, and even addict us to, repetitive, unpalatable tasks through meaningless rewards, thereby obviating the need and the effort to make such tasks less repetitive and more palatable in the first place. (As the cartoonist Zach Weinersmith quipped in an *SMBC* comic, it's as if Sisyphus were rewarded with meaningless points and progressed one level each time he reaches the summit and the rock rolls back down, providing him with more strength and also a bigger rock for his next try.) On the other hand, gamification can make learning easier and more enjoyable, for example, learning to handle or operate complex interfaces and machinery; it can help us find solutions to difficult problems; it can promote changes in our behavior and motivate us to choose long-term goals over short-term rewards for a more healthy lifestyle.

Extrinsic rewards—meant for the player development arc only, as a reminder—succeed almost universally for two reasons. On the one hand, they directly address the probably most basic principle of human behavior: to seek to repeat pleasurable experiences and avoid unpleasurable experiences. On the other hand, extrinsic rewards are highly abstracted, often in symbolic ways. Both characteristics in tandem make them work nearly independent of individual differences and personalities. The psychological model most intimately connected to this is behaviorism, and the motivational models and tools associated with it are classical and operant conditioning, reinforcements and rewards, and reinforcement and reward schedules. (Punishment, except for the moderate absence of rewards, is not part of this model, or of behaviorism in general. Punishment doesn't facilitate but prevents learning and lasting change.)

The most basic motivational drivers in terms of extrinsic rewards form the so-called PBL layer: points, badges, leaderboards. These should not be dismissed as mere lightweights. PBL fueled the early generations of video games, and they kept being relevant for a whole range of games and purposes precisely because they are highly abstracted, instantly comparable, and indifferent to personality or individual preferences. And they need not literally be points or badges or boards; they can be stars or souvenirs or trophies that can be collected throughout a game, or achievement and progress messages that are automatically posted on social media, or anything you can think of that fulfills the same symbolic function.

The PBL layer fertilizes the ground, so to speak, for the second layer of extrinsic rewards that resides on top of it. This layer was collected and condensed by Gabe Zichermann and Christopher Cunningham in *Gamification by Design* into the SAPS range: status, access, power, stuff. All four elements are still highly abstract and universally applicable, but they're not as purely symbolic anymore as PBL. SAPS is where success is transformed into the following assets: *status* to status items, bragging rights, prestige, and similar; *access* to special content, products, information, or services without monetary value (e.g., access to a level or character skin that is part of the game the player has already bought, or the right to buy a product in a certain color that isn't regularly available); *power* to certain functions like board master or event coordinator or moderator for a community, game forum, or game chat; and finally *stuff* to special content, products, information, or services that do have monetary value (but preferably not much).

PBL and SAPS are universally applicable and extremely versatile. They also complement each other: items from the PBL range can accumulate to items from the SAPS range, and items from the SAPS range can be displayed, indicated, and referred to by items from the PBS range as a kind of shorthand.

Now, of course, you have to fill your PBL and SAPS layers with life! If you have a cleverly devised PBL/SAPS-based extrinsic register, it can not only power your game's player development arc but even create and power an entire gaming community around your game.

Let's move on to the intrinsic reward register, to be applied to the story development arc and the character development arc. Intrinsic rewards do not operate universally. Much less abstract in nature than their extrinsic cousins, intrinsic rewards have to account for the emotional and cognitive complexity of individuals. For maximum versatility and effectiveness, intrinsic rewards need to spread out, so that the reward system can serve different types of behavior and different wants and needs, all of which fluctuate between one player and the next, and might also fluctuate from one day to the next for one and the same player. The psychological models intimately connected to these types of rewards are cognitivism, constructivism, and connectivism. The tools associated with these psychological models, in turn, are numerous and open-ended.

As our model is also supposed to work as an example, we will plug in a collection of specific tools and drivers. But these are just suggestions; you can fill in whatever suits you and works best for your game.

For your toolbox, you can use all kinds of applied motivation models and findings that are applicable to designing intrinsic rewards. The most obvious tools you can put here are Csíkszentmihályi's flow model and McGonigal's seven types of work model, which we had originally placed higher up in the "Achieve" slot to keep things simple at the beginning of this phase. As a reminder, the idea is not to offer all seven types of work—high-stakes, busy, mental, physical, discovery, team, and creative work—but a delightful and highly rewarding cocktail with handpicked ingredients. But you can offer some symbolic treatment for work types that are missing. If it's a single-player game, non-player characters could help the player character out in a coordinated team effort from time to time. If your game doesn't include creative work, give the player something to arrange or customize or individualize, whatever it is. If the game doesn't involve cognitive challenges, give the player some mental work like optimizing the use of their inventory space—many players *like* optimizing their inventory space in clever ways, so don't over-automatize to begin with. (There's even a puzzle game out there, *Save Room*, that is exclusively about managing a *Resident Evil*-style inventory.)

Next, you can add a player-type taxonomy, similar to the one originally researched by Richard Bartle and later expanded by himself and others. A player taxonomy is a highly useful tool, as long as you heed Bartle's admonition that *what* players do is less important for your design decisions than *why* they do it. Also, be aware that players need not conform to one particular type at all times. However, the most important caveat is that you probably can't simply pick a player taxonomy off the shelf for your game! Bartle's model and similar models are built on observations around certain playing situation, or game types. Thus, if you want to use one of these models, you have to adapt it by testing it against your game and modifying it, if necessary. Alternatively, you can take a general model, for example, any version of Timothy Leary's "interpersonal circumplex" classification of interpersonal behavior, observe players playing your prototype, and strip that general model down to an applied model that contains only those behaviors that the mechanics of your game actually allow. Either way, it's a lot of work. But if you know what player types your game permits and, in extension, what motivates them and what they perceive as rewarding and why, you can draw them in and keep them spellbound with well-chosen incentives.

Then, let's throw in the information gap model and the curiosity gap model by Daniel E. Berlyne and George Loewenstein, respectively. With the help of these and similar models, you can distribute and dispense information in specific ways so that seeking out new things and finding out what happened before or what happens in the end is perceived as a powerful reward.

Likewise, you can use set completion models like Ellen R. K. Evers's set stimuli and the pseudo-set framing from Kate Barasz and others. For that, items are arranged in true sets or pseudo-sets so that the player acquires each item not just for its own value, but also to complete the set. Holding the final piece of a puzzle, crossing off the last item from a list, completing your 1953 Bowman set at an auction, or putting the sixth and final gemstone into place is deeply rewarding because people love to bring about *completion*. This, for example, can be combined with Nunes and Dreze's endowed progress effect, when you give the player a few pieces of the puzzle, a few cards to start the collection, or a gemstone in advance, but increase the total the player has to collect, cross off, etc., by that exact same amount. The effect is that, even though both challenge and reward remain the same, the player displays more persistence toward reaching that challenge's goal and even perceives the reward as more satisfying. Set completion and collecting things in general, it should be added, have also extrinsic properties and can be used and abused with purely symbolic items like stars or coins or anything from the PBL range. But collecting something, especially if it has personal or narrative value, can be an enjoyable activity in and of itself, and completing such a collection is its own reward as well.

Moreover, as final suggestions, you can and should use agenda-setting and priming models from media psychology, which is addressed in the *Narrativity* territory, and everything that's attached to it, like foreshadowing. In the right circumstances, simply recognizing something, remembering something, or putting something to use can be perceived as satisfying and rewarding. To these ends, you can also play with the Zeigarnik effect that people remember uncompleted tasks better than completed tasks, to scale rewards for recognition over time.

None of these tools are particularly complicated, but it needs some knowledge of, and engagement with, social science research to apply them effectively. If that's not your cup of tea, and that's perfectly okay, then you might want to get someone on the team who has a background in social sciences. All these models and tools can not only power your game's reward system, it should be added. They are also exceptionally useful for level design and the purpose of player guidance. Which, alas, is outside the scope of this book.

In the driver section above the toolbox tier, you can again plug in any motivational drivers that suit your game and your purposes. For our example, we will plug in the three floors of our motivational building that we created earlier in this phase.

As reward drivers in the bottom layer, we can plug the "excite" floor with the four elements of our interactive playing experience model: the just-right amount of challenge (*Interactivity*), compelling aesthetics (*Plurimediality*), emotional appeal (*Narrativity*), and meaningful choices (*Architectonics*). But there's enough space on that floor to add more tenants. We can choose from many options, but let's pick unnecessary obstacles and epic scale as our examples.

Without unnecessary obstacles, which we addressed earlier in this level, games wouldn't be very rewarding. If players were allowed to put a number of balls into a number of holes by hand or suspend tetrominoes in midair and rotate them until they fit, neither the word "golf" nor the word "tetris" would ring any bells.

Epic scale, of any kind, is almost always experienced as rewarding. It can be anything from wide vistas to the formation of massive war parties to intense music to the sound of a rock that is dropped into a very deep well. (All four examples, incidentally, are staged in reverse order to great effect in Peter Jackson's *The Fellowship of the Ring*, when Pippin manages to alert the orcs of Moria to their presence.) With respect to rewards attached to epic scale, you can also utilize cutscenes in an enjoyable manner. Epic scale is where cutscenes can shine, and this includes embedded micro-cutscenes, which are less complex and costly and more suitable for indie games. In *More Than a Game*, Barry Atkins provides a range of examples. One of them is the demanding speedboat race through Venice's narrow canals in *Tomb Raider II*. There, successful moves are rewarded by what Atkins calls "personal mini-movies" or "cinematic vignettes" that are loaded with "epic" elements from cinematic tropes. As these mini-movies are always very brief and intimately tied to player actions, players still can see themselves in these mini-movies through emotions from the fear class (the situation players can see themselves in) and emotions from the fiero class (triumph and accomplishment).

For the rewards in the middle layer, we can plug in our "achieve" floor with the resolutions to the story, character, and player development arcs, as discussed earlier in this beat: the plot resolution (visible goal), the journey resolution (internal goal), and the gameplay resolution (proficiency goal). All these have to be rewarding in terms of player achievement.

For the rewards in the top layer, finally, we can plug in our "become" floor with autonomy/agency, mastery/performance, relatedness/community, and purpose/goal from our player motivation model. Each of these elements has a range of intrinsic rewards baked right into it. Having changed something for the better, getting good at something, being trusted, and doing something that makes sense is rewarding in ways that are empowering and memorable.

Finally, be aware that any reward experience from the "achieve" and "become" layers can be abstracted and symbolized by items from the PBL or SAPS range—think medals, for example, military and otherwise. Don't ever underestimate the power of symbolic representation.

STRATIFIED REWARD SYSTEM				
Intrinsic Register *Story Development Arc* *Character Development Arc* **INDIVIDUAL**	**Drivers**	**Layer III** *(Become)*	Autonomy/Agency Mastery/Performance, Relatedness/Community, Purpose/Goal	
		Layer II *(Achieve)*	Story, Character, and Player Development Arcs: Plot Resolution (Visible Goal); Journey Resolution (Internal Goal); Gameplay Resolution (Proficiency Goal)	
		Layer I *(Excite)*	Just-Right Amount of Challenge, Compelling Aesthetics, Emotional Appeal, Meaningful Choices; Unnecessary Obstacles, Epic Scale	
	Toolbox (ad libitum)		Flow; Types of Work; Player Types; Information Gap; Curiosity Gap; Set Completion; Agenda-Setting/Priming; etc.	
	Models		Cognitivism, Constructivism, Connectivism	
	Behavior/Needs		Increasing emotional and cognitive complexity	
Extrinsic Register *Player Development Arc* **HUMAN**	**Drivers**	**Layer II**	Status, Access, Power, Stuff (SAPS)	
		Layer I	Points, Badges, Leaderboards (PBL)	
	Toolbox		Classical and Operant/Instrumental Conditioning; Reinforcements and Rewards; Reinforcement and Reward Schedules	
	Model		Behaviorism	
	Behavior/Needs		Repeating Pleasurable Experiences and Avoiding Unpleasurable Experiences	

FIGURE 4.50   Stratified reward system.

That should do. Remember, it's a model, which you can change! And it's also just an example, so you can stick with the general model, but plug in different tools and drivers that are more suitable for your game.

Two final aspects of rewards before we close: loot rewards and save points.

As to loot rewards of value, be that gold coins, weapons, armor, spells, potions, electronic lock picks, a horse, a car, or a spaceship, never make them extraneous rewards. Extraneous in this context means that the player achieves something within the game and then looks around and "finds" something valuable that's not firmly connected to their actions. With extraneous rewards, the player will switch instantly into extrinsic reward mode—extraneous rewards are nothing more than glorified "drop" rewards of the kind mentioned previously. Every valuable item the player owns in-game should have been earned by the player in a plausible context as an intrinsic reward. Naturally, beyond the story and character development arcs, they will also be tied to the player development arc, as the player has to overcome obstacles or fight for these items. However, it's still an intrinsic reward. It's firmly tied to the game world and the narrative on the one hand, and it's neither symbolic like points or badges nor unspecific like gold or coins on the other.

For all the reasons discussed, if you want to reward your player for an extraordinary achievement in the player development arc and handle it as an extrinsic reward, you really want to keep that reward outside the game world as, for example, an item from the PBL or SAPS range along the examples given above. If that, in turn, directly or indirectly involves or reflects on in-game items, these should then be rather cosmetic and carefully chosen.

Then, save points. In the previous beat, we left the question hanging as to why some titles still retain a save point mechanic in the typewriter tradition, where certain items have to be found in the game world in order to save a game state manually—like cassette tapes in *Resident Evil 7: Biohazard* or wall consoles in *Alien: Isolation*.

As a hypothesis, such save point mechanics aren't related to player failure and punishment but are part of these games' reward systems. Looking closely, save point mechanics reward two things: exploration and survival. In the original *Aliens versus Predator* game, discussed in this context, the restrictive game save system actively discouraged exploration. And while it certainly rewarded survival, that reward amounted to nothing more than having beaten the level. In *Resident Evil 7: Biohazard* or *Alien: Isolation*, in contrast, exploration boosts the player's chances of survival. Finding a save point is an achievement and a reward at the same time.

Still, *Resident Evil 7: Biohazard* also has an autosave mechanic, which *Alien: Isolation* lacks. Predictably, not all players were happy about the latter, for all the good reasons enumerated in the preceding beat. Here, a great opportunity was lost. What if players in *Alien: Isolation* were allowed to decide for themselves if they want to switch autosave on or off? In the design spirit of games like *Legend of Grimrock*, where the "modern" automap feature can be disabled in favor of using a pen and graph paper, this would have given players the option to play the game in old-school fashion without depriving others of the convenience of autosaves.

It should be conceded that, on the whole, wall consoles are quite numerous in *Alien: Isolation*. But real-world punishment through time loss is still a thing. There always will be players who are unusually cautious, prone to being killed instantaneously after having spent an inordinate amount of time hiding away in a locker.

Outlook

Congratulations! If you beat this phase's first level and final level on integral perspectives, traveled through the open-world levels in between for everything that's relevant for your game, and properly documented all your design decisions, you have beaten the Process phase and advanced your game concept to a *game treatment*! We will talk about what a game treatment is a bit more in the upcoming Proposition phase, but the most important thing about it is that everything is typed out, not just sketched, and not merely residing in your head.

At the very least, you should now have a thorough description of your game's three dramatic development arcs, its goal structure, and its reward system. Depending on your game type and the territories through which you traveled, you might also have detailed descriptions of your game's rule system, conflict dynamics, and task system; its learning curves, challenges, and emotions over the course of the game; its style, space, and sound elements, dynamics, and intensities; a collection of powerful memorable moments; and its dramatic structure and functional characters.

All of these elements will eventually contribute to your game's overall *pacing framework*. Pacing isn't just about plot, and it's a framework because you can't simply *set* the pacing of your game as you would for a book or a movie. You can't fully control the player development arc, and you can't control how players will approach your game to begin with—as creepers, blazers, or completists from Stevens and Raybould's range mentioned earlier, or with other behaviors from a different attribute range that is applicable to your game. (To learn more about a game's pacing framework, Jacek Wesołowski's *Game Developer* feature "Beyond Pacing: Games Aren't Hollywood" is a good place to start.)

Then, with your game treatment in front of you, you can ask yourself questions that you couldn't ask yourself before:

- Is your concept strong enough to keep you motivated and enthusiastic over very long stretches of time, probably years, in good times and in bad times, in times of plenty and in times of depleted budgets?
- Is that concept strong enough to make skilled and experienced creatives—from developers to artists to possibly game writers and sound artists and beyond—want to join your team?

If that's the case, if you can imagine that, then you have really accomplished something.

What's lying before you now is the Proposition phase, the last stretch of your journey. It will prepare you for the final boss fight: your pitch presentation!

Phase 05

Propositions

Introduction

Welcome to the Proposition phase!

This is where it all comes together. First, you will build a prototype, or even several prototypes, and you will test them and iron out the kinks. Then, you will build your pitch presentation, based on everything you have accomplished so far. Finally, you will prepare your delivery of that pitch presentation. Except for the Postmortem phase, which revolves around references, rightsholders, and responses, this is the final stage of your journey. Yet, don't rush it. It would be too sad if you impaled yourself on your proposal after all the work you put into it. Odysseus didn't land in Ithaca after ten years of travels to immediately crash into his palace, guns a-blazin'. He meticulously prepared for killing it, so to speak, caring about every detail. So should you.

One of the first things you will need is a so-called elevator pitch. It should describe your game in one snappy sentence within 10 seconds or less, reveal what differentiates your game from other games like it, focus on the playing experience and not on features, and evoke an emotion. You will need your elevator pitch every time someone asks you what you're working on, preferably accompanied by a quick conceptual demonstration—of any kind—on a mobile device that you conjure up within seconds. It's how you get people interested in your game, and it's how you demonstrate your dedication to your game. How difficult is it to forge an irresistible elevator pitch? Very difficult. Brainstorm the heck out of it. Look at industry examples, log lines, and headlines. Let people comment on your game, earnestly ask them how they would describe it. Don't stop until you've created something that rocks. Then, go and refine it further!

The second thing is some copyright stuff you need to consider: the copyright of your work and the copyrights of contributions to your work. Naturally, we can only touch the surface here, and none of the following amounts to legal advice in any way. They're just observations worth sharing.

Let's start with the copyright of your work. Way back, at the beginning of your journey, you started out with a *game idea*. From this idea, you extracted the core idea for a *game plan* and then built a *game concept* around it during the Procedure phase. Now, after the Process phase, you have much more than a concept: what you have is a *game treatment*. But, to repeat, you only have a game treatment *if you typed everything out*! It doesn't count if it's only in your head. Legally, a game treatment is neither an idea nor a concept. An idea is not copyrightable, only the artistic expression or embodiment of it. A concept, in legal terms, is treated similar to ideas, log lines, titles, etc., all of which are not copyrightable. Besides finished works, only a treatment is.

DOI: 10.1201/9781003334682-24

If you're in the United States, you can take your typed-out treatment, register and submit it online to the Copyright Office of the Library of Congress as a video game treatment, pay an application fee (as of 2023, $45 for single author, same claimant, one work, not for hire; otherwise $65), and boom, it's copyrighted—with a date stamp as proof that you came up with it first. It's that simple! (You can even copyright a website that way, so don't be shy.) In Europe, everything's more complicated, especially in Germany. Despite an unalienable *Urheberrecht* (more on that in a minute), no legal option exists to publicly secure the copyright of a work, with proof that you came up with it first, without having it published. Which makes you wonder. For other areas and countries, you have to sound out the legal procedures yourself. The important point is, if you typed it out, it's not a concept anymore. If you typed it out, it's a *thing*.

Then, about the copyrights of contributions to your work. If you hire a writer or an artist for a fee, for example, to create or polish certain elements of your prototype or your pitch presentation or proposal document, legal aspects are involved that you should know about. But again, the following is not legal advice. It's merely a compilation of more or less common knowledge that could be *wrong* in your particular case, so beware. It only serves the purpose of giving you a general sense of direction, nothing more, nothing less.

Always make a contract about who obtains or retains what rights with the exact consequences all this entails, whenever you hire a writer, an artist, a programmer, a composer, and so forth. In case of major or regular contributions, you should always be generous within the framework of what your present situation allows. You should also see to it that you don't throw your contributors under the bus in advance, effectively, when your game happens to become a surprise hit later and makes a lot more money than expected. But there's the case of minor third-party contributions that you immediately pay for, and for that, you might want to apply a certain type of contract to ensure that the resulting work fully belongs, in terms of copyright, to you and your team. In the United States, you have to set up a Work Made for Hire contract that all parties must sign, which specifically states that the commissioned work—text, image, bunch of code, sound loop, whatever it is—is Work Made for Hire. This isn't possible for stand-alone works of art, only for contributions to audiovisual and/or collective works, for example, a video game. Of course, if any such work is created for you by someone who works for you as a regular employee, and whose task indeed is to produce that kind of work, that's Work Made for Hire by default. In European countries, in contrast, such a Work Made for Hire option often doesn't exist. In Germany, especially, the creators' right—*Urheberrecht*—is an inalienable personal right that a creator cannot transfer to their client by design. (Though major news publishers there are very crafty in designing contract models and, indeed, drafting *legislation*, to systematically corrode these creators' rights.) Here, the only way for you to "own" a minor commissioned work is to acquire the exclusive and unlimited rights to use that work in question, either through a contract or an employment agreement that makes this very explicit, and this might also contain a so-called buy-out passage which means that as yet unknown types of use are also covered.

Work Made for Hire contracts should be the exception, not the rule. It's a two-edged sword. The good side of its blade prevents successful projects from being milked by grotesque lawsuits. The evil side of its blade freezes out creatives from getting a decent cut when their work contributes to a game's success, no matter whether that success was anticipated or not. The latter happens all the time. It's an appalling industry habit that needs to change.

So be discriminate, and judicious! Whatever you do when you commission a work, give everyone their due in relation to their contributions on the one hand, and see to it that usage rights won't come around later and haunt you on the other.

Level One

Prototyping

Opening

First, let's break the whole process of prototyping down into a small number of simple steps, employing a slightly modified version of the design philosophy Donald R. Lebeau once posted on the AtariAge forums. According to Lebeau, you can break down everything you do into four simple steps:

1. Make it.
2. Make it work.
3. Make it work reliably.
4. Make it work reliably and X.

Lebeau's original fourth step is "Make it work reliably and fast." But for our purposes, that needs to be more flexible, so you can adapt it to your game. Your compass for that is your work from the Preparation phase. Depending on the dimension where your USP resides, the fourth step for your prototype might look similar to this:

- Game-Mechanical USP: Make it work reliably and smoothly.
- Ludological USP: Make it work reliably and intuitive.
- Cinematological USP: Make it work reliably and pretty.
- Narratological USP: Make it work reliably and polished.

These are just serving suggestions—you have to find your own "X" that applies to your game. But whatever it is, following these four steps will make your life easier and your work more focused.

Beat 1: Assemble

Basically, there are three types of game prototypes in the world: the proof-of-concept prototype, the vertical slice prototype, and the pre-production prototype. Always make sure you know what you're talking about, and always make sure others know what you're talking about.

As this book doesn't cover the development process, the pre-production prototype won't concern us here. It is part of the development process, the first thing you build after green-lighting. It could, and some say should, absorb 20% or even 25% of the entire development cycle.

What we're concerned with here are the proof-of-concept prototype and the vertical slice prototype. The proof-of-concept prototype is the prototype you build for yourself, to check if the playing experience you have in mind turns out as you hoped, and if the game is actually worth playing. The vertical slice prototype is the prototype you will need for your pitch. (Some, to make it more confusing, also call the vertical slice prototype "demo.")

Both your proof-of-concept prototype and your vertical slice prototype need to be laser-focused on those elements that differentiate your game from other games. But the former takes a lot less cost and effort to build. Only the most important elements that make the playing experience different have to be

DOI: 10.1201/9781003334682-25

in there; it can be rough and sprinkled with placeholders; it can be a horizontal instead of a vertical slice; and it can be analog instead of digital. Your vertical slice, in contrast, has to be a polished and playable digital level that contains sample elements from all the ingredients your game will consist of. Don't worry, we'll go into the weeds to discuss all that soon.

Will you need a proof-of-concept prototype? It depends, but it is recommended. You can probably build one yourself, or with very little help, on your own budget. As mentioned in the Preliminary phase, even the proudest concepts might ignite violently and turn to ashes when hit by the harsh light of reality. There are at least four things you can get out of a proof-of-concept prototype. First, if all goes well, it will give you some confidence that your game is enjoyable to play in principle. Then, you learn a lot about what it would take to realize parts of the game on a more comprehensive scale. Next, if it's playable and enjoyable, you might be able to secure some funds for your next step. Finally, you can pitch it to assemble a team! Thus, building a proof-of-concept prototype is well worth the effort.

Will you need a vertical slice prototype? In almost all cases, the answer should be yes. First of all, it provides a much more advanced and sophisticated reality check than your proof-of-concept prototype. If the elements that make your game different don't work as intended, if your treatment can't be translated into a fresh and exciting playing experience, that prototype will tell you, and there will be no doubt about it. There's another reason, though, that's even more important. If you and your team don't have a string of successful games under your belts, how would anyone know that you're capable of building that game? As Brian Upton put it in his GDC 2017 presentation "30 Things I Hate About Your Game Pitch," without a reasonable amount of presentable experience, the only thing that can attest to your abilities and those of your team is a playable and polished prototype. Also, while you're at it, watch Rebekah Saltsman's GDC 2019 talk "So You're Ready to Pitch to a Publisher? (You're Not)," which also touches on this and several other topics in this level.

To sum it up, your vertical slice prototype must show proof of two related, but different things: that the game you want to make is worth making, and that you and your team can make it. Now, how do you fund your prototype? You've probably already discerned from the general logic of the situation that publishers don't bankroll prototypes! As available options vary wildly from country to country and even from state to state, and this book isn't about funding in any case, you have to do your own research. Savings; loans; investments from friends, family, or interested people; startup grants; government grants and action programs; and, particularly, freelance work on the side. (Crowdfunding might also be an option in case you've created well-received work before *and* excel in skills like marketing and PR.)

It's time to dive into the details. We'll look at the proof-of-concept prototype first; it has more options and fewer constraints, and it comes first in any case.

There are two decisions you need to make before you can start to build a proof-of-concept prototype. The first decision concerns creating a vertical slice or a horizontal slice, also known as vertical layer and horizontal layer. A vertical slice contains representative bits and pieces from almost everything that your game will contain. A horizontal slice showcases one major aspect of your game more in-depth. Translated into *Ludotronics* parlance, a vertical slice showcases bits and pieces from all four dimensions, while a horizontal slice focuses on one particular dimension. The second decision concerns creating an analog prototype or a digital prototype.

For each decision, there is a criteria set that you can use. For vertical vs. horizontal, the criteria set consists of your gameplay loop, your USP, and your core idea. For digital vs. analog, the criteria set consists of the particular dimension your game is focused on.

Let's begin with the criteria set for your vertical vs. horizontal decision.

Gameplay loop. If your prototype can't demonstrate what the player will be doing again and again, for hours and days and weeks, then it's worthless. Your gameplay loop should be the first thing on your mind when you start planning your prototype. In general, it is probably more difficult to integrate your gameplay loop into a horizontal slice that focuses on one single dimension than into a vertical slice. But if it's possible in principle and supported by other criteria, go for it. Whatever you do, though, never forget that your prototype must be able to demonstrate the gameplay loop.

USP. If your prototype can't communicate what differentiates your game from similar games, that's also a huge problem, but not as huge as a missing gameplay loop. As discussed in the Preparation phase, your USP is your game's most important value characteristic. If it falls into one of the four dimensions of the *Ludotronics* map—*Game Mechanics*, *Ludology*, *Cinematology*, or *Narratology*—and you want to highlight your USP, that could be a good reason for a horizontal slice that presents this particular dimension in greater detail. Provided, of course, you can also integrate your gameplay loop! If your USP is a fresh and exciting combination of value characteristics from all four dimensions instead, you should obviously decide on building a vertical slice.

Key values. If your prototype can't demonstrate the other key values beyond your USP, that's a bummer too. But it's not as vital as demonstrating your gameplay loop or your USP. In general, the more compelling your key values are, the more you should be in favor of building a vertical slice. In case your key values are concentrated on one particular dimension, however, there's nothing wrong with building a horizontal slice that focuses on your game's most compelling and innovative aspects—without surrounding it, and possibly diluting it, with a host of more pedestrian elements from the other dimensions.

Next, let's go through the criteria set for your digital vs. analog decision.

Game mechanics. If your USP resides in the game-mechanical dimension, that leaves your options open for either a digital or an analog prototype. In case of the latter, mechanics and rule sets and rules can often be meaningfully mapped to the typical materials and actions of analog prototypes, be that paper, cardboard, sticky notes, coins, dice, playing cards, index cards, game pieces, counters, miniatures, grid/hexagon graph paper, whiteboards and magnets, building blocks, or physical player actions and player decisions, all of which can be supported by pen and paper–like probability distributions as discussed at length in the Process phase. Even pacing can be simulated! In *Players Making Decisions*, Zack Hiwiller relates the example of an analog version of *Tetris*, where players had to scramble to catch or pick up "tetromino cards" that were thrown at them, and process them racing against time.

Ludology. If your USP resides in the ludological dimension, that will almost always call for a digital prototype. The ludological dimension is all about the interactions between player and game or between player and player, which usually involves the game's controls and interfaces, kinesthetic learning, input-dependent cognitive tasks (aka puzzles), control scheme–specific coop or multiplayer action, and so on. It is highly unlikely that any of these can be simulated with the analog materials and actions enumerated above. None of these materials or actions would convey how actual controller input would feel, and how the game would react to that input. There might be cases where an analog prototype can communicate ludological elements, possibly around certain player vs. player interactions. But that would be an exception, not the rule.

Cinematology. If your USP resides in the cinematological dimension, which involves graphical style, music, sound, camera movement, and so on, to convey aesthetics, atmosphere, and emotions through its environment, that again will in most cases call for a digital prototype. Short of converting a whole conference room into a game level, firing up a playlist and showing a collection of pictures won't cut it.

Narratology. If your USP resides in the narratological dimension, that leaves your options open once more for either a digital or an analog prototype. For the analog option, you can use narrative authoring tools or create a short pen and paper adventure, and then combine your interactive narrative with a map or other kind of terrain, game pieces, counters, cards, etc. But be sure to create your prototype around a meaningful chunk of narrative with its own stand-alone plot structure, maybe introduced by a three paragraph–roll-up, as discussed in the Process phase, so that it's gripping and emotionally satisfying. Explanations and expositions are invariably clumsy and boring and will torpedo your objective.

To sum it up, if your USP falls into the game-mechanical or the narratological dimension, the decision to create a digital or an analog proof-of-concept prototype is up to you. If your USP falls into the ludological or the cinematological dimension, it is strongly recommended that your proof-of-concept prototype be digital, barring very distinguished circumstances.

For an analog prototype, all the materials and actions mentioned so far could be suited, plus anything your imagination comes up with, depending on your game type. For a digital prototype, you have three basic options. If you don't have any coding experience, you can use an authoring tool with a visual editor and drag-and-drop functionality; these yield good results without forcing you to invest large amounts of time to wrap your head around scripting or programming. If you have scripting experience, you can use a scripting language to build your prototype. If you're a seasoned programmer, you can use whatever game engine and development kit you like. All three solutions are fine; it always depends on the type and scope of the game you have in mind.

Next, what about the vertical slice prototype, the one that you need for your publisher pitch? It's everything we discussed so far for the proof-of-concept prototype, except that it has to be a vertical slice, it has to be digital, and it's a lot more demanding.

It should be fully playable, polished, and enjoyable, which also means that it has to be perfectly self-explanatory. After you distributed it in the context of a pitch, you won't be present when people play it.

To accomplish that, you need to know how to prepare your prototype conceptually. Your prototype should be able to test and assess the differentiating elements of your game on the one hand, and present your game in attractive ways on the other. Thus, you have to decide what to include on a granular level. Figuring this out is not altogether different from deciding what artwork to include in a portfolio, or which sample to send out from a manuscript. The following three principles should always be your guide:

- The prototype should be representative.
- The prototype should be engaging and exciting.
- The prototype should be accessible.

The beginning and the ending of your game, as you imagine them at this point, are not well suited. They're almost by definition not representative of what the player will experience over the course of the game. Also, they're not that exciting either. Endings have accumulated too much context and invested practice and emotions to serve as an involving stand-alone example. Beginnings are rarely exciting because you need exposition to get things going. On the other hand, everything that's not in the close vicinity of the beginning of your game might not be accessible enough in terms of game mechanics and your game's control scheme. If any of that isn't taken into account, your prototype will neither help you test and assess nor present and impress.

The solution to all this, in most cases, is to compose a prototype that uses well-chosen bits and pieces from your game treatment and create a compelling playing sequence that, in all likelihood, won't be part of your actual game later on. That's perfectly normal. If you look at successful prototypes or talk to people who created them, you will quickly realize that the playable sequences from these prototypes almost never made it into the final game. The sequence should be about 10–15 minutes long. If it continually dazzles the mind, you can get away with less.

Treat your mechanics, your player interactions, your aesthetics, your dramatic development arcs, your goal and reward systems, your learning curves, and your style intensity arc as a buffet from which to pick a powerful memorable and emotional moment that showcases everything that's important in your game. You can take something from the very beginning of the learning curve and some very early tasks, combine them with something a bit more advanced in terms of story and style dynamics, and top everything off with a peak from your intensity curve around an emotional moment. What you have to do, basically, is create a gourmet teaser that is representative, engaging, and accessible.

Don't take this lightly. Your decisions can and will make the difference between acceptance and failure.

Now decide what kind of prototype you need, sketch it, and make it!

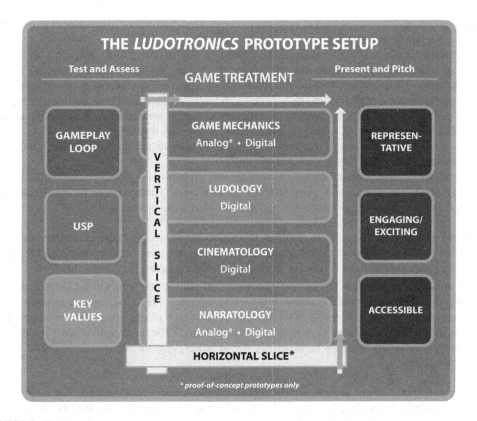

FIGURE 5.1 Prototype setup.

In the following two beats, you will learn how to test your prototype, and how to balance and adjust your prototype for your pitch presentation.

Beat 2: Assess

What principal function playtests serve is a frequent source of confusion, so the following needs to be spelled out early and clearly:

- Conducting playtests is not about asking for opinions, it is about learning what's wrong with your design.

That's it. Everything else follows from there. It *doesn't* mean that you shouldn't ask your playtesters for their opinions, far from it. But the interesting thing is not their opinions. The interesting thing is what their opinions tell you about the strengths and weaknesses of your design.

Then, playtesting should not be confused with quality assurance testing. QA testing is conducted by a team of QA testers, who are professionals and intimately familiar with the game, for the completely different purpose of quality control as an essential part of the development cycle. Equally, playtesting should not be confused with game user research. GUR looks at actual player behavior "in the wild" with telemetry data, analytics, and metrics. It's also part of the development cycle but includes—depending on game type, platform, and budget—maintaining, balancing, or expanding the game with new content after release.

In this beat, some approaches to playtesting will be mentioned that are too complicated and costly for an indie game prototype, no matter if it's a proof-of-concept or a vertical slice. But it's not labs and budgets that count, it's procedures and attention to detail. Thus, just follow along and scale everything down to the level you can manage.

The first question is how playtests should be conducted. The most common approach is to confront playtesters with a prototype or a new build, observe them playing, with think-aloud comments or without, make notes, ask questions about their experience with a prepared questionnaire or with open questions, possibly record everything, and then sit down and analyze the data. There's nothing wrong with all this, that's more or less how it should be done! It's under the surface where misconceptions lurk. What game designers often fail to realize is that such tests are, for all practical purposes, social science research. And to obtain test results that are valid, reliable, significant, and relevant, in other words, actually useful, these tests must follow a number of rules.

The first rule of playtesting is, you have to meticulously prepare every playtest in advance. There are two different sets of preparations for two different question types. These types differ epistemologically with regard to the nature of knowledge and how that knowledge can be obtained.

> **The unknowns**. The first type are questions that you already have, for example: are there enough clues for the player to find the hidden path to the tower? Are there enough enemies to keep the player engaged? Will the number of enemies overwhelm the player?
>
> **The unknown unknowns**. The second type are questions that you don't know exist, for example: does the player correctly interpret the level objective? (Playtesters miss the hidden path to the tower not because they can't find it, but because they misinterpret the level objective.) Would the player rather go exploring instead of fighting? (The number of enemies is perfect, but playtesters aren't happy because they would rather enjoy the scenery or go exploring at this point.)

As a general rule, you can answer the first type of questions with testing methods that fall under the label of quantitative research, and the second with testing methods that fall under the label of qualitative research. These technical terms are not important; important is how you proceed in each case. Let's have a look at both types of research and their associated methods in detail.

For the first type, collect everything you already *know* you want to know, and translate that into questions in such a way that each question asks *exactly one thing*, and one thing only. As you might have noticed, the example question above with respect to the correct number of enemies was split in two (too many enemies to maintain control? Not enough enemies to keep engaged?) for that very reason. Then, if you have your set of questions, create a *hypothesis* for each question that, again, hypothesizes exactly one thing! There's no need to create your hypothesis according to what you believe to be true. On the contrary—your results might be more reliable when you try to *disprove* something with your hypothesis that you believe to be true. Also, be imaginative—different hypotheses will teach you different things! Let's say your question is: "Does the player find the hidden path to the tower?" There's a great number of possible hypotheses for this question. For example, with separate mirror-hypotheses in parentheses: "Players will miss (find) the path to the tower." "X percent of all players will find (will miss) the path to the tower." "If players recognize at least two clues (fail to recognize two or more clues), they will find (they will miss) the path to the tower." And so on. Whatever hypothesis you pick, it should be the one with the greatest potential to expand your knowledge effectively and efficiently for subsequent design decisions.

Now, why go through all this trouble to ask a simple question? There are three major reasons.

> **Focus.** The first reason is that you need to focus. You cannot simply observe something and be aware of all the details, neither live nor in replay. Yet for playtesting, it's the details that count. Almost all of what you're not directly focused on will be gone. Sensory data, as you might remember from the Process phase, is first stored in sensory memory, where it decays rapidly— visual and haptic data will last from a few milliseconds to a maximum of 2 seconds, and audio data up to 3 seconds, if you're lucky. And the vast majority of that data isn't forwarded to working or long-term memory to be processed. It's dismissed because you're focused on something else. To give you a sense of impact, there's the famous selective attention test by Daniel J.

Simons of Harvard University, more popularly known as "gorilla test." Up to half of the participants' sensory memories fail to forward, and the participants therewith fail to remember, an actor in a gorilla costume—who moves openly and deliberately through a group of six ball players divided into two teams. That's because participants are occupied, as instructed, with counting the passes between the two teams. (A more recent study by Polly Dalton and Nick Fraenkel with unprimed and unattended sensory input produced evidence to that effect also for the auditory domain.)

Judgments. The second reason is that human thought processes are riddled with systematic errors in judging and thinking. These errors, called cognitive biases, make up convincing reasons to dismiss the undesired and embrace the expected on the spot. Watertight hypotheses make it as tough as possible for our brains to give in to these biases and weasel out of the results and the consequences of our observations. Also, never change your hypothesis after the test! Maybe it turns out your hypothesis wasn't a good fit for your setup or your results, or you realize it was sloppily formulated. Whatever the reason, it doesn't matter. Throw away the test results, create a better hypothesis, and run a new test from scratch. Otherwise, your biases will beat you every time.

Resources. The third reason is that you will have a much better idea of how many playtesters you will need, what kind of playtesters you will need, how many observers and assistants you will need, what kind of testing equipment and technologies you will have to employ, and how, overall, you can allocate your resources in the most effective manner.

When you're sure that you're testing what you actually want to be testing (that's the "validity" part), you should then see to it that the conditions are exactly the same for every session and every playtester from a particular setup (your test needs to produce similar results under consistent conditions to pass the "reliability" check). Playtesters should play with the same equipment; different rooms or the same room at different times should have roughly the same noise level, temperature, and lighting conditions; the welcome and introduction should be the same; and whatever else applies to your setup should always remain consistent. In the same manner, following up on a topic discussed in the Process phase's *Interactivity* territory, you can't have random (or rather pseudo-random) events in your prototype's test setup if you want to get results that can be compared and interpreted in a meaningful manner. Except, of course, you want to test a pseudo-random event!

Finally, after your test players have finished playing, you can and should ask them prepared questions to verify your observations and to stress-test your hypothesis. These questions should be the same for every player; in other words, they should be "standardized." That way, the answers from all your playtesters from a particular test setup can be turned into a data set and compared, analyzed, and interpreted.

That should suffice for the first type of research, the "quantitative" type.

The second type of research, the "qualitative" type, needs a completely different kind of setup: the semi-structured or unstructured interview. Remember, with this type it's about questions you don't yet have, questions you don't yet know exist. So you can't just go and ask them! Here, in stark contrast to your preparations for the first type of research, you only prepare a very loose and very broad set of questions, all of which should be *as open as possible*. You can ask these questions after or even during a playtest (more on that below), individually with each playtester or with several playtesters as a group (also called "focus group"). You can ask all of your loosely prepared questions, or only a few, in whatever order you like, and you can and should pursue interesting prompts with new or follow-up questions that you make up on the spot.

In *Players Making Decisions*, Zack Hiwiller makes the very important point that you need to keep questioning. About our own work and our own accomplishments, we all have the tendency to answer questions and to correct wrong assumptions. And we want to be helpful! But when your playtester asks questions or makes bad assumptions or needs help, you should keep questioning instead—questions like, to take a few examples from Hiwiller, "Why would you think that?" or "What did you think at that moment?" or "Why did that bother you?" or "Why would you want to do X at that point?" and similar. For unstructured or semi-structured interviews, this is good advice to drill down to and lay bare the really interesting stuff.

A very effective method, briefly mentioned before, is K. Anders Ericsson and Herbert A. Simon's "Think Aloud Method" or "Think Aloud Protocol," proposed in their 1980 paper "Verbal Reports as Data." With this method, the "interview" is conducted while the playtester is playing, and the "interviewer" has one task, and one task only: to keep the playtester talking about what they're doing and why they're doing it. You can't ask questions that are more open than that! Should your playtesters be playing in their own homes, they can record their comments and impressions in so-called diaries. Which is still an effective method, even if you can't nudge them on from time to time.

But whatever method you employ for this second type of questions, always make sure you don't overprepare. The whole reason is to elicit from your playtesters interesting observations and experiences that tell you something about your design you haven't thought of yet, to shed light on the "unknown unknowns."

Finally, there's the question of multiplayer and coop testing for both types of research. In most cases, you want to have a setup where one playtester or one team of playtesters plays against, or together with, carefully instructed players from your developer team. Your own players could play cautiously, aggressively, professionally, naively, annoyingly, or in any manner you instruct them to, so that you can observe the behavior and reactions of your playtester or playtesters in different emotional circumstances. Only by isolating playing behavior, and by reducing the amount of events and variables you need to track, will you be able to accomplish your test objectives in coop or multiplayer setups. There might be exceptions to this. But if you want to let loose a group or groups of playtesters against each other, be sure to have a great set of hypotheses for that.

That's enough with respect to methods. Next up, you have to decide what kind of playtesters you need. This, of course, depends on your particular game, the state of your prototype, your test setup, and your questions. But to make sense, all conceivable scenarios should have at least two elements in common: the correct target audience and the correct tester type.

> **Target audience**. Your playtesters must belong to your primary target audience. Otherwise, testing doesn't make sense for a whole raft of reasons, some of which we discussed in the context of difficulty and familiarity in the Process phase. Playtesting with players that don't belong to your primary target audience works both ways, so to speak, and not in your favor. On the one hand, you don't learn about the strengths and weaknesses of your design for players that will actually play your game. On the other hand, you might end up fixing things that don't need fixing. Imagine you rebuild your entire interface because it took your playtesters too long to figure it out, but your primary target audience would have adapted to your original design in a snap. That's a lot of resources that went into what could be called, very generously, a medium priority item.

> **Tester type**. For each setup, you have to determine whether you need playtesters who already have some experience with your game, either from earlier tests or because they have seen some of it in action, or so-called "tissue testers," playtesters who come fresh to your game and cannot be used again for this or any other setup that calls for this type of testers. (But they can later be used for other setups that do not involve tissue testers.)

Obviously, it can be difficult to find not only good playtesters, but the right playtesters for your prototype and for your particular test setup. If that helps, you're not the only one with this problem! Not just playtesting, but social science research in general has been plagued by the problem of "convenience samples" since forever. But shortcuts of this kind won't get you anywhere in the end, neither in research nor for playtesting purposes.

When you have found the right playtesters for your project, you can mix and match all the different testing methods discussed above as you please. But don't push your playtesters past exhaustion. Also, there's the question of recompense. During development and with a budget, it should go without saying that playtesters are paid. But even for a proof-of-concept prototype at only the meagerest of budgets, it's good manners to offer some recompense when you're trying to recruit playtesters. You don't have to shower them with silver and gold. But playing a prototype riddled with issues and answering whole catalogs of questions *isn't a reward in itself*. So think of something that would be appreciated. (Promises of a copy of the final game, years away in a highly uncertain future, don't count.)

Now that we have discussed playtesting methods and playtesters, let's move on to test data. From your playtests, you should always record as many data points and as many types of data as you can and meticulously document everything. For your proof-of-concept or vertical slice prototype, this will most certainly not include elaborate technical tools like automatically recorded, graphable event data, heat maps and hot spot measuring, physiological tests that measure electrodermal activity or muscle activity, or a split testing infrastructure, to name a few. Or artificial neural networks that you train to play and break your game! Yet, there's still a lot you can do and record with a minimum of effort.

To begin with, you should track time, record everything that is said during tests and interviews, and record physical events with a camera. The gameplay should also be recorded, obviously, but there's more. Take the in-built computer camera, or any old mounted cell phone, and record the facial expressions of your playtesters. Later, you can run these recordings side-by-side with your gameplay recordings to review these sessions in detail. Facial expressions, prominently so-called micro-expressions, will tell you a lot about emotional reactions, from confusion and annoyance to flow and fiero. And don't forget fitness trackers—even run-of-the-mill models can record several types of physical data that you can correlate with in-game events later! Finally, there should always be an assistant present whose *one job* it is to watch and take notes about everything noteworthy, from peculiarities to irregularities, with regard to setup and procedure.

After making sure you have all the data you need, the last step is analysis and interpretation. From the four parameters of sound scientific research we mentioned earlier in this beat, we already touched upon "valid" and "reliable" in the methods section. When it comes to analysis and interpretation, the other two become important: "significance" and "relevance."

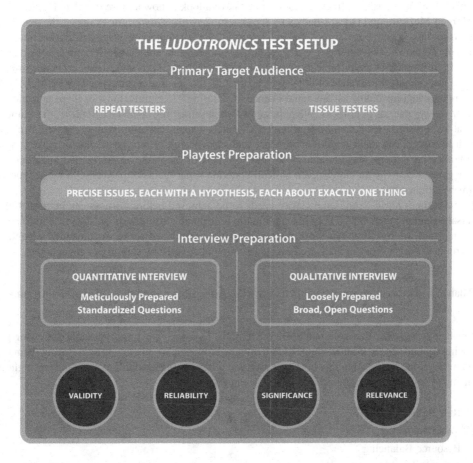

FIGURE 5.2   Test setup.

A high significance means that the result has a low probability to have come about randomly, or by error. (It's a bit more complicated than that, but it'll do for our purposes.) One of the strongest indicators for shaky significance is a very low number of playtesters, or a number of wrong playtesters (in terms of target audience, repeat or tissue testers, and so on). Without the complex math social scientists apply to setups and analyses, you can't do much about it, except for being careful and considerate. Yet, being careful and considerate goes a long way. You do not want to put a lot of time and effort into redesigning parts of your prototype, or later your game, on the basis of a faulty test result.

The final parameter, relevance, means exactly what it seems to mean. A test can be reliable and valid, and its results significant, but the results might not matter enough to warrant action, or even matter at all. Don't waste your resources on findings that are not relevant.

All this, from methods to playtesters to data to evaluation, is certainly not exhaustive. But it should give you a head start. In any case, it should be more than enough to give you ideas, and some orientation, for testing your prototype.

Beat 3: Adjust

For the probability of any given event to occur, you can always substitute numbers for time. Suppose your game has a very rare imbalance that makes the red team invincible once every 10,000 years. With several hundred thousand active players, the red team will be invincible about once a week. Hence, in our definition, balancing is everything you carry out to lower the probability of undesired events in your game.

If this sound ominously abstract, it should! Let's have a look at how a more tangible definition fares. For Morgan McGuire and Odest Chadwicke Jenkins in *Creating Games*, for example, the goal of balancing is to make a game *fair*, *stable*, and *engaging*—a succinct, comprehensive description that should universally apply. The two latter properties are largely uncontested, and they're also covered by our more abstract definition (both an unstable game and a bored player qualify as undesired events, for sure). But there's a surprisingly wide range of objections against the notion that a game needs to be "fair," which McGuire and Jenkins define as "an equal chance of winning." Certainly, most of these objections are based on interpretations of fairness. What, how, and when something could be called fair in a game, and on what level or meta-level, can be legitimately disputed. Quantities of unfairness that conform to the rules, it is argued, can make a game more tense and suspenseful, or more realistic. Or make it *appear* more fair! What's more, cheating can be an intrinsic part of the game, as in the pen and paper role-playing game *Paranoia*, and might even willfully provide some agents or players with more opportunities to cheat than others.

To sum it up, a lot of definitional clarity needs to be achieved before fairness can be accepted as a universal balancing goal. Thus, notwithstanding the indisputable usefulness of McGuire and Jenkins's balancing triad, we'll stick to our more abstract definition introduced above. As an added advantage, it leaves room for other types of undesired events that are not covered by stability or engagement.

> Balancing is everything you carry out to lower the probability of undesired events in your game.

For obvious reasons, this beat can't tell you how to balance your prototype and later your game. Balancing depends on such a huge range of individual factors that any attempt at aggregating them would become encyclopedic. Instead, this beat will give you a basic overview with regard to *what* might need balancing in your game, structured into four neat categories:

- Rule Balancing
- Value Balancing
- Resource Balancing
- Agent Balancing

These four categories are good places to start, and they cover a lot of ground. Still, they're far from exhaustive. Some particular balancing questions might resist being defined by any of these four categories, or by one category alone. Then, as with the previous beat, some approaches will be mentioned that are certainly overkill in your current context. It's difficult to draw the line—depending on game type, some of the more complex balancing schemes might turn out to be necessary for your prototype after all. Luckily, you already know what you need to test and how you can test it! Provided you heeded the advice, given in the introduction to the Process phase, to sketch testing and balancing procedures for every game element you introduce. From there, take this beat as a general overview, a map that points you in all kinds of directions that you can pick from, to explore now or at some point in the future. Following these premises, we will now go through all four categories one at a time.

Let's start off with a small but fairly typical selection of *rule balancing* cases. Certainly, your rule system shouldn't create unintended advantages or disadvantages for any game world agent, including players, in any situation. The operative word is *unintended*—of course you can lavish advantages or disadvantages on your game world agents and players at will to make your game more enjoyable! Unintended advantages are a different matter, and they're often hard to detect. And when you detect them, they're often hard to eradicate. A good example is the notorious "first move advantage" in turn-based games and particularly combinatorial games, i.e., turn-based games without randomness (no luck involved) and with perfect information (no hidden moves), as touched upon in the Process phase. It can take years to find out if the opening move confers an advantage, how strong that advantage is, in statistical terms, and how it can be balanced. In some cases, a handicap rule will solve the problem, or compensation points, like in the game of Go. In other cases, a rule that puts a clever constraint on the first move will do the trick. But every game needs its own solution.

Another typical problem source are rules in asymmetrical games like *StarCraft* or baseball, also discussed in the Process phase. In any game, new strategies are being developed all the time. But in asymmetrical games, new strategies almost always cause problems because they cannot simply be mirrored by the other party or parties during any particular match. The new strategy soon becomes dominant, everybody uses it, and matches become predictable. For asymmetrical games, as long as that game has a substantial player base, the need for balancing never stops. No problem is predictable, every solution is unique.

A third classic in this category, equally touched upon in the Process phase, is balancing luck and skill in a way that will make the game enjoyable for the widest range of players from your target audience. If a game is only about skill, beginners and casual players are rarely able to enjoy it. But the more luck is involved, the less enjoyable it becomes for advanced or more ambitious players. In a way, the luck component imposes an unwanted "handicap" on more advanced players, and a handicap problem cannot be solved with a handicap. Multiplayer arena shooters are a good example, which we discussed in a different context before. The more precise the weapons are, the more skill they will require, and the game becomes less enjoyable for beginners or casual players. And vice versa. The less precise and more "spammy" the weapons are, the less incentive the game provides for more ambitious players to practice and become better. One solution would be to introduce a new rule that only players of roughly equal ability are allowed to compete in any given match, and then introduce a matchmaking system to enforce this rule. Another option would be to tweak the values instead, with a well-balanced combination of precise and spammy weapons that enables weaker players to get lucky from time to time, but without taking away anyone's incentive to learn and become more proficient. Solutions based on one or the other principle can also be applied to strategy games, racing games, and many other game types where skill and luck need to be balanced.

The biggest issue in this category is complexity and synergetic effects, often called "emergent gameplay." It's both a boon and a curse. It makes a game more interesting, but also very difficult to control. As again discussed in the Process phase, if you want to build a complex system of interacting subsystems that create such synergetic effects, you should always start from simple beginnings, add one subsystem at a time, and increase the degree to which these subsystems interact with one another very carefully. Here, you need a much higher number of test runs than you can achieve with playtesters alone; what you need are simulations, a topic we will discuss further below. Complexity, moreover, can itself create a particular variant of luck that we haven't mentioned so far, which Cameron Browne calls a "failure of resilience" in his catalog of viability criteria in *Evolutionary Game Design*. A complex game that is not resilient, following Browne's definition, has become so opaque that the probability of gaining an advantage or winning by random moves matches or exceeds the probability of gaining an advantage or winning by skilled play. So that's another property that you might need to balance and test for, that your game is resilient to random play!

A final example that almost appears trivial in comparison is the matter of match length. But this isn't trivial at all. Match length has to align with your target audience's playing habits. A game that is enjoyable but drags on past concentration levels, or past bedtime, isn't well-balanced at all. What needs to be balanced here, first and foremost, is the gameplay loop, another topic we discussed in-depth in the Process phase. Match lengths for multiplayer games can last, for example, from around 10 minutes in traditional arena shooters to about 30–45 minutes in MOBAs, or be as short as 30 seconds in casual free-to-play online games. (Whereby free-to-play games often feature gameplay loops with shorter and longer paths, precisely balanced to match their target audience's physical playing locations and time constraints.) Match lengths or the length of the gameplay loop are not necessarily balancing points for single player PC or console games. Nevertheless, a level or a game that is too short or too long with respect to its target audience's expectations can't be called well-balanced in that regard.

These examples don't cover all possible rule balancing problems, far from it. But they're fairly typical and common enough. In all likelihood, you will encounter at least some of them.

Next, let's have a look at *value balancing* situations. Mostly, this is about balancing values from and between interacting subsystems, like the health packs/ammunition example in our *Shroom!* shooter in the Process phase, where interacting values from different subsystems enabled a lock-on-victory strategy. On a more general level, this comprises balancing player and player character proficiency levels and equipment levels against the capabilities of game world agents. Then, it comprises balancing nontransitive relationships between three or more competing game elements, based on the rock–paper–scissors mechanic. All in all, *everything* that has values needs to be balanced against *everything else* that has values! Damage values, health values, armor values, range values, unit capabilities, character classes, how fast anything can move, how high and how far anything can jump, and much, much more.

The more elements are involved, and the more values these elements are endowed with for competing advantages and disadvantages in different contexts, the more tricky and time-consuming it becomes to make them less vulnerable to exploits and dominant strategies. Some value balancing problems are more treacherous than others. Consider, for example, the frequent complaint that this or that value in a game (a weapon, a unit, a spell, an ability, and so on) is "overpowered." Maybe that's not the problem at all. Maybe that element merely *looks* overpowered because it's too easy to learn or too easy to acquire, or something along these lines, in comparison to other elements.

Again, your particular game treatment will generate its own individual problems for which you will need to find your own individual solutions. But to set you up for value balancing success, the path to follow is Tynan Sylvester's "key property" design approach from *Designing Games*. According to this approach, every element should have a key property, and the value of that key property should be set as high as possible. If the key property of an element is speed or jump-height or protection or ground combat, this element then should be designed by default to move spectacularly fast, jump spectacularly high, be spectacularly impenetrable, or be unbeatable in infantry engagements, respectively. To begin with, every element will be distinctly valuable. Then, level designers can incorporate them with a clear purpose. Next, players can easily remember them and apply them in appropriate situations. Finally, and that's our critical aspect for balancing, you relegate value balancing to each element's *ancillary* advantages and disadvantages and leave their respective key values alone, which saves you time and headaches.

As a real-life example, let's look at *Unreal Tournament 2003/2004* and the sniper rifle, the eternal bone of contention in multiplayer arena shooters. There, the classic sniper rifle from the original *Unreal Tournament* game was turned into a "Lightning Gun" that signaled the shooter's position visibly across the map. Later, the classic sniper rifle was reintroduced, but now it triggered conspicuous puffs of smoke with each shot. While neither solution was particularly satisfying, you can see the "key property" principle at work: the developers *didn't* tweak long-range lethality, the rifle's key property in an arena game. What they tried to tweak instead was its ancillary advantage of being hard to spot. (Trained and clever shooters are always hard to spot, but it's amplified with distance.)

This approach has another benefit, as Sylvester points out. If all your value balancing attempts come to naught and the only option left is to lower the value of an element's key property, then that's an indicator, a warning sign even, that you should throw that element out. Besides being of questionable usefulness, elements that have their key properties nerfed are neither distinct nor interesting.

A real-life example for this, again from the transition of the original *Unreal Tournament* game to its successor games, is the notorious "Ripper." The Ripper's primary fire mode fills a room with razor-sharp discs that ricochet uncontrollably *six times* from walls and obstacles before disappearing, indiscriminately killing enemies, friends, and more often than not the shooter as well. It is perhaps the most spammy non-nuclear weapon ever devised in any game, and that is certainly its key property. Instead of nerfing its key property for later incarnations of the franchise, the developers took it out of the game altogether. (But it saw a comeback later in community contributions.)

If you follow this principle, you can create complex non-transitive sets of elements in your game without confusion or overlapping values. Still, details are important, and there will be no shortage of demanding value balancing tasks *despite* following the key property path. Many of these balancing tasks, again, cannot be accomplished with playtesters alone, and we will come back to that.

There's one more major value balancing area that needs your attention, and that's terrain, or maps. Terrain or maps, if you look closely, are effectively collections of values! Terrains must be designed in a way that all territories or positions have a balanced mix of advantages and disadvantages. You have to make sure that no territory or position is more "valuable" in context-independent ways than the others, and thus vulnerable to being exploited for a dominant strategy. This applies to practically every multi-player map in strategy games, 4X games, arena shooters, tactical shooters, MOBAs, and so on. It involves the clever distribution of resources and logistics and also the prevention of areas conducive to camping or spawnkills, where applicable. Depending on your game type, you might even be able to apply the key property rule for your terrain and map design!

Again, as a caveat, all this doesn't cover every possible problem associated with value balancing. Nevertheless, they're typical, they're common, and you will most likely encounter some of them.

Then, the matter of *resource balancing*, which applies to the virtual economies of a huge range of game types from business, management, or life simulation games to shooters to racing games to role-playing games to strategy games to 4X games, and so on, and especially free-to-play games with in-game purchases. Virtual economies, moreover, often generate player-controlled real-world economies, or the game itself has a real-world economy attached to it that turns real-world money into "hard" in-game currency, as opposed to "soft" in-game currency that can be earned through play. Resource balancing warrants its own book-length treatise, so we will keep it brief by providing a structural framework without pursuing the details. For the latter, good places to start are Wolf's *Case Histories and Analyses of Synthetic Economies* or Vili Lehdonvirta and Edward Castronova's *Virtual Economies*.

In *Fundamentals of Game Design*, Ernest Adams breaks virtual economies down into four principal drivers which he calls sources, drains, converters, and traders. This makes good sense, and we will adopt this principle with a slightly different nomenclature: *source*, *sink*, *switch*, and *swap*. These four drivers keep virtual economies running in the following ways.

Source. Resources are generated from renewable or non-renewable sources in six major ways: from natural sources that regrow like plants or berries or wildlife; from reaping the fruits of labor players spent on mining, farming, research, and similar; from invisible game world agents in the form of periodically spawning resources like health vials or ammunition or power-ups or social game–typical "gifts"; from visible game world agents that provide items voluntarily (rewards) or involuntarily (loot), often in the form of gold coins or wads of cash; or creating in-game resources by injecting real-world resources (money) into the game economy.

Sink. Resources are used up through decay, ruination, consumption, or devaluation. Decay comprises game world conditions like rotting crops and regular wear and tear that demand maintenance and repair. Ruination is caused by natural disasters like storm, fires, or earthquakes, and by player activities like pollution, land clearing, or overfishing. Consumption comprises agent interactions, including player activities, that make a resource disappear by using it, like consumed food, burned-out tires, fired ammunition, or cracked shields. Devaluation comprises

inflation, deflation, stagnation, stagflation, and similar dynamics that devalue virtual curren-
cies, labor, or resources, all of which can be an unintended or intended part of the rule system;
unintentionally triggered by cumulative player behavior; or intentionally triggered by individual players.

Switch. Resources are turned into other resources through transformation, manufacturing, and
crafting processes, like turning ore into weapons, crops into food, rubber into racing tires,
herbs into potions, or runes into spells. One single resource can be turned into a different
resource this way, but in more interesting switch setups, a collection of different base resources
is needed to obtain one specific target resource. All this can be effected by any game world
agent including players, the latter especially through crafting systems.

Swap. Resources are exchanged through buying, selling, bartering, lending, borrowing, giving
away, stealing, and auctioning off, either between players or between players and non-player
game world agents.

Thus, resource balancing comprises two different tasks. Both are demanding. You have to balance
the quantities and qualities of all the resources in your game with respect to their specific functions in
the game world and for your gameplay loop. Then, you also have to balance your economic system as a
whole by balancing your *source*, *sink*, *switch*, and *swap* dynamics. Within these parameters, there are
hosts of problems to solve and factors to balance, notably those related to player behavior in multiplayer
games. The most damaging factors among them are overproduction; hoarding and other forms of manu-
factured scarcity; supply and demand manipulation; hyperinflation as has happened in *Diablo 3*; bugs
and exploits like those that almost broke the economy of *GTA V* early on; or emerging black markets that
almost invariably form around MMOs, from *Ultima Online* to *Lineage* to *World of Warcraft* to *Diablo
Immortal*'s tenth circle of economic hell.

For a more in-depth introduction, Wolf's already mentioned *Case Histories and Analyses of Synthetic
Economies* is recommended reading. As a warning, everything comes down to math at the end of the
day. And unless you hire an economist, this particular kind of math falls squarely into your responsibilities as a game designer! Later, in the development phase, and this is especially true if your game is an
MMORPG or any kind of persistent multiplayer game, you will need to create an integrated system that
collects, prepares, and stores data points representative of what's going on in your in-game economy
on the one hand, and develop metrics to analyze and interpret these data points on the other to counter
detrimental developments and keep your game's economy balanced in the long run.

Finally, *agent balancing*. As defined back in the Process phase, the term "agent" comprises simple
processes, complex in-game AI, and players. Once more, let's create a basic structure first. Roughly, we
can differentiate four typical areas for agent balancing: *players*, *tasks*, *rewards*, and *game AI*.

Beginning with *players*, agent balancing is about what players are allowed to do and when, so that
they can enjoy playing without gaming the system, dominating other players, or dropping out of the flow
channel, as discussed in the Process phase.

Next, *tasks* must be balanced toward your intended share of physical, cognitive, and empathic tasks,
both for the game as a whole and as a balanced cocktail in any given dramatic unit larger than a beat.
This is also discussed in the Process phase. Closely related, as a kind of subcategory, are tasks balanced
for different player types, also already touched upon. This can be Richard Bartle's expanded *killer*,
achiever, *socializer*, *explorer* model or any other player type model that fits your game type, including
one you create and test yourself. It should make your game interesting for different kinds of player types,
maybe even make it attractive for a wider range of players, and keep certain player types from dominating other player types.

The third area that needs your attention is *rewards*, equally a topic examined in the Process phase.
Like your tasks, your rewards need to be distributed in well-balanced proportions over the entire game
and over each dramatic unit. But that's not all! You must also see to it that extrinsic rewards, as discussed,
don't seep into the player or character development arcs. That's no small feat.

The fourth area is *game AI*. Your game AI should neither serve headshots from the far end of the map
nor get stuck in every other doorway. They should neither take the action out of the player's hands nor run
helplessly into enemy fire. Balancing game AI is hard—it's for a reason that escort missions are among

the tasks players loath most. (And when it works out, as in *The Last of Us* or 2018 *God of War*, you can no longer call it an escort mission.) Balancing game AI also comprises balancing the "computer player" in games like *Pong*, chess programs, and similar.

In all four areas of agent balancing, unsurprisingly, specific demands that require specific solutions are attached to different player/agent configurations across single-player, coop, multiplayer, and MMO games.

Certainly, many challenges in this agent balancing category can and must be solved by tweaking rules or values or economic conditions. Yet, it's not a particular rule, value, or economic condition that's causing you problems, but matters related to agent activities and behavior. Still, all four superordinate categories—rule balancing, value balancing, resource balancing, and agent balancing—are malleable enough and permeable enough that you can shift types, tasks, or areas between categories to accommodate the precise balancing demands of your game.

Luckily, the demands imposed on your proof-of-concept or vertical slice prototype are far less severe than on your pre-production prototype later on, not to speak of your actual game. During development,

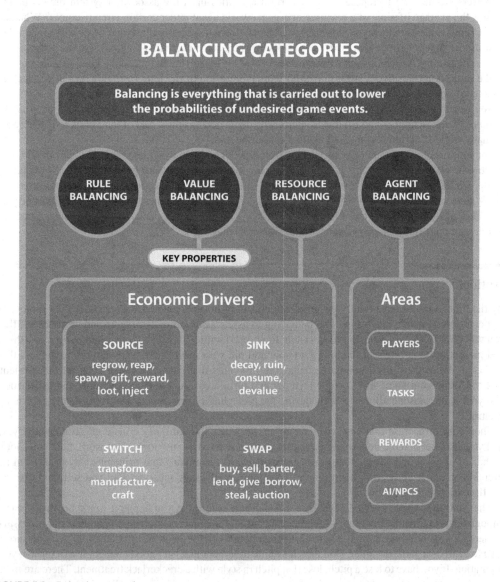

FIGURE 5.3 Balancing categories.

you will also have a lot more tools at your disposal. For example, you might be able to balance your game through A/B testing with very small, very controlled changes that affect one particular aspect of your game. Or, on the contrary, you can make huge, sweeping changes and split-test both versions, which is fairly typical of mobile game development.

As announced earlier, and to conclude this beat, let's have a look at one of the most powerful balancing tools you can wield later during development. It substitutes numbers for time through automated simulations that run millions of players or matches or both. The most popular tool to run such simulations is the common spreadsheet.

In a nutshell, for any game element you want to test, you determine the numerical values, probabilities, and dependencies involved; put these values and the formulas that connect these values into a spreadsheet; and define the number of iterations. When you're done, fire it up and see what happens. How many resources of a certain type will players have accumulated after a certain time on average? Will some players have accumulated much more of that resource than other players? How will the game's experience/leveling-up curve turn out for huge numbers of players over time? How many game world agents or players would have to repeat or avoid certain activities until the associated system breaks down? What's the average lifetime of a resource or a game world agent under certain circumstances? What are the extreme values at which your formulas will break down, especially those that involve exponential or logarithmic functions? Are there extreme results that lurk somewhere in a long tail? Do the probabilities of your non-transitive relationships behave as expected? If two different units duke it out that are not part of the same non-transitive relationship, who wins more often in the long run? How are match lengths affected if you increase or decrease the spawn frequency for a certain resource? And so on.

You can find a detailed and very beginner-friendly introduction to spreadsheet balancing in *Game Balance* by Ian Schreiber and Brenda Romero, who dedicated an entire part of their book to it. There are so many wonderful things you can do with a spreadsheet!

For your proof-of-concept or vertical slice prototype, again, you won't need this. But you should have made yourself familiar with this powerful balancing tool by the time your game enters the development phase. Undesirable results in terms of clustering, runaway effects, curious convergence patterns, and many more, all these become visible, and you can correct them by either tweaking your values or your formulas, or by introducing new elements or removing others. In this one case, you can indeed become a god, with your spreadsheets as your own universes to play with.

Outlook

By the time you will have built your proof-of-concept prototype, created your vertical slice prototype, and conducted enough playtesting and balancing to assess your game's strengths and weaknesses, then you will have to make a momentous decision: to proceed with your project toward preparing, polishing, and presenting your pitch, or to abort. Did you, and did your playtesters, enjoy the prototype less than expected? Were there insurmountable balancing problems that gave you pause? Did all the elements that constitute your game fail to come together and form a coherent and enjoyable playing experience? Did your game, despite all your efforts during the preceding phases, feel derivative instead of fresh and exciting?

Should it be the case that you will have to answer such and similarly crucial questions with "yes," and you also feel that the underlying issues are not easily fixed by investing more work, then you should be honest about it and abort. Always remember Richard Feynman's first principle, way back from the Preparation phase at the very beginning of your journey: that you must not fool yourself, and that you are the easiest person to fool.

That your prototype isn't as enjoyable or as fresh and exciting as you hoped it would be, that's reason enough to abort already. But there's even more at stake, which makes aborting imperative and necessary.

Here's a lesson for you from the field of writing, notably the screenwriting profession, that you should take to heart as a game designer. Don't pitch a game treatment that isn't good enough. It will tarnish your reputation. If you have to lose a pitch, lose that pitch in style with a crackerjack treatment. There are many reasons why treatments fail to win a pitch—too many similar games in the pipeline, incompatibility with recent brand decisions and the company's future plans, market forces and developments you couldn't possibly predict, financial or capacity constraints, and many more. All that shouldn't bother you as long as you deliver a top-notch treatment with your pitch. Because that will earn you reputation and future invites! In the long run, it's not a game treatment that you pitch, but your abilities as a game designer. In the long run, your game treatment is not the commodity. You are.

Thus, if there's anything wrong with your game treatment that became visible during prototyping, testing, and balancing, go back to work on it—in the Process phase, in the Procedure phase, even in the Preparation phase if need be. Or, if its flaws seem irredeemable, cut yourself loose from it and start from scratch. Create something new and exciting, building on everything you've learned.

However, if your vertical slice prototype does knock your socks off, and if it knocks your friends' and your playtesters' socks off as well, then go ahead! Put on your boots and prepare for battle.

Level Two

Polishing

Opening

It's time to pack your bag. In this level, you will collect everything you have created so far, polish it, and process it for your pitch presentation and proposal handout.

Adopting Trevor Longino's "Honesty, Creativity, Delight" paradigm from his 2013 GDC Europe talk "PR Quest! The Adventure to Make Your Game Famous" with a small modification, the pitch presentation you'll be preparing should be built upon *honesty*, *meaning*, and *delight*.

Honesty. Obviously, you should be honest. Nothing good will come out of it if you try to kick off a long-term future relationship with a deceit. Also, honesty makes your presentation more personal and less self-centered.

Meaning. The meaning must be in the message. That your game treatment is meaningful to you doesn't miraculously transmute it into being meaningful for your prospective publishing partner. You always have to ask yourself: what's in it for them? If it's not meaningful to them, you're throwing away the time, trust, and goodwill they've invested in you with their invite.

Delight. To delight your audience with your game treatment and your presentation, being honest and meaningful is a great start. But true delight comes with exceeding expectations. This can be an extraordinarily well-conceived element of your treatment, your USP, your gameplay loop, your grasp of economic factors, or your treatment's perfect portfolio fit. Or it could be you—by creating the lasting impression with your top-notch presentation that you have the skills and the personality to lead a game development project to success.

Now, what about the original "creativity" part from Longino's PR and marketing paradigm? In a pitch presentation, it should always be your *treatment* that represents the creative part, not your presentation. Indeed, your presentation should downright not be creative. It should follow general industry rules, and possible house rules, to the letter.

Then, as mentioned, always remember that you're not only pitching your game treatment but also yourself and your team. As Brian Upton puts it in his GDC 2017 talk "30 Things I Hate About Your Game Pitch," your pitch has to answer two questions, not one:

1. Is This Game Worth Making? (Uniqueness)
2. Can Your Team Make This Game? (Execution)

Honesty, meaning, delight, uniqueness, execution—all that should guide your preparations for the final stretch of your journey. With respect to structure, your presentation will also need a beginning, a middle, and an end (yes, Aristotle again). Each is represented by its own beat in this level around a "shaking up" metaphor: hypocenter, epicenter, propagation. The hypocenter is where the seismic wave is created by the core elements of your *concept*. The epicenter is where the seismic wave is felt through *action*, which is your presentation of the playing experience. The propagation finally is about the economic *conditions* that will support your wave. In other words: you say what it is, show what you have, and specify what you need.

DOI: 10.1201/9781003334682-26

Be attentive, accurate, and cautious! That way, you won't forget anything or become cocky. A good way to keep that in mind, always, is to rehearse "confident, cocky, lazy, dead" (a mantra from Tad Williamson's *Sea of Silver Light*). Just handle everything with great care, and you'll be doing fine.

Beat 1: Hypocenter

Creating the Wave

Your pitch presentation starts with the core elements of your concept: title, tagline, and logo; vision statement and synopsis; USP, target audience, and platform. Let's go through preparing each of these elements one by one.

If you haven't already done so, now is the time to create your **working title**. Aim for something short, emotional, and vivid, perhaps with a subtle literary or cultural reference, that meets your game's overall theme and mood. Later, that working title might change when a release title will be negotiated that meets both your game's creative vision and its marketing requirements. Nevertheless, you should give your working title your best shot—which includes exhaustive research whether a game with that title already exists, or some other media product like a book, movie, or TV series.

Your **tagline** will serve as your advertising hook. Create something catchy and descriptive that refers to your game's most important aspects—theme, mood, USP, or gameplay loop. Think *Halo*'s "Combat Evolved," *Asura's Wrath*'s "Rage Never Dies," or *Dark Soul*'s "Prepare to Die." Or, less succinctly, but forcefully nonetheless, *Warhammer 40K*'s "In the grim darkness of the far future, there is only War." Or *Heavy Rain*'s "How far are you prepared to go to save someone you love?" If you created an elevator pitch, as recommended at the beginning of this phase, you already have something to work with, and you might be able to condense it even further toward a tagline.

A **provisional logo** will give your title and tagline more weight, and it will serve your presentation as a visual anchor. You can follow the same basic rules that apply to your working title. You should give it your best shot, but it's not a release logo. No one expects it to meet your game's vision and marketing angles perfectly.

As an aside, for your working title, your tagline, possibly your provisional logo, and your pitch presentation and proposal handout as a whole, you should also choose the right fonts that serve your purpose best. Most likely, Arial or Times New Roman won't be it. If you don't have any experience with typography, you can either read up on it or ask someone who has! (While font licensing needs to be sorted out during development, it isn't an issue right now as you're not publishing anything or displaying it publicly.)

Your title, tagline, and logo slide should remain up throughout your **crisp introduction**. Your introductory words shouldn't be about how great it is to be here, how grateful you are for the opportunity, or some such. As Alejandro Cremades put it in *The Art of Startup Fundraising*, you should start "clear and strong"—with words your audience will remember. For a game pitch, these clear and strong words will be your vision statement and your synopsis, so keep everything that precedes it brief and snappy. Succinctly introduce yourself, the team you represent, and the game you're going to pitch. (You will

> **Pitch Presentation Part I**
> *Concept*
>
> 1. Title, Tagline, Logo
> 2. Crisp Introduction
> 3. Vision Statement
> 4. Synopsis (Log Line)
> 5. USP (Hook)
> 6. Target Audience
> 7. Platform and Engine

FIGURE 5.4 Pitch presentation part I: Concept.

introduce yourself and your team more in-depth during the third part of your pitch; we'll come to that.) While this introduction will be no longer than a few sentences, you should prepare these sentences very thoroughly. First impressions go a long way.

The next thing you have to prepare is your *vision statement*, which is a reworked and polished version of your desire-driven goal that you developed in the Procedure phase. You need to rework it until it matches everything you accomplished in the Process phase, and you need to polish it until it sounds really exciting and fresh, but also natural and authentic, without bombast and braggadocio.

Then, you have to prepare your *synopsis*, or log line, which is a reworked and polished version of your design-driven goal, also developed in the Procedure phase. What you need to rework especially are its three key elements "growth," "insight," and "experience," so that your synopsis matches your work from the Process phase and succinctly summarizes your game's projected playing experience, its central conflict, its mood, and the goal the player will have to pursue. What your synopsis should also contain at this point in time is the overall playing time you're aiming at, with rough estimates for creepers, blazers, and completists, or for a similar taxonomy that makes sense for your game.

The final triad of elements in this beat consists of your *USP*, which in this context is also often called the "hook"; your *target audience*; and your *platform and engine*. You'll find all of it in your documentation from the Preparation phase. They made sense back then, but you'd better check if that's still the case. Do they still correspond with everything you sketched out during the Process phase? Some conceptual changes might be obvious, others might be so subtle that you barely noticed them. Is it still the right game for the right players with the right key values and your USP at the center? That's what you have to ask yourself. And don't be nonchalant about your platform and engine choices either. With regard to platforms, justify your choices with clear evidence that each is a perfect fit for your USP and your target audience and makes economic sense. With regard to engines, justify your choice with your platform or platforms, your game type, and your value set.

Finally, you can use your USP, target audience, and platform and engine to establish what Oren Klaff calls the "Why Now?" frame in *Pitch Anything*, to demonstrate that the game you're pitching is not only fresh and exciting but takes advantage of current economic, social/cultural, and technological market opportunities. All of which you will be able to back up in your proposal handout, with a summary of the research you did in the Preparation phase.

This first part of your pitch presentation is where you create the wave, where you have to catch everyone's attention and interest. Work on it as hard as you can.

Beat 2: Epicenter

Feeling the Wave

The second part of your pitch presentation, the middle, is about presenting what the player will do and experience. This comprises your gameplay loop, your game's general aesthetics and mood, its dramatic structure, and a presentation of your prototype and your playtest results.

Up front, one point of critical importance.

It's a pitch presentation, not a show and tell session, so established game mechanics, also called "pillars," are of no interest to anyone. Don't pelt your audience with well-known features like your quest-giving mechanic, crafting system, AI behavior, monetization scheme, and similar. The only elements that count in this department are those that *differentiate* your game from other games aimed at your target audience, not tried-and-true industry standards.

First off, are you allowed to reference other games during this part? Absolutely. You can pick some data points from the value matrix you built in the Preparation phase, to demonstrate what inspired you, what you did differently, and what you tried to avoid. But never disparagingly! That's the important thing. It's perfectly acceptable to point out weaknesses in other games, but it's perfectly unacceptable to bad-mouth them.

The first three elements, gameplay loop, aesthetics/mood, and dramatic structure, need to be distilled from what you accomplished in the Process phase. The final element will be a clip of your prototype.

PITCH PRESENTATION PART II

Action	Differentiating Elements (e.g.)
Gameplay Loop	Mechanics, Interactions, AI, Difficulty…
Aesthetics/Mood	Styles, Interfaces, Artistic Abstractions…
Dramatic Structure	Development Arcs, World Narrative…
Prototype Clip	Commentary, Learnings from Playtests…

FIGURE 5.5 Pitch presentation part II: Action.

The *gameplay loop* is essential. Prepare to describe what the player will do again and again in vivid detail. For extras, you might want to throw in some innovative rules, mechanics, input methods, interactions, difficulty options, or similar that you created in the Process phase. But mind the operative word "innovative." Don't present any stock features!

For your game's *aesthetics and mood*, you need outstanding examples from your artwork that present your game's genre, period, and presentation styles and evoke memorable gameplay moments. In other words, you need to present original concept art and meticulously composed and refined images from your actual prototype that aren't merely screenshots, all of them technically impeccable, professional, and inspiring. On top of it, again, you can throw in anything noteworthy, be that interface details, camera handling, or elements related to sound or speech. (If audio of any kind is crucial for the playing experience, and you want to present a brief sample, make sure you'll have excellent speakers at your disposal during your presentation, or provide them yourself.) Once again, that an element is important, or even exciting, doesn't justify its place in your pitch presentation. It must be differentiating and innovative, compared to similar games aimed at your target audience.

For your *dramatic structure*, you should prepare the most relevant elements from your game's development arcs. If your game is dramatically complete, that would be elements from your story development, character development, and player development arcs. Be snappy. Limit yourself to the defining and most relevant elements of each arc. Rule number one, which you probably already heard and will hear again and again: no lore. Nobody's interested in the biography of your characters or the history of your game world. That doesn't mean you can't present a story point or a character detail or a specific skill your player has to learn—but only if it truly differentiates your game from similar games directed at your target audience. Finally, is your game's theme of any interest here? Not in and of itself. But if you can use it to explain important design decisions, so that your audience gets a better sense of what you're trying to achieve, then sure, go ahead and reveal your theme.

For your *vertical slice prototype*, prepare a well-edited video with the parts that illustrate the gameplay loop, the USP, the mood, and other vital elements of your game, and make it as polished as you can so that it doubles as a terrific in-game trailer. All in all, your video should not exceed 2 minutes. Which sounds short, but it will feel a lot longer in a pitch presentation. Everything about the presentation of your prototype should be *professional*, including sound mixing. Also, if it needs commenting on, you don't want to stage a shouting match between yourself and the speakers during your presentation. Instead, edit necessary comments right into your video for the pitch version, preferably with both audio overlays and captions or subtitles.

Follow up the presentation of your prototype with an ultrabrief overview of the learnings you gathered from playtesting.

Again, make everything shine, but stay honest, especially with regard to your prototype and playtests. Talking of honesty, there's the question of creating and showing a cinematic game trailer. The recommended answer is, prepare a cinematic trailer only if it's explicitly expected by your host. The skills to create a great game and the skills to create a great cinematic trailer do not necessarily intersect, and a cinematic game trailer can never address the hard question whether the game's actual gameplay is enjoyable and exciting. This is a question only an in-game trailer can address and demonstrate, besides playing the prototype.

Pitch Presentation Part III
Conditions
1. Yourself and Your Team
2. Competitive Analysis
3. Time Frame and Costs
4. Risks and Contingency Plans
5. Additional Opportunities
6. Contract/Partner Wish List
7. Title, Tagline, Logo

FIGURE 5.6   Pitch presentation part III: Conditions.

Beat 3: Propagation

Amplifying the Wave

The third and final part of your pitch presentation is about yourself and the team; a competitive analysis; time and cost estimates; and the project's possible risks, constraints, and opportunities. After that, your presentation should end *exactly* how it started: with your title, tagline, and logo. Once more, let's look at each element in more detail.

You will have to introduce ***yourself***, who you are and what you did and your most relevant projects so far, both in terms of overall importance and in relation to your proposal. Preparing to introduce yourself goes beyond presenting facts from your résumé, and also beyond the actual introduction itself. As a matter of fact, you need to prepare your whole pitch as an elaborate introduction to your personality! In the literature, you'll find various lists of personal qualities you need to convey during a pitch presentation. There are William Draper's eight qualities in *The Startup Game*, for example, that comprise brains and education, energy and passion, expertise and vision, integrity, and sense of humor; or you can pick David S. Rose's ten characteristics from his 2007 TED Talk "How to Pitch to a VC." Let's have a thorough look at the latter.

As Rose famously put it in his talk, the single most important thing in a pitch presentation is *you*. This applies to video game pitches as well. Are you the right person to lead that project to success? Rose lists ten personal characteristics that you have to convey during your pitch, of which the most important one is *integrity*, and the most important three are *integrity*, *passion*, and *experience*. All three are hard to fake when facing a room full of industry veterans who've seen it all. For the experience, you will have to acquaint the audience with the most relevant projects you worked on in the past, and you should *always* do that, regardless of how sure you are that everybody in the room knows exactly who you are and what you did. (Spoiler: they don't.) Then, never conceal past failures. Not only would that be dishonest and count against your integrity, it deprives you of showing that you have learned from your mistakes and thus gained more experience. How much experience should you have? Well, all else being equal, that's a question of scale and proportions. The project you propose should be built on prior experience and not exceed it by a large margin. It should be ambitious with respect to your prior career, but not flamboyantly so. The next two characteristics are *knowledge* and *skill*. Both you should convey through your game treatment and your knowledge about its economic conditions. But as you can't have all the knowledge and all the skills that your project demands, *leadership* is another vital characteristic that you need to convey. Can you develop, inspire, and motivate a team and lead it to success? Your résumé will vouch for you, hopefully, and your overall performance during the pitch. Also, there's the team or part of a team that you assembled to build your prototype, that you will introduce right after you introduced yourself, and if it's a quality team, that will vouch for you too. Then, you need to convey *commitment*, that you won't jump ship when worse comes to worst. A good indicator for that is how much time, effort, money, and other resources you have already committed to your game. Then, both *vision* and *realism* should inform everything you present. Finally, you should prepare the impression that you have what Rose calls *coachability*, denoting your openness to recommendations and advice. Yes, that's a whole lot to incorporate in your pitch. But that's what it comes down to if you want to successfully pitch not just your game treatment, but also yourself as the bearer of its vision.

Closely related to the matter of yourself is the matter of your **team**, which you will introduce after you introduced yourself. Describe their experiences and accomplishments, and why they're the exact right people to build this game.

For the presentation of yourself and your team, the same rule kicks in that we applied in the Process phase in the context of skill, style, and subject matter: limit yourself to highlighting only outstanding experiences and accomplishment. Just like target audiences, people listening to your pitch will build averages in their heads, not sums. This has also been recognized in the literature on pitching, with Oren Klaff's already cited *Pitch Anything* as an example.

If you managed to collect commitments from experienced developers, artist, writers, and so on, for a capable core team, that's terrific news. Because if you inspired them to commit in principle, that's a powerful indicator for the viability of your proposal *and* attests to your personality. But what if you have a team that isn't very experienced, and maybe you're not that experienced either? It comes down to what's already been discussed—your prototype must come to the rescue. It's another point stressed by Brian Upton in his GDC 2017 presentation, mentioned earlier in this level. Without a reasonable amount of presentable experience, the only thing that can attest to your abilities and those of your team is a terrific prototype that is both playable and polished. That's the thing that will speak for you, and it's the only thing that can speak for you under such circumstances.

For the **competitive analysis**, you're well-prepared already with the data points from your value characteristics table that you developed in the Preparation phase. Putting your entire value matrix on a presentation slide amounts to overkill, Harvey Balls or no, but you can include it in your proposal handout (more on that later in the level on presenting). For your pitch, just prepare the most important points that support your key value decisions.

For your preparation of the next two elements, estimates for your time frame and costs, this book cannot give you detailed calculations or formulas for your specific game and team. Actually, no book can do that. It can only provide you with a basic framework, and you need to flesh out that framework for yourself. Besides having experience, which goes a long way, you can find and ask domain experts for the specific parameters you need to know in the context of the type and scope of your game and the size of your team. Go to conferences, developer meetings, indie meet-ups, and trade fair shows, and prepare in advance whom you want to meet and what you want to ask. Also, you can send polite inquiries per e-mail! And don't forget social messaging and microblogging platforms like Mastodon or Twitter. These are repositories full of illustrious industry natives who'll be glad to answer your questions, as long as you pick and ask the right people the right questions in non-annoying ways.

Let's start with how you prepare your **time frame**. During your pitch, you should be able to present an estimate for completion that is well-supported by facts and based on typical development cycles for your type of game, its scale, its platform, and so on, and on projected time allocations for everything from story development to casting, cinematics, and voice recording to testing and QA and localization, if applicable. To do that, you have to break literally *everything* down into person hours and distribute them over your project plan. Factor in all known dependencies. Adjust for the average number of sick days and vacation days. Even after that, don't stack everything too tightly—the number of team members might need to fluctuate at times, for example, and not everything or everybody might always materialize on schedule. Adjust for that, too. The more scrupulous your estimate, the better. Will you need projected milestones for your pitch? It depends—chances are your pitch will be based on an innovative idea where change is inevitable, and that calls for an agile approach. So instead of milestones, you might want to lay out a rough schedule for a number of viable but elastic interim products that allow for course corrections. Beyond your general time estimate, should you include a projected launch window? Probably not, as this rarely makes sense. First, the publisher will analyze your time estimate and refine it. Then, the publisher's own organization will add several parameters to the mix. Finally, launch times are not merely determined by completion! It's the publisher's marketing professionals who will determine the best possible launch window for your game.

Then there's your preparation of the **cost** estimate. Don't ever let that become the elephant in the room. The better and more specific your time frame estimate, the better and more specific your budget estimate will be. Still, it's a formidable task, because you might not be aware of all the costs your project entails.

Here's a handful of elements to consider for your preparations (many of them courtesy of Thomas Friedmann, managing director at Funatics). Everybody who's working on the project should be able to pay their rents and fill their fridges and pay their taxes over the project's life span, and don't forget social security and insurance contributions. Basically, you take all the person-hours from your time estimate and attach price tags to each. Then, depending on your type of game, there might be third-party costs toward casting, actors, voice talent, localization, and similar. Or writers—for everything from menus to quick-start guides to story, plot, dialogues, and descriptions in a dramatically complete game. Next, calculate what equipment you will need, hardware and software alike, and if you want to license an engine or music or other assets of any kind. Be particularly clear on licensing fees for music; these can vary from free to grotesque, and no one can calculate that for your game but you. Then, there are several types of operating costs: office rent, heat, electricity, telecommunications, hosting services, cleaning services, insurance, tax consulting, to name a few. These aren't directly devoured by your project but needed to maintain it. Add to that all kinds of expenses, including travel expenses for research, presentations, meetings, and so forth. Also, you need to adjust for the location where your project will take place! There are measurable differences in rent, transportation, and cost of living, depending on the country and the city where you reside. As an example, there's a famous Twitter conversation where industry legend Tim Schafer, alias @TimofLegend, explains how his San Francisco-based team of 12 people in a two-year development cycle and with fixed costs of $200,000 for music, voice talent, localization, etc., burned through $3 million without even a hint of extravaganza.

Lastly, should you offer cost alternatives, for example, different scope options with different budgets attached to them? Generally, don't. Pitch your best plan. First off, options and alternatives are detrimental to pitching a clear and compelling vision. (You wouldn't pitch alternative aesthetic styles or different options for your game mechanics either.) Then, scope and budget alternatives can be negotiated later, unhurriedly and with all the numbers on the table. Finally, "option fatigue" is a thing. Requiring fewer choices—Daniel H. Pink calls it "The Less Frame" in *To Sell Is Human*—appeals to people a lot more than you think. Plus, the more options, the more messy human decision-making gets; Dan Ariely's talk "Are We in Control of Our Own Decisions?" provides an illuminating and entertaining introduction.

Then, after having prepared both your time and budget estimates, apply some math. How do these figures compare to the economic data of competing games that you analyzed in the Preparation phase, both in terms of development costs and sales? And, importantly, do these parameters correlate with the price range you have in mind for your game? While all that market data is far from reliable, it might at least give you a warning if your economical projections seem to be far off the mark. If everything checks out, put the data into your proposal handout and your results into your pitch.

Next up, you need to sketch the possible ***risks*** of your project for your presentation. To be able to do that, you need to make your homework and learn everything about the industry that is even remotely relevant to your specific game and its development cycle. There can be technological risks, when your game requires hardware or software that will only be available in the future—or so you hope. Effectively, there's always a technological risk involved. If you want to play it safe and plan exclusively for hardware, software, or graphics specs that already exist, your game will look dated when it comes out in two years. Which is just another form of risk! Then there are industry uncertainties, from sudden price hikes for hardware (think graphic cards) to ubiquitous consumer software going up in flames (think Adobe Flash back in the days) to strikes (think Activision Blizzard). Or, there might be a potential threat that the market will be flooded with similar games before yours is release-ready. Or that there will be dozens of cheap knockoffs with similar names two months after release. Parts of the risk package are also foreseeable constraints that are specific to your game type, your content, and your release markets. This could be age and content ratings, console manufacturer requirements, and all kinds of localization issues. Particular to regional cultures and legal environments all over the globe, there's a shockingly wide range of factors to consider, running from the reasonable to the quaint to the outright bizarre. It's not just about sex, violence, and gambling, mind. The more issues you are aware of, the better. Thus, do your homework. For all of these possible risks, be thorough with your preparations. Find them, substantiate them, explain how you plan to deal with them, and what your contingency plans are. Being conscientious will score you a lot of points in the personality department discussed above.

PITCH PRESENTATION		
Part I: Concept	*Part II: Action*	*Part III: Conditions*
1. Title, Tagline, Logo	1. Gameplay Loop	1. Yourself and Your Team
2. Crisp Introduction	2. Aesthetics/Mood	2. Competitive Analysis
3. Vision Statement	3. Dramatic Structure	3. Time Frame and Costs
4. Synopsis (Log Line)	4. Prototype Clip	4. Risks and Contingency Plans
5. USP (Hook)		5. Additional Opportunities
6. Target Audience		6. Contract/Partner Wish List
7. Platform and Engine		7. Title, Tagline, Logo

FIGURE 5.7   Pitch presentation.

From there, you should follow up with additional mid-term or long-term *opportunities* that your treatment might support. The stress is on *additional*—everything that is cool about your game as such doesn't belong here! Instead, ask yourself whether it could accommodate DLCs, sequels, spin-offs, adaptations for other genres, adaptations for different media, licensing, merchandizing, or what you can think of. But whatever it is, be specific and produce numbers. Don't just go and proclaim that your game could be easily adapted to other media, for example, a graphic novel. Explain why that's the case, and do that by showing that you're *intimately familiar* with graphic novels' narrative, aesthetic, and economic conditions and how these would work for you. Vague, unsupported statements won't do you any favors. (While the question of intellectual property (IP) rights is outside the scope of this book, there will be a few thoughts on that topic further below.)

You're almost there, but one important point remains: your *contract/partner wish list*. What services do you need from the publisher? What services do they offer? Financial investment, obviously. But three more things are almost always on that list, and available: marketing, production, and release management. Marketing usually includes public relations, advertising, and event management, but possibly also community management. Production generally includes QA testing, localization, porting, and often sound, particularly music and speech. Release management can include retail, promotional programs, and merchandise. Maybe you're able to handle some of these items yourself. But perhaps you'd rather want to focus on developing your game. Also, publishers have the expertise and the infrastructure in place to handle these things more efficiently.

After that, the only thing left is to wrap everything up with your final slide that contains your *title*, *tagline*, and *logo*, just like your first slide, and serve it to your audience with a plain verbal "thank you." That's it. Everything beyond, from profuse testimonies of gratitude for listening to you, to a final slide cluttered with personal and networking information, distracts from your cause and looks unprofessional. Anything anybody might ever want to know about you and your communication channels belongs into your proposal handout (more on that in the upcoming level). Don't ask if there are any questions, or proclaim that you're looking forward to answering them. You will be asked questions, don't worry, and everybody expects you to answer them! Simply conclude your presentation with your title, tagline, and logo on the screen, and say "thank you." It's not hard. Everything else will develop from there.

Outlook

Before you break camp and set out, let's close this level with a few words concerning IP, or IP rights, and how to handle negotiations. If you're pitching to a reputable indie publisher, it's rarely a problem; you will almost always keep your IP by default. With some major publishers, though, this might be different, and you should be prepared.

IP rights won't be part of your pitch, but you should have a clear goal in mind to guide you through contract negotiations later. (On negotiations after a successful pitch in general, you can find an entire chapter in *The Business of Indie Games* by Josef, Van Lepp, and Carper.) What you need to develop is what's called a BATNA in negotiation theory: your *best alternative to a negotiated agreement*. It's not a bottom line. A bottom line is certainly useful, but it makes you inflexible during negotiations and leaves no wiggle room for imaginative solutions. As Roger Fisher and William Ury put it in *Getting to Yes*, you should think through and calculate all the possible choices you have, so that you're neither too optimistic nor too pessimistic about viable alternatives, and know exactly the limits of these alternatives. During negotiations, then, you can always measure the result of any proposed agreement against the result of your best alternative, your BATNA, and decide accordingly—while remaining flexible toward imaginative "out of the box" proposals. These often come about through "broadening the options," as has been mentioned before in a different context. In the context of IP rights, this could be scope or time limits or interesting compensations and conditions. Whatever it is, you can always measure it against your BATNA!

Why is that important? Because IP rights are *immeasurably* important. Once you have given away your IP, you've made yourself more dependent on your publisher than might be advisable in the long run. Now, it doesn't mean your IP could *never* come back to you—maybe you negotiated a time limit after which it will return to you. Or you can buy it back—IO Interactive's management buyout from Square Enix in 2017, for example, included buying back the *Hitman* IP under terms that were called "supportive." But such examples are rare. Some will make you believe that relinquishing your IP for a publisher deal is industry standard, but that's simply not the case. Shahid Kamal Ahmad, who headed Sony UK's Strategic Content division for over a decade and commissioned hundreds of titles from indie developers for the PlayStation 4, Vita, and VR, put it very succinctly in "Pitching Is Courtship": *you want to own your IP in as many cases as you reasonably can*. To sum it up, if you have a BATNA with respect to your IP, both you and your negotiation partner should be doing fine. And there's yet another angle. If you've built up your IP from humble beginnings, by self-publishing a less ambitious game, by having written stories related to that IP that sold reasonably well, or comics or a graphic novel, or a web video series, or whatever you're good at, that would strengthen your position. Not only is your IP then something that already exists, it's also a tangible asset you bring to the negotiation table.

Level Three

Presenting

Opening

This final level of the Proposition phase will be brief and relaxed. It will give you general recommendations for the look and fitness of your slides, your personal demeanor during your pitch, and your proposition handout. Some parts will be applicable to on-site presentations only; others to both on-site and virtual presentations. There is no dedicated section for virtual pitch presentations for two reasons: no clearly established rules for virtual pitch presentations exist as yet, and virtual presentations are often more conversational to begin with, particularly with indie publishers. Thus, in case of a virtual pitch presentation, inquire as to what you have to provide and expect.

Now let's step back a bit and start from the beginning. Only try to get invites from the right publisher or publishers. The *right* publisher is a publisher whose portfolio is a match for your game, and whose portfolio would be enriched by it. If you find such a publisher, apply for a pitch presentation. This might entail handing in a high-level paper, about two or three pages long, compiled from your pitch content discussed in the previous level. It certainly should contain information about you and your team, the reasons why you think they're the right publisher for your game, and what you hope they can do for you. Whatever else you need to provide, they—or their web page or web form—will tell you. All in all, keep everything snappy. And tasty! You might even want to use your elevator pitch instead of your full vision statement or synopsis. Then, somewhat less formally, if you make a pitch at a games convention or trade show, you generally won't have to provide a high-level paper in advance. But you might have considerably less time for your actual pitch instead of the usual 20 minutes plus questions. Wherever you are, though, don't waste anyone's time. Don't pitch to a publisher for the sole reason that their representatives happen to be there. Pitch to a publisher because it's the right publisher for your game!

Then, the matter of who needs to sign what. Here, misconceptions abound. On the one hand, there's the non-disclosure agreement, or NDA, which no publisher will sign for your pitch ever. Then there's the submission agreement, which you will have to sign for your pitch pretty much always.

Let's unravel this from the tail end. By signing the submission agreement, you have no legal recourse in case your pitch is unsuccessful, but a game similar to what you pitched is released by that publisher at some point in the future. The reason is that ideas and inventions aren't created in a vacuum. They're created in a cultural context. Similar ideas and inventions tend to bubble up in different places around the same time. Your personal risk would be that the publisher takes your idea and develops it without you, a risk that is minuscule for reasons we'll get into in a minute. But on the publisher's side, a game with elements similar to what you're pitching might already be in production. The sheer chance and legal risk involved with that is orders of magnitude larger than the imaginary risk that a publisher steals your idea. Also, if you invented a hammer, everything will look to you like a hammer. You will see similarities left and right where there are none, or only superficial similarities, or even unavoidable similarities. Publishers have to protect themselves. And for the exact same reasons, they certainly won't sign an NDA.

Now, what about you and your precious game idea? First off, as mentioned, the risk you take pitching to a publisher is microscopic. But beyond that, if you do it right, you need not fear that anyone will take your idea from you because *you're not pitching an idea but a treatment*, as discussed in this phase's introduction. If you were pitching an idea, that would be different. You can't copyright ideas. Actually, nobody can own an idea! So everybody can take your idea, and that's perfectly legal, create a work based on it, make a million dollars, and—as the film teacher Dov Simens put it—go to heaven.

DOI: 10.1201/9781003334682-27

The chances that a reputable publisher takes your game treatment and develops it without you against your will are infinitesimal. Not only is it a risk no publisher in their right mind would be willing to take. It would also be completely at odds with a publisher's business model.

Beat 1: Display

What You Show

Almost everybody is perpetually exasperated with terrible slides, and almost everybody produces terrible slides. Almost everybody gives advice to take a lesson from Apple, and almost nobody takes a lesson from Apple. Is there a law of nature that your slides have to be terrible? No. Here's the first rule:

- Make it one idea, one slide.

What an idea is, that's up to you. An idea can be that your treatment has four incredible advantages. Then put all four on one slide, maybe making them appear line by line for greater impact. Or, you can treat each of these four advantages as an idea by itself. Then distribute them over four different slides. Or, one feature has a defined set of elements that aren't too numerous. Then put these elements together on a slide. It's the *concept* of one idea, one slide that counts. It helps you structure your set in the most impressive way possible, both cognitively and emotionally, by making you *think*. The second rule:

- Make it highly legible.

Legibility is a matter of font, font size, and contrast. Use a classic presentation font that is easy to read, with large font sizes, breathing space between elements, and high contrast against the background. Arial or Times New Roman aren't presentation fonts. If in doubt what to use, read up on this or ask someone with typography skills. As a rough guideline, don't make text smaller than 24pt or headlines larger than 44pt (but individual fonts might need adjustment). And don't cram elements too close to each other! Don't be that person who apologizes to the audience, "I know you can't read this, but I wanted to put all twelve points on one slide." (Which actually happened at a game-based learning conference, of all places.) Don't combine background colors with text colors or element colors that don't stand out clearly, don't match, or cause problems for people with color blindness. Again, read up on it or ask a designer what fits your presentation best. (The default black-on-white arrangement isn't lacking in contrast, for sure. But it's terribly lacking in style.) This is followed by the rule:

- Make it instantly graspable.

Think of well-designed highway billboards. They don't feature sentences with more than six simple words because people are busy driving; they neither have the time nor the cognitive capacity to read and digest difficult words or complex sentences. Your audience in a pitch presentation is also "driving." They're busy listening to your presentation and analyzing your treatment! They, too, have neither the time nor the cognitive capacity to read and digest dense and long-winded prose on the screen. The best approach to make every slide instantly comprehensible is to follow billboard rules and use clear, simple sentences with not more than six words; crisp artwork that adds meaning, clarification, or emphasis; or a combination of both. (And don't use clip art or stock images. This is a pitch proposal, not a road safety presentation at your local children's library.) Finally:

- Make it zero errors.

No spelling, grammar, or punctuation errors. Immaculate typography with all hyphens, n- and m-dashes where they belong; correct double and single quotation marks or Guillemets or corner brackets that match your language; uniform and consistent line heights, tabs, indents, margins, and so on; and

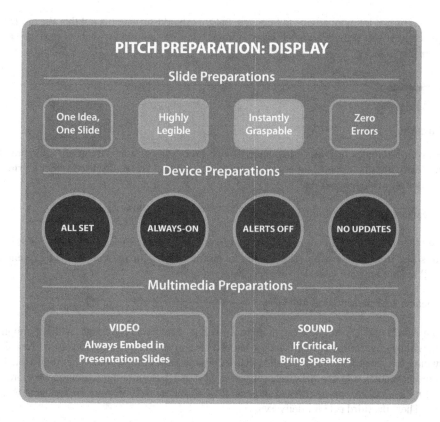

FIGURE 5.8 Pitch preparation: Display.

every element aligned to an invisible baseline grid. If you're not scrupulous with your presentation, why should anyone think you'll be scrupulous with your game?

That's about it, at least for the slides. From the technical side, there are also a handful of rules:

- Have your presentation device fully charged and booted up, your presentation app running, and your slide set ready to launch before you enter the room.
- Kill any power management features so your device won't go into screensaver or sleep mode while you're answering a question.
- Use a presentation device where you can reliably mute all internal and external messages.
- Use a presentation device that will not begin to install updates or reboot during your pitch.

These things happen all the time, and they're not funny. Make checking for them part of your preparation routine, always.

The last set of rules is about video and sound:

- Don't run videos from the internet or in different applications, so that you have to switch apps, trawl through folder structures or your overpopulated desktop, revisit your Wi-Fi settings, accidentally close the prepared browser tab, and similar embarrassments. Instead, embed videos right into your presentation slides.
- If sound is of the essence, and you're not absolutely sure what's available in the presentation room, bring a pair of cutting-edge speakers to the session.

In case you bring your playable prototype for a subsequent hands-on session, don't even think of using your presentation device. Provide dedicated devices that you have prepared in advance.

There's certainly a lot more advice to be given, but this should suffice. It's not that the bar is particularly high, sadly. If you manage to meet these ten rules, your presentation will shoot past the audience's expectations like a rocket.

Beat 2: Delivery

What You Say

Whether given 5 minutes or 20 or a full hour, almost everybody assumes that their slide presentation will fit perfectly into the allotted time slot. It almost never does. You really need to get a grip on this! Therefore, delivery rule number one:

- Rehearse your presentation for time.

Don't be that presenter who overruns the time limit, speed-reads the last 15 slides, or skips whole chunks of slides in a state of panic. If you can't be on time with your presentation, why should anyone think you'll be on time with your deliverables? Next up:

- Rehearse your presentation for clarity.

Go from A to B to C and so on, straight up to Z, without leaving anything out, without jumping back and forth, without digressing. Know exactly what you have to say with respect to your current slide, and what you have to say with respect to the slide that will follow your current slide. That way, a quick glance at your presenter notes will always suffice, if you need it at all. Stumbling, searching for words, losing focus, getting lost, and dropping the ball in general won't reflect well on your management and leadership skills. Then, the third rule for delivery:

- Rehearse your presentation for presence.

Never look at the projection screen, except when your prototype video is playing. Be 100% present and connected to your audience all the time. Your slides should illustrate and emphasize what you say. Don't turn this on its head by making it look as if you were commenting on and clarifying your slides! The only thing you should be looking at, at every given moment, is your audience. When you rehearsed your presentation often enough, your own words will become your anchor, and you won't be tempted to cling to your slides on the screen like a cartoon sailor to the mast in a thunderstorm. Finally, the last delivery rule:

- Rehearse your presentation for flow.

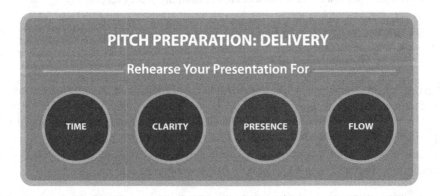

FIGURE 5.9   Pitch preparation: Delivery.

Memorize essential wordings, phrases, and sequences by rehearsing them over and over, so that your audience will be pleased and excited just by listening to you. Different words, grammar, and syntax have different meanings and different rhetorical properties. Always use what's most effective, cognitively and emotionally. Never use what crossed your mind the first time around. Never rely on improv.

Then, two rules concerning audience questions.

Questions in between. Should someone ask a question while you're still presenting, don't be annoyed. Take it as an opportunity to clarify something that wasn't clear, and later rework your presentation to preempt that question in case you'll be pitching to another publisher. Be brief—answer questions crisply or communicate that you'll be going into that in a minute, if that's the case. Don't let a question lead you on a wild tangent. And remember, your presentation should lead from A to Z in a straight, logical line, which makes interruptions for clarification much less likely.

Questions after. As has been stressed before, don't ask if there are "any questions" at the end of your presentation, neither orally nor on your final slide, or proclaim that you're looking forward to answering them. Close by saying "thank you" and let the questions roll in. They will! Remember, you're not delivering a conference paper. In a pitch presentation, the audience isn't just allowed to ask questions, no. Your audience has the perfect right to comment, summarize, criticize, supplement, discuss, compare, analyze, or order pizza. You're not in charge! So don't generously invite their "questions."

Moreover, stay open and stay professional. Don't get defensive against criticism and suggestions, but don't treat them as revelations either. Just write everything down you haven't thought of yet, maybe on a notepad as your device is busy, and promise to check it out, think it through, and communicate the solution later.

Finally, and that should go without saying, all the rules for personal appearance, behavior, and attitude for speaking in public apply.

Beat 3: Documents

What You Provide

To accompany your pitch, you need to prepare a well-designed proposition handout, possibly around 15–30 pages long. The good news is, you already have three master documents from which to extract this handout—your *Ludotronics* inventory, your game treatment, and your pitch preparations.

Your handout should contain data, details, and documentation for every point you make in your pitch, as compiled in the previous level. It should contain your demographic breakdown, your competitor breakdown, your value set, and all your background figures, your target audience, your market research conclusions, and your time and cost projections, all fairly detailed. It should also contain all the screenshots, artwork, illustrations, and diagrams needed to understand what your game is about without having attended your pitch. Make enough high-quality copies for your presentation (when in doubt, ask in advance how many people will attend), put them in pocket folders, and keep a print-quality PDF handy to send around.

Don't distribute your handout at the beginning of your pitch if you want the audience to listen to your presentation. But to preempt mental distress, it's always a good idea to put your stack of handouts visibly on your desk when you start your presentation and hand them out after you're done. That way, everybody can give your presentation their full attention in the knowledge that all the data and all the details and all the documentation will be available to them in written form right after.

There's absolutely no need for your handout to look and feel like a slick upmarket magazine. But like everything else you provide, your handout should look and feel *professional*, not like something spawned in the layout and typography hell of a singularly unsuited word processor. Use professional tools, either yourself or a designer from your team. It's the *form* that makes difficult matter legible, comprehensible, and exciting.

Your prototype is also a kind of "document" that you need to provide. Put it online for download, and also your walkthrough video and your proposition handout. Provide links, and protect them against unauthorized access. If there's a hands-on session after your presentation, bring suitable devices along, as mentioned earlier. Also, provide over-ear headphones, not in-ear headphones, for reasons that should be immediately obvious, and a pack of baby wipes to clean them before handing them to another person. (Regular disinfectant wipes might be irritating to both your earphones and your audience's ears.)

Outlook

This is the end of your journey. But a subsequent, grander journey is waiting for you, right after your pitch and your contract negotiations. That grander journey is the development cycle, and that's where our ways part. But look around, and you will certainly find another helper to accompany you across that next magical threshold and beyond.

So goodbye, and good luck.

Your great adventure has barely begun.

Phase 06

Postmortems

Introduction

Welcome to the Postmortem phase!

For several reasons, the following sections are not simply relegated to this book's "back matter" but constitute levels, and a phase, in their own right.

The first level, *References*, is not just a list of works mentioned throughout the text. Many if not all the works cited deserve and even demand to be read, watched, or followed up on in general. As a reminder, the *Ludotronics* paradigm is a methodology, nothing more, nothing less, which is first and foremost about *procedures* and *processes* and much less about *artistic intent* and *execution*. For the latter, engaging these listed sources is indispensable. Also, many of these sources contain valuable information for beginners on the one hand, and specialized information for professionals on the other, neither of which this book is focused on.

Similarly, the second level on *Rightsholders* is not just a list of games and movies mentioned throughout the text. It's a cross section of works of art that provide information and illumination, patterns and paradigms, and important experiences both in terms of expertise and awareness for the game design profession.

The third and final level on *Responses* is not just about providing the means to "ask questions"; it's about providing the means to lead an ongoing conversation. In the Preliminary phase, right at the beginning of this book, an argument was made for the game design document to be a "living document," and that's what *Ludotronics* itself should aspire to as a shared perpetual project, reflected on *ludotronics.net* and the trail it leaves on the web and on social media.

DOI: 10.1201/9781003334682-28

Level One

References

Works Cited

Adams, Ernest. *Fundamentals of Game Design*. 2nd Ed. New Riders, 2010.

Ahmad, Shahid Kamal. "Pitching Is Courtship." YouTube, 2017.

Ames, Carole. "Classrooms: Goals, Structures, and Student Motivation." *Journal of Educational Psychology* 84.3, 1991. https://doi.org/10.1037/0022-0663.84.3.261

Anderson, Lorin W. & David R. Krathwohl (Eds.). *A Taxonomy for Learning, Teaching, and Assessing: A Revision of Bloom's Taxonomy of Educational Objectives*. Allyn & Bacon, 2001.

Anthropy, Anna & Naomi Clark. *A Game Design Vocabulary: Exploring the Foundational Principles Behind Good Game Design*. Pearson, 2014.

Ariely, Dan. "Are we in control of our own decisions?" EG3 Conference, 2008.

Ariely, Dan, Anat Bracha & Stephan Meier. "Doing Good or Doing Well? Image Motivation and Monetary Incentives in Behaving Prosocially." IZA Discussion Paper No. 2968, 2007. https://dx.doi.org/10.1257/aer.99.1.544

Aristotle. *The Complete Works of Aristotle: The Revised Oxford Translation* Vol. 2. Ed. Jonathan Barnes. Princeton UP, 1984.

Atkins, Barry. *More Than a Game: The Computer as Fictional Form*. Manchester UP, 2003.

Baranowski, Andreas M. & Heiko Hecht. "The Auditory Kuleshov Effect: Multisensory Integration in Movie Editing." *Perception* 46.5, 2017. https://doi.org/10.1177/0301006616682754

Barasz, Kate, Leslie K. John, Elizabeth A. Keenan & Michael I. Norton. "Pseudo-Set Framing." *Journal of Experimental Psychology: General* 146.10, 2017. https://doi.org/10.1037/xge0000337

Barrie, J. M. *Peter and Wendy*. Hodder & Stoughton, 1911.

Barron, Kenneth E. & Judith M. Harackiewicz. "Achievement Goals and Optimal Motivation: A Multiple Goals Approach." In: *Intrinsic and Extrinsic Motivation: The Search for Optimal Motivation and Performance*. Eds. Carol Sansone & Judith M. Harackiewicz. Academic P, 2000.

Bartle, Richard. "Hearts, Clubs, Diamonds, Spades: Players Who Suit MUDs." mud.co.uk, 1996.

Bartle, Richard. "Understanding the Limits of Theory." In: *Beyond Game Design*. Ed. Chris Bateman. Course Technology, 2009.

Bates, Bob. *Game Design*. 2nd Ed. Course Technology, 2004.

Bedau, Mark. "Weak Emergence." In: *Philosophical Perspectives: Mind, Causation, and World* Vol. 11. Ed. James E. Tomberlin. Blackwell, 1997. https://doi.org/10.1111/0029-4624.31.s11.17

Beedie, Christopher J., Peter C. Terry & Andrew M. Lane. "Distinctions between Emotions and Mood." *Cognition and Emotion* 19, 2005. http://dx.doi.org/10.1080/02699930541000057

Beldoch, Michael. "Sensitivity to Expression of Emotional Meaning in Three Modes of Communication." In: *Social Encounters: Contributions to Social Interactions*. Ed. Michael Argyle. AldineTransaction, 2009.

Berlyne, Daniel E. *Conflict, Arousal, and Curiosity*. McGraw–Hill, 1960.

Bhatty, Michael. *Interaktives Story Telling: Zur historischen Entwicklung und konzeptionellen Strukturierung interaktiver Geschichten*. Shaker, 1999.

Birdwell, Ken. "The Cabal: Valve's Design Process for Creating Half-Life." *Game Developer* December 10, 1999.

Bloom, Benjamin S. et al. (Eds.). *Taxonomy of Educational Objectives: The Classification of Educational Goals; Handbook I: Cognitive Domain*. David McKay, 1956.

Bogost, Ian. "Persuasive Games: Familiarity, Habituation, and Catchiness." *Game Developer* April 2, 2009.

DOI: 10.1201/9781003334682-29

Brown, Rennie & Dave King. *Self-Editing for Fiction Writers: How to Edit Yourself Into Print.* 2nd Ed. HarperCollins, 2004.

Browne, Cameron. *Evolutionary Game Design.* Springer, 2011.

Bullinger, E. W. *Figures of Speech Used in the Bible: Explained and Illustrated.* E. & J. B. Young, 1898.

Campbell, Joseph. *The Masks of God Vol. I: Primitive Mythology.* Martin Secker & Warburg, 1960.

Campbell, Joseph. *The Power of Myth: A Conversation with Bill Moyers.* Doubleday, 1988.

Campbell, Joseph. *The Hero with a Thousand Faces.* Princeton UP, 2004.

Collins, Karen. *Game Sound: An Introduction to the History, Theory, and Practice of Video Game Music and Sound Design.* MIT, 2008.

Corning, Peter A. "The Re-emergence of 'Emergence': A Venerable Concept in Search of a Theory." *Complexity* 7.6, 2002. https://doi.org/10.1002/cplx.10043

Costikyan, Greg. *Uncertainty in Games.* MIT, 2013.

Crawford, Chris. "Barrels o' Fun." *The Journal of Computer Game Design* 8, 1995.

Crawford, Chris. *The Art of Computer Game Design.* Washington State U, 1997.

Crawford, Chris. *Chris Crawford on Game Design.* New Riders, 2003.

Crawford, Chris. *On Interactive Storytelling.* New Riders, 2005.

Csikszentmihalyi, Mihaly. *Flow: The Psychology of Optimal Experience.* Harper & Row, 1990.

Csikszentmihalyi, Mihaly. *Finding Flow: Psychology of Engagement with Everyday Life.* Basic, 1997.

Dalton, Polly & Nick Fraenkel. "Gorillas We Have Missed: Sustained Inattentional Deafness for Dynamic Events." *Cognition* 124, 2012. https://doi.org/10.1016/j.cognition.2012.05.012

de Bono, Edward. *Teach Your Child to Think.* Penguin, 1994.

Deci, Edward L. & Richard M. Ryan. *Intrinsic Motivation and Self-Determination in Human Behaviour.* Plenum, 1985.

Domsch, Sebastian. *Storyplaying: Agency and Narrative in Video Games.* de Gruyter, 2013.

Dood, Maximilian. "YoVideogames Aliens: Colonial Marines Review (WTF HAPPENED?!)." YouTube, 2013.

Draper, William H. III. *The Startup Game: Inside the Partnership between Venture Capitalists and Entrepreneurs.* Palgrave Macmillan, 2012.

Dutton, Donald G. & Arthur P. Aron. "Some Evidence for Heightened Sexual Attraction under Conditions of High Anxiety." *Journal of Personality and Social Psychology* 30.4, 1974. http://dx.doi.org/10.1037/h0037031

Egri, Lajos. *Dramatic Writing: Its Basis in the Creative Interpretation of Human Motives.* Touchstone, 2004.

Ekman, Paul & Daniel Goldman. *Knowing Our Emotions, Improving Our World: A Conversation.* Audio-CD. More Than Sound Productions, 2007.

Ericsson, K. Anders & Herbert A. Simon. "Verbal Reports as Data." *Psychological Review* 87.3, 1980. https://doi.org/10.1037/0033-295X.87.3.215

Evers, Ellen R. K. *Sets: How the Organization of Stimuli Affects Judgments & Choice.* Tilburg U, 2014.

Falstein, Noah. "Understanding Fun: The Theory of Natural Funativity." In: *Introduction to Game Development.* Ed. Steve Rabin. Charles River Media, 2005.

Farrell, David & David Moffat. "Applying the Self Determination Theory of Motivation in Games Based Learning." In: *Proceedings of the 8th European Conference on Games Based Learning.* Ed. Carsten Busch. ACPI, 2014.

Feynman, Richard P. "Cargo Cult Science: Some Remarks on Science, Pseudoscience, and Learning How to Not Fool Yourself." Caltech Commencement Address, 1974.

Field, Syd. *Screenplay: The Foundations of Screenwriting.* First published 1979. Rev. Ed. Delta, 2005.

Fisher, Roger & William Ury. *Getting to Yes.* Penguin, 1983.

Forster, E. M. *Aspects of the Novel.* Mariner, 1956.

Foucault, Michel. "Of Other Spaces: Utopias and Heterotopias." First published in *Architecture/Mouvement/Continuité* no.5, October 1984, based on a lecture at the Conférence au Cercle d'études architecturales, Tunis, March 1967. Transl. Jay Miskowiec. *Diacritics* 16.1, 1986.

Fox, Andrew S. et al. (Eds.). *The Nature of Emotion: Fundamental Questions.* Oxford UP, 2018.

Frank, Allegra. "RPGs Need In-Game Recaps to Help Us Out." *Kotaku* July 31, 2018.

Freeman, David. *Creating Emotion in Games: The Craft and Art of Emotioneering.* New Riders, 2003.

Freytag, Gustav. *Technik des Dramas.* S. Hirzel, 1863.

Fullerton, Tracy. *Game Design Workshop: A Playcentric Approach to Creating Innovative Games.* 4th Ed. CRC, 2019.

Gall, John. *General Systemantics: An Essay on How Systems Work, and Especially How They Fail.* Quadrangle, 1977.

Gardner, Howard. *Intelligence Reframed: Multiple Intelligences for the 21st Century.* Basic, 2006.

Gardner, Howard. *Multiple Intelligences: New Horizons.* Basic, 2006.

Gardner, Howard. *Frames of Mind: The Theory of Multiple Intelligences.* First published 1983. 10th Anniv. Ed. Basic Books, 2011.

Garrido, Sandra. *Why Are We Attracted to Sad Music?* Palgrave, 2017.

Genette, Gérard. *Narrative Discourse: An Essay in Method.* Transl. Jane E. Lewin. Cornell UP, 1980.

Gerrig, Richard J. & Allan B. I. Bernardo. "Readers as Problem-Solvers in the Experience of Suspense." *Poetics* 22, 1994. https://doi.org/10.1016/0304-422X(94)90021-3

Ginsburg, Herbert & Sylvia Opper. *Piaget's Theory of Intellectual Development.* 3rd Ed. Pearson, 1983.

Goleman, David. *Emotional Intelligence: Why It Can Matter More Than IQ.* First published 1995. 10th Anniv. Ed. Bantam, 2005.

Grime, James. "Non-Transitive Dice." singingbanana.com. n.d. Correction attributed to Jon Chambers. In: *Wikipedia*: "Intransitive Dice: Corrected Grime Dice." Rev. May 26, 2016.

Grimshaw, Mark & Gareth Schott. "A Conceptual Framework for the Analysis of First-Person Shooter Audio and Its Potential Use for Game Engines." *International Journal of Computer Games Technology.* 2008. https://dx.doi.org/10.1155/2008/720280

Guardiola, Emmanuel. "The Gameplay Loop: A Player Activity Model for Game Design and Analysis." In: *Proceedings of the ACE 2016.* ACM, 2016. http://dx.doi.org/10.1145/3001773.3001791

Hallford, Neal & Jana Hallford. *Swords & Circuitry: A Designer's Guide to Computer Role-Playing Games.* Prima, 2001.

Harrow, Anita J. (Ed.). *A Taxonomy of the Psychomotor Domain: A Guide for Developing Behavioral Objectives.* David McKay, 1972.

Hearn, Lafcadio. "The Boy Who Drew Cats." In: *Japanese Fairy Tale* Vol. 23. Transl. Lafcadio Hearn. Hasegawa Takejirō, 1898.

Hiwiller, Zack. *Players Making Decisions: Game Design Essentials and the Art of Understanding Your Players.* New Riders, 2015.

Hocking, Clint. "Ludonarrative Dissonance in Bioshock." *Click Nothing: Design From a Long Time Ago,* 2007.

Homer. *The Odyssey.* Transl. Emily Wilson. Norton, 2017.

Hui, Yu-Chun Lorena. *Japanese Noh Theatre: The Aesthetic Principle of Jo-Ha-Kyu in the Play* Matsukaze. U of Hong Kong, 1999.

Huizinga, Johan. *Homo Ludens: A Study of the Play-Element in Culture.* Routledge & Kegan Paul, 1943.

Iyengar, Shanto, Mark D. Peters & Donald R. Kinder. "Experimental Demonstrations of the 'Not-So-Minimal' Consequences of Television News Programs." *The American Political Science Review* 76.4, 1982. https://doi.org/10.2307/1962976

Johnson, Daniel. *Game Design Companion: A Critical Analysis of Wario Land 4.* Stolen Projects, 2013.

Josef, Alex, Alex van Lepp & Marshal D. Carper. *The Business of Indie Games: Everything You Need to Know to Conquer the Indie Games Industry.* CRC-Press, 2022.

Jung, C. G. *Archetypes and the Collective Unconscious. The Collected Works of C. G. Jung.* Transl. R. F. C. Hull. 2nd Ed. Bollingen, 1968–1972.

Juslin, Patrik N. & John A. Sloboda (Eds.). *Handbook of Music and Emotion: Theory, Research, Applications.* Oxford UP, 2010.

Katkoff, Michail. "Clash of Clans—The Winning Formula." *Deconstructor of Fun,* September 16, 2012.

Kim, W. Chan & Renée Mauborgne. *Blue Ocean Strategy: How to Create Uncontested Market Space and Make the Competition Irrelevant.* Harvard Business School, 2005.

Klaff, Oren. *Pitch Anything: An Innovative Method for Presenting, Persuading, and Winning the Deal.* McGraw-Hill, 2011.

Kleist, Heinrich von. *Michael Koolhaas.* In: Erzählungen (1. Band). Realschulbuchhandlung, 1810.

Koster, Raph. "Tools don't stifle art!" *Raph Koster's Website.* August 13, 2013.

Krathwohl, David R., Benjamin S. Bloom, & Bentram B. Masia (Eds.). *Taxonomy of Educational Objectives: The Classification of Educational Goals; Handbook II: Affective Domain.* 2nd Ed. Longman, 1999.

Lacan, Jacques. "The Subversion of the Subject and the Dialectic of Desire In: *Écrits: The First Complete Edition in English.*" Transl. Bruce Fink. Norton, 2006.

Lacoste, Remi. "Creating an Emotionally Engaging Camera for Tomb Raider." GDC Europe, 2013.

Lazzaro, Nicole. "Why We Play Games: 4 Keys to More Emotion." GDC, 2004.

Lazzaro, Nicole. "Understand Emotions." In: *Beyond Game Design: Nine Steps toward Creating Better Videogames*. Ed. Chris Bateman. Course Technology, 2009.

Lazzaro, Nicole. "Games and the Four Keys to Fun: Using Emotions to Create Engaging Design." AIGAdesign, 2016.

Leary, Timothy. *Interpersonal Diagnosis of Personality: A Functional Theory and Methodology for Personality Evaluation*. Resource Publications, 2004.

Lebeau, Donald R. "Ring Buffer Introduction." *AtariAge Forum* January 30, 2008.

Lee, Harper. *To Kill a Mocking Bird*. J. B. Lippincott, 1960.

Lee, Ken & Stephen M. Silverman. "Michelle Rodriguez Gets 60 Days in Jail." *People* May 22, 2006.

Lehdonvirta, Vili & Edward Castronova. *Virtual Economies: Design and Analysis*. MIT, 2014.

Levin, Ira. *The Stepford Wives*. Random House, 1972.

Levine, Ken. "Narrative Legos: Building Replayable Narrative Out of Lots of Tiny Pieces." GDC, 2014.

Loewenstein, George. "The Psychology of Curiosity: A Review and Interpretation." *Psychological Bulletin* 116.1, 1994. http://dx.doi.org/10.1037/0033-2909.116.1.75

Loewy, Raymond. *Never Leave Well Enough Alone*. Simon & Schuster, 1951.

Longino, Trevor. "PR Quest! The Adventure to Make Your Game Famous." GDC Europe, 2013.

Luhmann, Niklas. *Soziologische Aufklärung Bd.3: Soziales System, Gesellschaft, Organisation*. Westdeutscher Verlag, 1981.

Mabinogion. Compiled from oral traditions in the 12–13th centuries. Transl. Sioned Davies. Oxford UP, 2007.

Massimini, Fausto & Massimo Carli. "The Systematic Assessment of Flow in Daily Experience." In: *Optimal Experience: Psychological Studies of Flow in Consciousness*. Eds. Mihaly Csikszentmihalyi & Isabella Selega Csikszentmihalyi. Cambridge UP, 1988.

McCarthy, Cormac. *The Road*. Knopf, 2006.

McCloud, Scott. *Understanding Comics: The Invisible Art*. HarperPerennial, 1994.

McEntee, Chris. "Rational Design: The Core of Rayman Origins." *Game Developer* March 27, 2012.

McGonigal, Jane. *Reality Is Broken: Why Games Make Us Better and How They Can Change the World*. Penguin, 2011.

McGuire, Morgan & Odest Chadwicke Jenkins. *Creating Games: Mechanics, Content, and Technology*. AK Peters, 2008.

McMillan, Luke. "The Rational Design Handbook: An Intro to RLD." *Game Developer* August 6, 2013.

Meadows, Mark Stephen. *Pause and Effect: The Art of Interactive Narrative*. New Riders, 2003.

Miller, Carolyn Handler. *Digital Storytelling: A Creator's Guide to Interactive Entertainment*. Focal, 2004.

Morricone, Ennio & Sergio Miceli. *Composing for the Cinema: The Theory and Praxis of Music in Film*. Transl. Gillian B. Anderson. Lanham, 2013.

Nicieza, Fabian et al. "Deadpool." In: *New Mutants #98*. Marvel Entertainment, 1991.

Nunes, Joseph C. & Xavier Dreze. "The Endowed Progress Effect: How Artificial Advancement Increases Effort." *Journal of Consumer Research* 32, March 2006. https://doi.org/10.1086/500480

Oba, Junko. "Jo-ha-kyū." In: *The SAGE International Encyclopedia of Music and Culture*. Ed. Janet Sturman. SAGE, 2019.

Perry, David & Rusel DeMaria. *David Perry on Game Design: A Brainstorming Toolbox*. Charles River, 2009.

Phillips, Melanie Anne & Chris Huntley. *Dramatica: A Theory of Story*. 4th Ed. Screenplay Systems, 2008.

Pichlmair, Martin & Christoffer Holmgård. "You Say Jump, I Say How High? Operationalising the Game Feel of Jumping." FDG Digra, 2017.

Pink, Daniel H. *Drive: The Surprising Truth About What Motivates Us*. Riverhead, 2009.

Pittman, Jamey. "The Pac-Man Dossier." *Game Developer* February 23, 2009.

Poe, Edgar Allen. "The Purloined Letter." In: *The Gift: A Christmas, New Year, and Birthday Present*. Carey and Hart, 1845.

Qin, Hua, Pei-Luen Patrick Rau & Gavriel Salvendy. "Effects of Different Scenarios of Game Difficulty on Player Immersion." *Interacting with Computers* 22.3, 2010. http://dx.doi.org/10.1016/j.intcom.2009.12.004

Rigby, Scott & Richard M. Ryan. *Glued to Games: How Video Games Draw Us In and Hold Us Spellbound*. Praeger, 2011.

Robinson, Michael D. et al. (Eds.). *Handbook of Cognition and Emotion*. Guilford, 2013.

Rogers, Scott. *Level Up! The Guide to Great Video Game Design*. Wiley, 2010.

Rogers, Tim. "Action Button Reviews: *The Last of Us*." YouTube, 2020.

Romero, John. "It's supposed to be you." Rome.ro Game Talk Forum. "Doom Marine's Name" Reply #5. July 08, 2002.

Rose, David S. "How to Pitch to a VC." TED, March 2007.

Rouse, Richard III. *Game Design: Theory & Practise*. Wordware, 2005.

Ryan, Marie-Laure. "Beyond Myth and Metaphor: The Case of Narrative in Digital Media." *Poetics Today* 23.4, 2002. http://dx.doi.org/10.1215/03335372-23-4-581

Ryan, Marie-Laure. "Interactive Narrative, Plot Types, and Interpersonal Relations." In: *First Joint International Conference on Interactive Digital Storytelling* ICIDS 2008. Eds. Ulrike Spierling & Nicolas Szilas. Springer, 2008.

Ryan, Richard M. & Edward L. Deci. *Self-Determination Theory: Basic Psychological Needs in Motivation, Development, and Wellness*. Guilford, 2017.

Salen, Katie & Eric Zimmerman. *Rules of Play: Game Design Fundamentals*. MIT, 2004.

Saltsman, Rebekah. "So You're Ready to Pitch to a Publisher? (You're Not)." GDC, 2019.

Schell, Jesse. *The Art of Game Design: A Book of Lenses*. 2nd Ed. CRC, 2015.

Schreiber, Ian & Brenda Romero. *Game Balance*. CRC, 2022.

Sheldon, Lee. *Character Development and Storytelling for Games*. Course Technology, 2004.

Simens, Dov. *Hollywood Film School Course: Screenwriting, Producing, Directing, Editing, Budgeting, Distributing*. Lesson 2: Screenwriting A–Z. DVD. Dov Simens, 2000.

Simons, Daniel J. & Christopher F Chabris. "Gorillas in Our Midst: Sustained Inattentional Blindness for Dynamic Events." *Perception* 28.9, 1999. https://doi.org/10.1068/p281059

Sir Gawain and the Green Knight. In: *The Poems of the Pearl Manuscript*. Eds. Malcolm Andrew & Ronald Waldron. Exeter UP, 1996.

Smith, Ed. "In the Army Now: The Making of Full Spectrum Warrior." *Vice* August 24, 2016.

Stevens, Richard & Dave Raybould. *The Game Audio Tutorial: A Practical Guide to Sound and Music for Interactive Games*. Focal, 2011.

Suits, Bernard. *The Grasshopper: Games, Life and Utopia*. Toronto UP, 1978.

Summers, Chanel. "Making the Most of Audio in Characterization, Narrative Structure, and Level Design." In: *Level Design: Processes and Experiences*. Ed. Christopher W. Totten. CRC, 2017.

Sylvester, Tynan. *Designing Games: A Guide to Engineering Experiences*. O'Reilly, 2013.

Takahashi, Dean. "Blizzard CEO Mike Morhaime on the Last 25 Years of Games—And the Next 25." *VentureBeat* February 8, 2016.

Tarasti, Eero. *Semiotics of Classical Music: How Mozart, Brahms, and Wagner Talk to Us*. de Gruyter, 2012.

Tavinor, Grant. *The Art of Videogames*. Wiley-Blackwell, 2009.

The Book of the Thousand Nights and a Night. Transl. & ed. Richard Francis Burton. Kama Shastra Society, 1888.

Tolkien, J. R. R. *The Lord of the Rings*. George Allen & Unwin, 1954–5.

Tolkien, J. R. R. *The Silmarillion*. George Allen & Unwin, 1977.

Tolstoy, Leo. *Anna Karenina*. The Russian Messenger, 1878.

Tost, Miles & Nikolas Kolm. "*The Witcher 3*: Crafting a Compelling Narrative in a Believable Open World— Between Location and Content." TNG Big Techday 8, 2015.

Tremblay, Kaitlin & Alan Williamson. *Escape to Na Pali: A Journey to the Unreal*. Five Out of Ten, 2014.

Tyng, Chai M., Hafeez U. Amin, Mohamad N. M. Saad & Aamir S. Malik. "The Influences of Emotion on Learning and Memory." *Frontiers in Psychology*, 8, 2017. https://doi.org/10.3389/fpsyg.2017.01454

Upton, Brian. "30 Things I Hate About Your Game Pitch." GDC, 2017.

van Geelen, Tim. "Realizing Groundbreaking Adaptive Music." In: *From Pac-Man to Pop Music: Interactive Audio in Games and New Media*. Ed. Karen Collins. Ashgate, 2008.

Vogler, Christopher. *The Writer's Journey: Mythic Structure for Writers*. M. Wiese Productions, 2007.

Weinersmith, Zach. *SMBC*, May 2, 2014.

Wesołowski, Jacek. "Beyond Pacing." *Game Developer* May 21, 2009.

Wilde, Oscar. *The Picture of Dorian Gray*. Lippincott, 1890.

Williamson, Tad. *Sea of Silver Light*. DAW, 2001.

Wolf, Christopher Alexander. *Case Histories and Analyses of Synthetic Economies*. Kent State ETD, 2013.

Wolfram von Eschenbach. *Parzival Bd.1–2*. Ed. & transl. Wolfgang Spiewok. Reclam, 1992.

Worch, Matthias & Harvey Smith. "What Happened Here: Environmental Storytelling." GDC, 2010.

Zdanowicz, Gina & Spencer Bambrick. *The Game Audio Strategy Guide: A Practical Course.* Routledge, 2020.

Zeigarnik, Blume. "Das Behalten erledigter und unerledigter Handlungen." *Psychologische Forschung* 9, 1927.

Zhu, Feng. "A Live Art Demonstration of Creating Worlds through Design Thinking." GDC, 2015.

Zichermann, Gabe & Christopher Cunningham. *Gamification by Design: Implementing Game Mechanics in Web and Mobile Apps.* O'Reilly, 2011.

Level Two

Rightsholders

With due attributions, this level lists every intellectual property mentioned throughout this book for purposes of analysis, criticism, and scholarly reference under the Fair Use doctrine. They are copyrighted or trademarked by their respective rightsholders and owners.

Games and Video Games

AI Dungeon. Latitude. 2019.

Alan Wake. Remedy Entertainment. Microsoft Game Studios. 2010.

Alien: Isolation. Creative Assembly. Sega. 2014.

Aliens: Colonial Marines. Gearbox Software. Sega. 2013.

Aliens versus Predator. Rebellion Developments. Fox Interactive. 1999.

Batman: Arkham Asylum. Rocksteady Studios. Eidos Interactive & Warner Bros. IE. 2009.

Bejeweled. PopCap Games. 2001.

BioShock. 2K Boston & 2K Australia. 2K Games. 2007.

Breakout. Atari. Atari & Namco. 1976.

Car Wars. Chad Irby & Steve Jackson. Steve Jackson Games, 1980.

Civilization. MPS Labs. MicroProse. 1991.

Clash of Clans. Supercell. 2012.

Connect Four. Howard Wexler & Ned Strongin. Milton Bradley. 1974.

The Crew. Ivory Tower & Ubisoft Reflections. Ubisoft. 2014.

Crusader Kings III. Paradox Development Studio. Paradox Interactive. 2020.

Cyberpunk 2077. CD Projekt Red. CD Projekt. 2020.

Dark Souls. FromSoftware. Namco Bandai Games & FromSoftware. 2011.

Dead Space. EA Redwood Shores. Electronic Arts. 2008.

Defense of the Ancients. Eul, Steve Feak, & IceFrog. 2003.

Desert Golfing. Blinkbat Games. 2014.

Deus Ex (Series). Eidos Montreal. Square Enix. 2011–6.

Diablo III. Blizzard Entertainment. 2012.

Diablo Immortal. Blizzard Entertainment & NetEase. Blizzard Entertainment. 2022.

Dishonored. Arkane Studios. Bethesda Softworks. 2012.

Dishonored 2. Arkane Studios. Bethesda Softworks. 2016.

Donkey Kong. Nintendo. 1981.

Doom. id Software. GT Interactive Software. 1993.

Doom II. id Software. GT Interactive Software. 1994.

Doom 3. id Software. Activision & Aspyr Media. 2004.

Dragon Age: Inquisition. BioWare Edmonton. Electronic Arts. 2014.

Dwarf Fortress. Tarn Adams. Bay 12 Games. 2006.

Dying Light. Techland. Warner Bros. IE & Techland Publishing. 2015.

Elden Ring. FromSoftware. Bandai Namco Entertainment & FromSoftware. 2022.

Fallout 4. Bethesda Game Studios. Bethesda Softworks. 2015.

Far Cry. Crytek. Ubisoft. 2004.

Far Cry 2. Ubisoft Montreal. Ubisoft. 2008.

Final Fantasy. Square/Square Enix. 1987–2018.

Final Fantasy Legend II. Square. Gameboy & Square. 1991.

Forza Motorsport. Turn 10 Studios, Playground Games, & Sumo Digital. Microsoft Studios. 2005–17.

Full Spectrum Warrior. Pandemic Studios & Mass Media. THQ. 2004.

Gears of War. Epic Games. Microsoft Game Studios. 2006.

Gears of War 2. Epic Games. Microsoft Game Studios. 2008.

God of War. Santa Monica Studio. Sony CE & Capcom. 2005.

God of War. Santa Monica Studio. Sony Interactive Entertainment. 2018.

God of War Ragnarök. Santa Monica Studio. Sony Interactive Entertainment. 2022.

GoldenEye 007. Rare. Nintendo. 1997.

Gone Home. The Fullbright Company. 2013.

Grand Prix Legends. Papyrus Design Group. Sierra Sports. 1998.

Grand Theft Auto V. Rockstar North. Rockstar Games. 2013.

Grim Fandango. LucasArts. 1998.

Guitar Hero. Harmonix. RedOctane. 2005.

Half-Life. Valve. Sierra Studios. 1998.

Halo: Combat Evolved. Bungie. Microsoft Game Studios. 2001.

Heavy Rain. Quantic Dream. Sony CE. 2010.

Hellblade: Senua's Sacrifice. Ninja Theory. 2017.

Hex. Piet Hein; John Nash (independently). Parker Brothers. 1952.

Hitman: Blood Money. IO Interactive. Eidos Interactive. 2006.

I Have No Mouth, and I Must Scream. The Dreamers Guild. Cyberdreams, 1995.

Ico. SCE Japan Studio & Team Ico. Sony CE. 2001.

Kill.Switch. Namco USA. Namco. 2003.

The Last Express. Smoking Car Productions. Brøderbund. 1997.

The Last of Us. Naughty Dog. Sony CE. 2013.

League of Legends. Riot Games. 2009.

Left4Dead. Valve South/Valve. Valve. 2008–09.

Legend of Grimrock. Almost Human. 2012.

The Legend of Zelda: Breath of the Wild. Nintendo EPD. Nintendo. 2017.

The Legend of Zelda: Phantom Hourglass. Nintendo EPD. Nintendo. 2007.

Life Is Strange. Dontnod Entertainment. Square Enix. 2015.

Lineage. NCSOFT. 1998.

Mafia III. Hangar 13. 2K Games. 2017.

Mario. Nintendo. 1981–2017.

Mario Kart 64. Nintendo EAD. Nintendo. 1996.

Mass Effect. BioWare. Microsoft Game Studios & Electronic Arts. 2007.

Mass Effect 2. BioWare. Electronic Arts. 2010.

Mass Effect 3. BioWare. Electronic Arts. 2012.

Medal of Honor: Allied Assault. 2015, Inc. EA Games. 2002.

Metal Gear. Konami. 1987.

Metal Gear Solid 3: Snake Eater. Konami CE Japan. Konami. 2004.

Metal Gear Solid: The Twin Snakes. Konami CE Japan & Silicon Knights. Konami. 2004.

Middle-Earth: Shadow of Mordor. Monolith Prod. Warner Bros. IE. 2014.

Mirror's Edge. EA DICE. Electronic Arts. 2008.

Myst. Cyan. Brøderbund. 1993.

NASCAR Racing 2003 Season. Papyrus Design Group. Sierra Entertainment. 2003.

NieR. Cavia. Square Enix. 2010.

Nightslink. Noiseminded. 2021.

Operation Flashpoint. Bohemia Interactive & Codemasters. Codemasters. 2001.

Overwatch. Blizzard Entertainment. 2016.

Oxenfree. Night School Studio. 2016.

P. T. 7780s Studio. Konami. 2014.

Pac-Man. Namco. Namco & Midway. 1980.

Paranoia. Greg Costikyan, Dan Gelber, & Eric Goldberg. WestEnd Games. 1984.

Phoenix Command. Barry Nakazono & David McKenzie. Leading Edge Games, 1986.

Planescape: Torment. Black Isle Studios. Interplay Entertainment. 1999.

Pong. Atari. 1972.

Prince of Persia. Brøderbund. 1989.

Prince of Persia: The Sands of Time. Ubisoft Montreal. Ubisoft. 2003.

Quake. id Software. GT Interactive. 1996.

Quake II. id Software. Activision. 1997.

Red Dead (Series). Rockstar. Rockstar Games. 2004–19.

Resident Evil. Capcom. 1996.

Resident Evil 4. Capcom Production. Capcom. 2005.

Resident Evil 5. Capcom. 2009.

Resident Evil 7: Biohazard. Capcom. 2017.

Revolution 60. Giant Spacekat. 2014.

Rise of the Tomb Raider. Crystal Dynamics. Square Enix. 2015.

Save Room. Fractal Projects. 2022.

Sekiro: Shadows Die Twice. FromSoftware. Activision. 2019.

Shadow of the Tomb Raider. Eidos Montréal. Square Enix. 2018.

Shenmue. SEGA AM2. SEGA. 1999.

Silent Hill (Series). Team Silent (Konami CE Tokyo). Konami. 1999–2004.

The Sims. Maxis. Electronic Arts. 2000.

Space Invaders. Taito. Taito & Midway. 1978.

S.T.A.L.K.E.R.: Shadow of Chernobyl. GSC Game World. THQ & GSC World Publishing. 2007.

Star Ship. Atari. 1977.

Star Trek: Klingon. Jonathan Frakes. Simon & Schuster: 1996.

StarCraft. Blizzard Entertainment. 1998–2017.

The Suffering. Surreal Software. Midway Games, Encore, & Zoo DP. 2004.

Super Mario Odyssey. Nintendo EPD. Nintendo. 2017.

Syberia. Microïds. 2002.

Tetris. Alexey Pajitnov. Game Boy Version: Bulletproof Software & Nintendo. Nintendo. 1989.

Thief: The Dark Project. Looking Glass Studios. Eidos Interactive. 1998.

Threes. Sirvo. 2014.

Titanfall. Respawn Entertainment. Electronic Arts. 2014.

Tomb Raider. Core Design. Eidos Interactive. 1996.

Tomb Raider. Crystal Dynamics. Square Enix. 2013.

Tomb Raider II. Core Design & Westlake Interactive. Eidos Interactive & Aspyr. 1997.

Train. Brenda Romero. 2009.

Twilight: 2000. Frank Chadwick et al. 2nd Ed. Game Designer's Workshop. 1990.

Ultima Online. Origin Systems. Electronic Arts. 1997.

Uncharted. Naughty Dog. Sony IE. 2007–17.

Uncharted 4: A Thief's End. Naughty Dog. Sony IE. 2016.

Uncharted: The Lost Legacy. Naughty Dog. Sony IE. 2017.

Unreal. Epic MegaGames, Digital Extremes, & Legend Entertainment. GT Interactive. 1998.

Unreal Tournament. Epic Games & Digital Extremes. GT Interactive. 1999.

Unreal Tournament 2003. Epic Games & Digital Extremes. Infogrames. 2002.

Unreal Tournament 2004. Epic Games & Digital Extremes. Atari & MacSoft. 2004.

Warcraft: Orcs & Humans. Blizzard Entertainment. 1994.

Wario Land 4. Nintendo R&D1. Nintendo. 2001.

The Witcher 2: Assassins of Kings. CD Projekt Red. CD Projekt. 2011.

The Witcher 3: Wild Hunt. CD Projekt Red. CD Projekt. 2015.

Wordfeud. Bertheussen IT. 2010.

World of Warcraft. Blizzard Entertainment. 2004.

Movies and TV Shows

Alien. Ridley Scott. 20th Century Fox. 1979.

Aliens. James Cameron. 20th Century Fox. 1986.

Alien³. David Fincher. Brandywine Productions. 1992.

Annie Hall. Woody Allen. United Artists. 1977.

Band of Brothers. Phil Alden Robinson et al. HBO Entertainment. 2001.

The Benny Hill Show. Benny Hill. Associated-Rediffusion. 1955–91.

Black Panther. Ryan Coogler. Marvel Studios/Walt Disney Studios. 2018.

Blade Runner. Ridley Scott. Warner Bros. 1982.

Casablanca. Michael Curtiz. Warner Bros. Pictures. 1943.

Children of Men. Alfonso Cuarón. Universal Pictures. 2006.

Dark City. Alex Proyas. New Line Cinema. 1998.

The Dark Knight. Christopher Nolan. Warner Bros. Pictures. 2008.

Ferris Bueller's Day Off. John Hughes. John Hughes & Tom Jacobson. 1986.

Flash Gordon. Mike Hodges. Starling Productions & Famous Films. 1980.

The Game. David Fincher. Propaganda Films. 1997.

Gladiator. Ridley Scott. DreamWorks Pictures & Universal Pictures. 2000.

GoldenEye. Martin Campbell. MGM/UA Distribution & United International Pictures. 1995.

GoodFellas. Martin Scorsese. Warner Bros. 1990.

Il grande silenzio. Sergio Corbucci. Adelphia Compagnia Cinematografica & Les Films Corona. 1968.

Groundhog Day. Harold Ramis. Columbia Pictures, 1993.

High Noon. Fred Zinnemann. Stanley Kramer Productions, 1952.

House of Cards. Paul Seed. BBC. 1990.

House of Cards. Beau Willimon, David Fincher et al. Netflix. 2013–7.

Indiana Jones and the Temple of Doom. Steven Spielberg. Paramount Pictures. 1984.

Invasion of the Body Snatchers. Don Siegel. Walter Wanger Productions. 1957.

Invasion of the Body Snatchers. Philip Kaufman. United Artists. 1978.

Kottan ermittelt. Peter Patzak. ORF. 1976–84.

Lock, Stock and Two Smoking Barrels. Guy Ritchie. PolyGram Filmed Entertainment et al. 1998.

The Long Goodbye. Robert Altman. United Artists. 1973.

The Lord of the Rings: The Fellowship of the Ring. Peter Jackson. New Line Cinema. 2001.

Mad Max: Fury Road. George Miller. Warner Bros. & Roadshow Films. 2015.

Mission: Impossible. Bruce Geller. Desilu Productions/Paramount Television. 1966–73.

Modern Times. Charlie Chaplin. Charlie Chaplin. 1936.

Moonlighting. Robert Butler et al. Disney–ABC Domestic Television. 1985–9.

Once Upon a Time in the West (C'era una volta il West). Sergio Leone. Euro International Film & Paramount Pictures. 1968.

The Pacific. Tim Van Patten et al. DreamWorks Television. 2010.

Peter Pan. Clyde Geronimi et al. Walt Disney Productions. 1953.

Raiders of the Lost Ark. Steven Spielberg. Lucasfilm Ltd. 1981.

Rogue One. Gareth Edwards. Walt Disney Studios Motion Pictures. 2016.

Se7en. David Fincher. Arnold Kopelson Productions. 1995.

The Sixth Sense. M. Night Shyamalan. Hollywood Pictures et al. 1999.

Some Like It Hot. Billy Wilder. Mirisch Company. 1959.

Star Wars. George Lucas. 20th Century Fox. 1977.

Star Wars: The Last Jedi. Rian Johnson. Lucasfilm. 2017.

The Sting. George Roy Hill. Universal Pictures & The Zanuck/Brown Company. 1973.

Thelma & Louise. Ridley Scott. Pathé Entertainment et al. 1991.

Titanic. James Cameron. Paramount Pictures & 20th Century Fox. 1997.

Tom and Jerry. Rudolf Ising et al. Metro-Goldwyn-Mayer. 1940–67.

Unforgiven. Clint Eastwood. Warner Bros. 1992.

The Usual Suspects. Bryan Singer. PolyGram Filmed Entertainment et al. 1995.

Vampire Hunter D: Bloodlust. Kawajiri Yoshiaki. Urban Vision & Nippon Herald Films. 2000.

The Wizard of Oz. Victor Fleming et al. Metro-Goldwyn-Mayer. 1939.

The X-Files. "War of the Coprophages." Season 3, Episode 12. Kim Manners. 20th Television. 1996.

Music and Songs

Bach, Johann Sebastian. "Canon per tonos." *Ein Musikalisches Opfer.* BWV 1079. Leipzig, 1747.

Bach, Johann Sebastian. "Chaconne." *Partita in D minor for solo violin.* BWV 1004. Köthen, 1720.

Barber, Samuel. Adagio for Strings. Premiere: NBC Studio 8H. 1938.

Iron Butterfly. "In-A-Gadda-Da-Vida." Atco Records. 1968.

Ligeti György. *Requiem.* Premiere: Stockholm, 1965.

Reich, Steve. "Clapping Music." Premiere: Houston, 1972.

Rich, James Q. "Spider" & Boots Randolph. "Yakety Sax." Monument Records. 1963.

Tanaka Hirokazu. "Korobeyniki" (trad. arr). Nintendo. 1989.

Wagner, Richard. *Die Meistersinger von Nürnberg*. Premiere: Munich, 1868.

Williams, John & Johnny Mercer. "The Long Goodbye." United Artists. 1973.

Company and Brand Names

The following company and brand names are copyrighted or trademarked by their respective owners.

Academy Award; Adobe Flash; AlphaGo; AlphaStar, Apple; Batman; Classic Tetris World Championship; Chicago Manual of Style; DC; E3 (Electronic Entertainment Expo); ESRA (Entertainment Software Rating Association); Funatics; GDC (Game Developers Conference); GDC Europe; iMuse; iPad; iPhone; Marvel; Merriam-Webster; Nemesis System; PlayStation; PlayStation Vita; Steam; Technicolor; TED Conferences (Technology, Entertainment, Design); Twitter; Unreal Engine; Valve; Walt Disney; Wargaming; Wi-Fi; Wii Remote, YouTube.

Level Three

Responses

If you want to get in touch, there's a huge range of options, all of which you will find listed, directly or indirectly, at *ludotronics.net*.

At *ludotronics.net*, you will also find a journal with occasional thoughts and amendments, and an errata section for rectifications and revisions. If you pointed out an error or made me change my mind about a particular model or topic, then your name will be listed together with the respective correction or change, if you like.

Finally, if you merely want to check out what I'm up to at any given moment in time, my blogs at *betweendrafts.com* and *voidpunk.com* will serve you well.

Let's keep everything dynamic, and our field in constant flow!

J.

DOI: 10.1201/9781003334682-31

Index